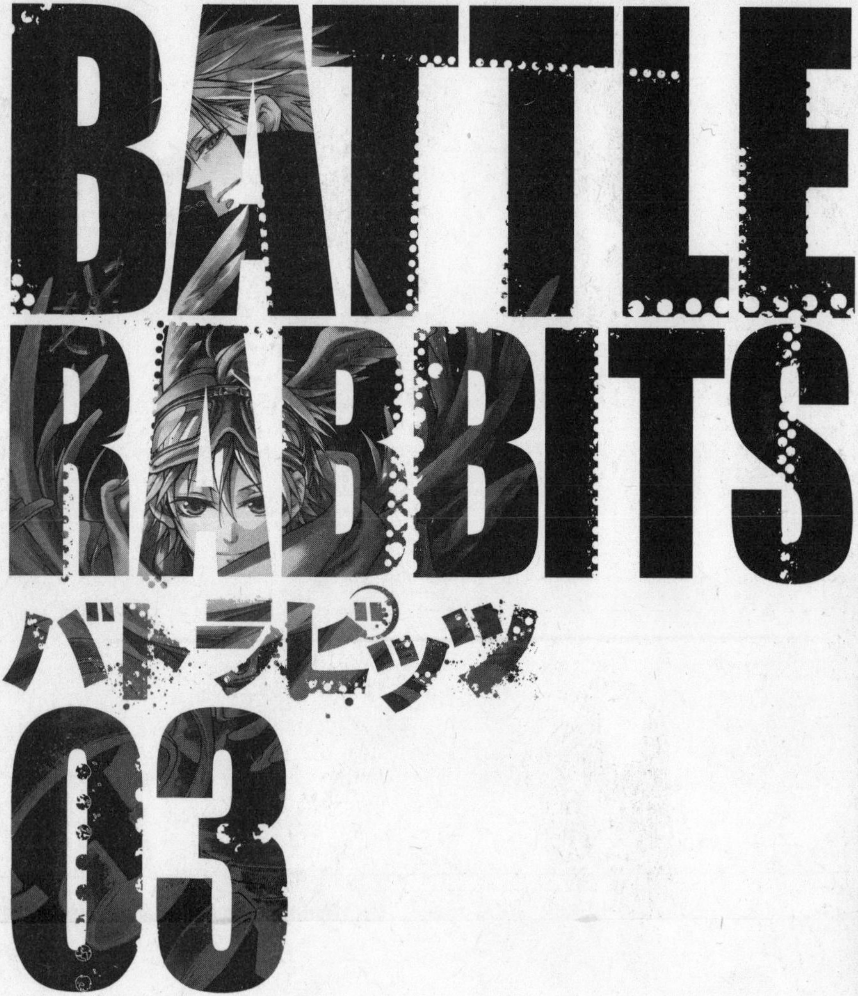
BATTLE
RABBITS
バトラビッツ
03

BATTLE RABBITS CHARACTERS

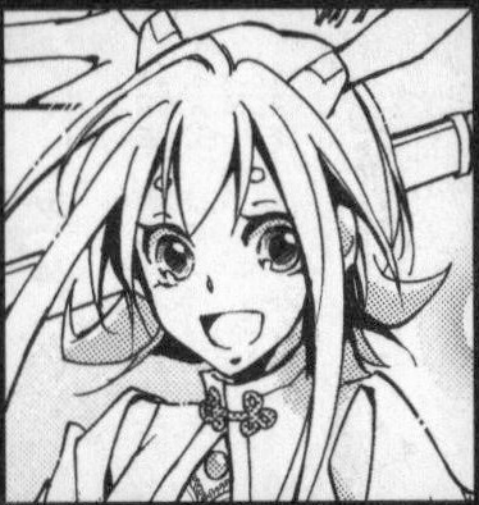

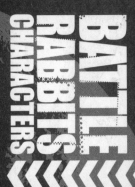

Domyoji Mao

A girl that was dispatched from the moon to protect the Earth. She adores Kaguya and serves as his bodyguard.

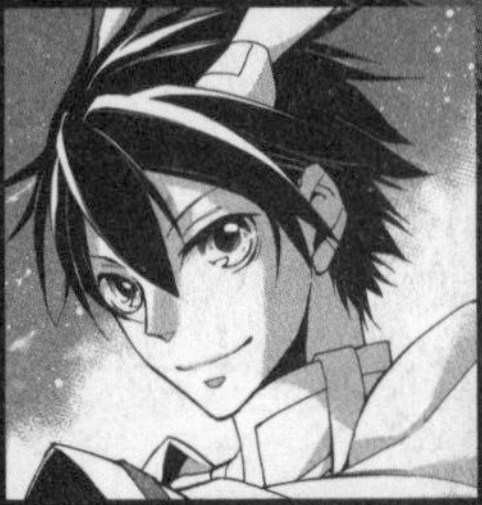

Kokuryuu Kaguya

A high school freshman who was raised without any knowledge that he was a citizen of the moon. He lost his family when he was very young.

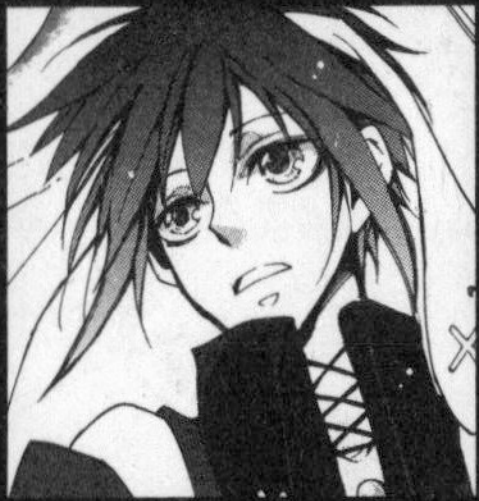

Kagura Nureha

A specialist with the ability to repair all of the body's cells by using an advanced medical technique.

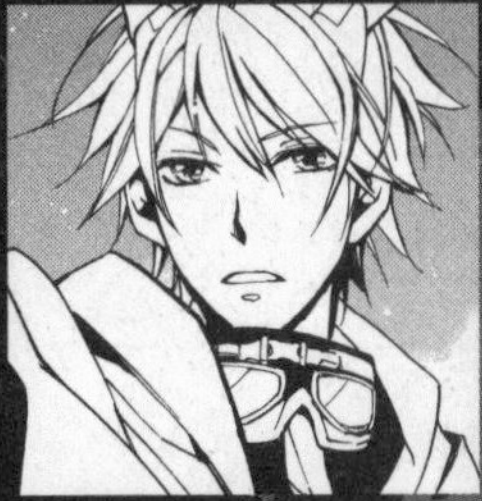

Hoshino Izumi

A citizen of the moon skilled at advanced fighting techniques. He also works as a top idol on Earth.

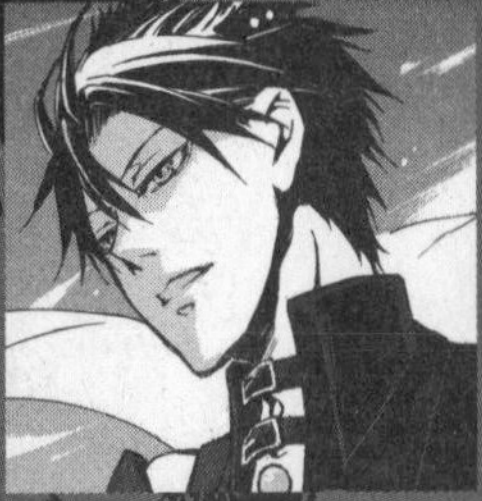

Takanomiya Hijiri

The Commander-in-Chief of the Earth Defense Force. He coerced Kaguya into joining their organization, and is responsible for his strict training.

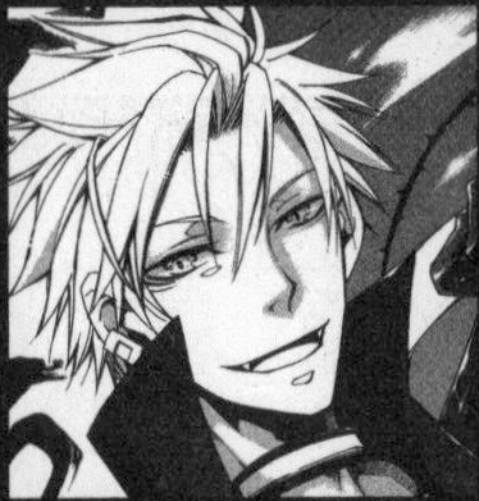

Shinigami (Death)

An otherworldly presence who maintains balance by collecting and guiding the souls of the dead.

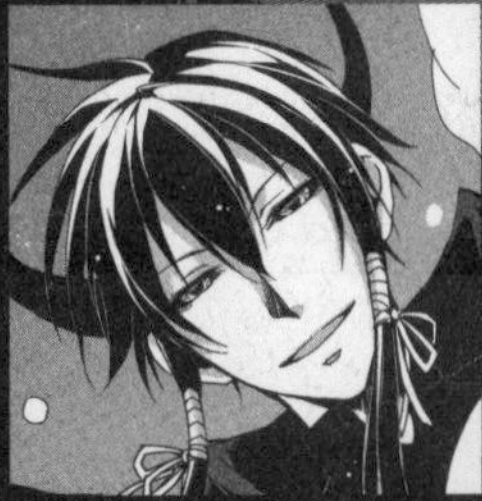

Rasetsu

An alien with the power to control ogres who feed on negative feelings. With this ability, he has destroyed many planets.

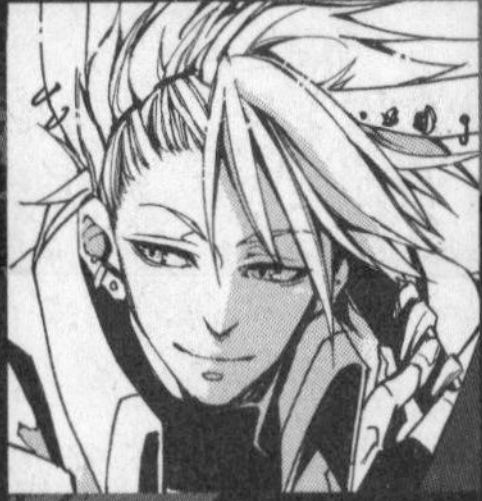

Kurogane Iori

A member of the elite Battle Rabbits force "Genou" with Hijiri, Izumi and Nureha. His abilities are unknown.

The Story So Far

After Kaguya is attacked by an ogre-possessed human, he learns of the existence of Battle Rabbits--citizens of the moon who have protected earthlings since ancient times. A glittering gold Rabi-Jewel appears on his chest, unleashing his sealed powers and proving that he himself is a citizen of the moon! He soon finds that his Rabi-Jewel is a treasure coveted by ogres, who could use it to gain unstoppable power. As the battle intensifies, the future of the universe hangs on the fate of Kaguya's Rabi-Jewel.

CHAPTER 11

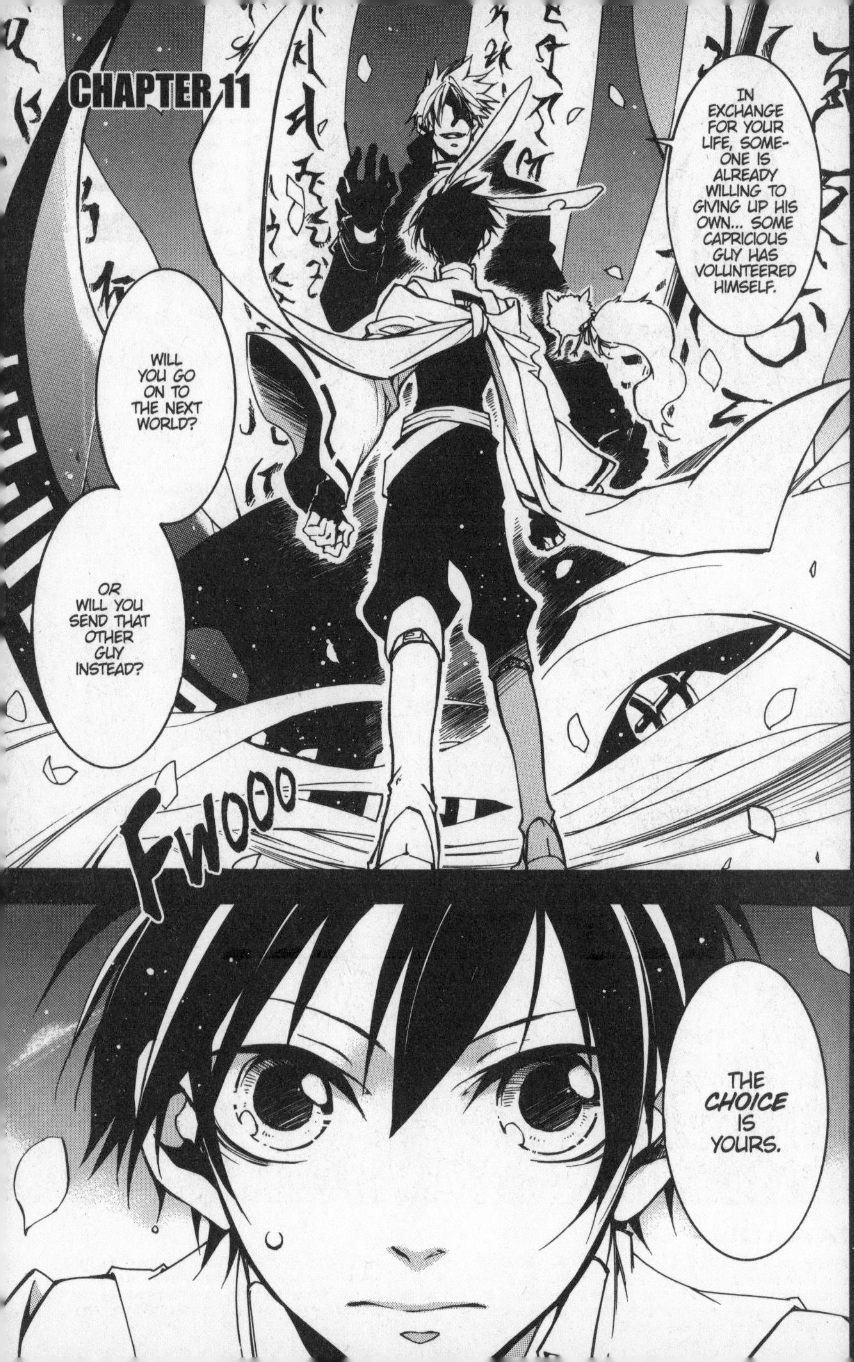
IN EXCHANGE FOR YOUR LIFE, SOMEONE IS ALREADY WILLING TO GIVING UP HIS OWN... SOME CAPRICIOUS GUY HAS VOLUNTEERED HIMSELF.
WILL YOU GO ON TO THE NEXT WORLD?
OR WILL YOU SEND THAT OTHER GUY INSTEAD?
FWOOO
THE *CHOICE* IS YOURS.

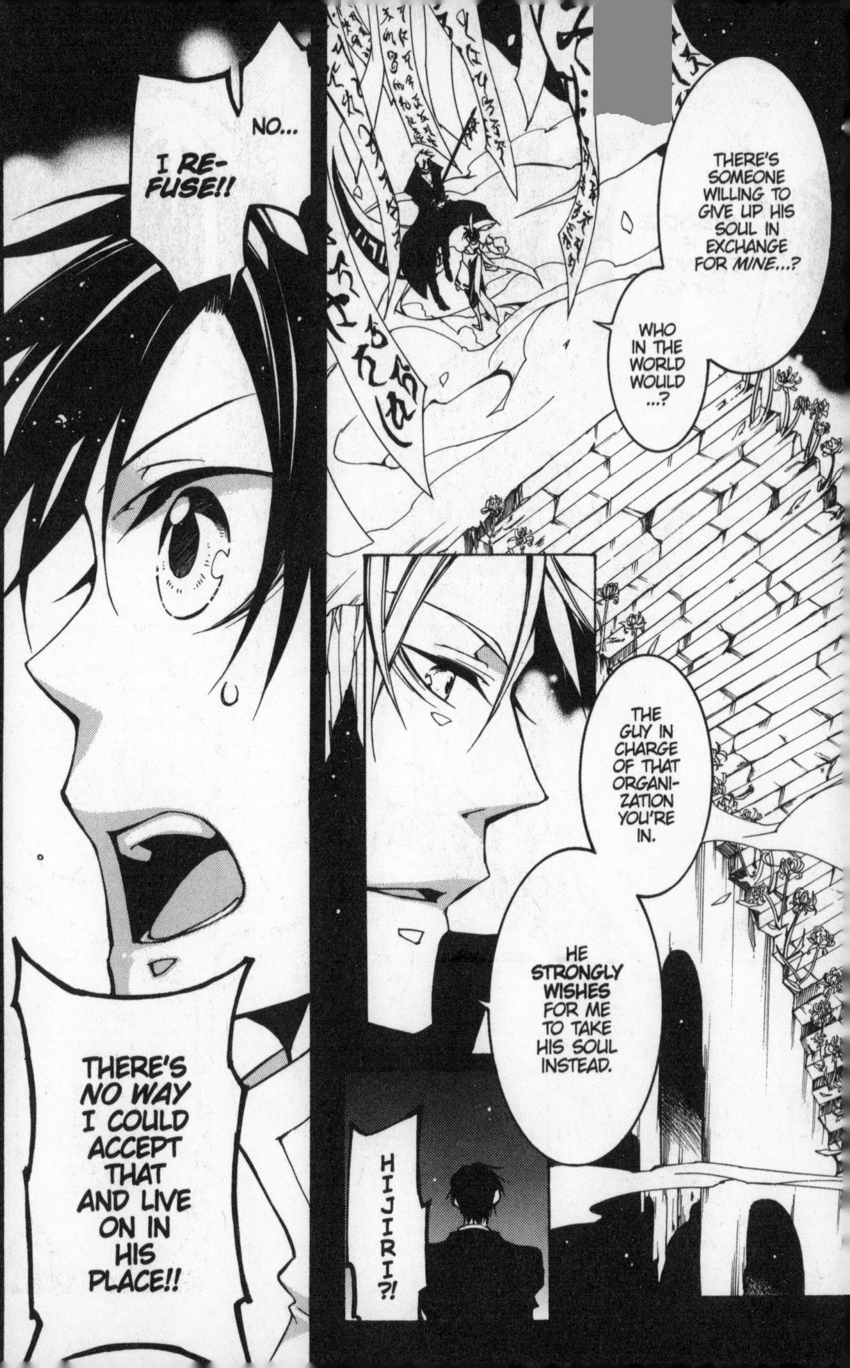
THERE'S SOMEONE WILLING TO GIVE UP HIS SOUL IN EXCHANGE FOR *MINE*...?
WHO IN THE WORLD WOULD ...?
THE GUY IN CHARGE OF THAT ORGANIZATION YOU'RE IN.
HE STRONGLY WISHES FOR ME TO TAKE HIS SOUL INSTEAD.
HIJIRI?!
NO...
I *RE-FUSE!!*
THERE'S *NO WAY* I COULD ACCEPT THAT AND LIVE ON IN HIS PLACE!!

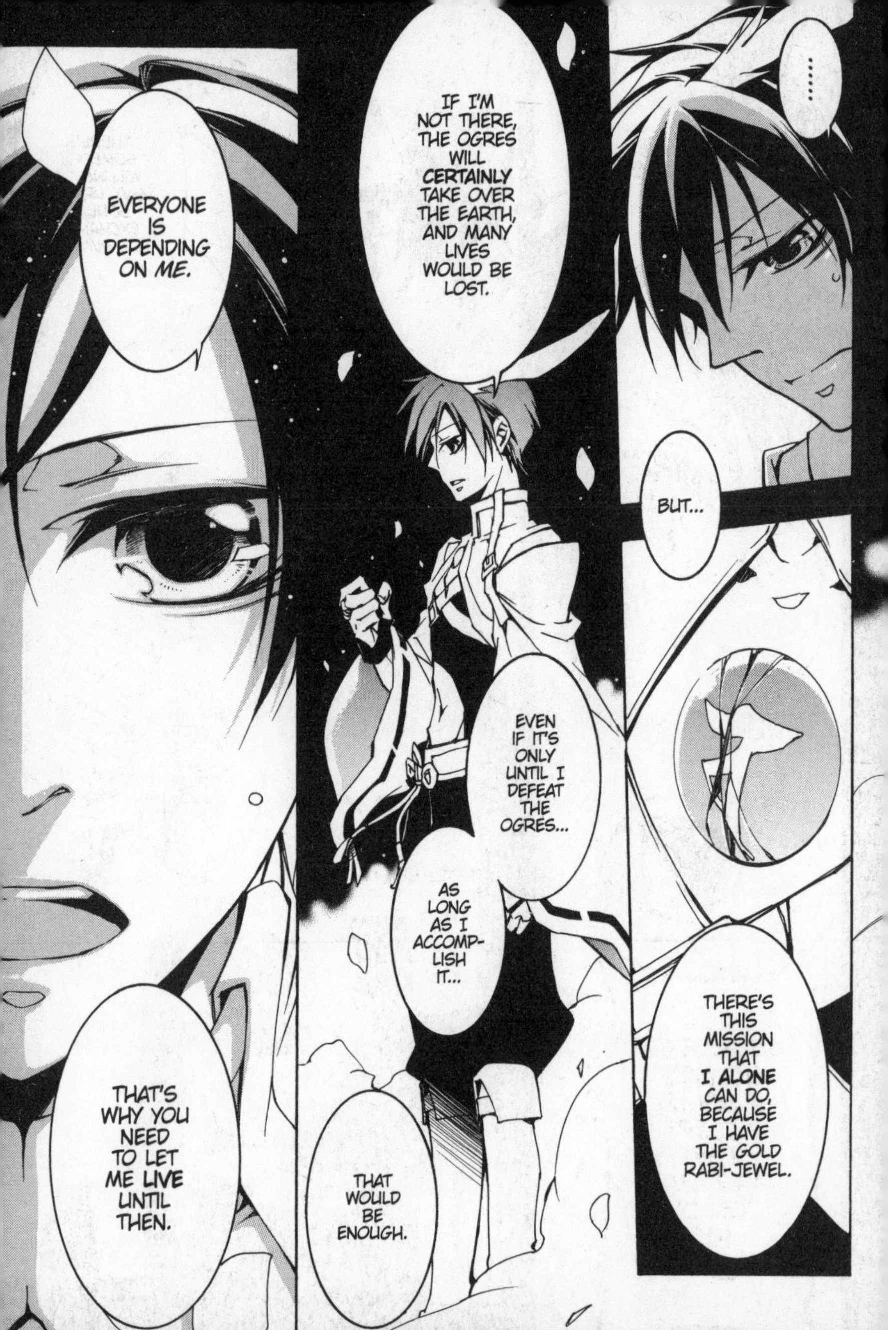
......
BUT...
THERE'S THIS MISSION THAT I ALONE CAN DO, BECAUSE I HAVE THE GOLD RABI-JEWEL.
IF I'M NOT THERE, THE OGRES WILL CERTAINLY TAKE OVER THE EARTH, AND MANY LIVES WOULD BE LOST.
EVEN IF IT'S ONLY UNTIL I DEFEAT THE OGRES...
AS LONG AS I ACCOMPLISH IT...
THAT WOULD BE ENOUGH.
EVERYONE IS DEPENDING ON ME.
THAT'S WHY YOU NEED TO LET ME LIVE UNTIL THEN.

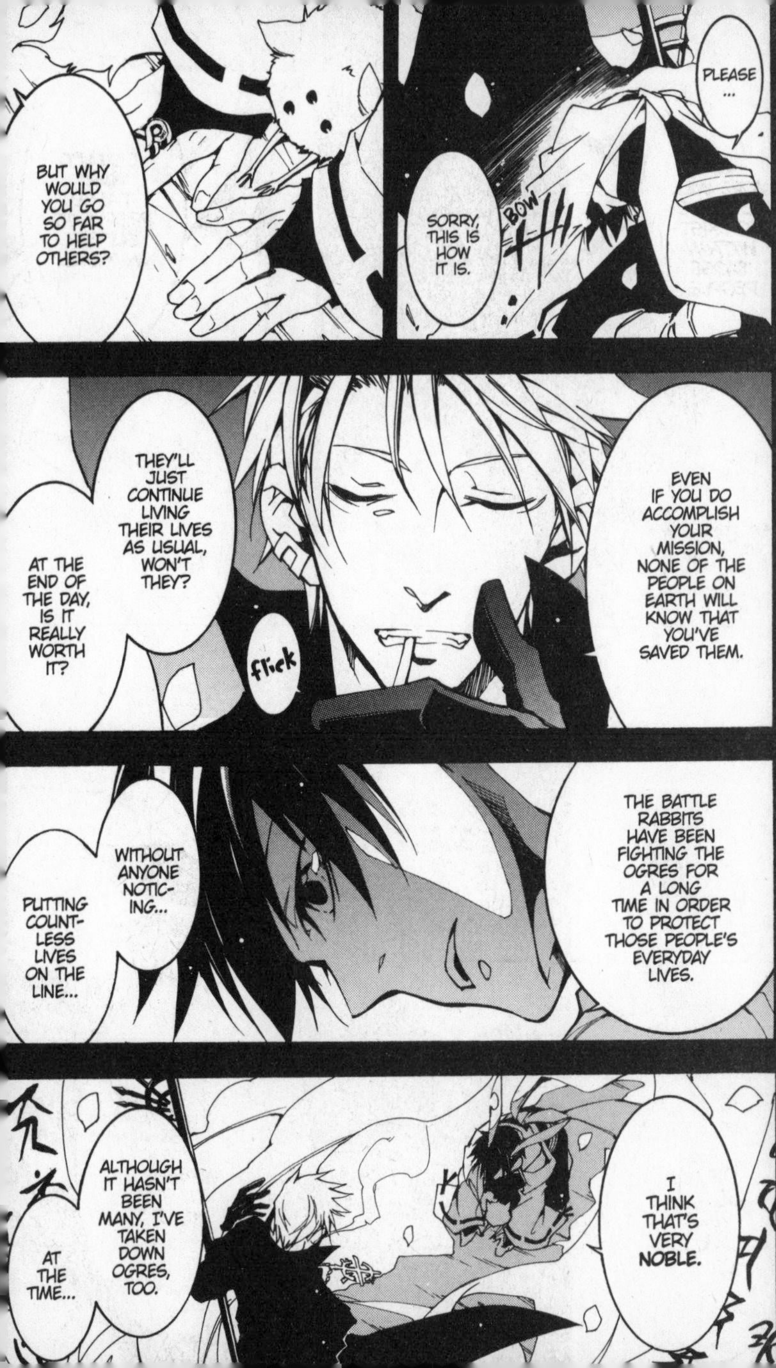
PLEASE ...
SORRY, THIS IS HOW IT IS.
BOW
BUT WHY WOULD YOU GO SO FAR TO HELP OTHERS?
EVEN IF YOU DO ACCOMPLISH YOUR MISSION, NONE OF THE PEOPLE ON EARTH WILL KNOW THAT YOU'VE SAVED THEM.
flick
THEY'LL JUST CONTINUE LIVING THEIR LIVES AS USUAL, WON'T THEY?
AT THE END OF THE DAY, IS IT REALLY WORTH IT?
THE BATTLE RABBITS HAVE BEEN FIGHTING THE OGRES FOR A LONG TIME IN ORDER TO PROTECT THOSE PEOPLE'S EVERYDAY LIVES.
WITHOUT ANYONE NOTIC-ING...
PUTTING COUNT-LESS LIVES ON THE LINE...
I THINK THAT'S VERY NOBLE.
ALTHOUGH IT HASN'T BEEN MANY, I'VE TAKEN DOWN OGRES, TOO.
AT THE TIME...

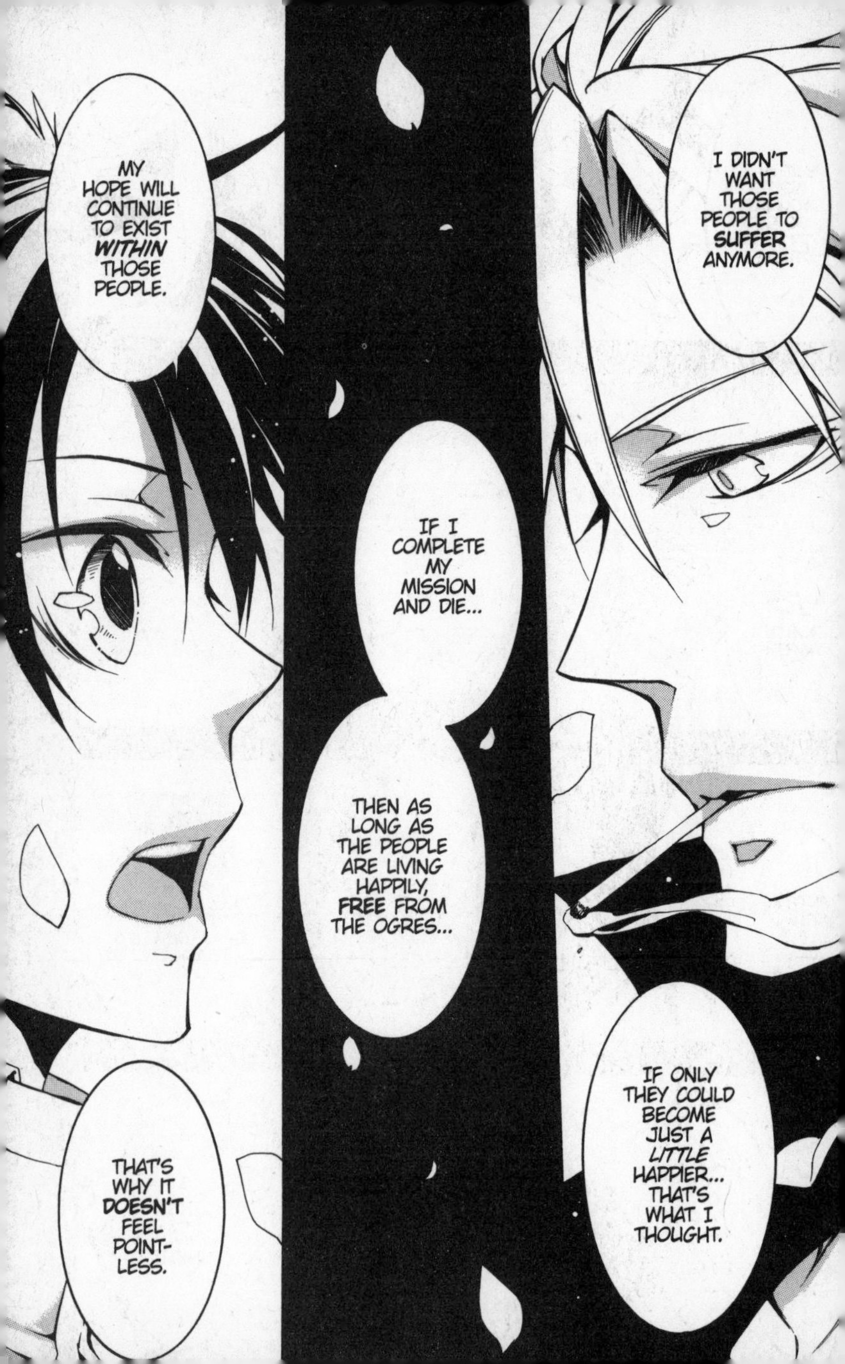
I DIDN'T WANT THOSE PEOPLE TO SUFFER ANYMORE.
IF ONLY THEY COULD BECOME JUST A LITTLE HAPPIER... THAT'S WHAT I THOUGHT.
IF I COMPLETE MY MISSION AND DIE...
THEN AS LONG AS THE PEOPLE ARE LIVING HAPPILY, FREE FROM THE OGRES...
MY HOPE WILL CONTINUE TO EXIST WITHIN THOSE PEOPLE.
THAT'S WHY IT DOESN'T FEEL POINTLESS.

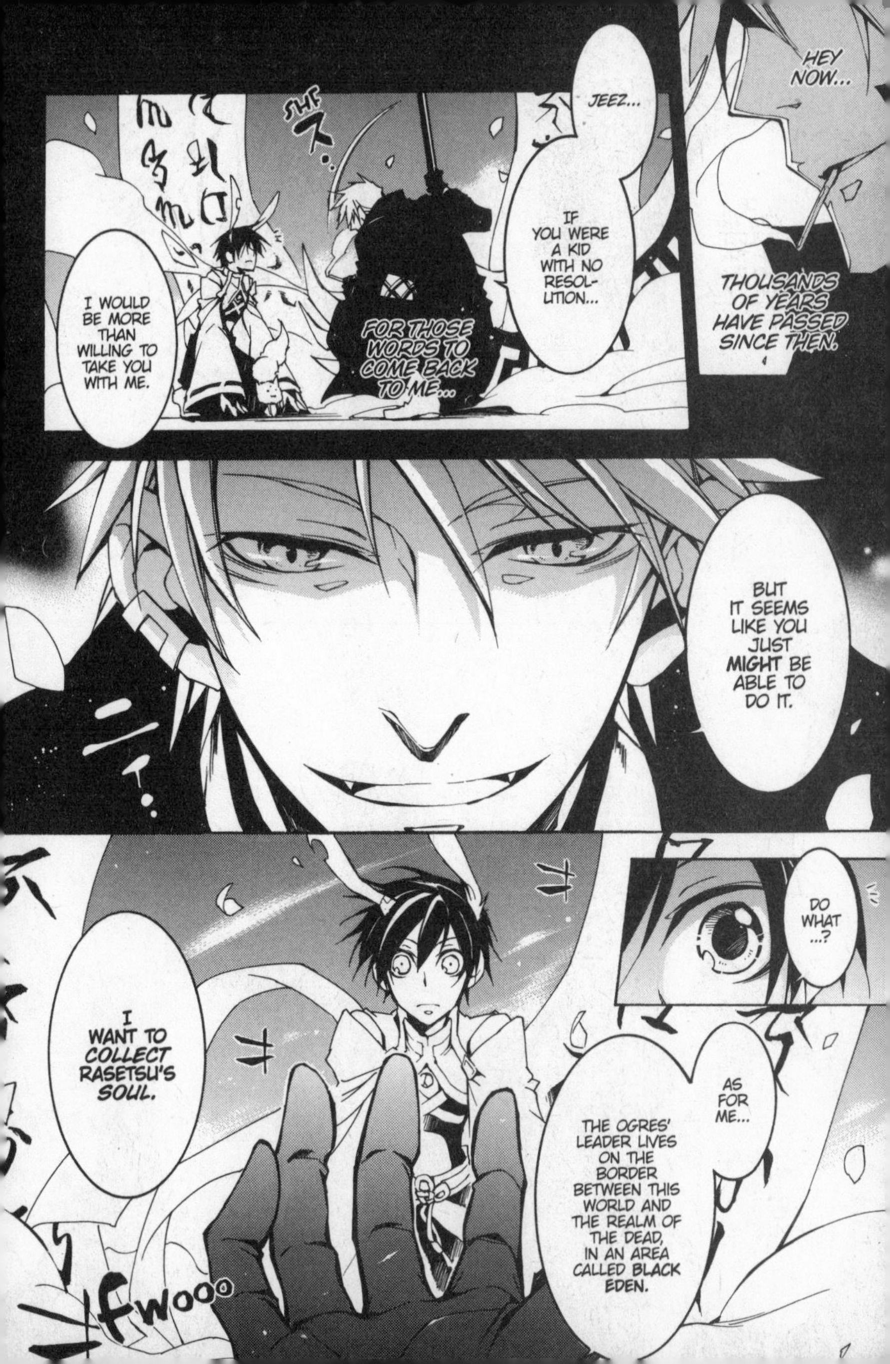
HEY NOW...
THOUSANDS OF YEARS HAVE PASSED SINCE THEN.
JEEZ...
IF YOU WERE A KID WITH NO RESOLUTION...
SHF
FOR THOSE WORDS TO COME BACK TO ME...
I WOULD BE MORE THAN WILLING TO TAKE YOU WITH ME.
BUT IT SEEMS LIKE YOU JUST MIGHT BE ABLE TO DO IT.
DO WHAT ...?
AS FOR ME...
THE OGRES' LEADER LIVES ON THE BORDER BETWEEN THIS WORLD AND THE REALM OF THE DEAD, IN AN AREA CALLED BLACK EDEN.
I WANT TO COLLECT RASETSU'S SOUL.
FWOOO

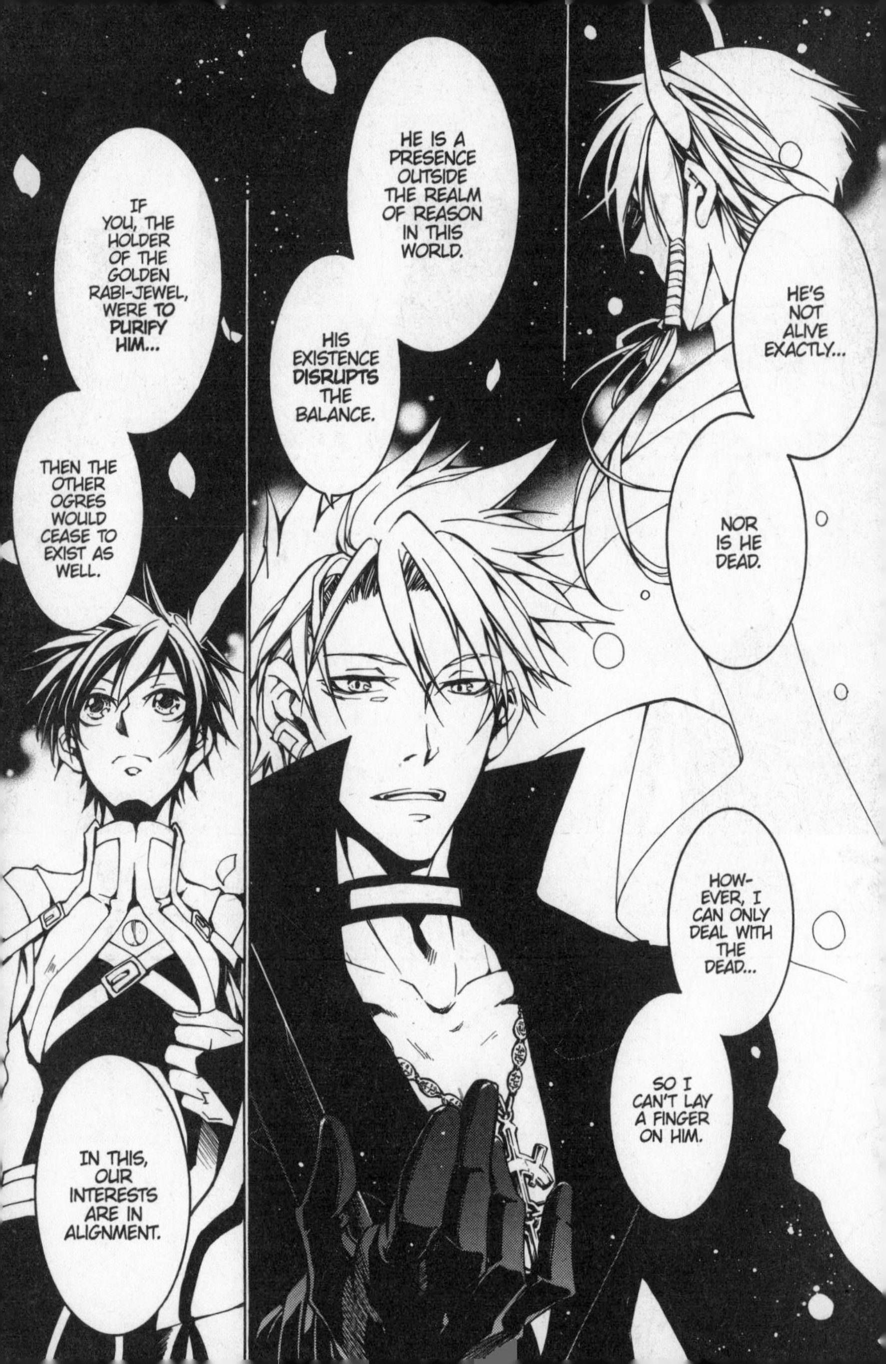
HE'S NOT ALIVE EXACTLY...
NOR IS HE DEAD.
HOW-EVER, I CAN ONLY DEAL WITH THE DEAD...
SO I CAN'T LAY A FINGER ON HIM.
HE IS A PRESENCE OUTSIDE THE REALM OF REASON IN THIS WORLD.
HIS EXISTENCE DISRUPTS THE BALANCE.
IF YOU, THE HOLDER OF THE GOLDEN RABI-JEWEL, WERE TO PURIFY HIM...
THEN THE OTHER OGRES WOULD CEASE TO EXIST AS WELL.
IN THIS, OUR INTERESTS ARE IN ALIGNMENT.

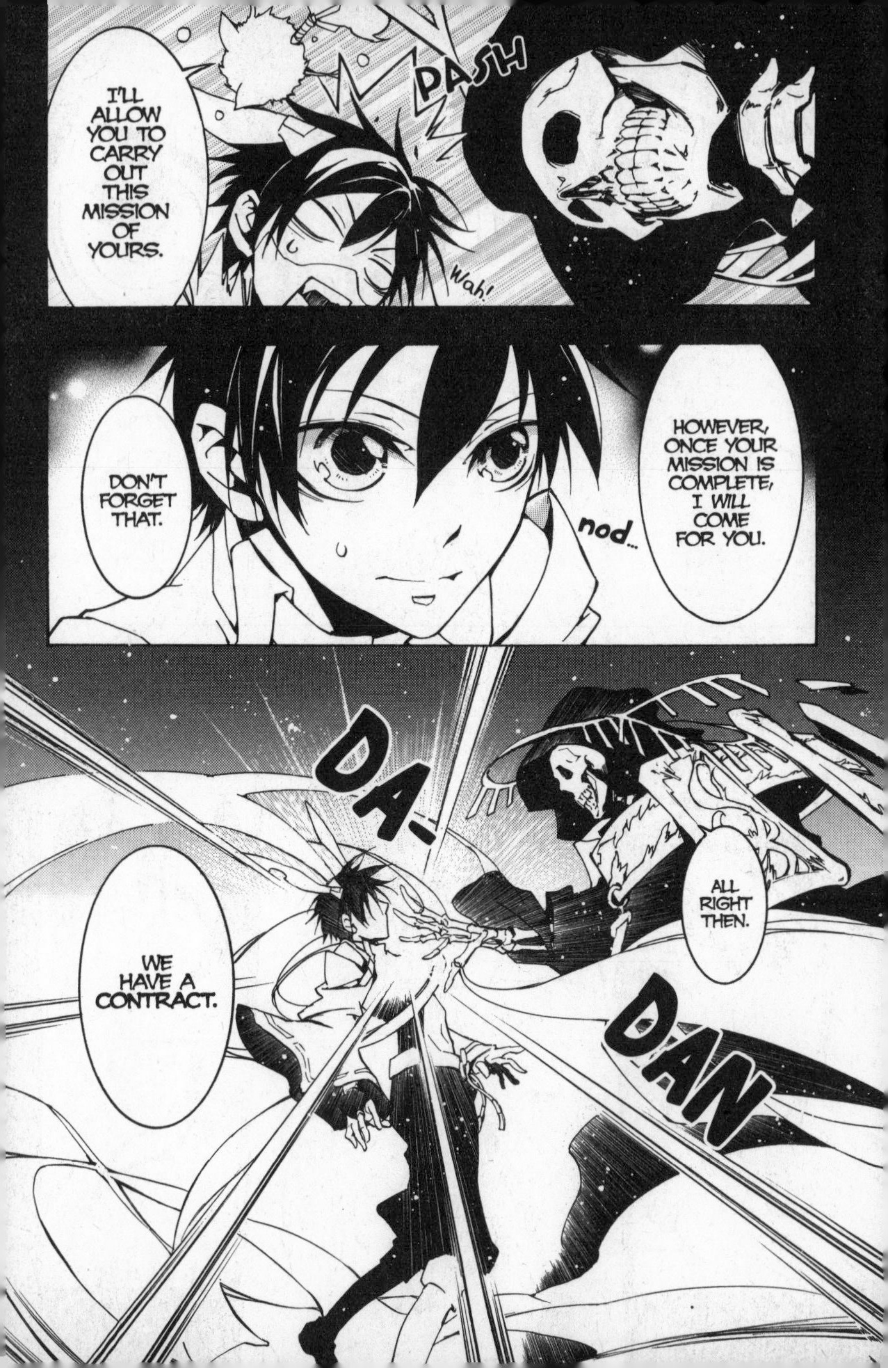
PASH
Wah!
I'LL ALLOW YOU TO CARRY OUT THIS MISSION OF YOURS.
HOWEVER, ONCE YOUR MISSION IS COMPLETE, I WILL COME FOR YOU.
nod...
DON'T FORGET THAT.
ALL RIGHT THEN.
DA-
DAN
WE HAVE A CONTRACT.

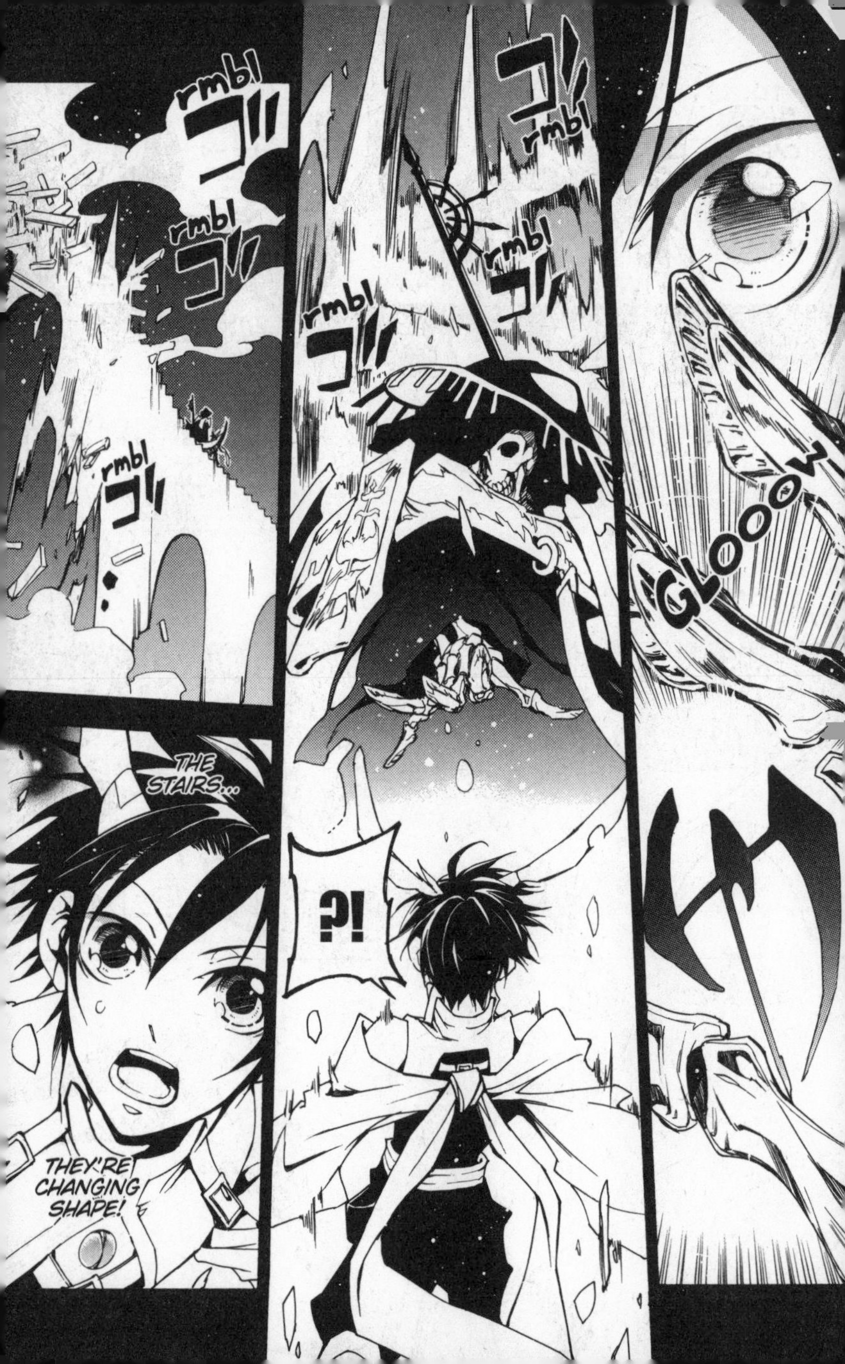
GLOOOW
rmbl
rmbl
rmbl
?!
rmbl
rmbl
rmbl
THE STAIRS...
THEY'RE CHANGING SHAPE!

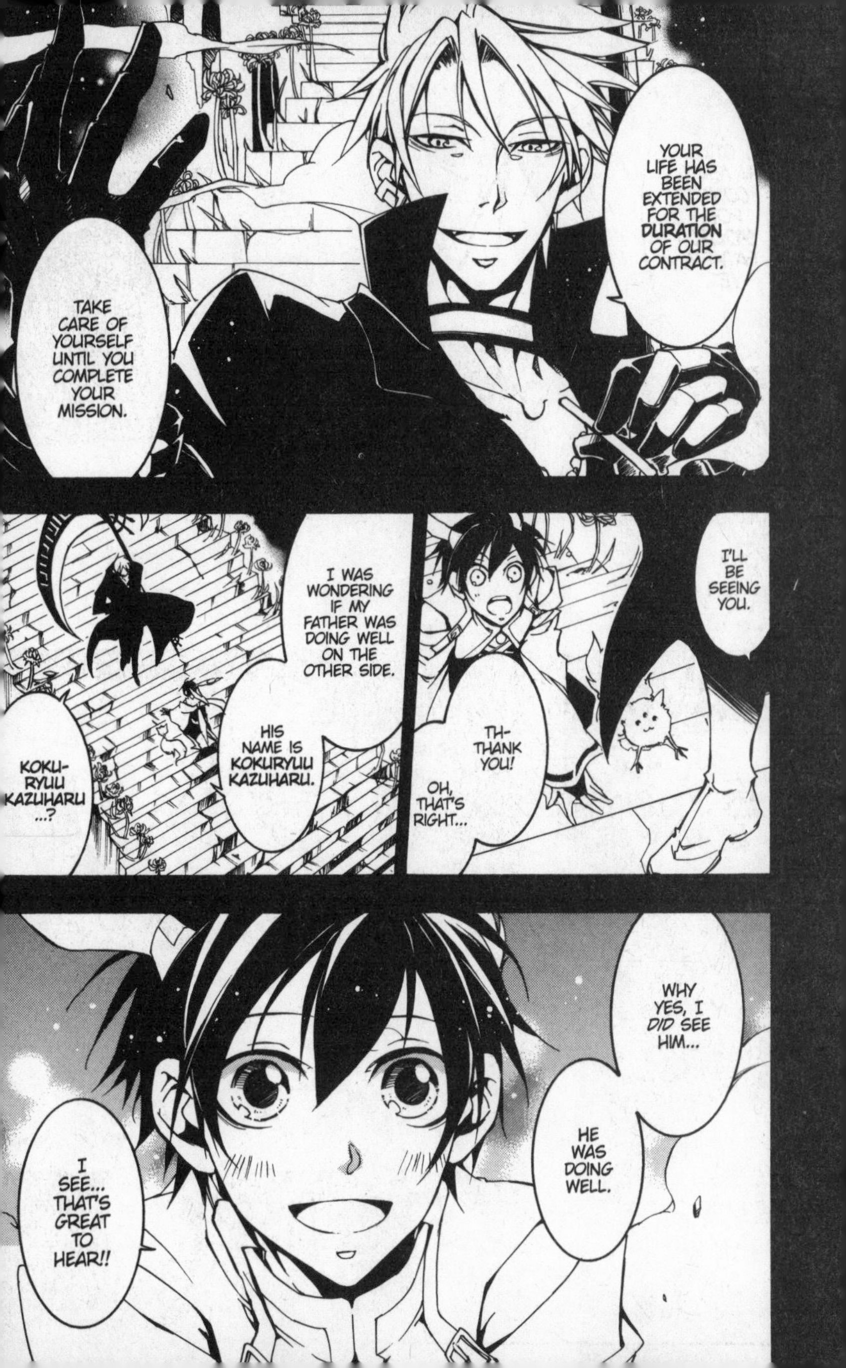
YOUR LIFE HAS BEEN EXTENDED FOR THE DURATION OF OUR CONTRACT.
TAKE CARE OF YOURSELF UNTIL YOU COMPLETE YOUR MISSION.
I'LL BE SEEING YOU.
TH-THANK YOU!
OH, THAT'S RIGHT...
I WAS WONDERING IF MY FATHER WAS DOING WELL ON THE OTHER SIDE.
HIS NAME IS KOKURYUU KAZUHARU.
KOKURYUU KAZUHARU...?
WHY YES, I *DID* SEE HIM...
HE WAS DOING WELL.
I SEE... THAT'S GREAT TO HEAR!!

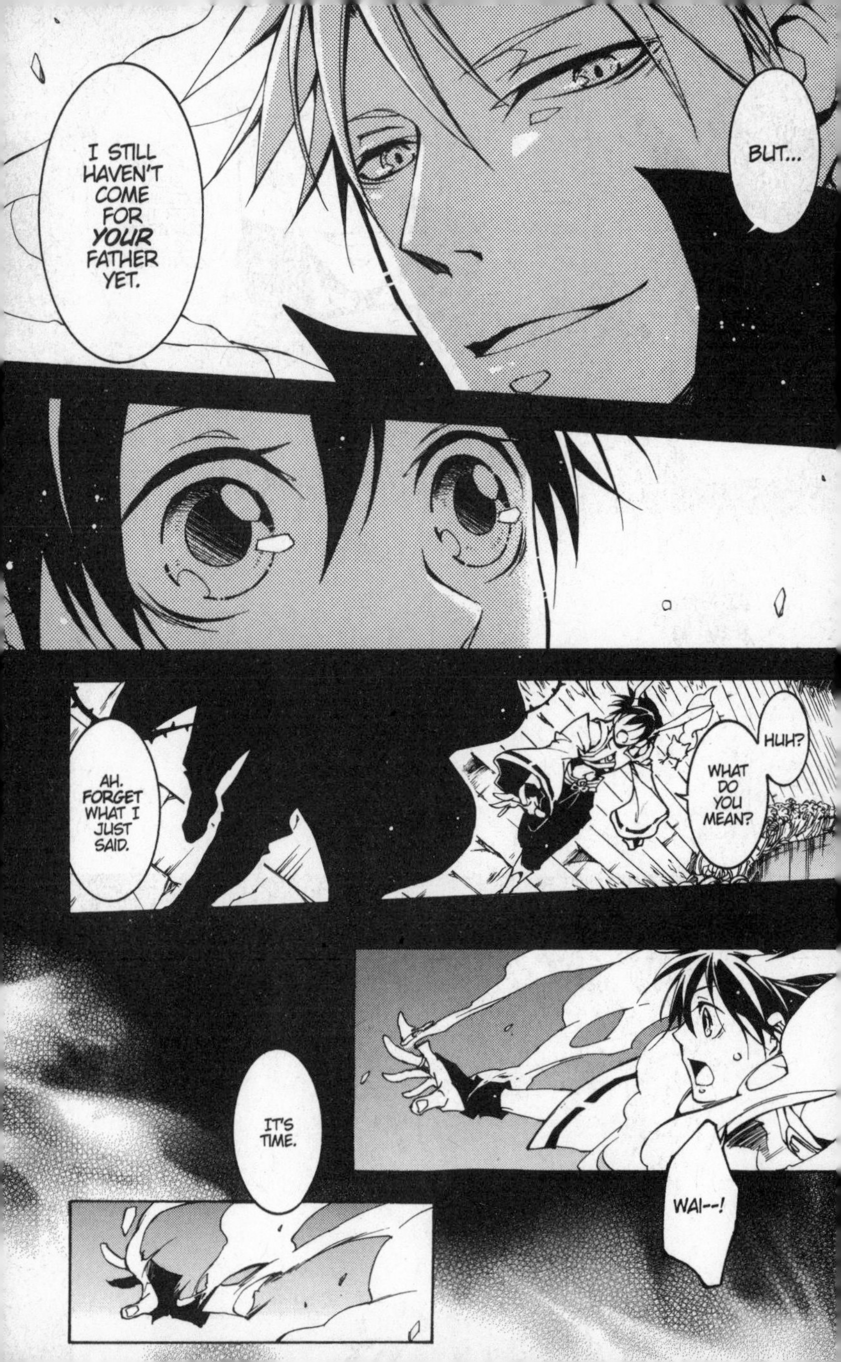
BUT...
I STILL HAVEN'T COME FOR **YOUR** FATHER YET.
HUH? WHAT DO YOU MEAN?
AH. FORGET WHAT I JUST SAID.
IT'S TIME.
WAI--!

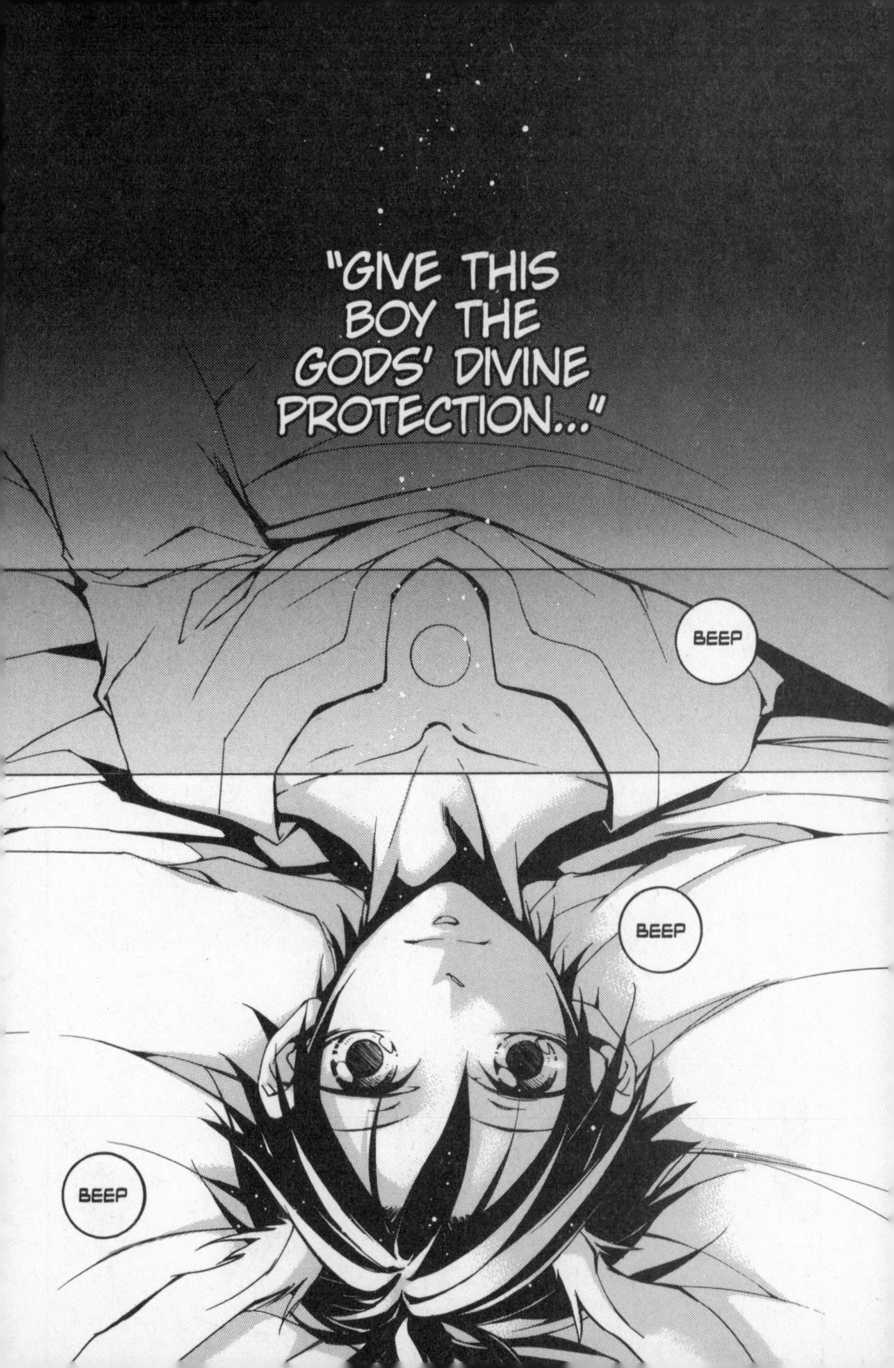
"GIVE THIS BOY THE GODS' DIVINE PROTECTION..."
BEEP
BEEP
BEEP

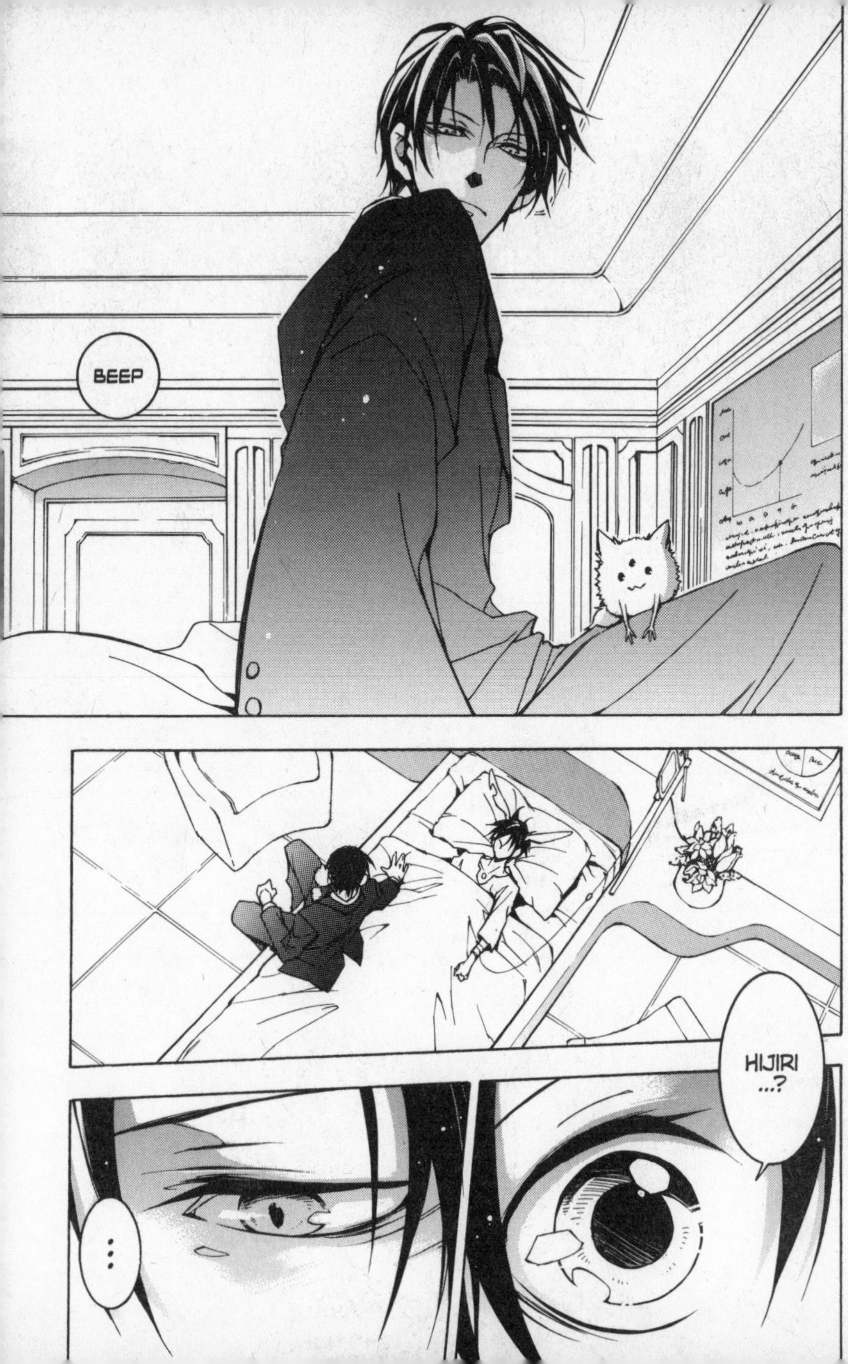
BEEP
HIJIRI ...?
...

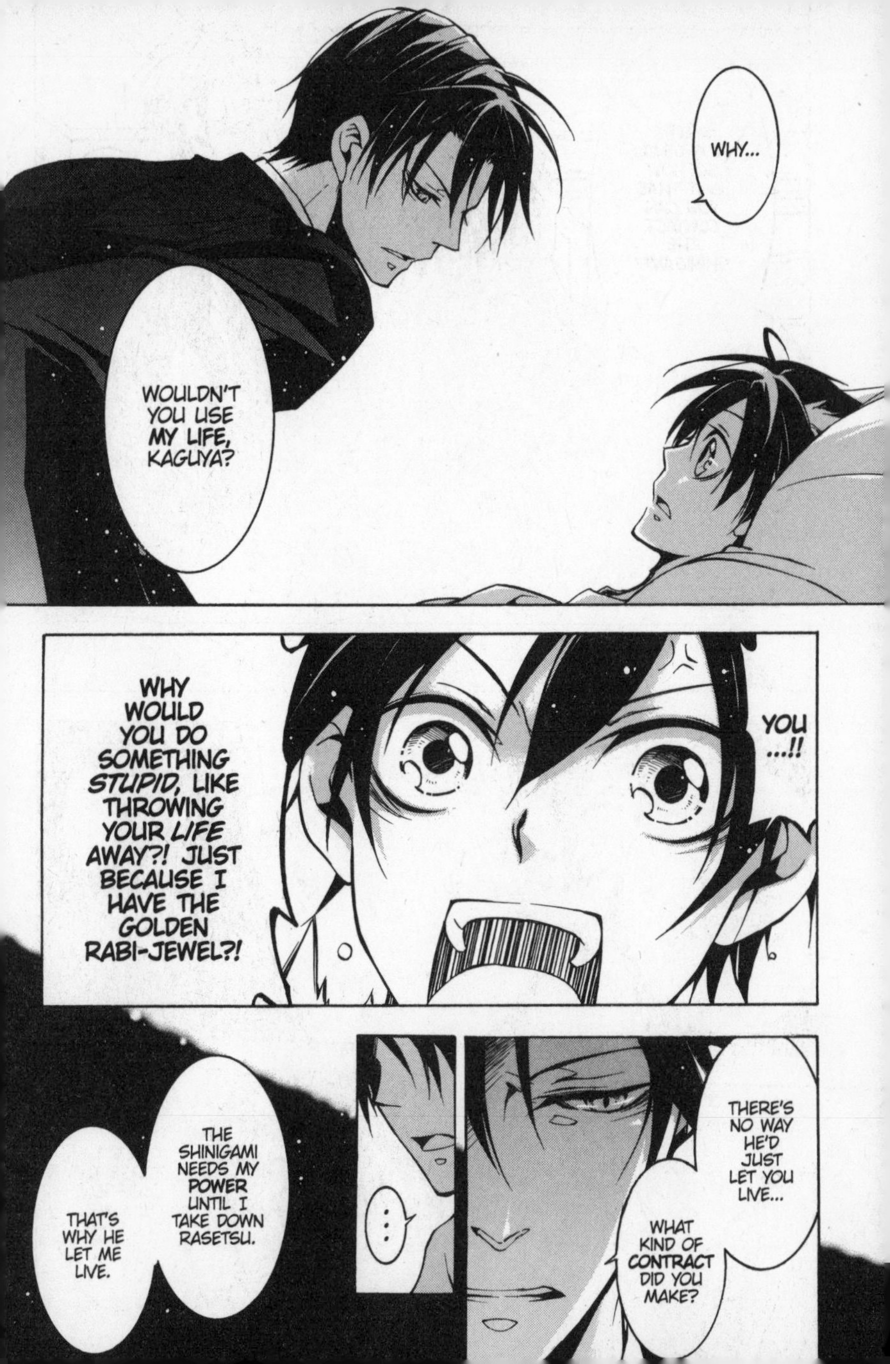
WHY...
WOULDN'T YOU USE MY LIFE, KAGUYA?
YOU ...!!
WHY WOULD YOU DO SOMETHING *STUPID*, LIKE THROWING YOUR *LIFE* AWAY?! JUST BECAUSE I HAVE THE GOLDEN RABI-JEWEL?!
THERE'S NO WAY HE'D JUST LET YOU LIVE...
WHAT KIND OF CONTRACT DID YOU MAKE?
...
THE SHINIGAMI NEEDS MY POWER UNTIL I TAKE DOWN RASETSU.
THAT'S WHY HE LET ME LIVE.

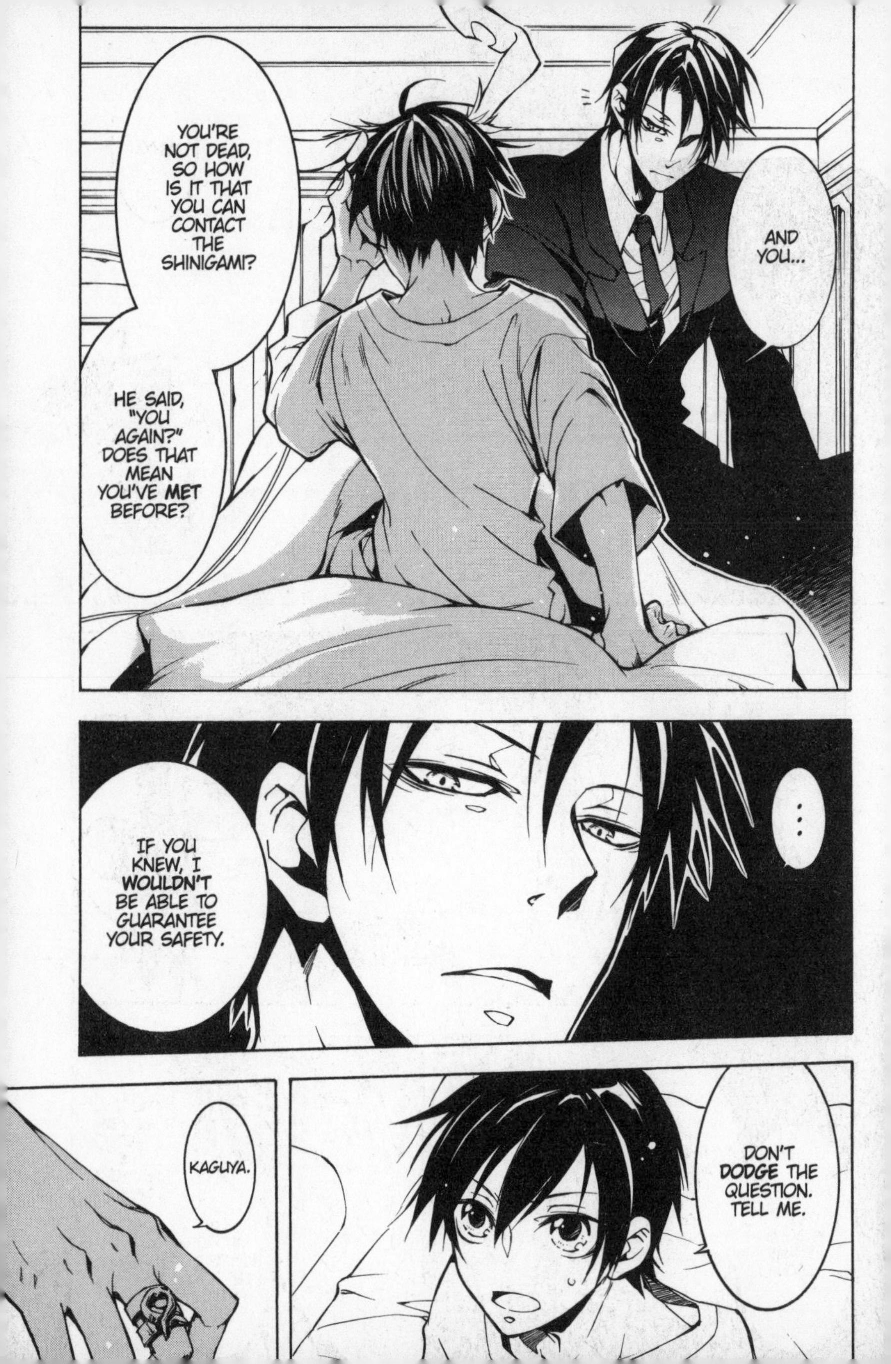
AND YOU...
YOU'RE NOT DEAD, SO HOW IS IT THAT YOU CAN CONTACT THE SHINIGAMI?
HE SAID, "YOU AGAIN?" DOES THAT MEAN YOU'VE MET BEFORE?
...
IF YOU KNEW, I WOULDN'T BE ABLE TO GUARANTEE YOUR SAFETY.
DON'T DODGE THE QUESTION. TELL ME.
KAGUYA.

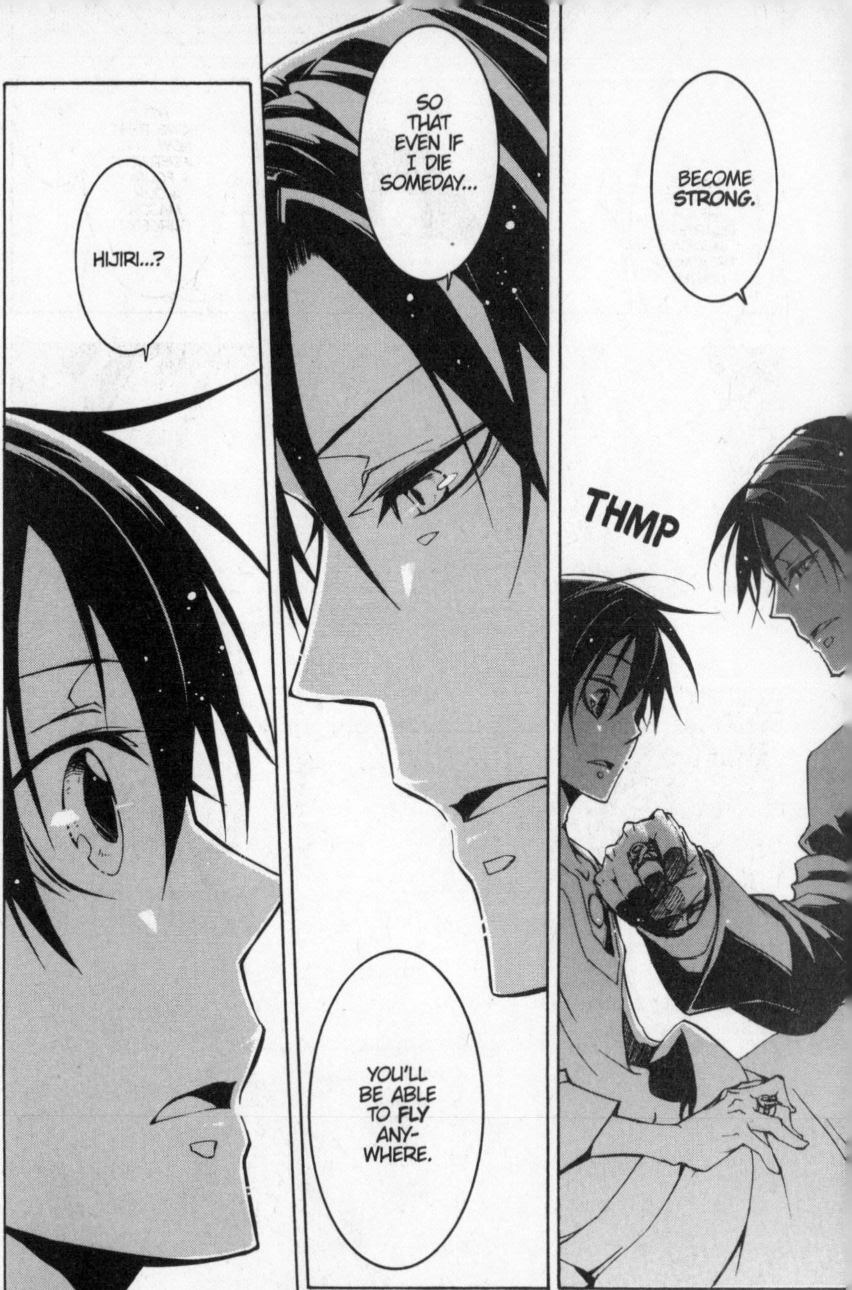
BECOME STRONG.
THMP
SO THAT EVEN IF I DIE SOMEDAY...
YOU'LL BE ABLE TO FLY ANY-WHERE.
HIJIRI...?

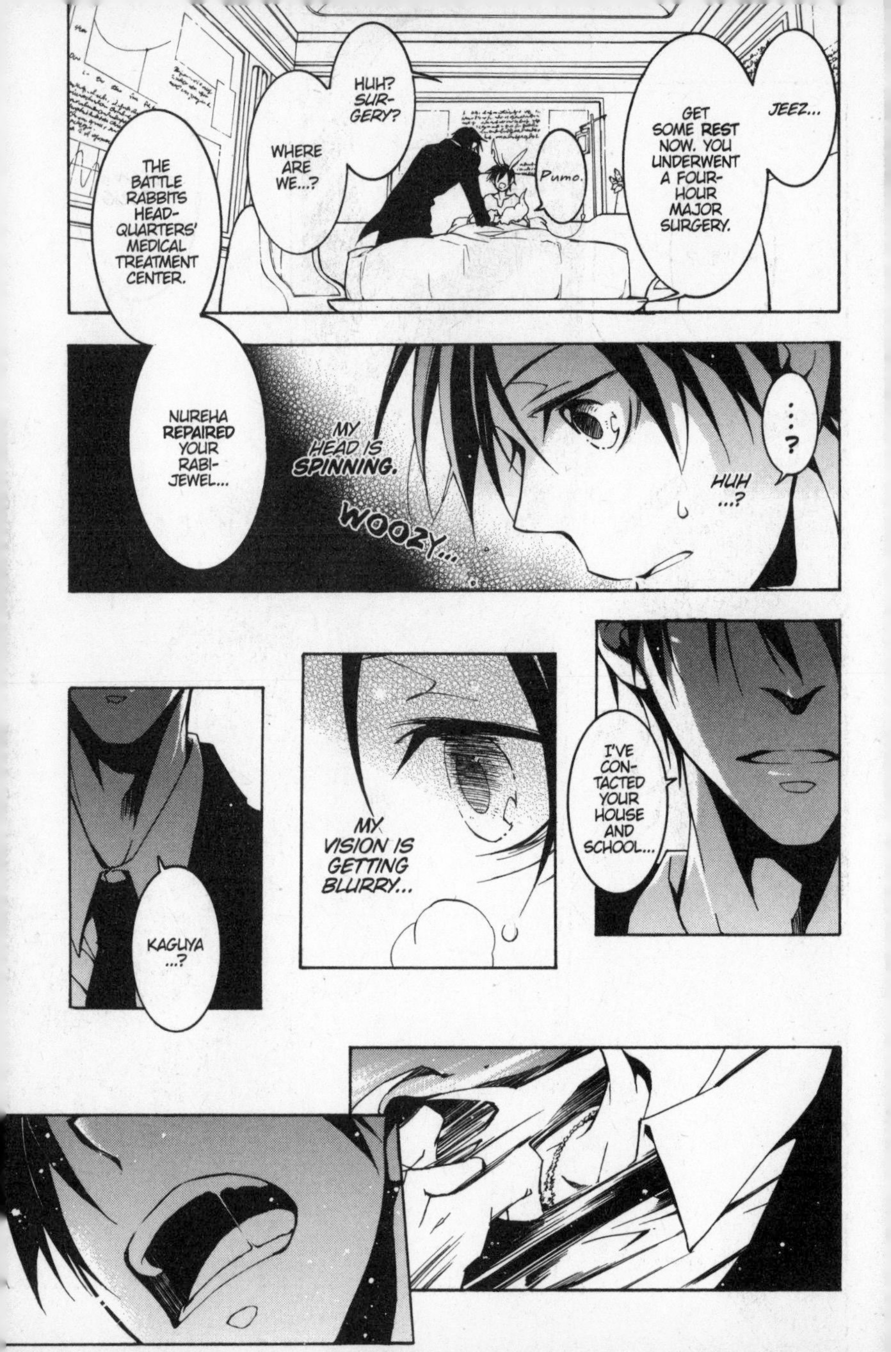
JEEZ...
GET SOME REST NOW. YOU UNDERWENT A FOUR-HOUR MAJOR SURGERY.
Pumo.
HUH? SURGERY?
WHERE ARE WE...?
THE BATTLE RABBITS HEADQUARTERS' MEDICAL TREATMENT CENTER.
...?
HUH ...?
MY HEAD IS SPINNING.
WOOZY...
NUREHA REPAIRED YOUR RABI-JEWEL...
I'VE CONTACTED YOUR HOUSE AND SCHOOL...
MY VISION IS GETTING BLURRY...
KAGUYA ...?

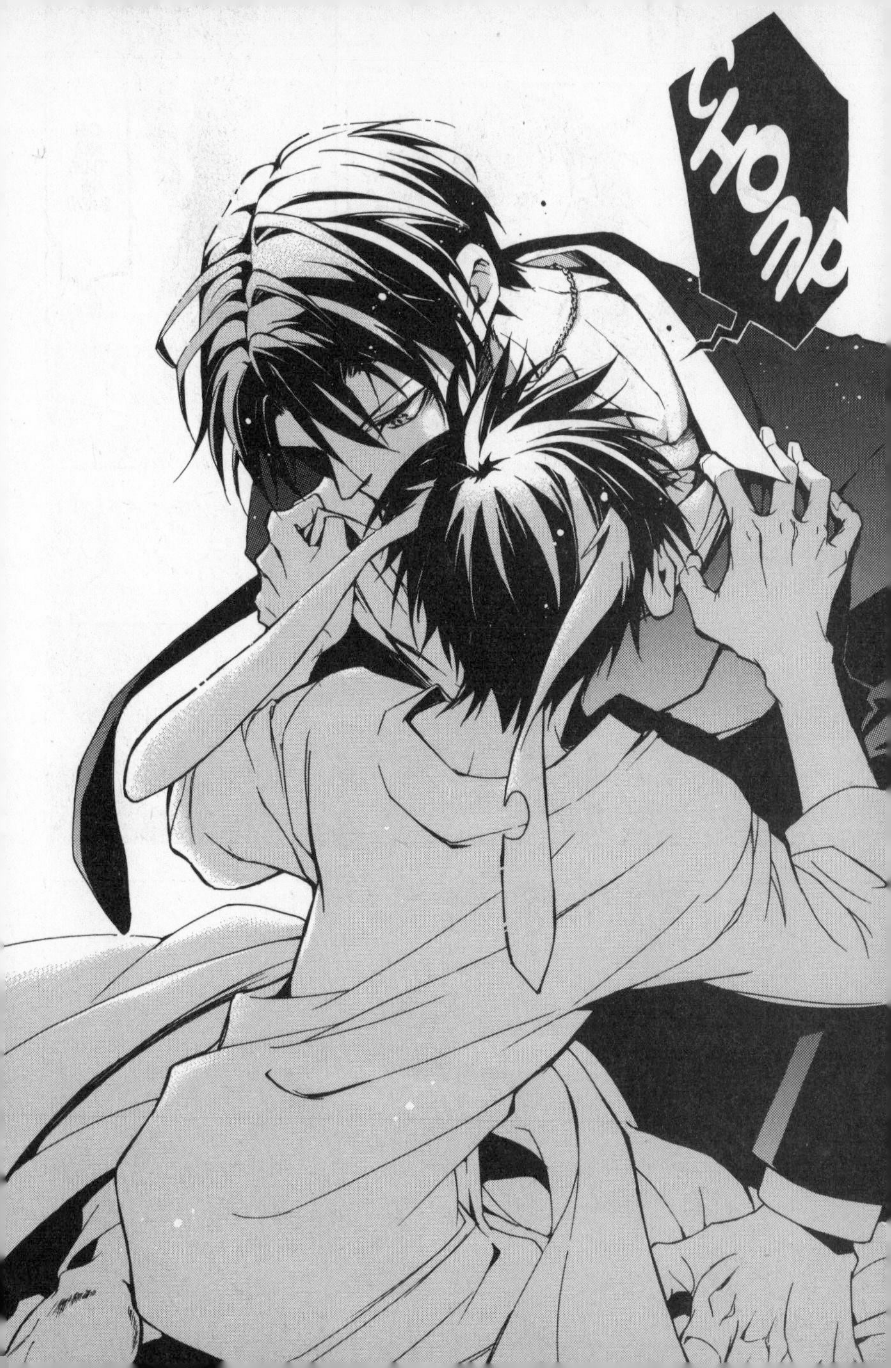
CHOMP

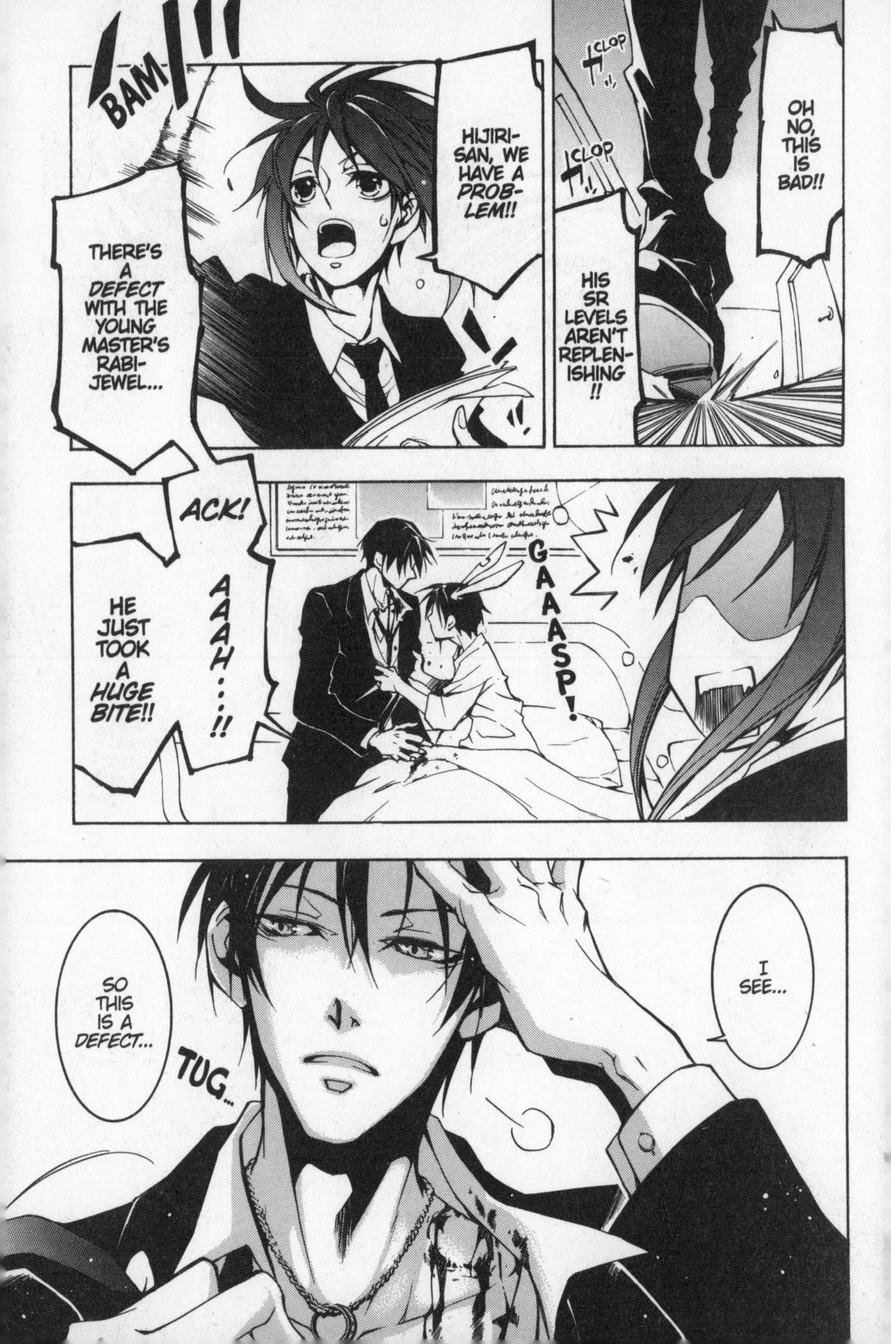
CLOP
CLOP
OH NO, THIS IS BAD!!
HIS SR LEVELS AREN'T REPLENISHING!!
BAM!!!
HIJIRI-SAN, WE HAVE A PROBLEM!!
THERE'S A DEFECT WITH THE YOUNG MASTER'S RABI-JEWEL...
GAAASP!
ACK!
AAAAH...!!
HE JUST TOOK A HUGE BITE!!
I SEE...
TUG...
SO THIS IS A DEFECT...

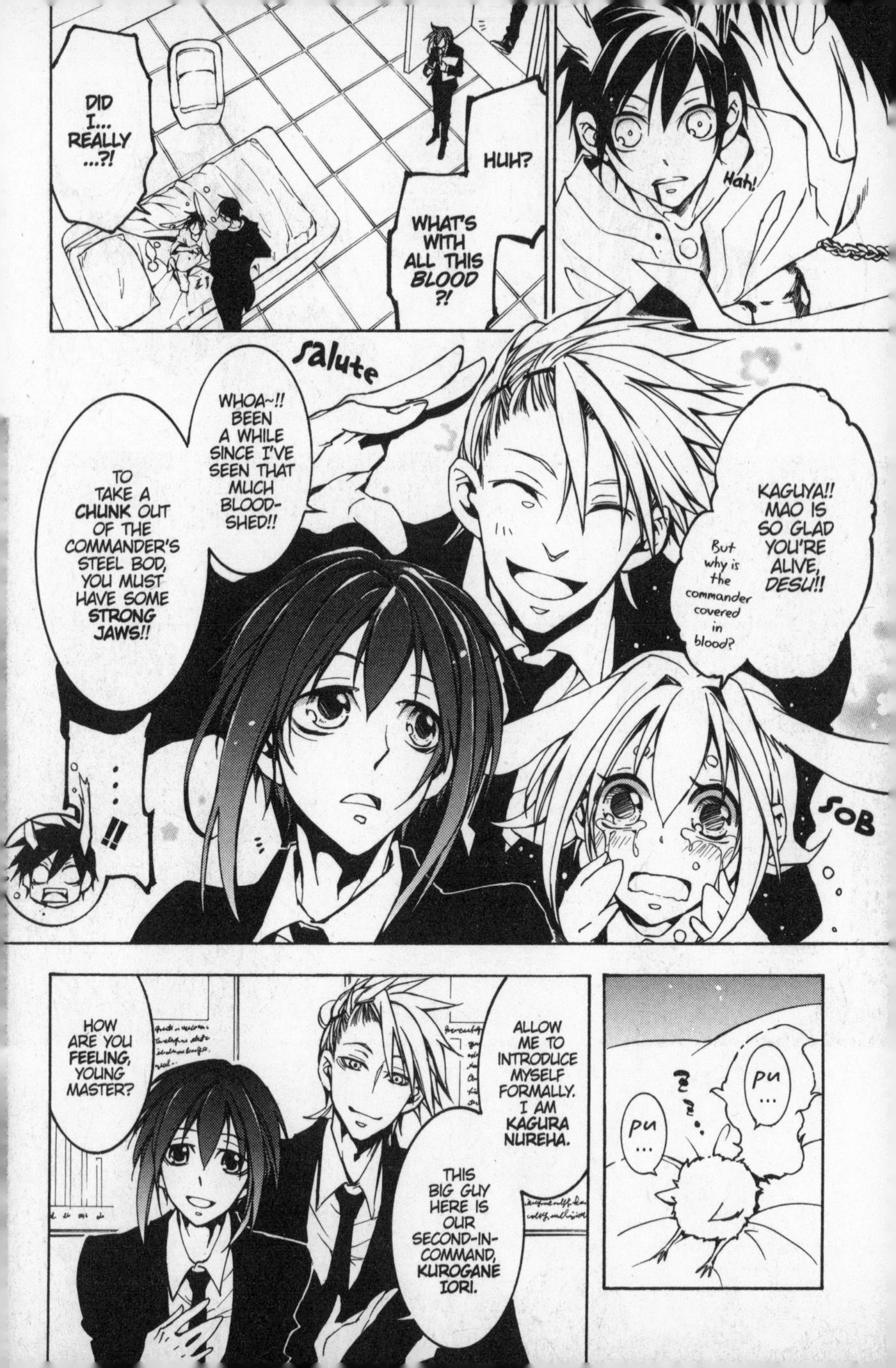
Hah!
HUH?
WHAT'S WITH ALL THIS BLOOD?!
DID I... REALLY...?!
KAGUYA!! MAO IS SO GLAD YOU'RE ALIVE, DESU!!
But why is the commander covered in blood?
salute
WHOA~!! BEEN A WHILE SINCE I'VE SEEN THAT MUCH BLOODSHED!!
TO TAKE A CHUNK OUT OF THE COMMANDER'S STEEL BOD, YOU MUST HAVE SOME STRONG JAWS!!
SOB
...!!
pu...
pu...
ALLOW ME TO INTRODUCE MYSELF FORMALLY. I AM KAGURA NUREHA.
HOW ARE YOU FEELING, YOUNG MASTER?
THIS BIG GUY HERE IS OUR SECOND-IN-COMMAND, KUROGANE IORI.

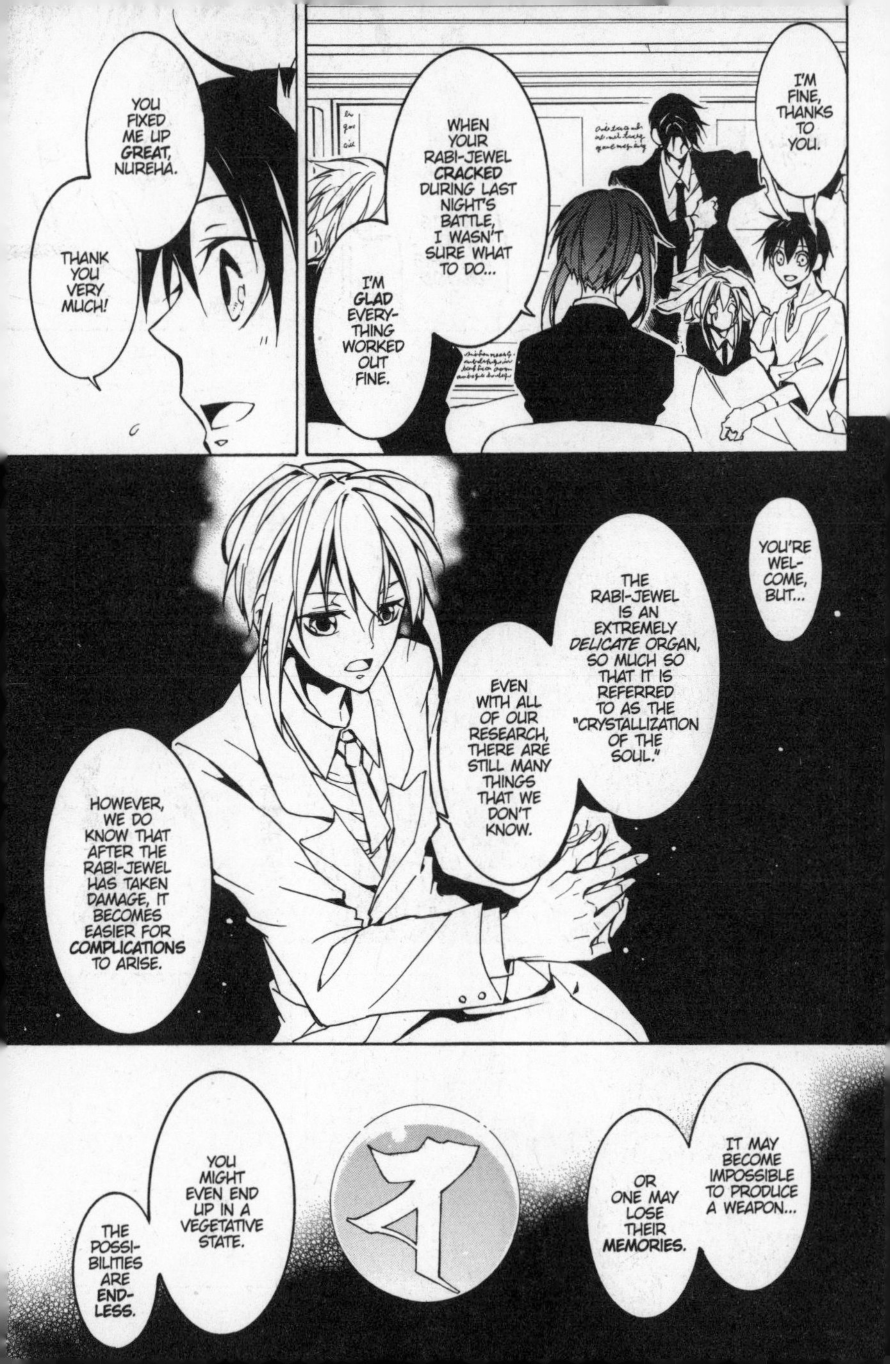
I'M FINE, THANKS TO YOU.
WHEN YOUR RABI-JEWEL CRACKED DURING LAST NIGHT'S BATTLE, I WASN'T SURE WHAT TO DO...
I'M GLAD EVERYTHING WORKED OUT FINE.
YOU FIXED ME UP GREAT, NUREHA.
THANK YOU VERY MUCH!
YOU'RE WELCOME, BUT...
THE RABI-JEWEL IS AN EXTREMELY DELICATE ORGAN, SO MUCH SO THAT IT IS REFERRED TO AS THE "CRYSTALLIZATION OF THE SOUL."
EVEN WITH ALL OF OUR RESEARCH, THERE ARE STILL MANY THINGS THAT WE DON'T KNOW.
HOWEVER, WE DO KNOW THAT AFTER THE RABI-JEWEL HAS TAKEN DAMAGE, IT BECOMES EASIER FOR COMPLICATIONS TO ARISE.
IT MAY BECOME IMPOSSIBLE TO PRODUCE A WEAPON...
OR ONE MAY LOSE THEIR MEMORIES.
YOU MIGHT EVEN END UP IN A VEGETATIVE STATE.
THE POSSIBILITIES ARE ENDLESS.

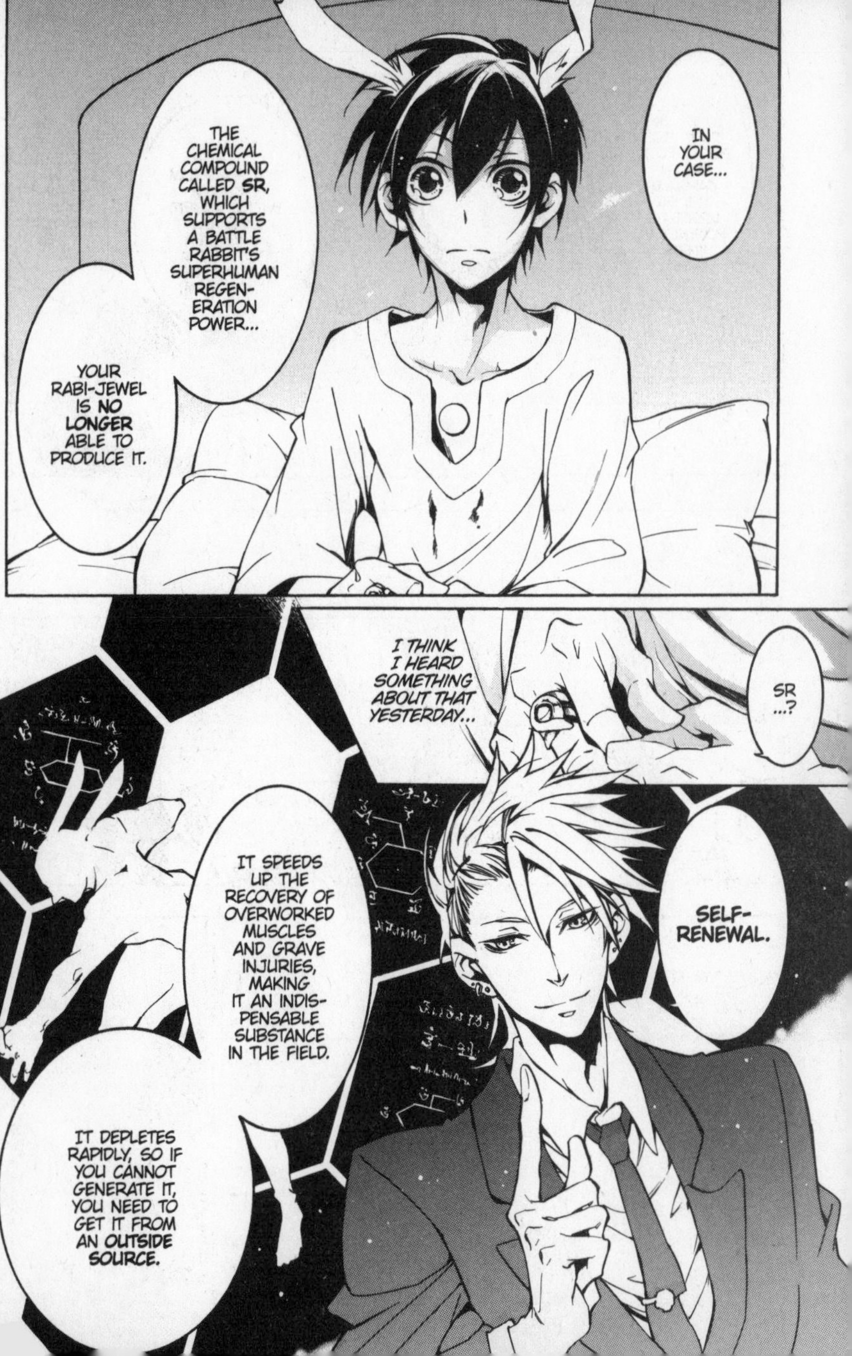
IN YOUR CASE...
THE CHEMICAL COMPOUND CALLED SR, WHICH SUPPORTS A BATTLE RABBIT'S SUPERHUMAN REGEN-ERATION POWER...
YOUR RABI-JEWEL IS NO LONGER ABLE TO PRODUCE IT.
SR ...?
I THINK I HEARD SOMETHING ABOUT THAT YESTERDAY...
SELF-RENEWAL.
IT SPEEDS UP THE RECOVERY OF OVERWORKED MUSCLES AND GRAVE INJURIES, MAKING IT AN INDIS-PENSABLE SUBSTANCE IN THE FIELD.
IT DEPLETES RAPIDLY, SO IF YOU CANNOT GENERATE IT, YOU NEED TO GET IT FROM AN OUTSIDE SOURCE.

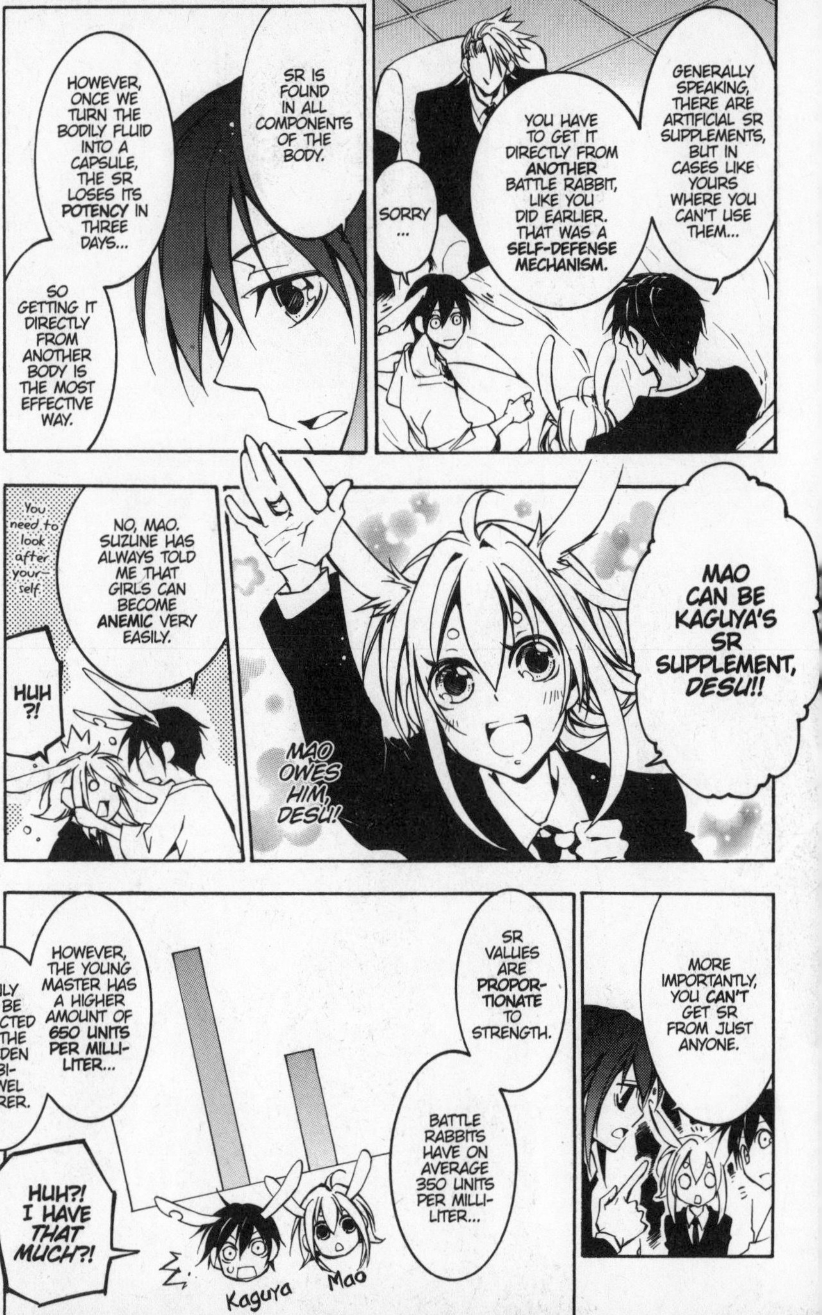
GENERALLY SPEAKING, THERE ARE ARTIFICIAL SR SUPPLEMENTS, BUT IN CASES LIKE YOURS WHERE YOU CAN'T USE THEM...
YOU HAVE TO GET IT DIRECTLY FROM ANOTHER BATTLE RABBIT, LIKE YOU DID EARLIER. THAT WAS A SELF-DEFENSE MECHANISM.
SORRY...
SR IS FOUND IN ALL COMPONENTS OF THE BODY.
HOWEVER, ONCE WE TURN THE BODILY FLUID INTO A CAPSULE, THE SR LOSES ITS POTENCY IN THREE DAYS...
SO GETTING IT DIRECTLY FROM ANOTHER BODY IS THE MOST EFFECTIVE WAY.
MAO CAN BE KAGUYA'S SR SUPPLEMENT, DESU!!
MAO OWES HIM, DESU!
NO, MAO. SUZUNE HAS ALWAYS TOLD ME THAT GIRLS CAN BECOME ANEMIC VERY EASILY.
You need to look after your-self.
HUH?!
MORE IMPORTANTLY, YOU CAN'T GET SR FROM JUST ANYONE.
SR VALUES ARE PROPORTIONATE TO STRENGTH.
BATTLE RABBITS HAVE ON AVERAGE 350 UNITS PER MILLILITER...
HOWEVER, THE YOUNG MASTER HAS A HIGHER AMOUNT OF 650 UNITS PER MILLILITER...
ONLY TO BE EXPECTED OF THE GOLDEN RABI-JEWEL BEARER.
Mao
Kaguya
HUH?! I HAVE THAT MUCH?!

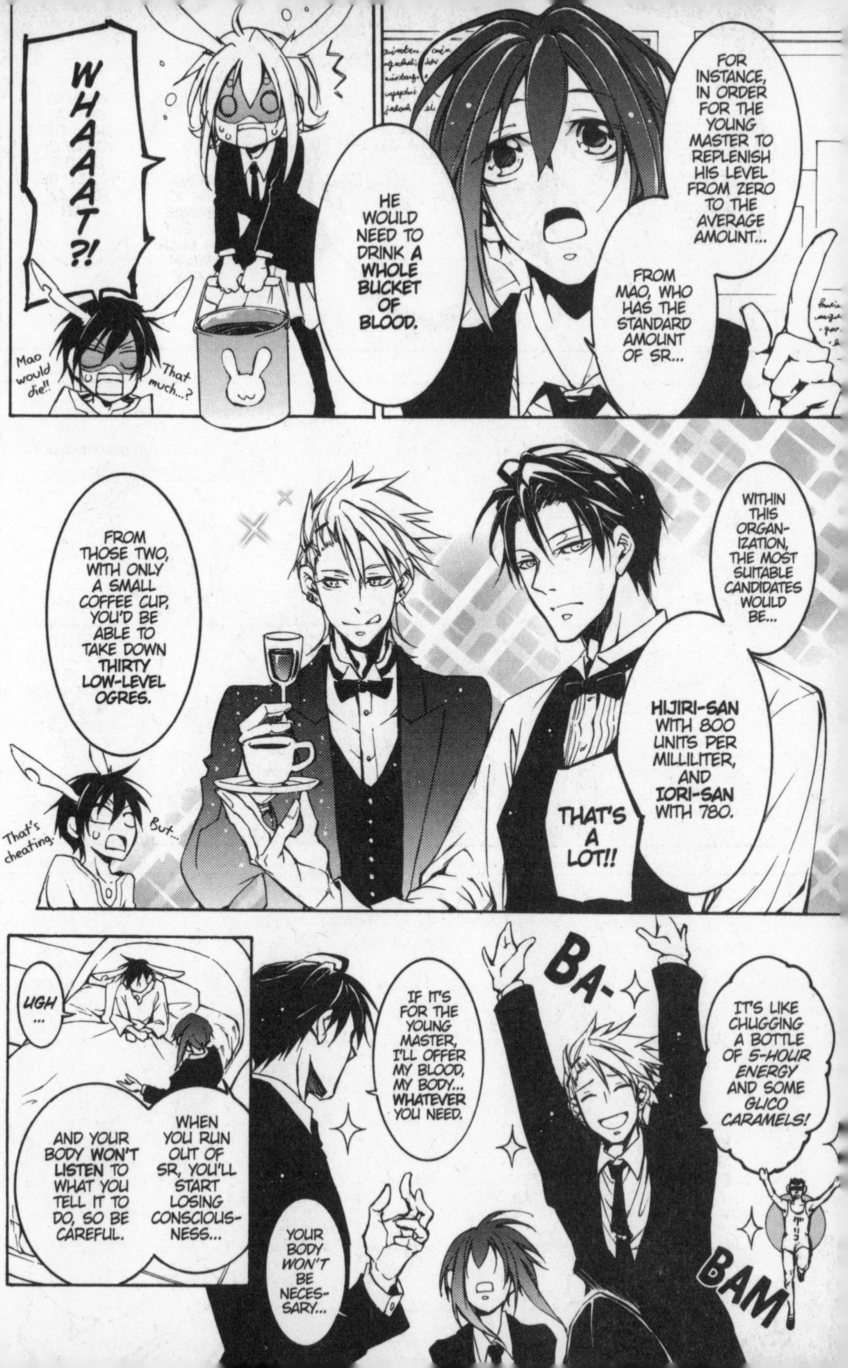
FOR INSTANCE, IN ORDER FOR THE YOUNG MASTER TO REPLENISH HIS LEVEL FROM ZERO TO THE AVERAGE AMOUNT...
FROM MAO, WHO HAS THE STANDARD AMOUNT OF SR...
HE WOULD NEED TO DRINK A WHOLE BUCKET OF BLOOD.
WHAAAAT?!
That much...?
Mao would die!!
WITHIN THIS ORGANIZATION, THE MOST SUITABLE CANDIDATES WOULD BE...
HIJIRI-SAN WITH 800 UNITS PER MILLILITER, AND IORI-SAN WITH 780.
THAT'S A LOT!!
FROM THOSE TWO, WITH ONLY A SMALL COFFEE CUP, YOU'D BE ABLE TO TAKE DOWN THIRTY LOW-LEVEL OGRES.
But...
That's cheating.
IT'S LIKE CHUGGING A BOTTLE OF 5-HOUR ENERGY AND SOME GLICO CARAMELS!
BA-
BAM
IF IT'S FOR THE YOUNG MASTER, I'LL OFFER MY BLOOD, MY BODY... WHATEVER YOU NEED.
YOUR BODY WON'T BE NECESSARY...
UGH ...
WHEN YOU RUN OUT OF SR, YOU'LL START LOSING CONSCIOUSNESS...
AND YOUR BODY WON'T LISTEN TO WHAT YOU TELL IT TO DO, SO BE CAREFUL.

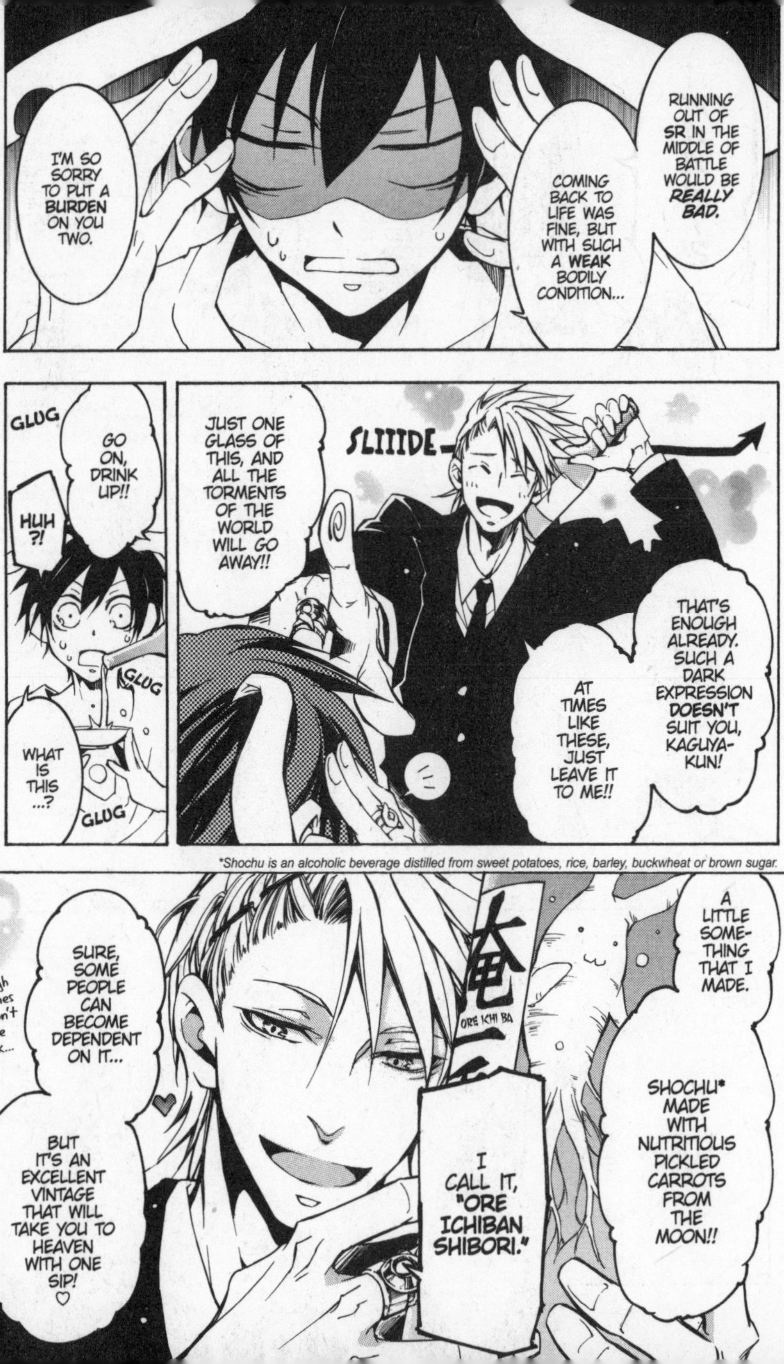
RUNNING OUT OF SR IN THE MIDDLE OF BATTLE WOULD BE REALLY BAD.
COMING BACK TO LIFE WAS FINE, BUT WITH SUCH A WEAK BODILY CONDITION...
I'M SO SORRY TO PUT A BURDEN ON YOU TWO.
THAT'S ENOUGH ALREADY. SUCH A DARK EXPRESSION DOESN'T SUIT YOU, KAGUYA-KUN!
AT TIMES LIKE THESE, JUST LEAVE IT TO ME!!
SLIIIDE
JUST ONE GLASS OF THIS, AND ALL THE TORMENTS OF THE WORLD WILL GO AWAY!!
GO ON, DRINK UP!!
GLUG
HUH ?!
GLUG
WHAT IS THIS ...?
GLUG
A LITTLE SOMETHING THAT I MADE.
SHOCHU* MADE WITH NUTRITIOUS PICKLED CARROTS FROM THE MOON!!
I CALL IT, "ORE ICHIBAN SHIBORI."
俺
ORE ICHI BA
SURE, SOME PEOPLE CAN BECOME DEPENDENT ON IT...
BUT IT'S AN EXCELLENT VINTAGE THAT WILL TAKE YOU TO HEAVEN WITH ONE SIP! ♡
Although sometimes you don't come back...

*Shochu is an alcoholic beverage distilled from sweet potatoes, rice, barley, buckwheat or brown sugar.

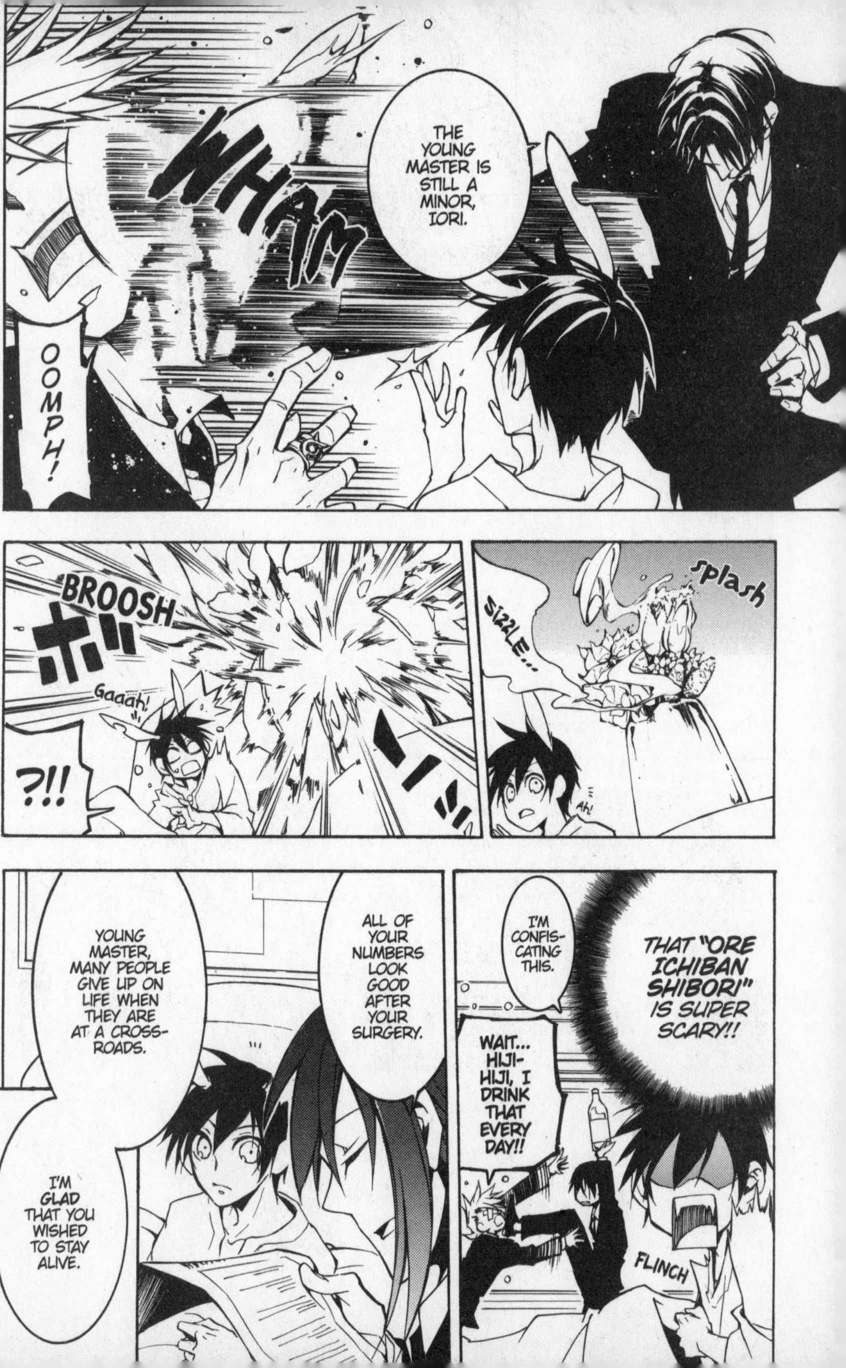
THE YOUNG MASTER IS STILL A MINOR, IORI.
WHAM
OOMPH!
splash
SIZZLE...
Ah!
BROOSH
Gaaah!
?!!
I'M CONFISCATING THIS.
THAT "ORE ICHIBAN SHIBORI" IS SUPER SCARY!!
WAIT... HIJI-HIJI, I DRINK THAT EVERY DAY!!
FLINCH
ALL OF YOUR NUMBERS LOOK GOOD AFTER YOUR SURGERY.
YOUNG MASTER, MANY PEOPLE GIVE UP ON LIFE WHEN THEY ARE AT A CROSS-ROADS.
I'M GLAD THAT YOU WISHED TO STAY ALIVE.

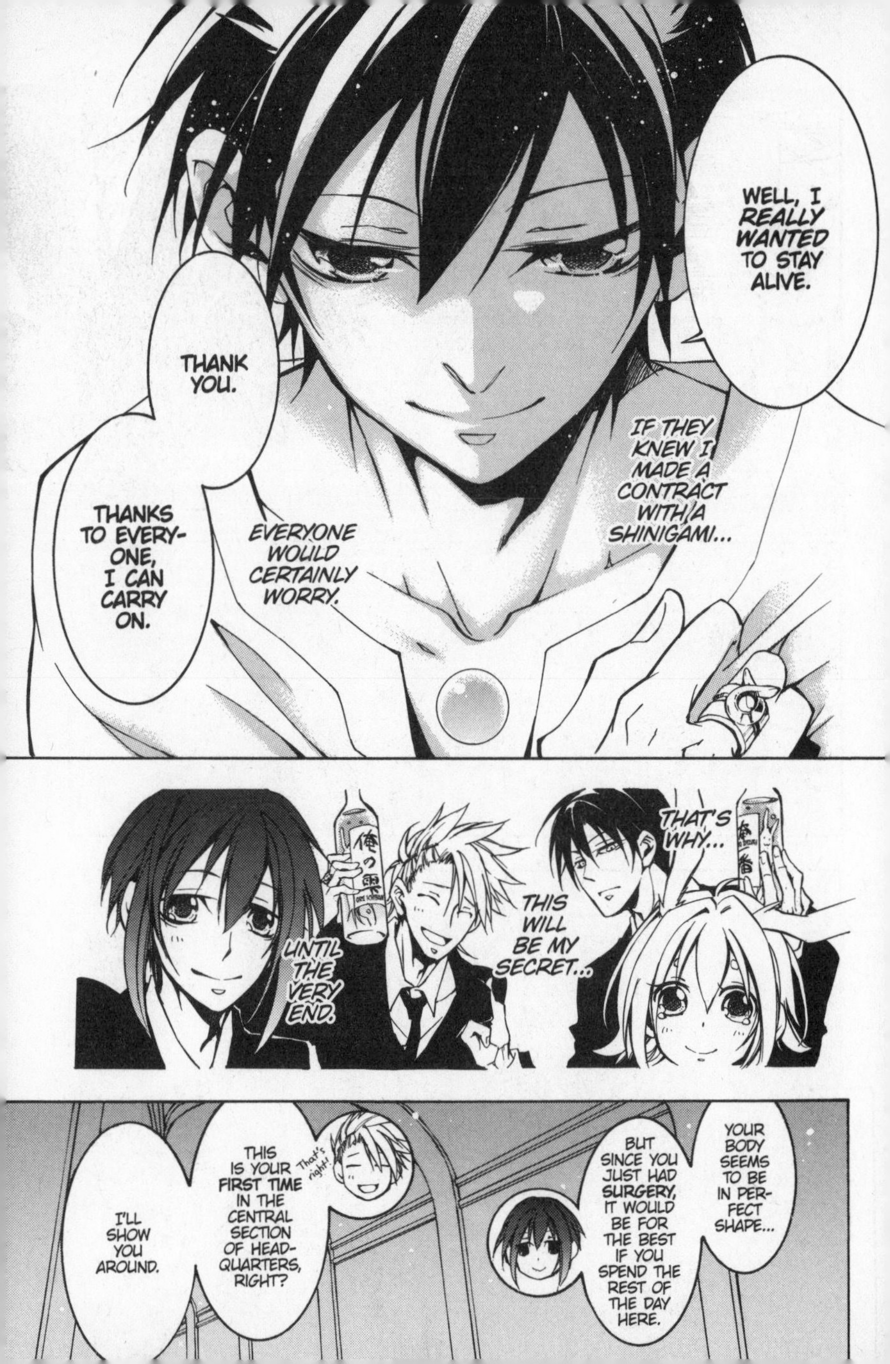
WELL, I REALLY WANTED TO STAY ALIVE.
IF THEY KNEW I MADE A CONTRACT WITH A SHINIGAMI...
EVERYONE WOULD CERTAINLY WORRY.
THANK YOU.
THANKS TO EVERY-ONE, I CAN CARRY ON.
俺の雫
THAT'S WHY...
THIS WILL BE MY SECRET...
UNTIL THE VERY END.
YOUR BODY SEEMS TO BE IN PER-FECT SHAPE...
BUT SINCE YOU JUST HAD SURGERY, IT WOULD BE FOR THE BEST IF YOU SPEND THE REST OF THE DAY HERE.
THIS IS YOUR FIRST TIME IN THE CENTRAL SECTION OF HEAD-QUARTERS, RIGHT?
That's right!
I'LL SHOW YOU AROUND.

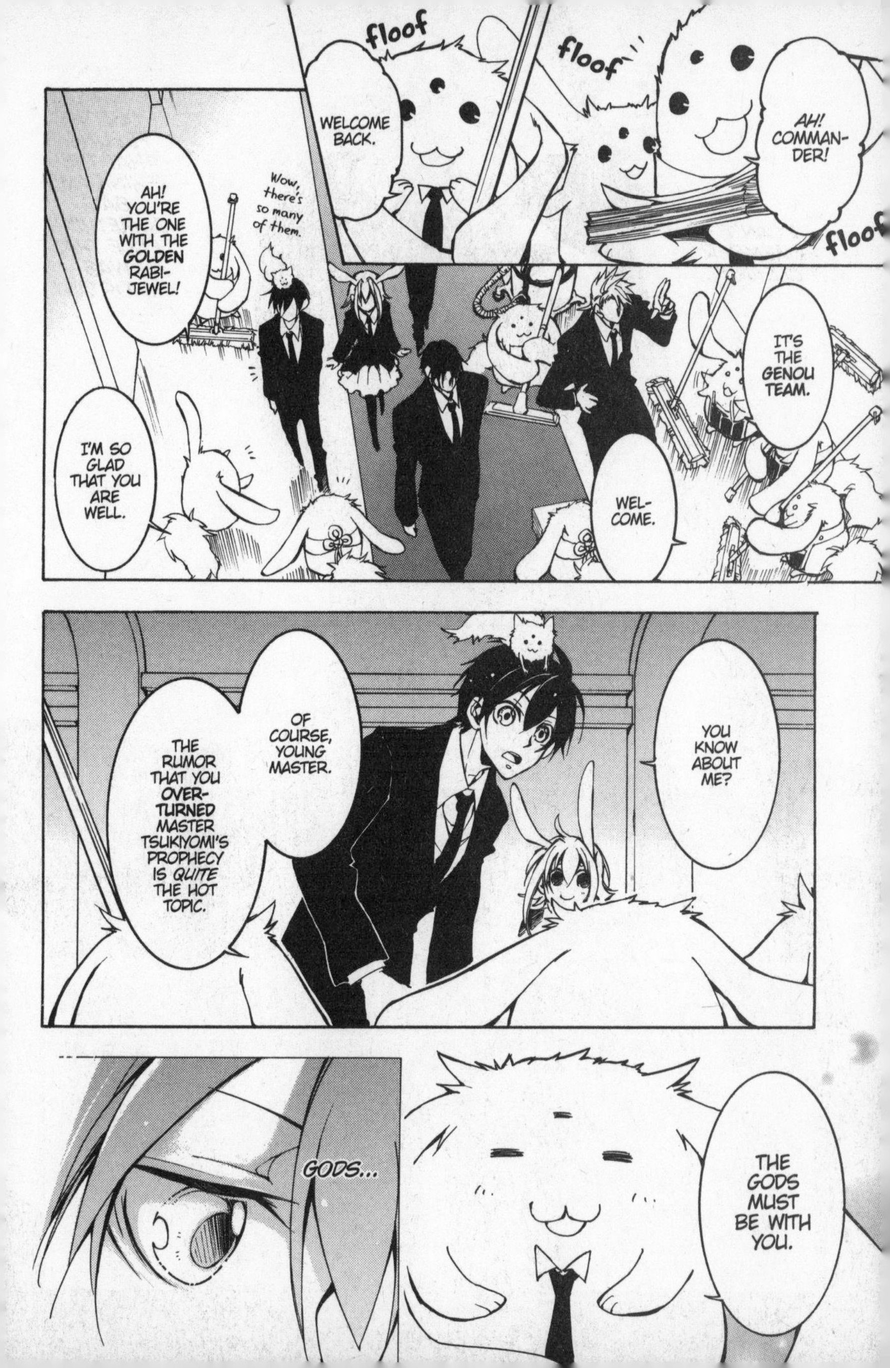
floof
floof
AH! COMMANDER!
floof
WELCOME BACK.
IT'S THE GENOU TEAM.
WEL-COME.
Wow, there's so many of them.
AH! YOU'RE THE ONE WITH THE GOLDEN RABI-JEWEL!
I'M SO GLAD THAT YOU ARE WELL.
YOU KNOW ABOUT ME?
OF COURSE, YOUNG MASTER.
THE RUMOR THAT YOU OVER-TURNED MASTER TSUKIYOMI'S PROPHECY IS QUITE THE HOT TOPIC.
THE GODS MUST BE WITH YOU.
GODS...

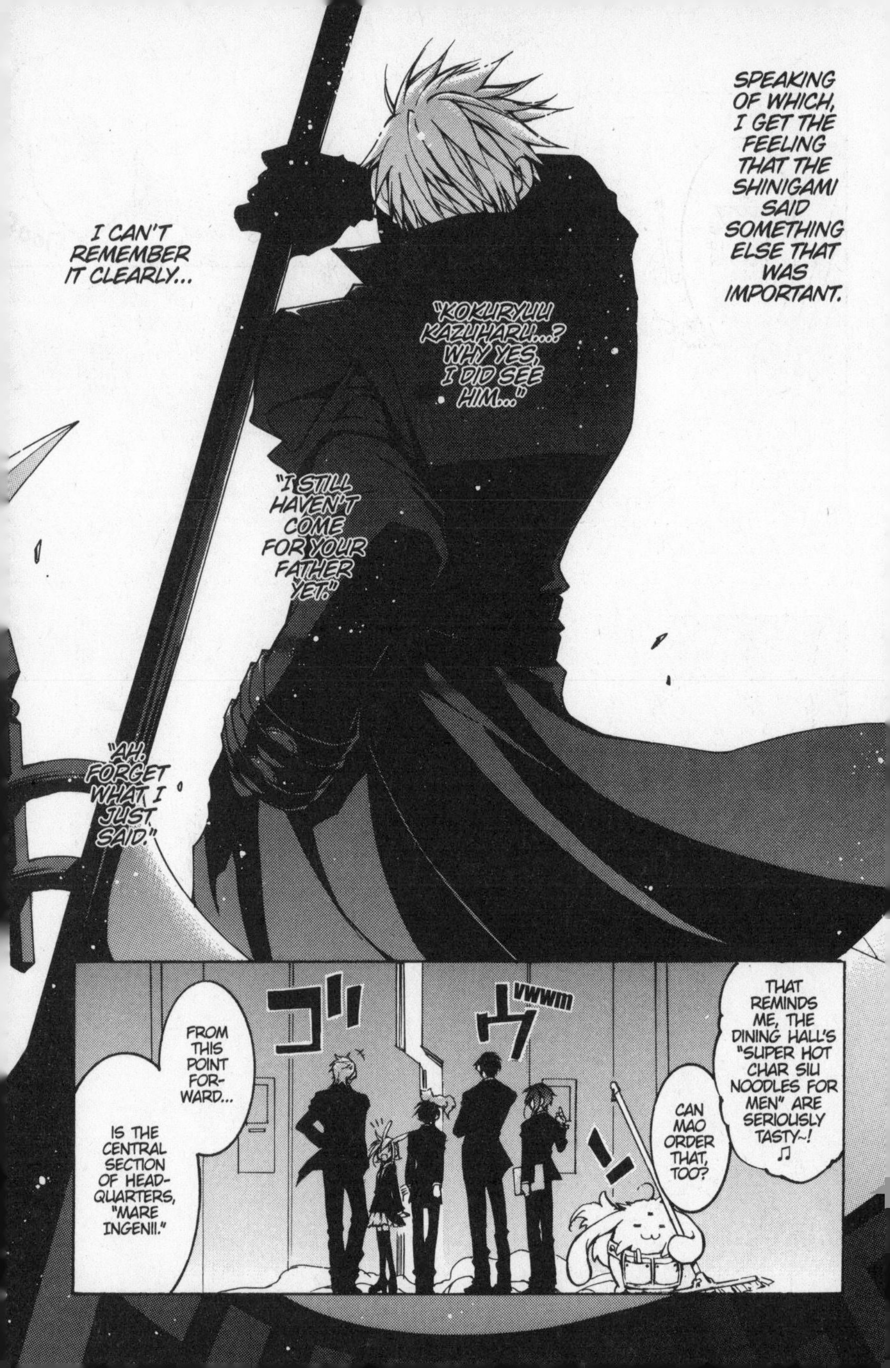
SPEAKING OF WHICH, I GET THE FEELING THAT THE SHINIGAMI SAID SOMETHING ELSE THAT WAS IMPORTANT.
I CAN'T REMEMBER IT CLEARLY...
"KOKURYUU KAZUHARU...? WHY YES, I DID SEE HIM..."
"I STILL HAVEN'T COME FOR YOUR FATHER YET."
"AH. FORGET WHAT I JUST SAID."
THAT REMINDS ME, THE DINING HALL'S "SUPER HOT CHAR SIU NOODLES FOR MEN" ARE SERIOUSLY TASTY~! ♫
CAN MAO ORDER THAT, TOO?
VWWM
FROM THIS POINT FOR-WARD...
IS THE CENTRAL SECTION OF HEAD-QUARTERS, "MARE INGENII."

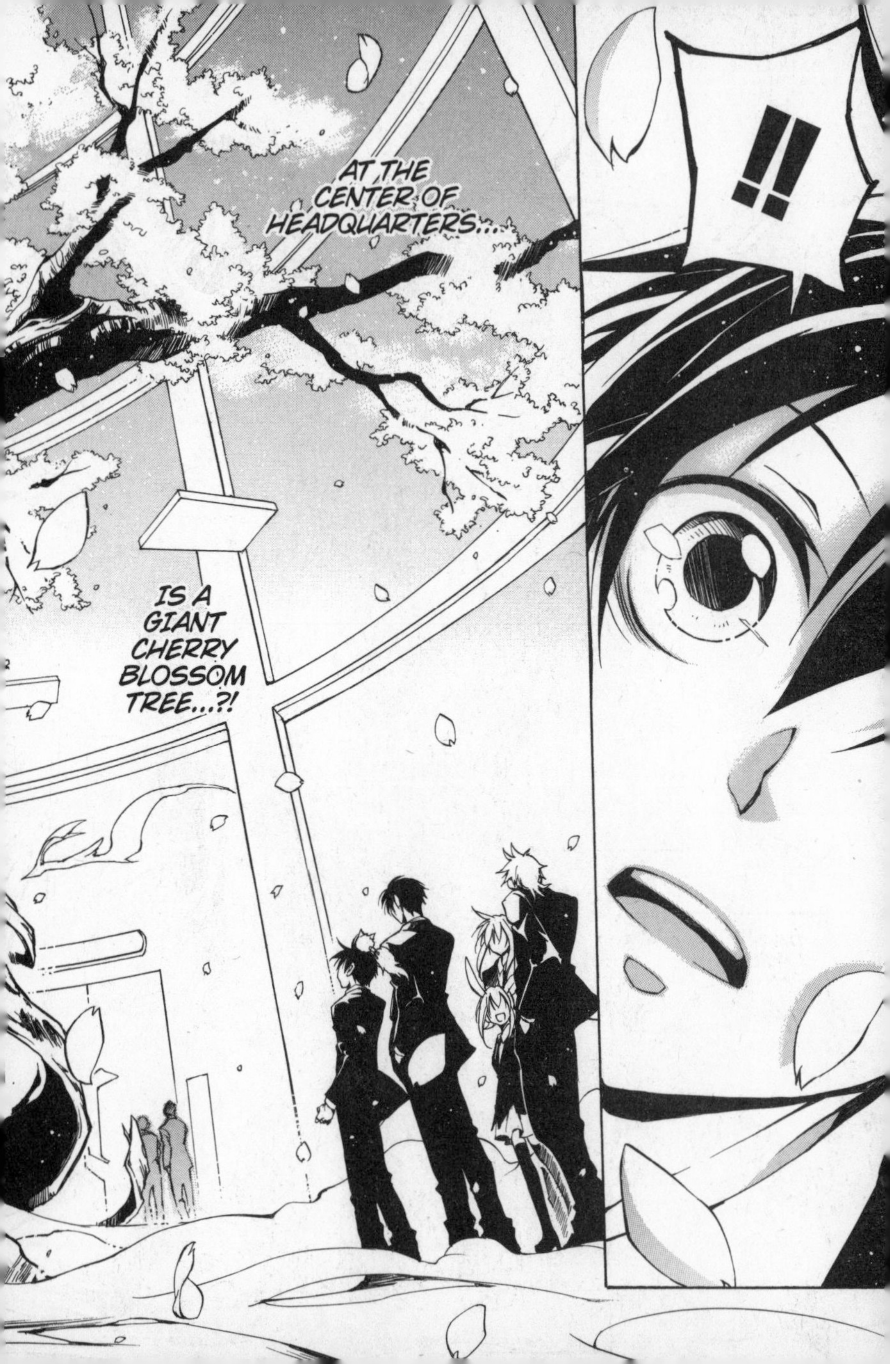
!!
AT THE CENTER OF HEADQUARTERS...
IS A GIANT CHERRY BLOSSOM TREE...?!

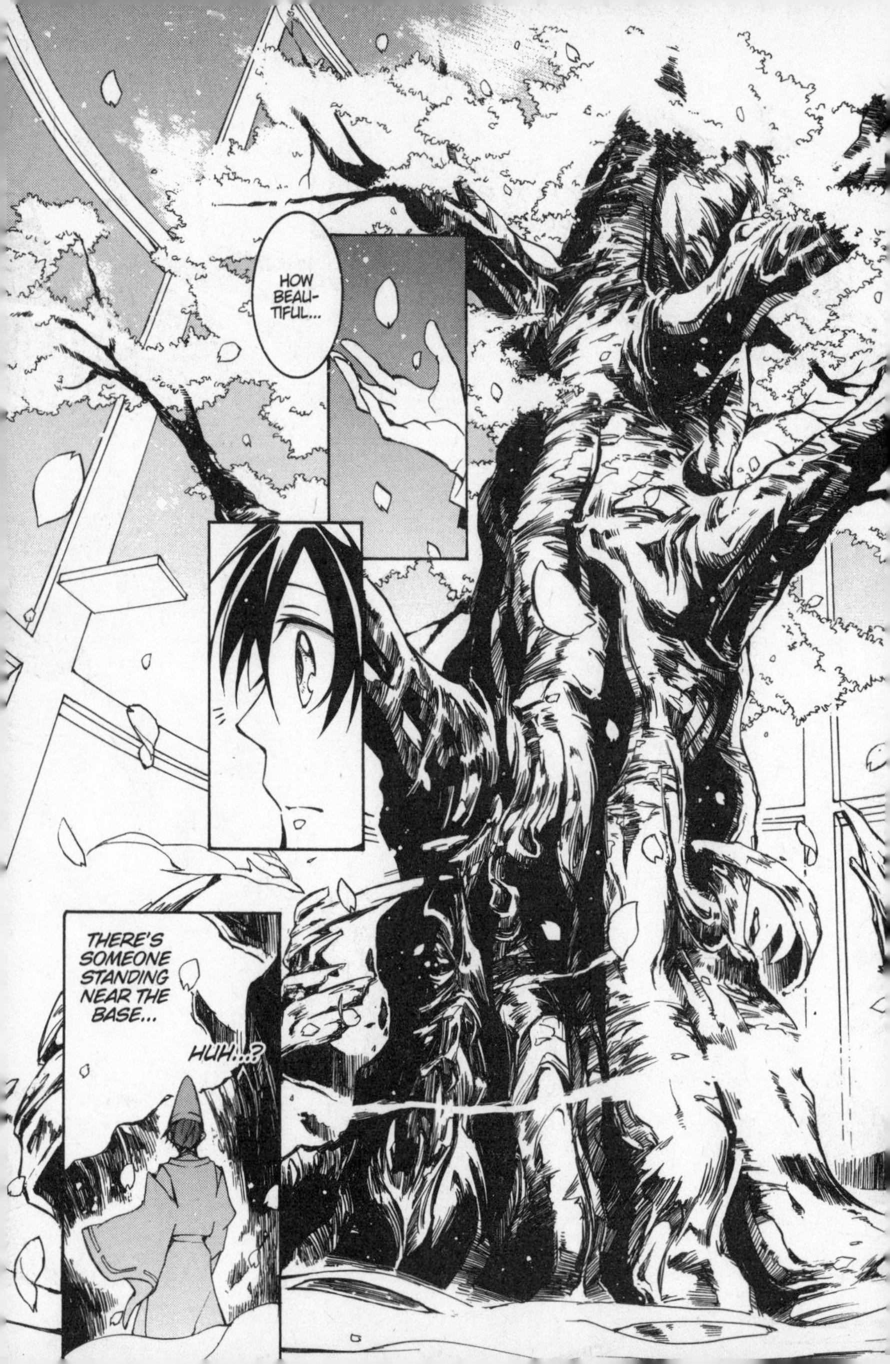
HOW BEAU-TIFUL...
THERE'S SOMEONE STANDING NEAR THE BASE...
HUH...?

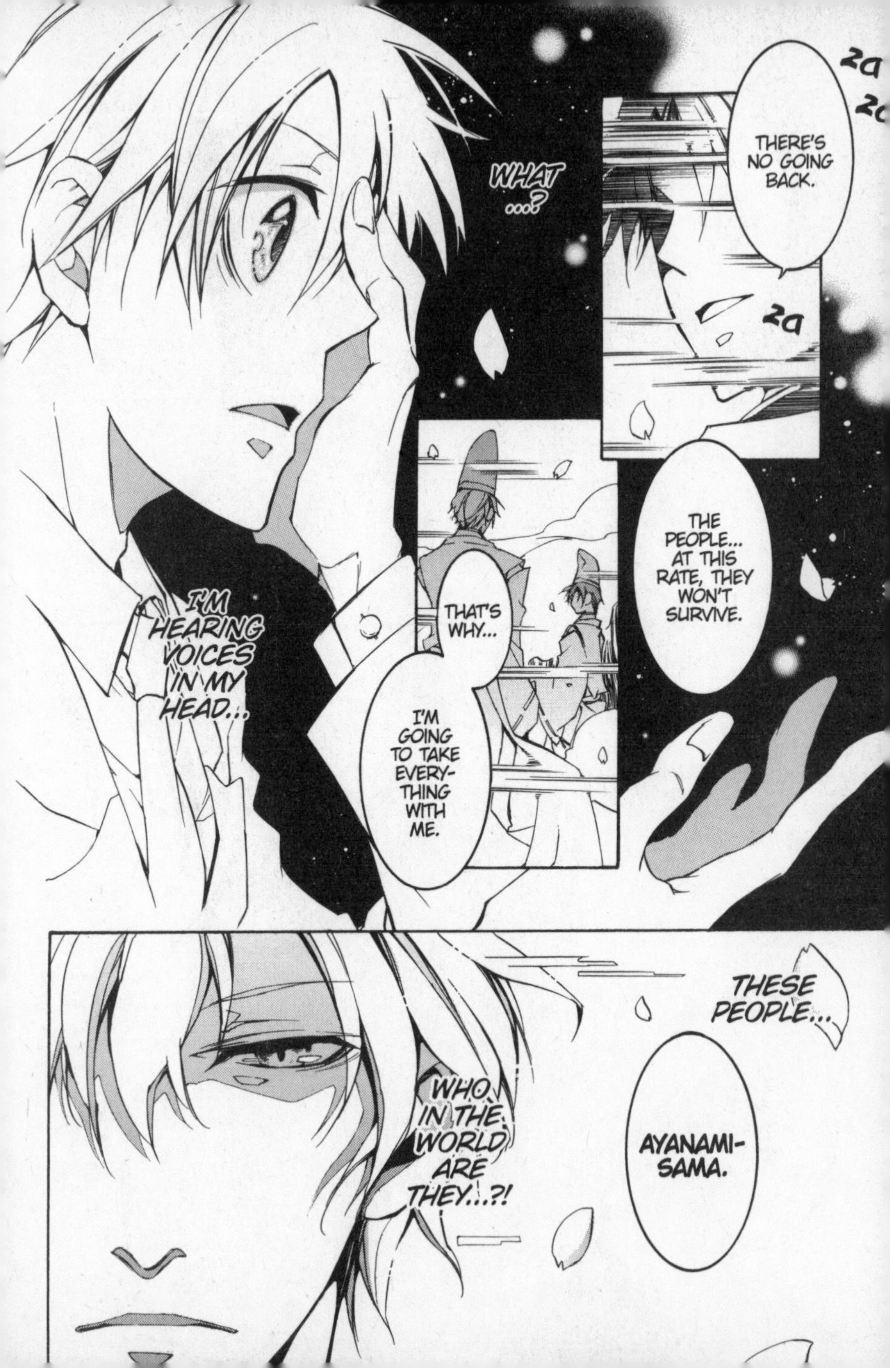
za
THERE'S NO GOING BACK.
za
THE PEOPLE... AT THIS RATE, THEY WON'T SURVIVE.
THAT'S WHY...
I'M GOING TO TAKE EVERYTHING WITH ME.
WHAT...?
I'M HEARING VOICES IN MY HEAD...
THESE PEOPLE...
AYANAMI-SAMA.
WHO IN THE WORLD ARE THEY...?!

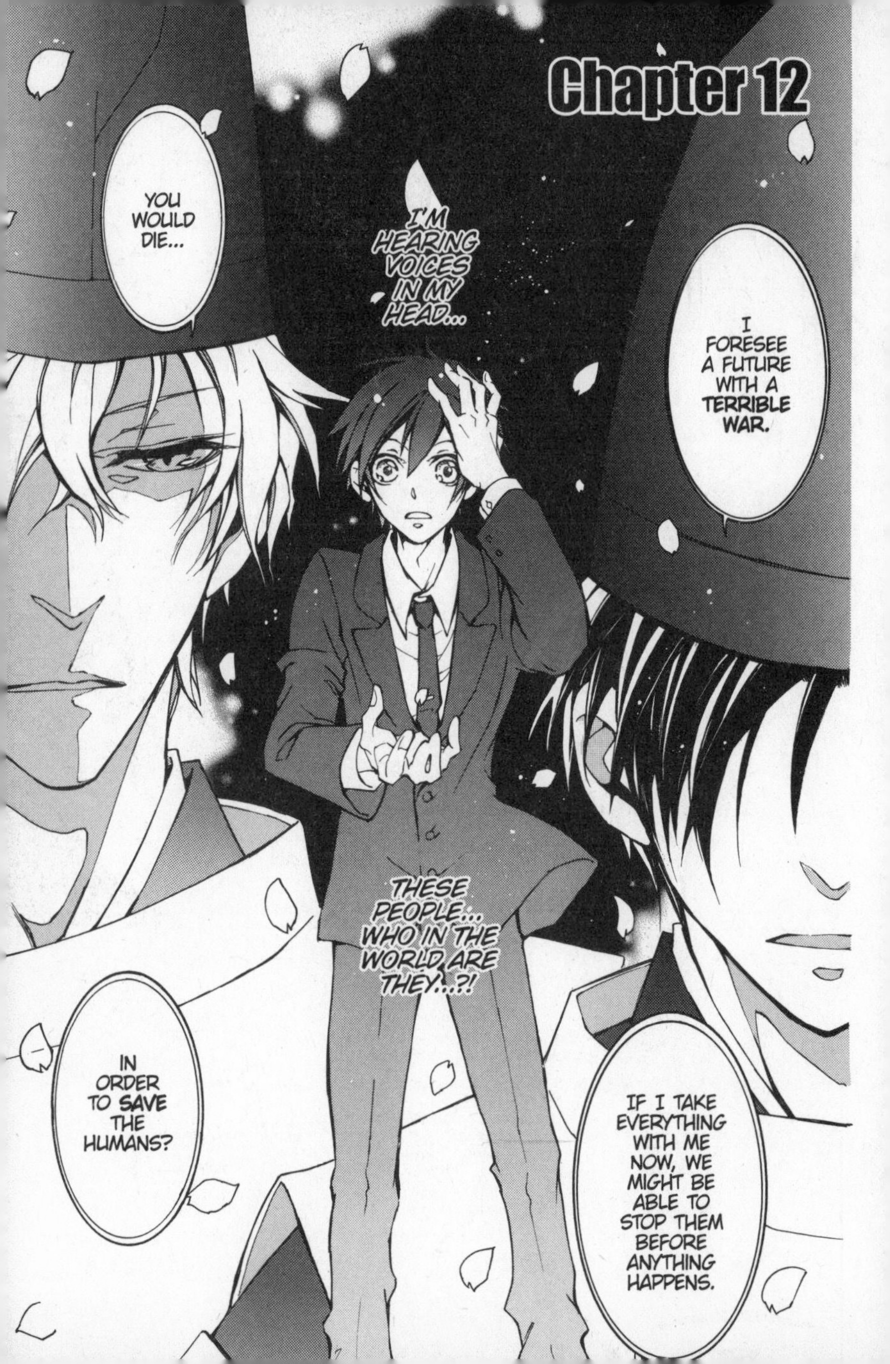
Chapter 12
I FORESEE A FUTURE WITH A TERRIBLE WAR.
I'M HEARING VOICES IN MY HEAD...
YOU WOULD DIE...
IF I TAKE EVERYTHING WITH ME NOW, WE MIGHT BE ABLE TO STOP THEM BEFORE ANYTHING HAPPENS.
THESE PEOPLE... WHO IN THE WORLD ARE THEY...?!
IN ORDER TO SAVE THE HUMANS?

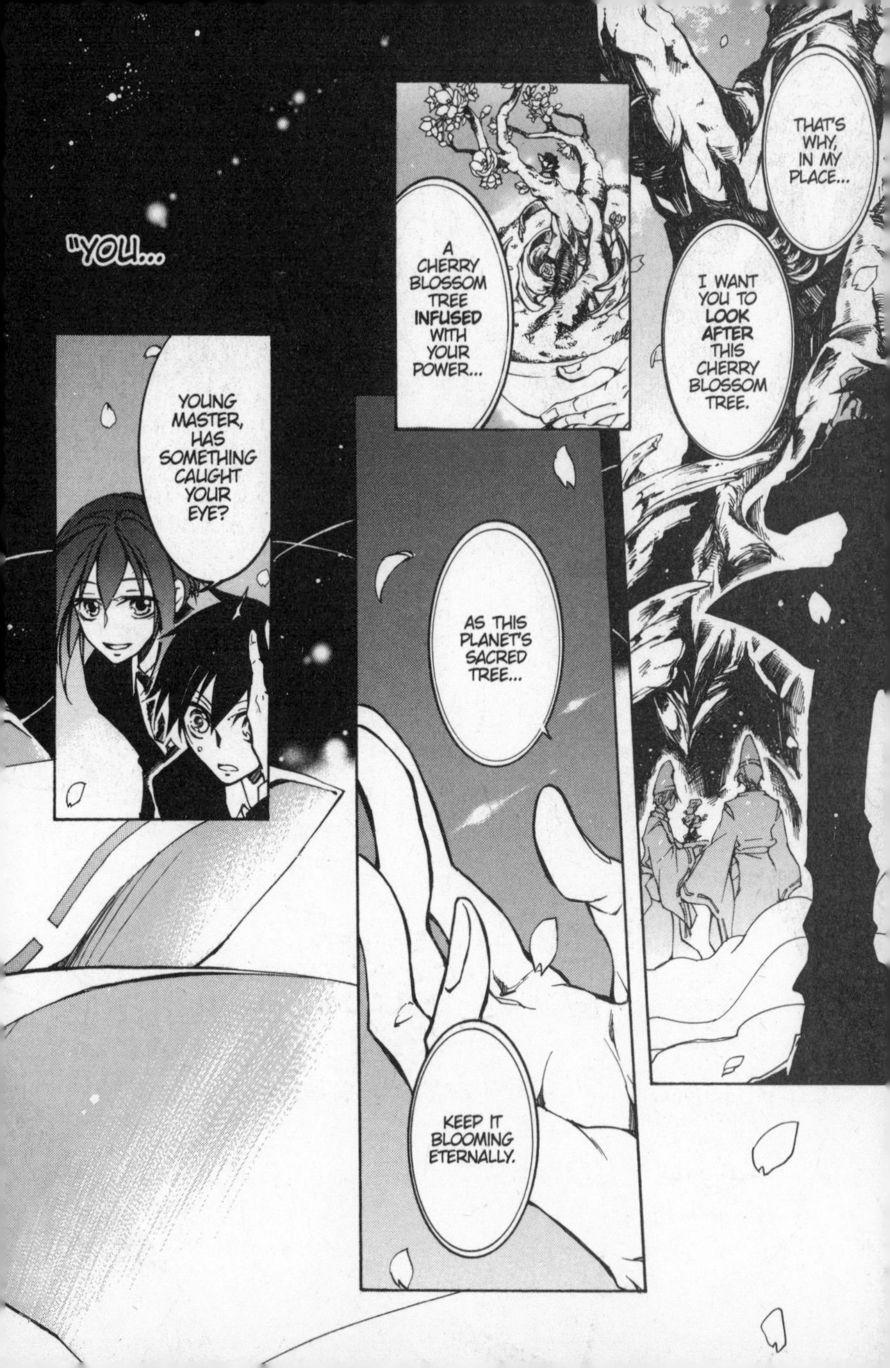
THAT'S WHY, IN MY PLACE...
I WANT YOU TO LOOK AFTER THIS CHERRY BLOSSOM TREE.
A CHERRY BLOSSOM TREE INFUSED WITH YOUR POWER...
"YOU...
AS THIS PLANET'S SACRED TREE...
KEEP IT BLOOMING ETERNALLY.
YOUNG MASTER, HAS SOMETHING CAUGHT YOUR EYE?

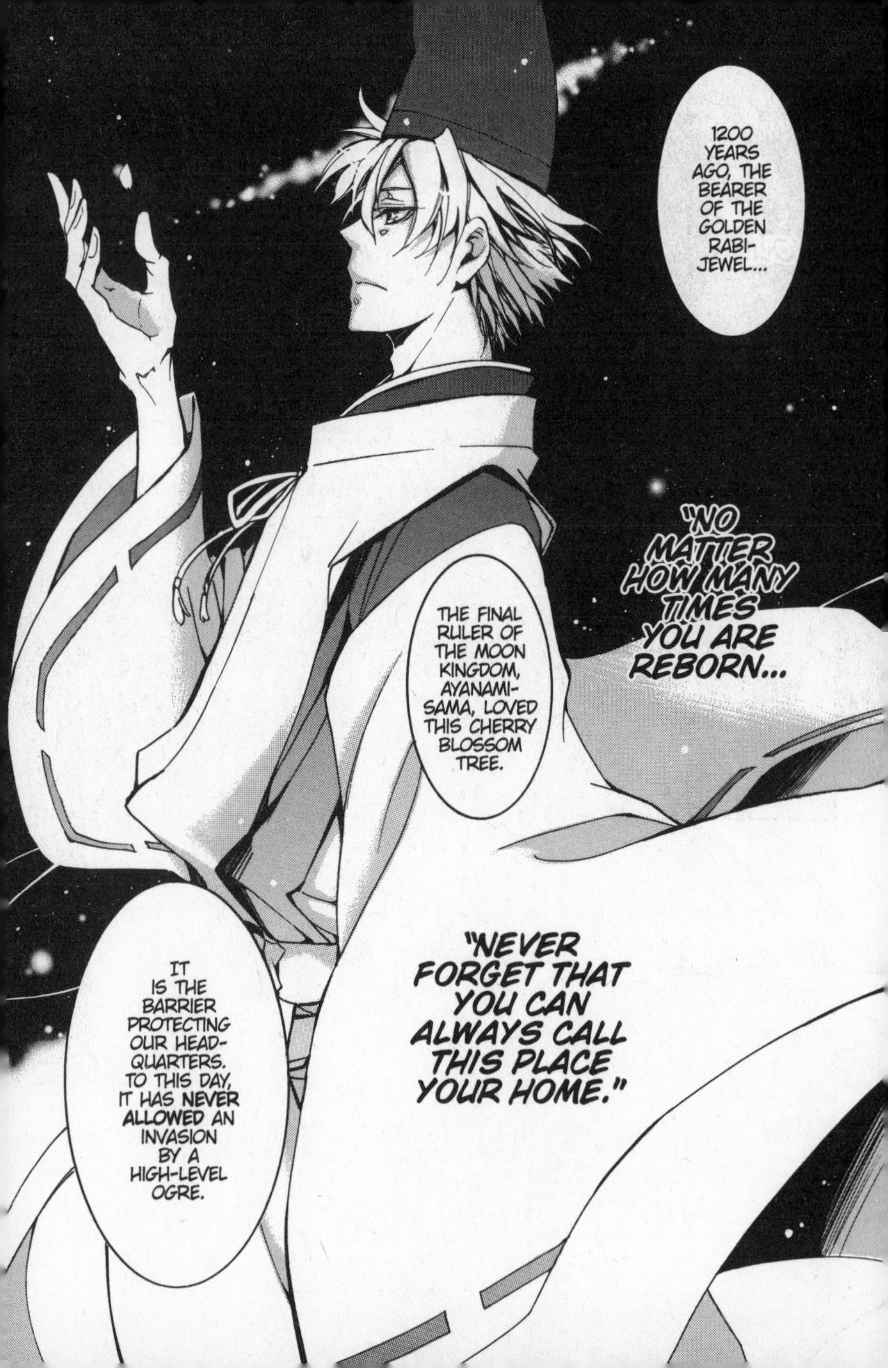
1200 YEARS AGO, THE BEARER OF THE GOLDEN RABI-JEWEL...
"NO MATTER HOW MANY TIMES YOU ARE REBORN...
THE FINAL RULER OF THE MOON KINGDOM, AYANAMI-SAMA, LOVED THIS CHERRY BLOSSOM TREE.
"NEVER FORGET THAT YOU CAN ALWAYS CALL THIS PLACE YOUR HOME."
IT IS THE BARRIER PROTECTING OUR HEAD-QUARTERS. TO THIS DAY, IT HAS NEVER ALLOWED AN INVASION BY A HIGH-LEVEL OGRE.

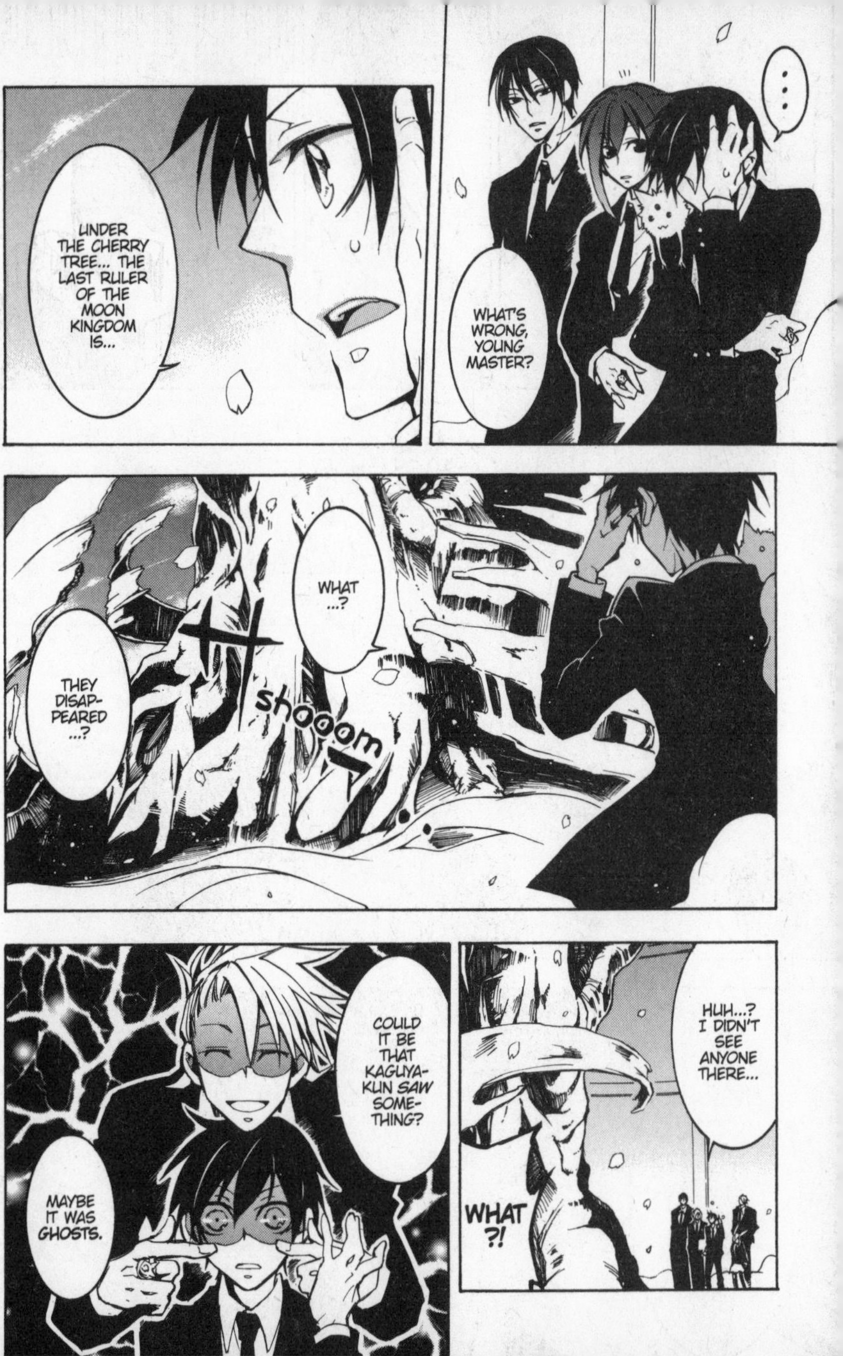
...
WHAT'S WRONG, YOUNG MASTER?
UNDER THE CHERRY TREE... THE LAST RULER OF THE MOON KINGDOM IS...
WHAT ...?
shoooom
THEY DISAP-PEARED ...?
HUH...? I DIDN'T SEE ANYONE THERE...
WHAT ?!
COULD IT BE THAT KAGUYA-KUN SAW SOMETHING?
MAYBE IT WAS GHOSTS.

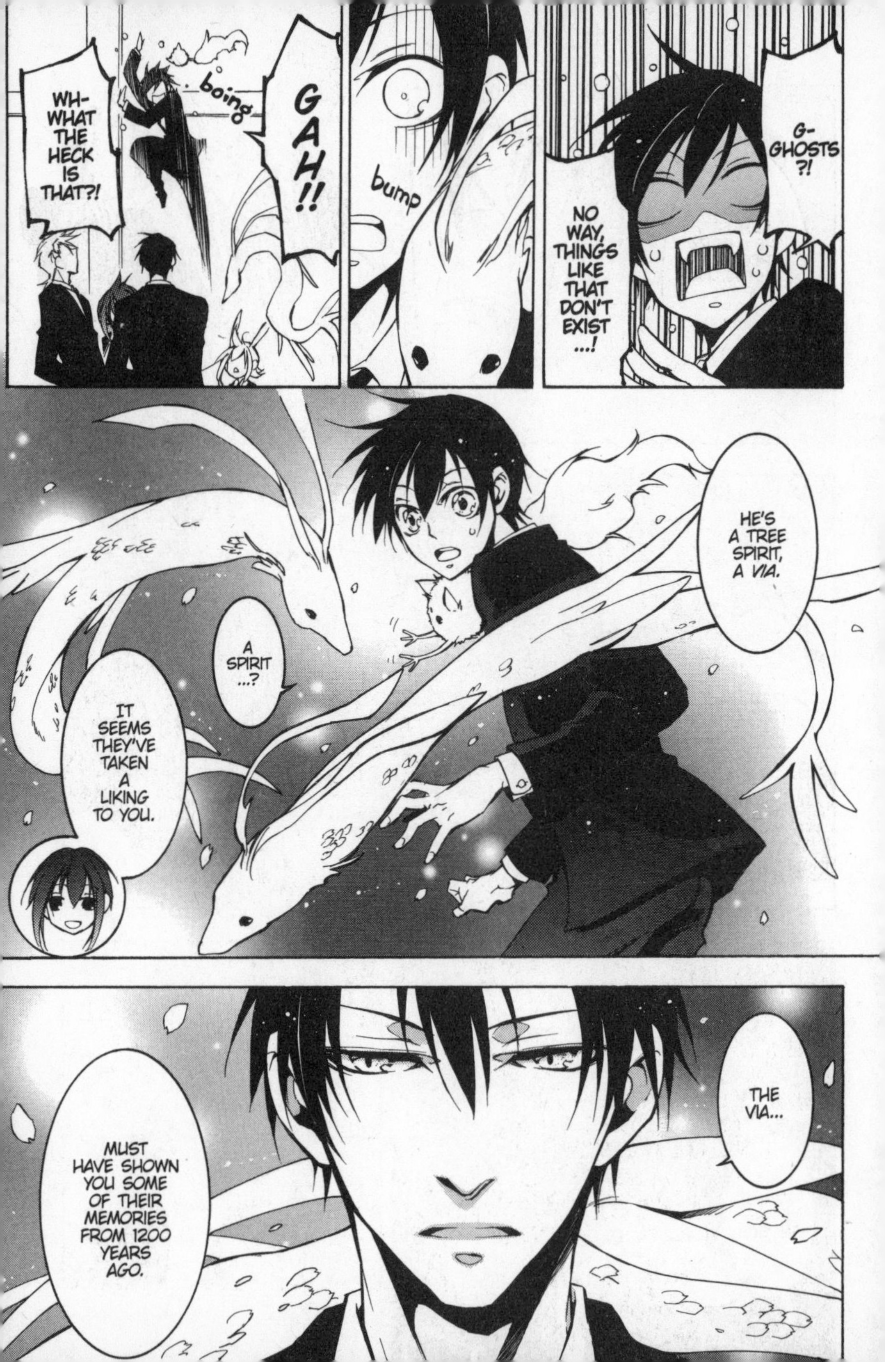
G-GHOSTS?!
NO WAY, THINGS LIKE THAT DON'T EXIST...!
GAH!!
bump
boing
WH-WHAT THE HECK IS THAT?!
HE'S A TREE SPIRIT, A VIA.
A SPIRIT...?
IT SEEMS THEY'VE TAKEN A LIKING TO YOU.
THE VIA...
MUST HAVE SHOWN YOU SOME OF THEIR MEMORIES FROM 1200 YEARS AGO.

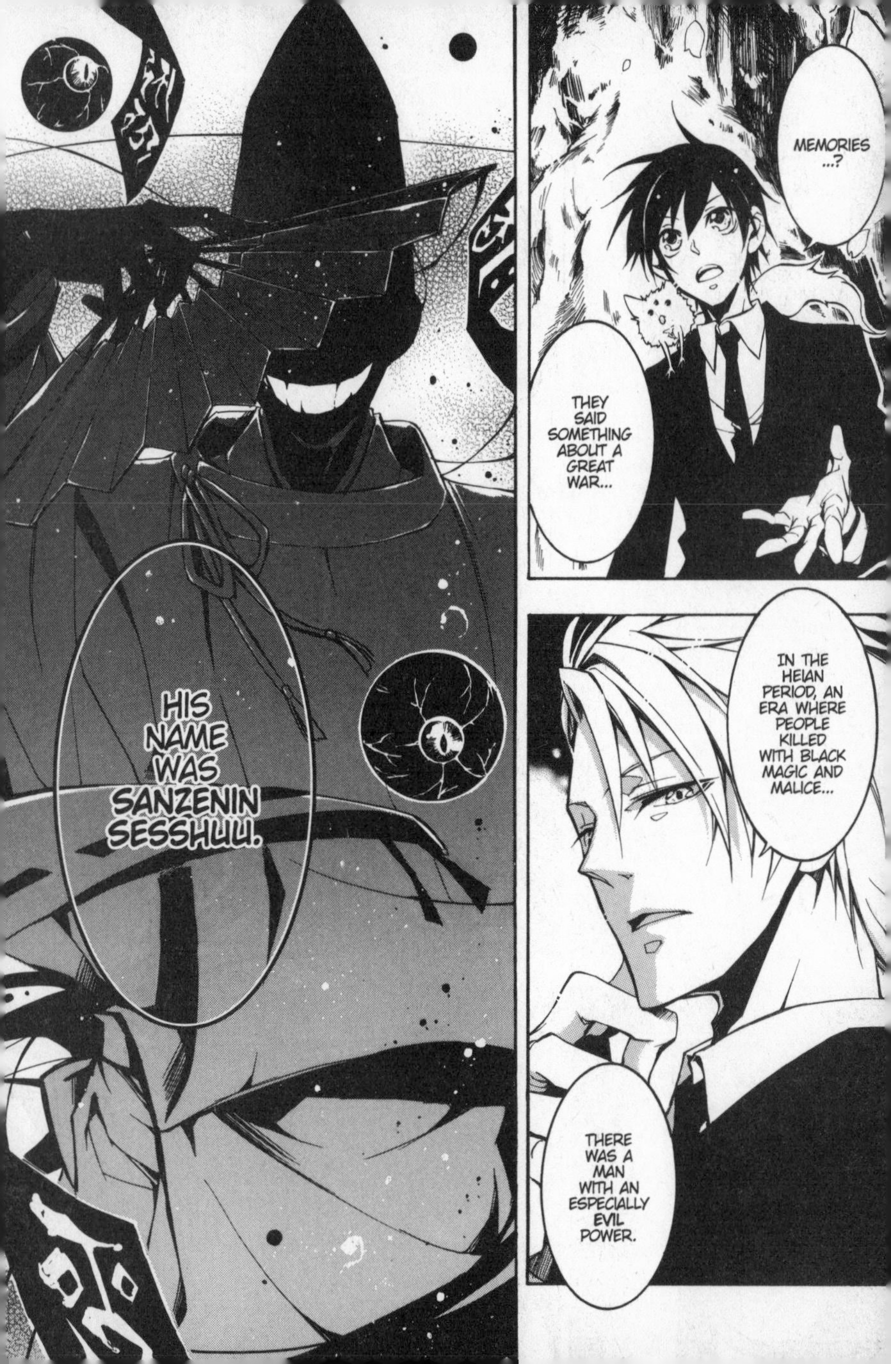
MEMORIES ...?
THEY SAID SOMETHING ABOUT A GREAT WAR...
IN THE HEIAN PERIOD, AN ERA WHERE PEOPLE KILLED WITH BLACK MAGIC AND MALICE...
THERE WAS A MAN WITH AN ESPECIALLY EVIL POWER.
HIS NAME WAS SANZENIN SESSHUU.

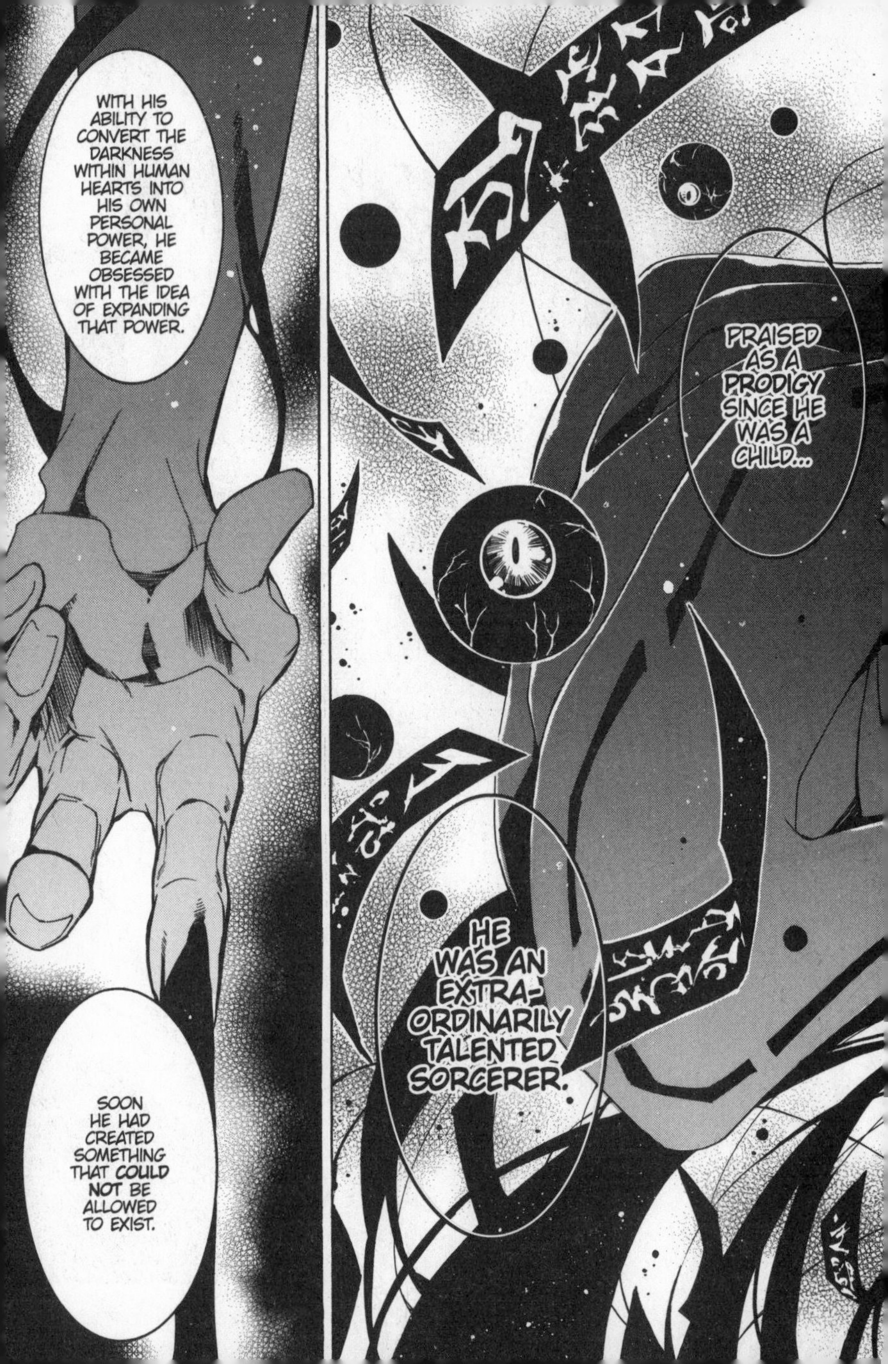
PRAISED AS A PRODIGY SINCE HE WAS A CHILD...
HE WAS AN EXTRA-ORDINARILY TALENTED SORCERER.
WITH HIS ABILITY TO CONVERT THE DARKNESS WITHIN HUMAN HEARTS INTO HIS OWN PERSONAL POWER, HE BECAME OBSESSED WITH THE IDEA OF EXPANDING THAT POWER.
SOON HE HAD CREATED SOMETHING THAT COULD NOT BE ALLOWED TO EXIST.

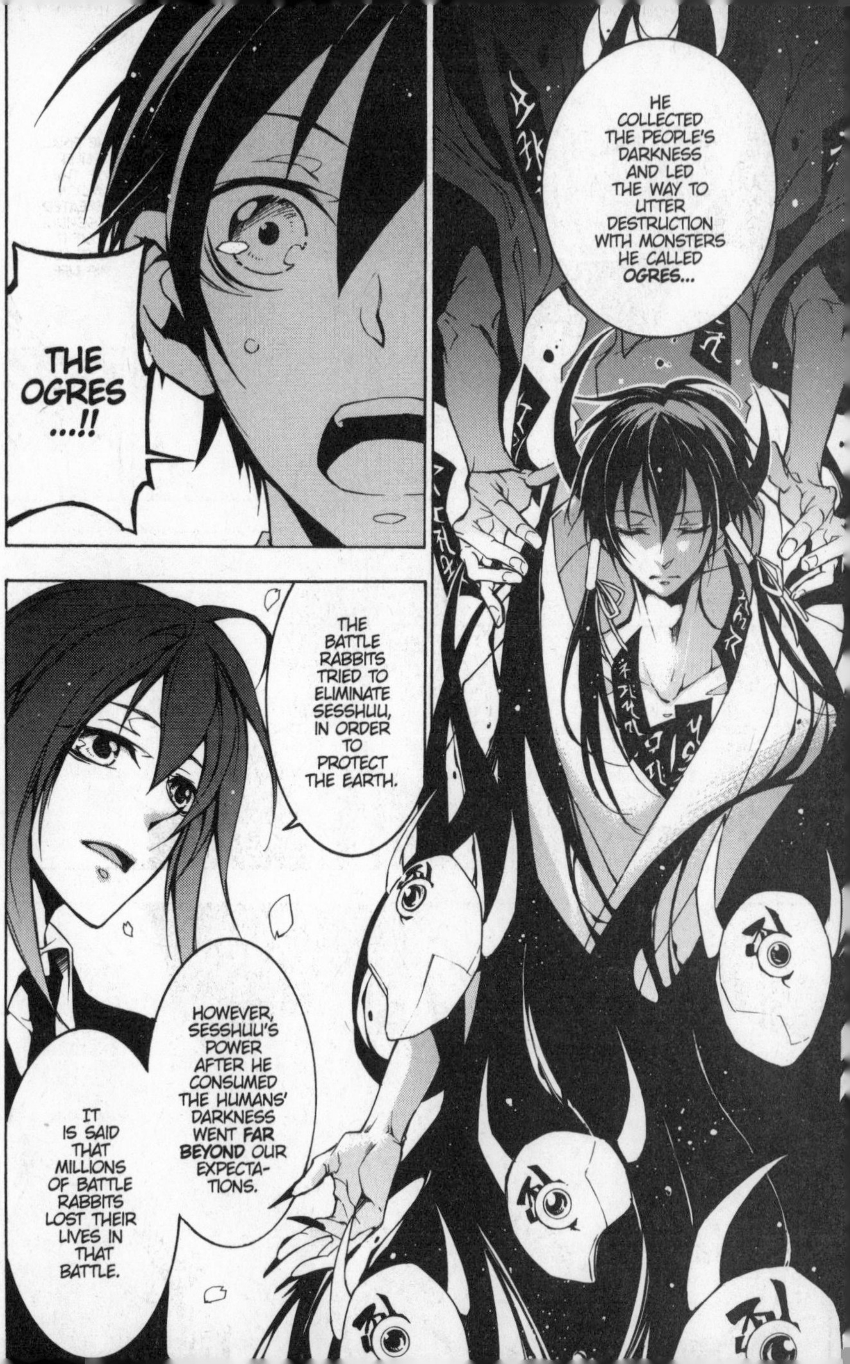
HE COLLECTED THE PEOPLE'S DARKNESS AND LED THE WAY TO UTTER DESTRUCTION WITH MONSTERS HE CALLED OGRES...
THE OGRES ...!!
THE BATTLE RABBITS TRIED TO ELIMINATE SESSHUU, IN ORDER TO PROTECT THE EARTH.
HOWEVER, SESSHUU'S POWER AFTER HE CONSUMED THE HUMANS' DARKNESS WENT FAR BEYOND OUR EXPECTATIONS.
IT IS SAID THAT MILLIONS OF BATTLE RABBITS LOST THEIR LIVES IN THAT BATTLE.

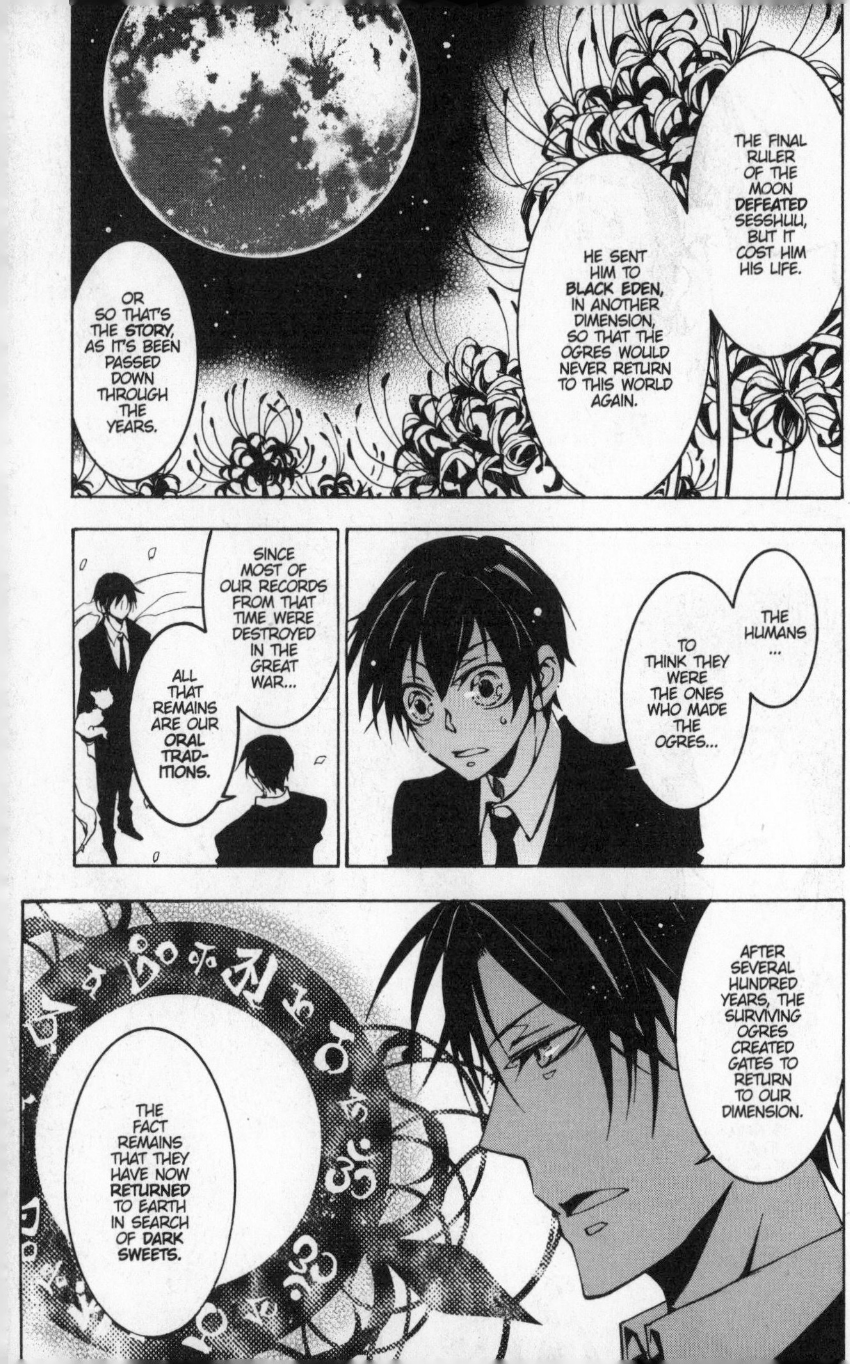
THE FINAL RULER OF THE MOON DEFEATED SESSHUU, BUT IT COST HIM HIS LIFE.
HE SENT HIM TO BLACK EDEN, IN ANOTHER DIMENSION, SO THAT THE OGRES WOULD NEVER RETURN TO THIS WORLD AGAIN.
OR SO THAT'S THE STORY, AS IT'S BEEN PASSED DOWN THROUGH THE YEARS.
THE HUMANS...
TO THINK THEY WERE THE ONES WHO MADE THE OGRES...
SINCE MOST OF OUR RECORDS FROM THAT TIME WERE DESTROYED IN THE GREAT WAR...
ALL THAT REMAINS ARE OUR ORAL TRADITIONS.
AFTER SEVERAL HUNDRED YEARS, THE SURVIVING OGRES CREATED GATES TO RETURN TO OUR DIMENSION.
THE FACT REMAINS THAT THEY HAVE NOW RETURNED TO EARTH IN SEARCH OF DARK SWEETS.

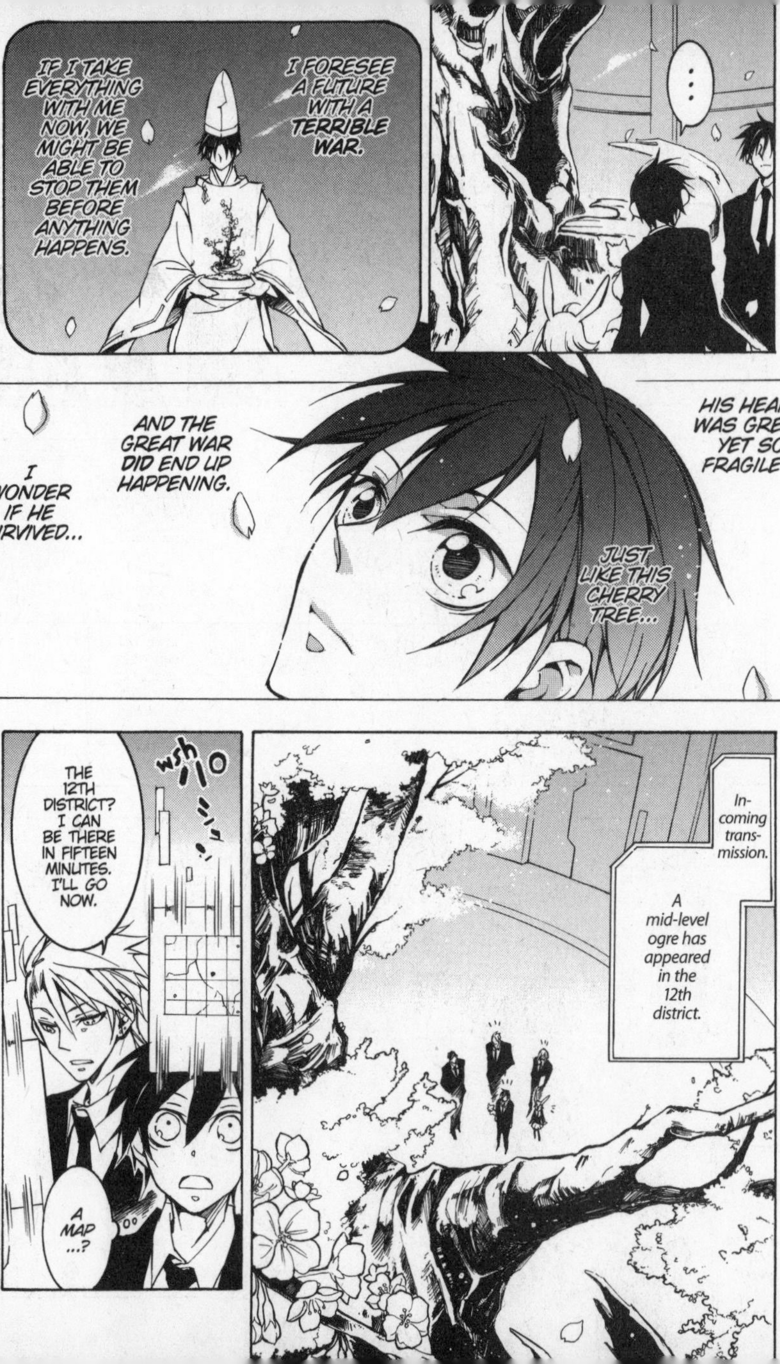
...
I FORESEE A FUTURE WITH A TERRIBLE WAR.
IF I TAKE EVERYTHING WITH ME NOW, WE MIGHT BE ABLE TO STOP THEM BEFORE ANYTHING HAPPENS.
HIS HEART WAS GREAT, YET SO FRAGILE...
JUST LIKE THIS CHERRY TREE...
AND THE GREAT WAR DID END UP HAPPENING.
I WONDER IF HE SURVIVED...
In-coming trans-mission.
A mid-level ogre has appeared in the 12th district.
wsh
THE 12TH DISTRICT? I CAN BE THERE IN FIFTEEN MINUTES. I'LL GO NOW.
A MAP ...?

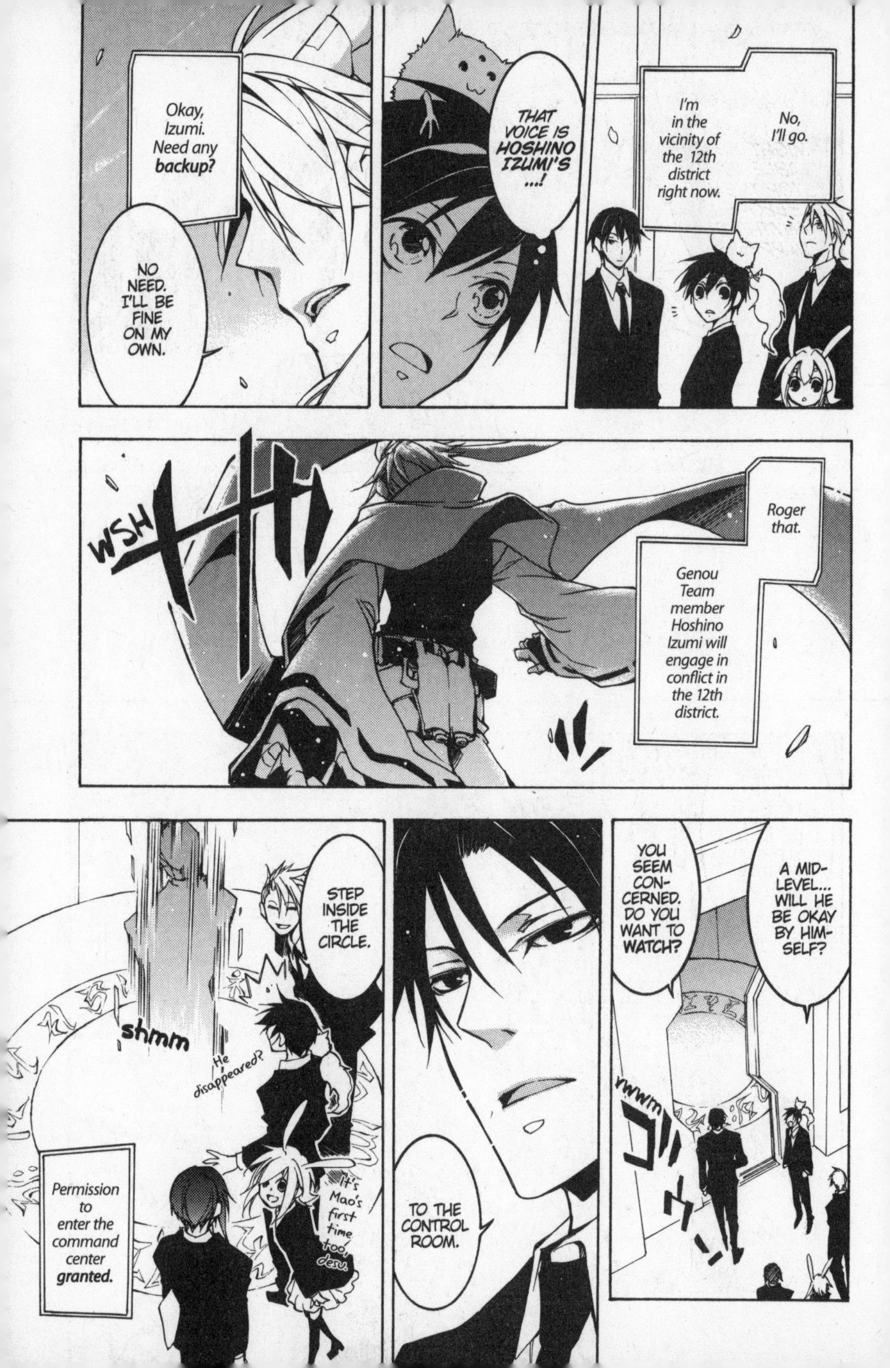
No, I'll go.
I'm in the vicinity of the 12th district right now.
THAT VOICE IS HOSHINO IZUMI'S ...!
Okay, Izumi. Need any **backup?**
NO NEED. I'LL BE FINE ON MY OWN.
Roger that.
Genou Team member Hoshino Izumi will engage in conflict in the 12th district.
WSH
A MID-LEVEL... WILL HE BE OKAY BY HIMSELF?
YOU SEEM CONCERNED. DO YOU WANT TO WATCH?
rwwm
TO THE CONTROL ROOM.
STEP INSIDE THE CIRCLE.
He disappeared?
shmm
It's Mao's first time too, desu.
Permission to enter the command center **granted.**

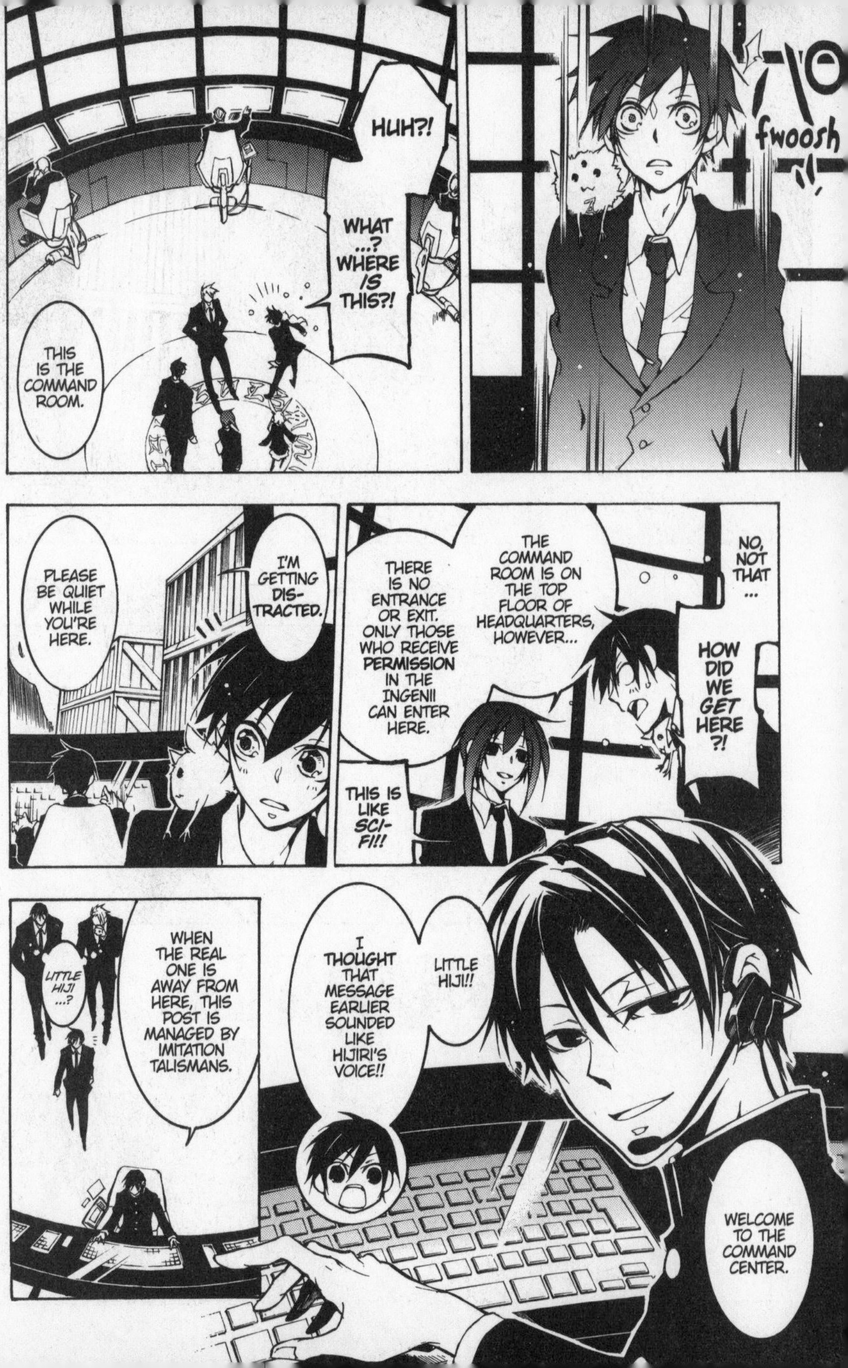
fwoosh
HUH?!
WHAT ...? WHERE IS THIS?!
THIS IS THE COMMAND ROOM.
NO, NOT THAT ...
HOW DID WE GET HERE?!
THE COMMAND ROOM IS ON THE TOP FLOOR OF HEADQUARTERS, HOWEVER...
THERE IS NO ENTRANCE OR EXIT. ONLY THOSE WHO RECEIVE PERMISSION IN THE INGENII CAN ENTER HERE.
THIS IS LIKE SCI-FI!!
I'M GETTING DIS-TRACTED.
PLEASE BE QUIET WHILE YOU'RE HERE.
WELCOME TO THE COMMAND CENTER.
LITTLE HIJI!!
I THOUGHT THAT MESSAGE EARLIER SOUNDED LIKE HIJIRI'S VOICE!!
WHEN THE REAL ONE IS AWAY FROM HERE, THIS POST IS MANAGED BY IMITATION TALISMANS.
LITTLE HIJI ...?

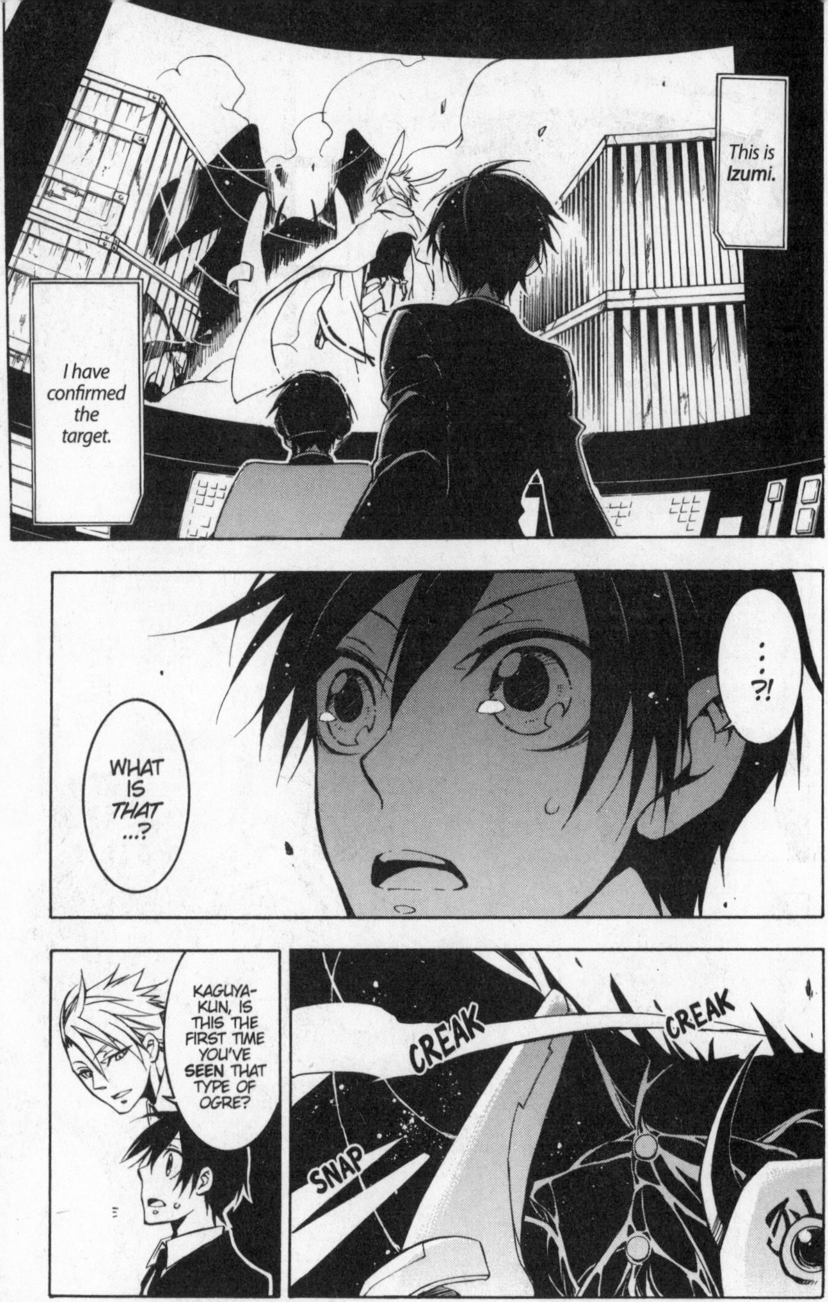
This is Izumi.
I have confirmed the target.
...?!
WHAT IS THAT...?
CREAK
CREAK
SNAP
KAGUYA-KUN, IS THIS THE FIRST TIME YOU'VE SEEN THAT TYPE OF OGRE?

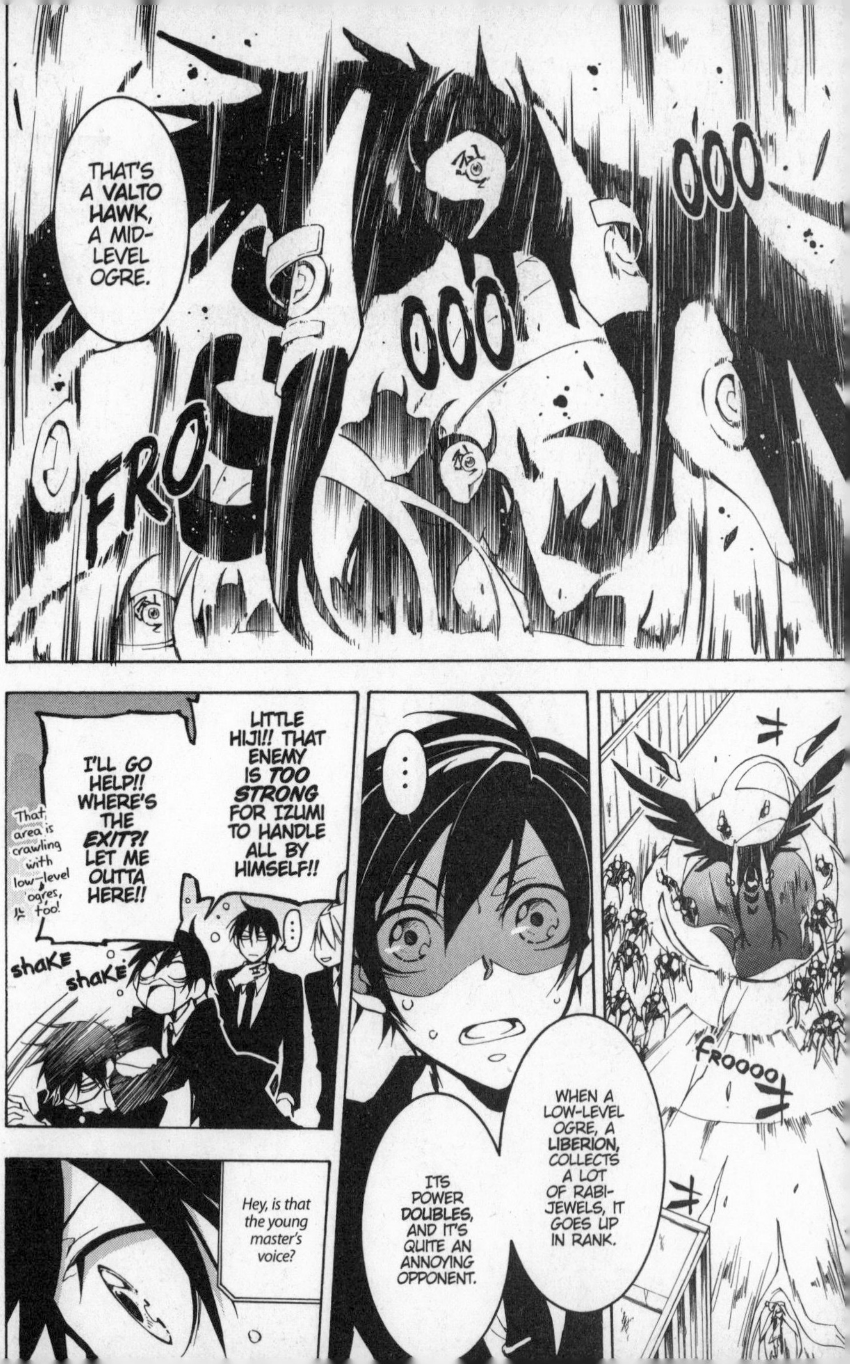
FRO
OOO
OOO
THAT'S A VALTO HAWK, A MID-LEVEL OGRE.
FROOOO
WHEN A LOW-LEVEL OGRE, A LIBERION, COLLECTS A LOT OF RABI-JEWELS, IT GOES UP IN RANK.
ITS POWER DOUBLES, AND IT'S QUITE AN ANNOYING OPPONENT.
...
LITTLE HIJI!! THAT ENEMY IS TOO STRONG FOR IZUMI TO HANDLE ALL BY HIMSELF!!
...
I'LL GO HELP!! WHERE'S THE EXIT?! LET ME OUTTA HERE!!
That area is crawling with low-level ogres, too!
shake shake
Hey, is that the young master's voice?

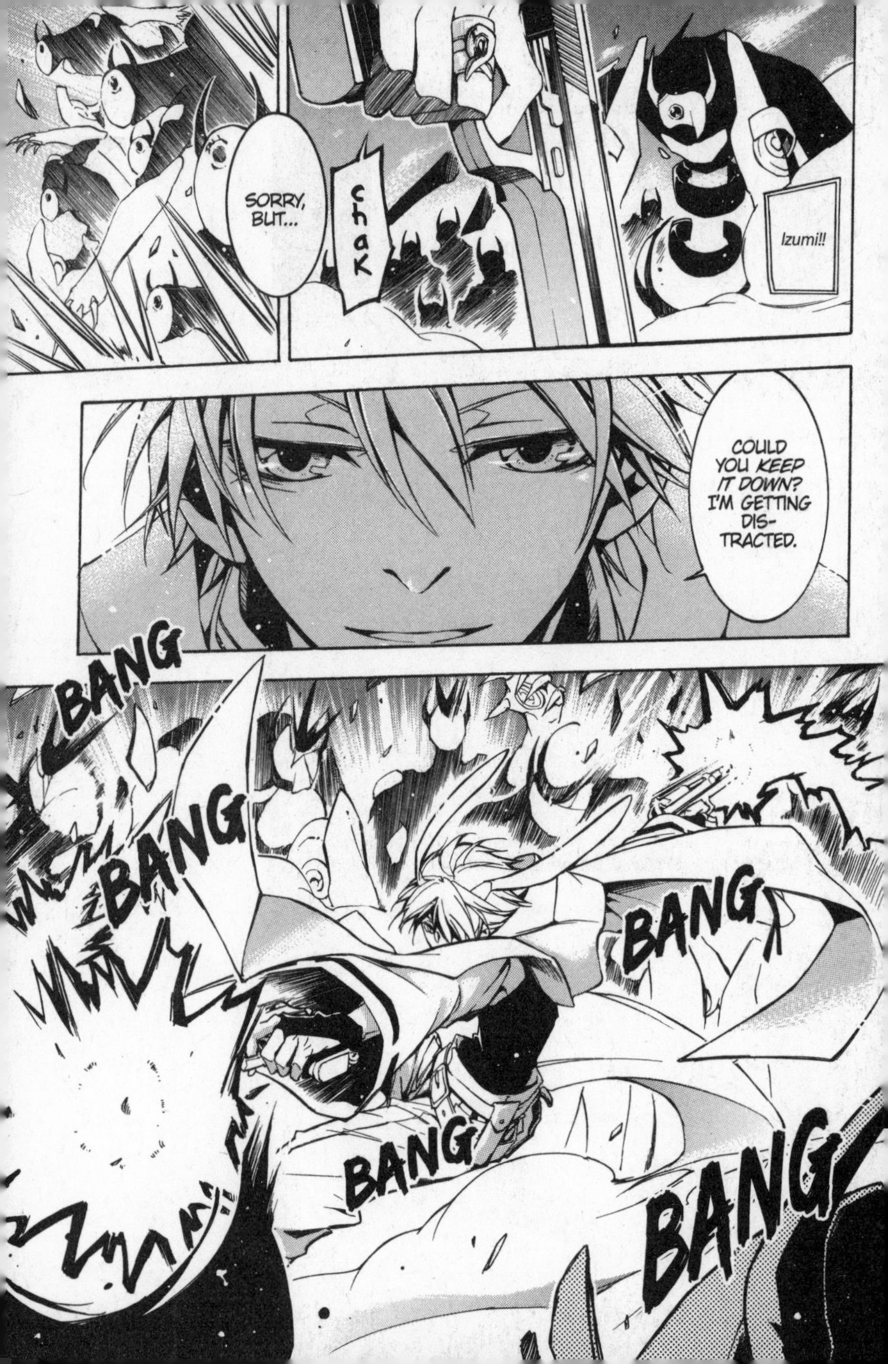

Izumi!!
chak
SORRY, BUT...
COULD YOU KEEP IT DOWN? I'M GETTING DIS-TRACTED.
BANG
BANG
BANG
BANG
BANG
BANG
BANG

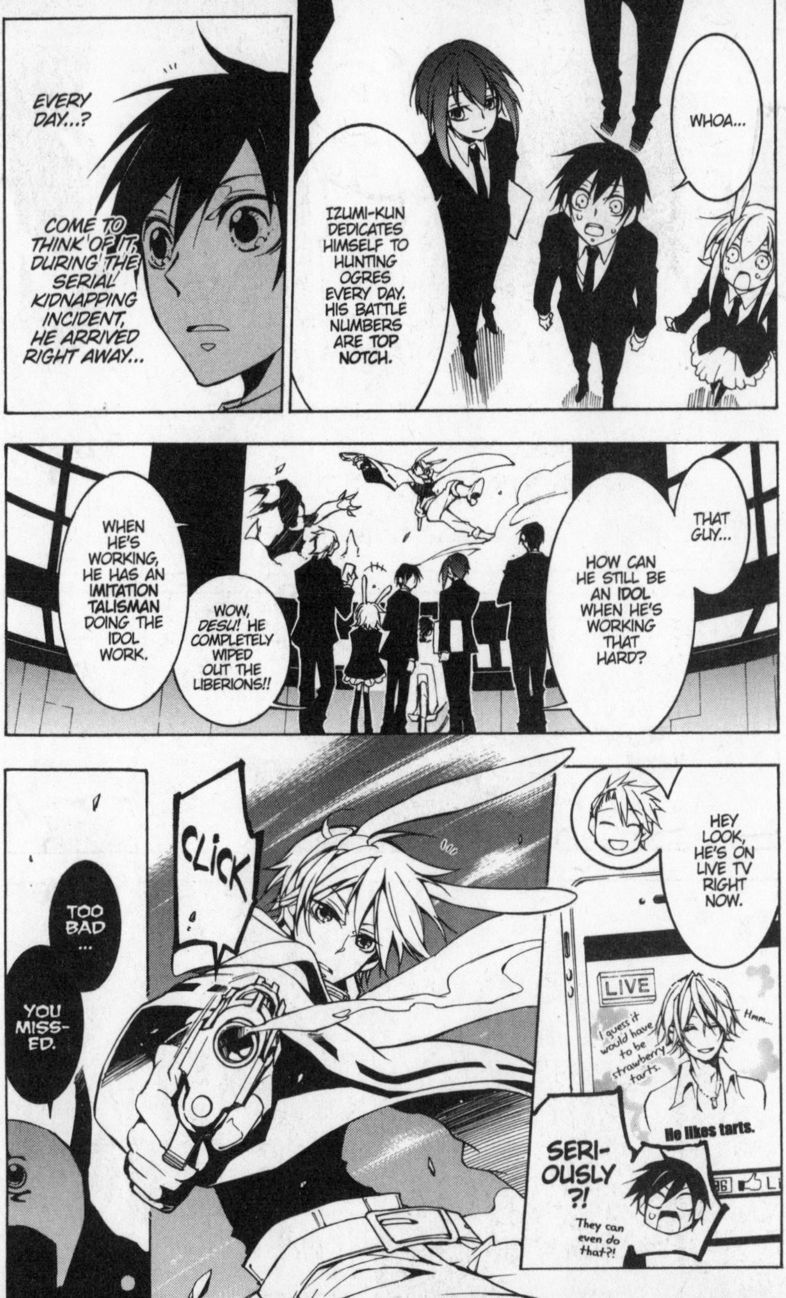
WHOA...
IZUMI-KUN DEDICATES HIMSELF TO HUNTING OGRES EVERY DAY. HIS BATTLE NUMBERS ARE TOP NOTCH.
EVERY DAY...?
COME TO THINK OF IT, DURING THE SERIAL KIDNAPPING INCIDENT, HE ARRIVED RIGHT AWAY...
THAT GUY...
HOW CAN HE STILL BE AN IDOL WHEN HE'S WORKING THAT HARD?
WOW, DESU! HE COMPLETELY WIPED OUT THE LIBERIONS!!
WHEN HE'S WORKING, HE HAS AN IMITATION TALISMAN DOING THE IDOL WORK.
HEY LOOK, HE'S ON LIVE TV RIGHT NOW.
LIVE
Hmm...
I guess it would have to be strawberry tarts.
He likes tarts.
SERI-OUSLY ?!
They can even do that?!
CLICK
TOO BAD ...
YOU MISS-ED.

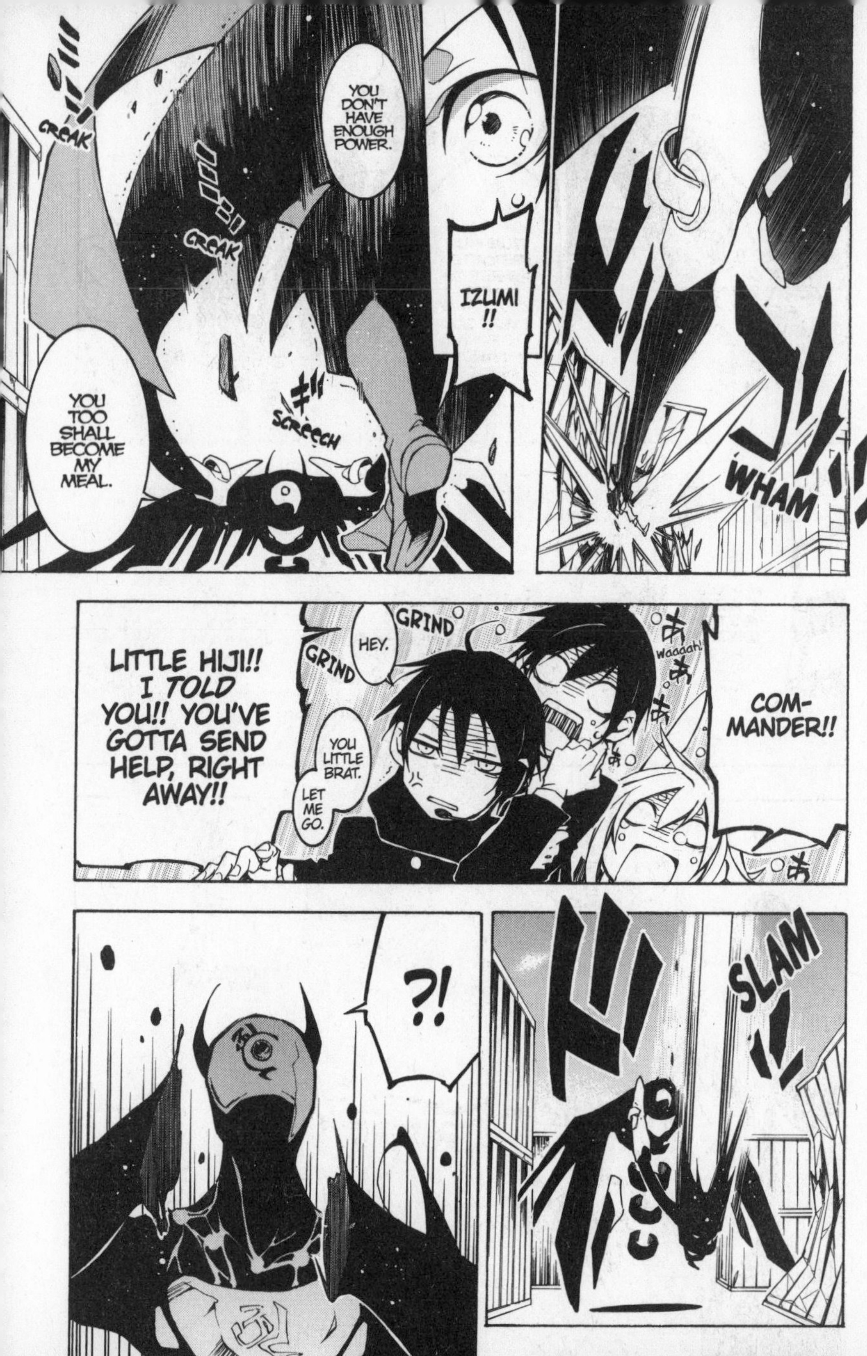
IZUMI!!
WHAM!!
YOU DON'T HAVE ENOUGH POWER.
CREAK
CREAK
SCREECH
YOU TOO SHALL BECOME MY MEAL.
COM-MANDER!!
Waaaah!
GRIND
GRIND
HEY.
YOU LITTLE BRAT.
LET ME GO.
LITTLE HIJI!! I TOLD YOU!! YOU'VE GOTTA SEND HELP, RIGHT AWAY!!
SLAM!!
?!

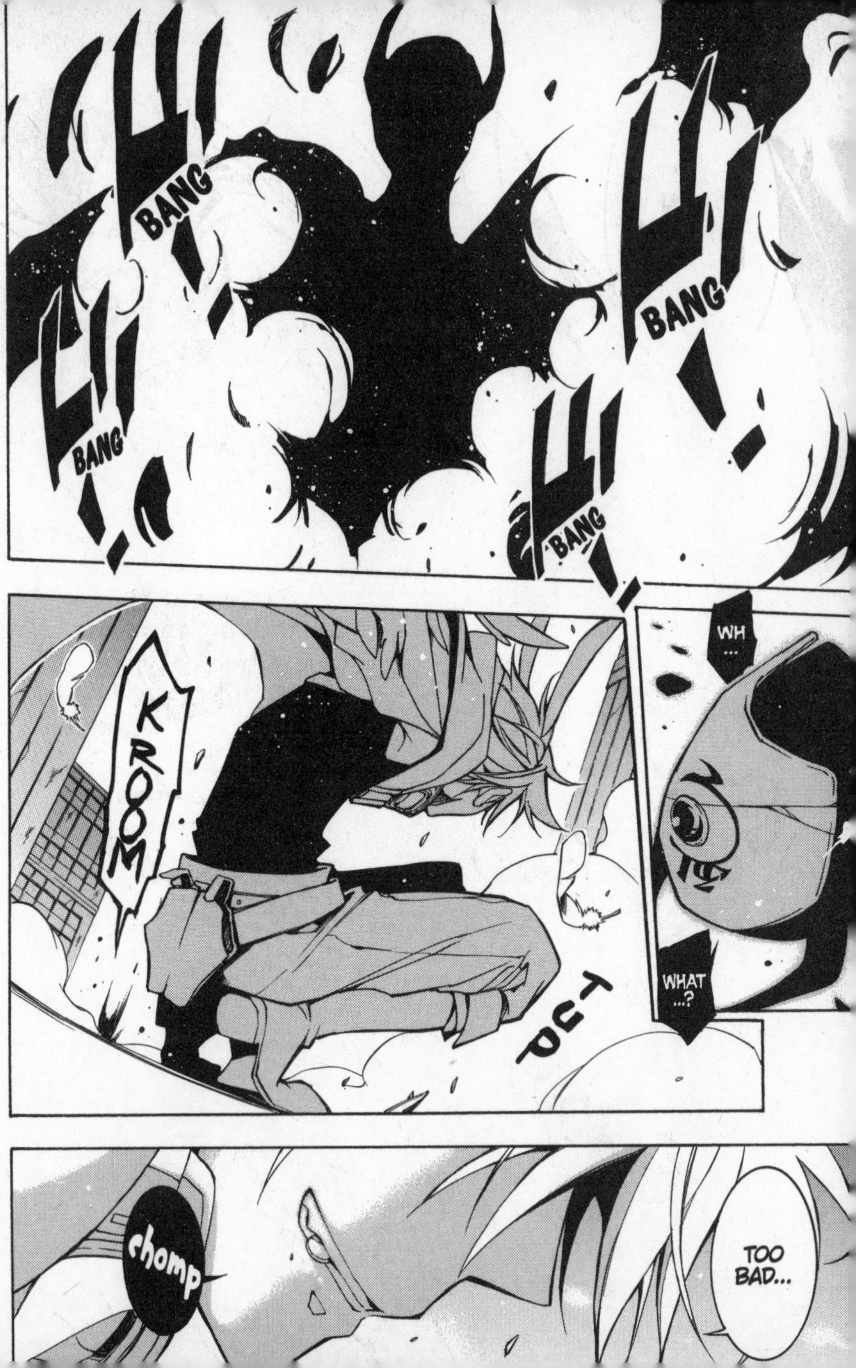
BANG
BANG
BANG
BANG
WH...
WHAT...?
KROOM
TUP
TOO BAD...
chomp

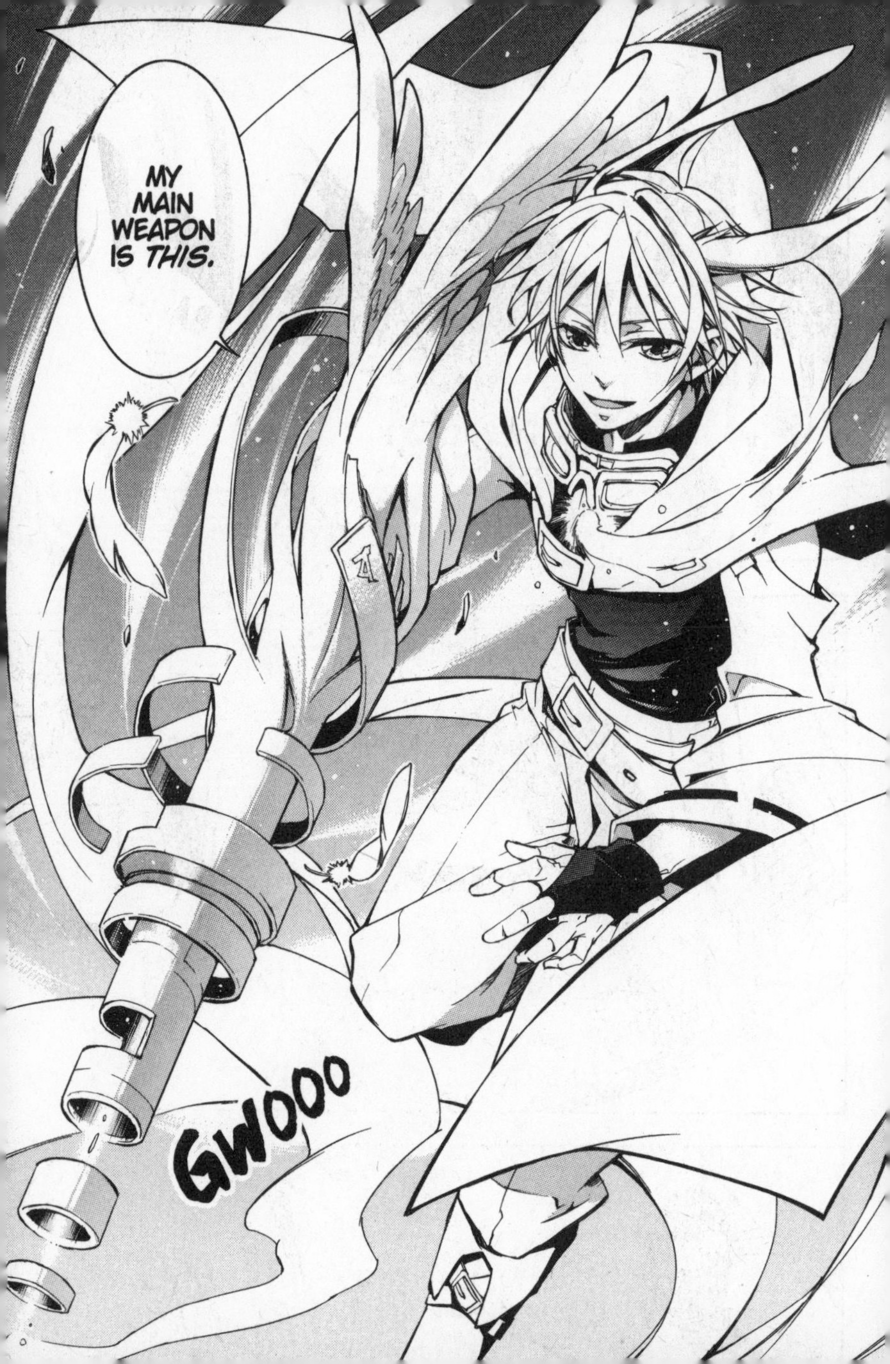
MY MAIN WEAPON IS *THIS.*
GWOOO

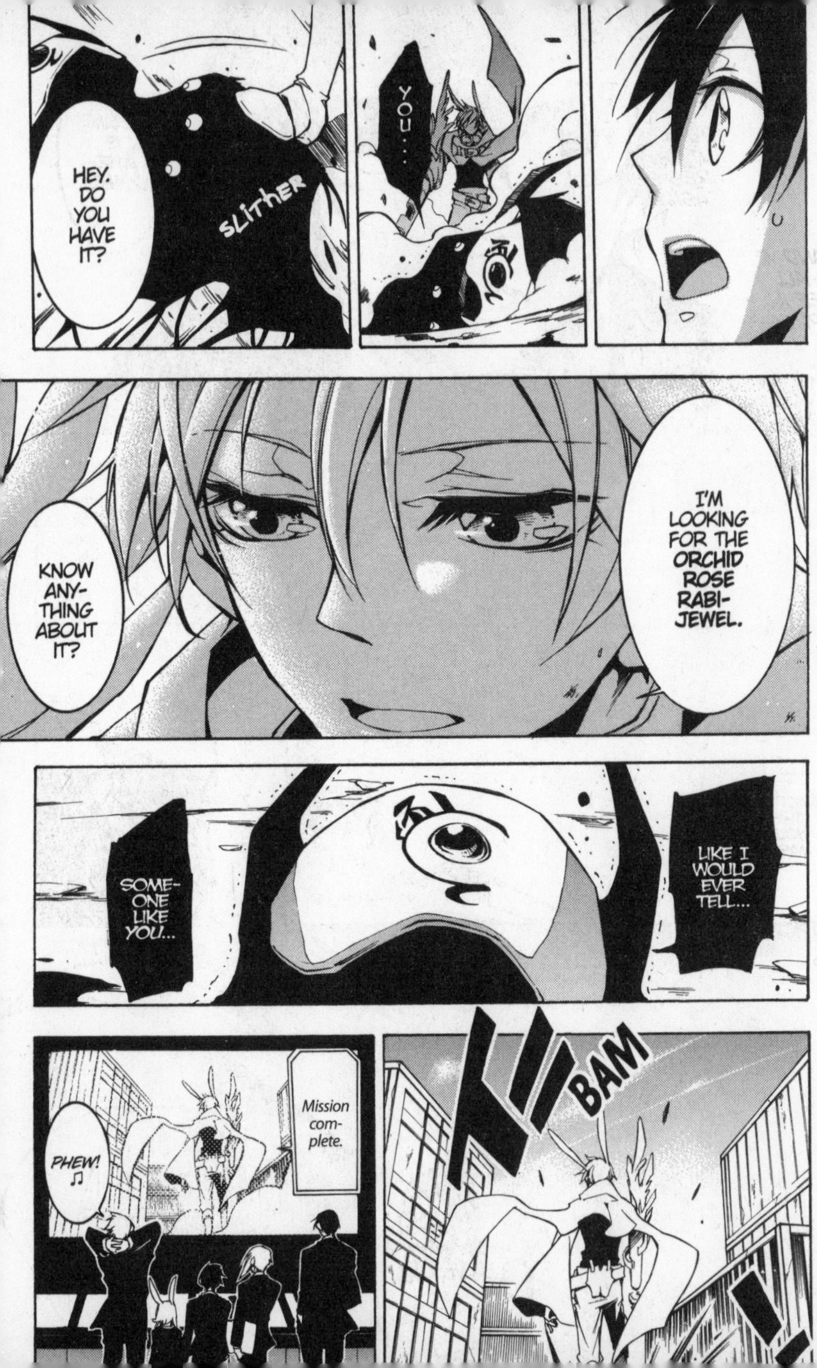
YOU...
HEY. DO YOU HAVE IT?
SLITHER
I'M LOOKING FOR THE ORCHID ROSE RABI-JEWEL.
KNOW ANYTHING ABOUT IT?
LIKE I WOULD EVER TELL...
SOMEONE LIKE YOU...
BAM
Mission complete.
PHEW! ♫

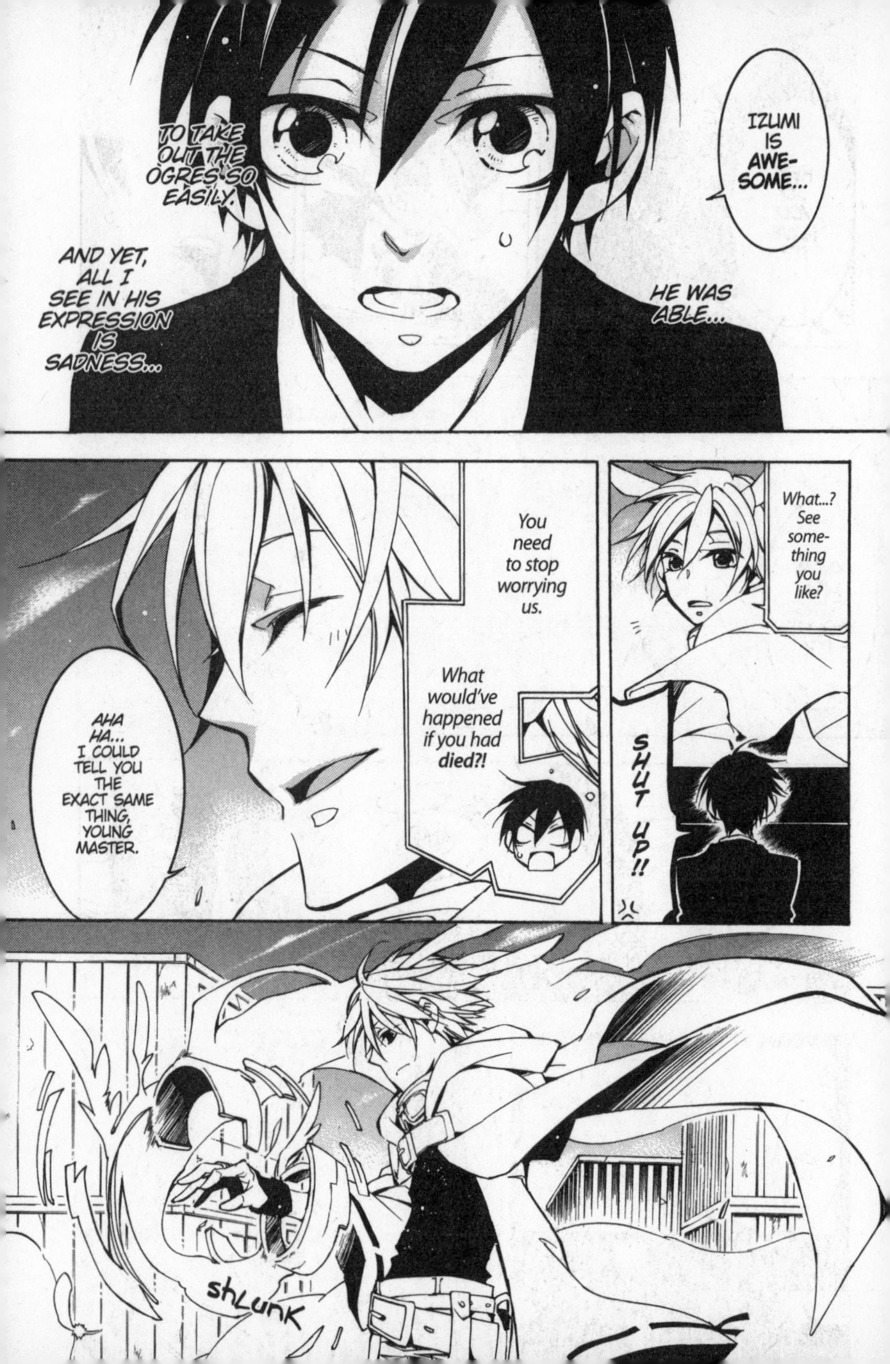
IZUMI IS AWE-SOME...
HE WAS ABLE...
TO TAKE OUT THE OGRES SO EASILY.
AND YET, ALL I SEE IN HIS EXPRESSION IS SADNESS...
What...? See some-thing you like?
SHUT UP!!
You need to stop worrying us.
What would've happened if you had died?!
AHA HA... I COULD TELL YOU THE EXACT SAME THING, YOUNG MASTER.
shLunk

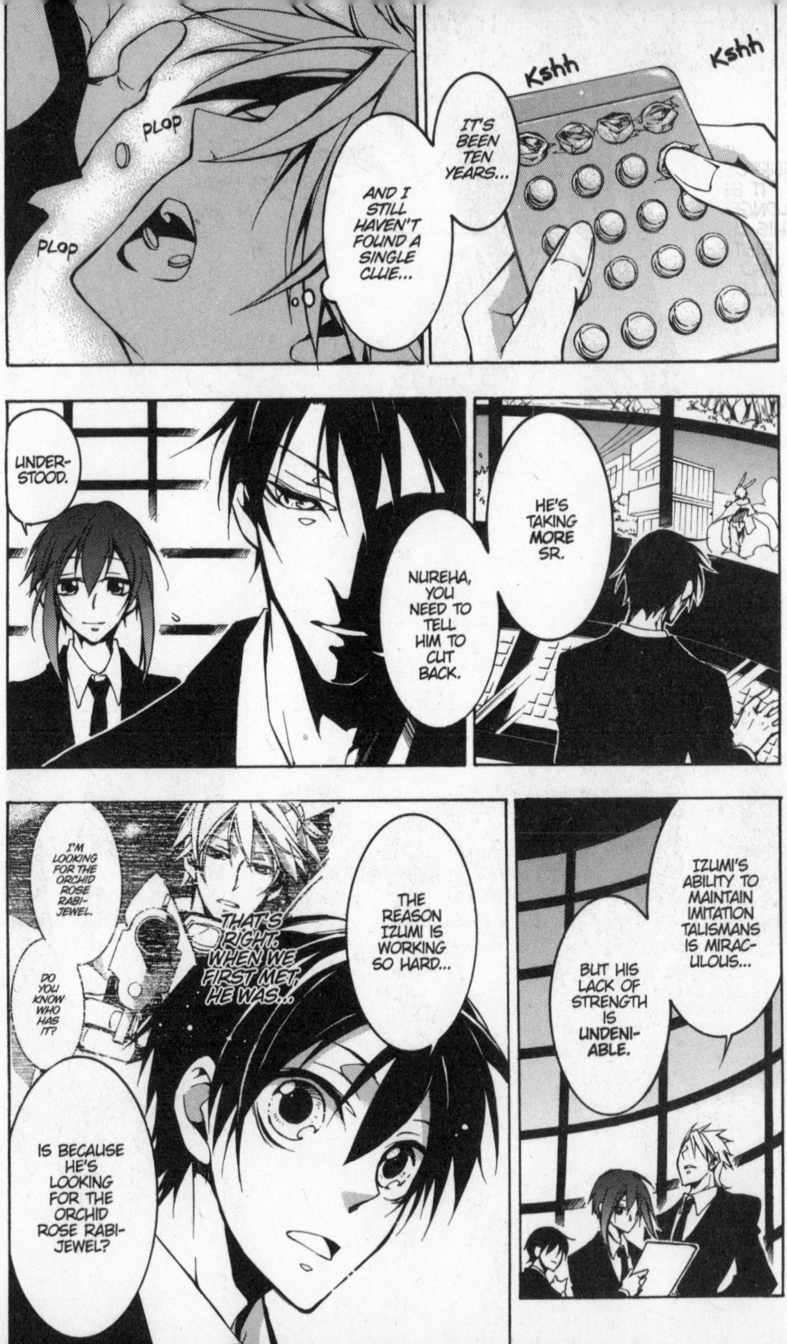
Kshh
Kshh
IT'S BEEN TEN YEARS...
AND I STILL HAVEN'T FOUND A SINGLE CLUE...
PLOP
PLOP
HE'S TAKING MORE SR.
NUREHA, YOU NEED TO TELL HIM TO CUT BACK.
UNDER-STOOD.
IZUMI'S ABILITY TO MAINTAIN IMITATION TALISMANS IS MIRACULOUS...
BUT HIS LACK OF STRENGTH IS UNDENI-ABLE.
THE REASON IZUMI IS WORKING SO HARD...
THAT'S RIGHT. WHEN WE FIRST MET, HE WAS...
I'M LOOKING FOR THE ORCHID ROSE RABI-JEWEL.
DO YOU KNOW WHO HAS IT?
IS BECAUSE HE'S LOOKING FOR THE ORCHID ROSE RABI-JEWEL?

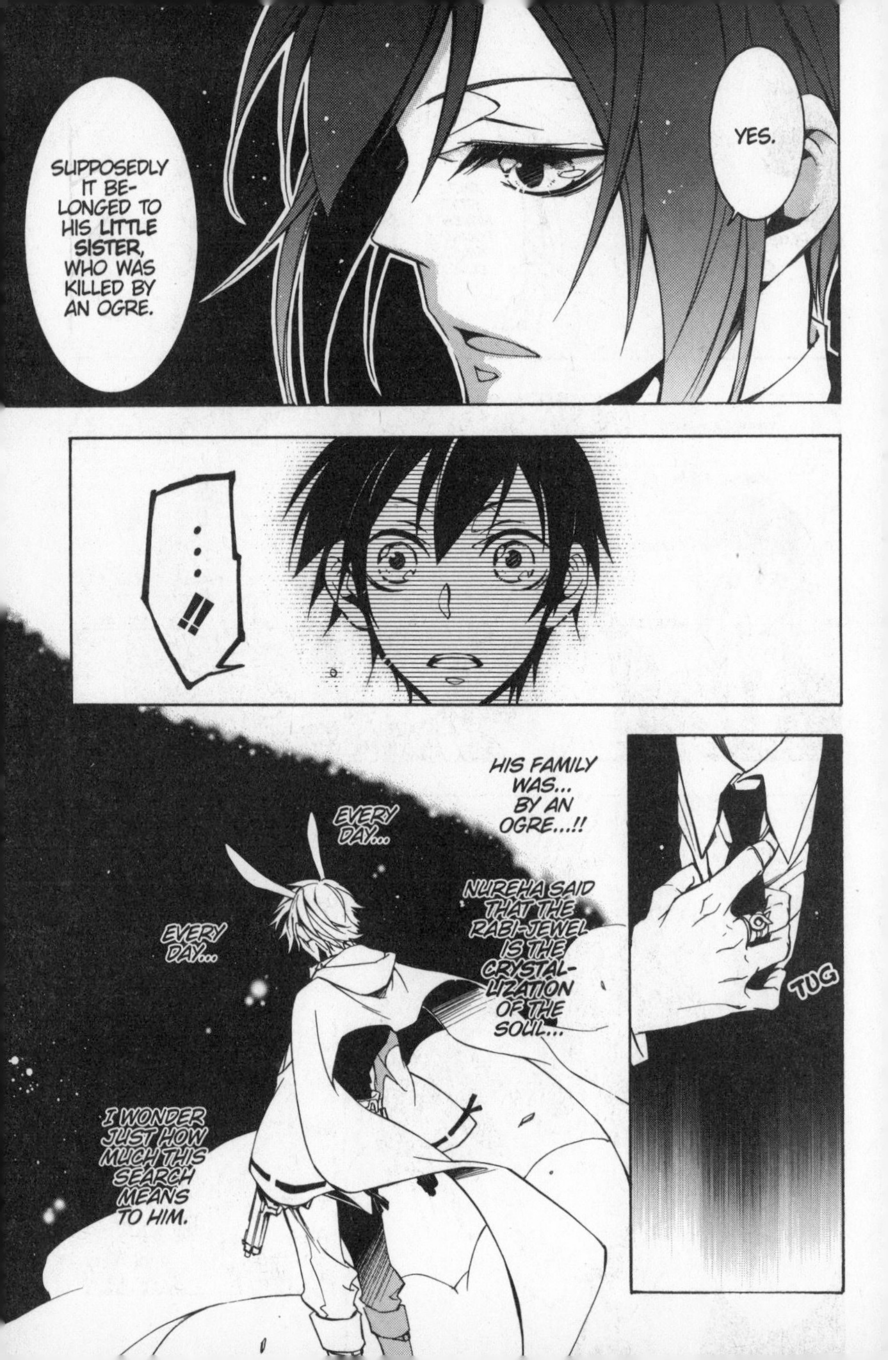
YES.
SUPPOSEDLY IT BELONGED TO HIS LITTLE SISTER, WHO WAS KILLED BY AN OGRE.
....!!
TUG
HIS FAMILY WAS... BY AN OGRE...!!
EVERY DAY...
NUREHA SAID THAT THE RABI-JEWEL IS THE CRYSTALIZATION OF THE SOUL...
EVERY DAY...
I WONDER JUST HOW MUCH THIS SEARCH MEANS TO HIM.

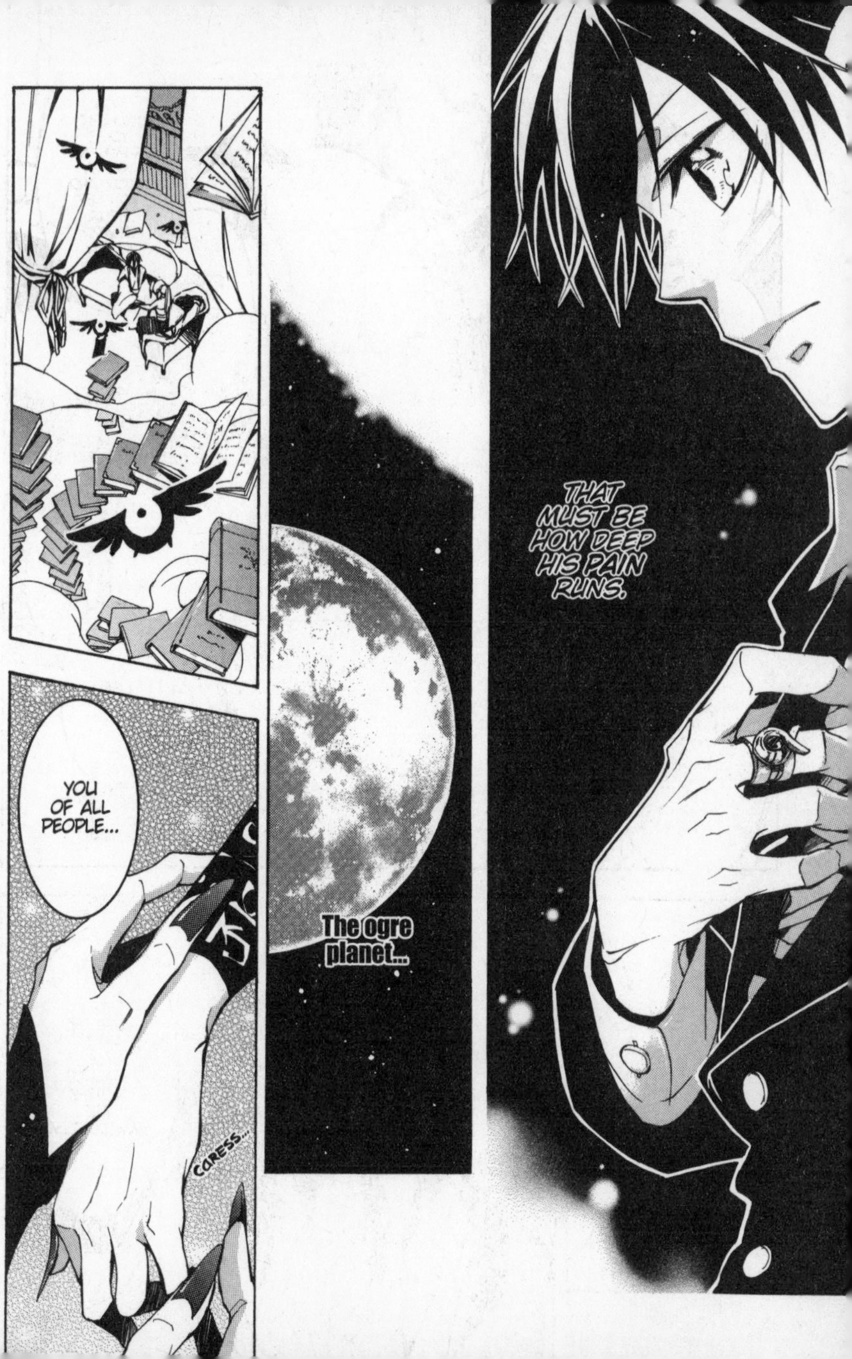
THAT MUST BE HOW DEEP HIS PAIN RUNS.
The ogre planet...
YOU OF ALL PEOPLE...
CARESS...

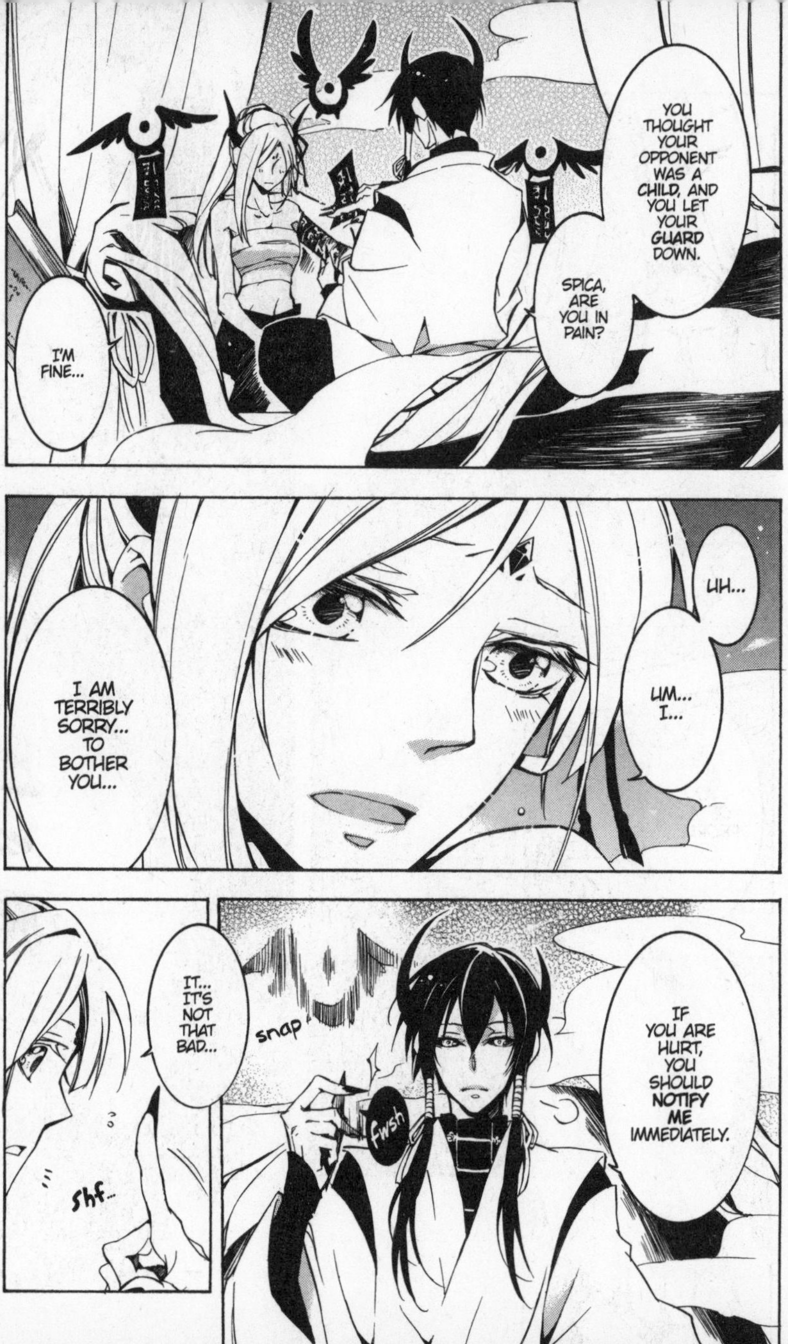
YOU THOUGHT YOUR OPPONENT WAS A CHILD, AND YOU LET YOUR GUARD DOWN.
SPICA, ARE YOU IN PAIN?
I'M FINE...
UH...
UM... I...
I AM TERRIBLY SORRY... TO BOTHER YOU...
IF YOU ARE HURT, YOU SHOULD NOTIFY ME IMMEDIATELY.
fwsh
snap
IT... IT'S NOT THAT BAD...
shf...

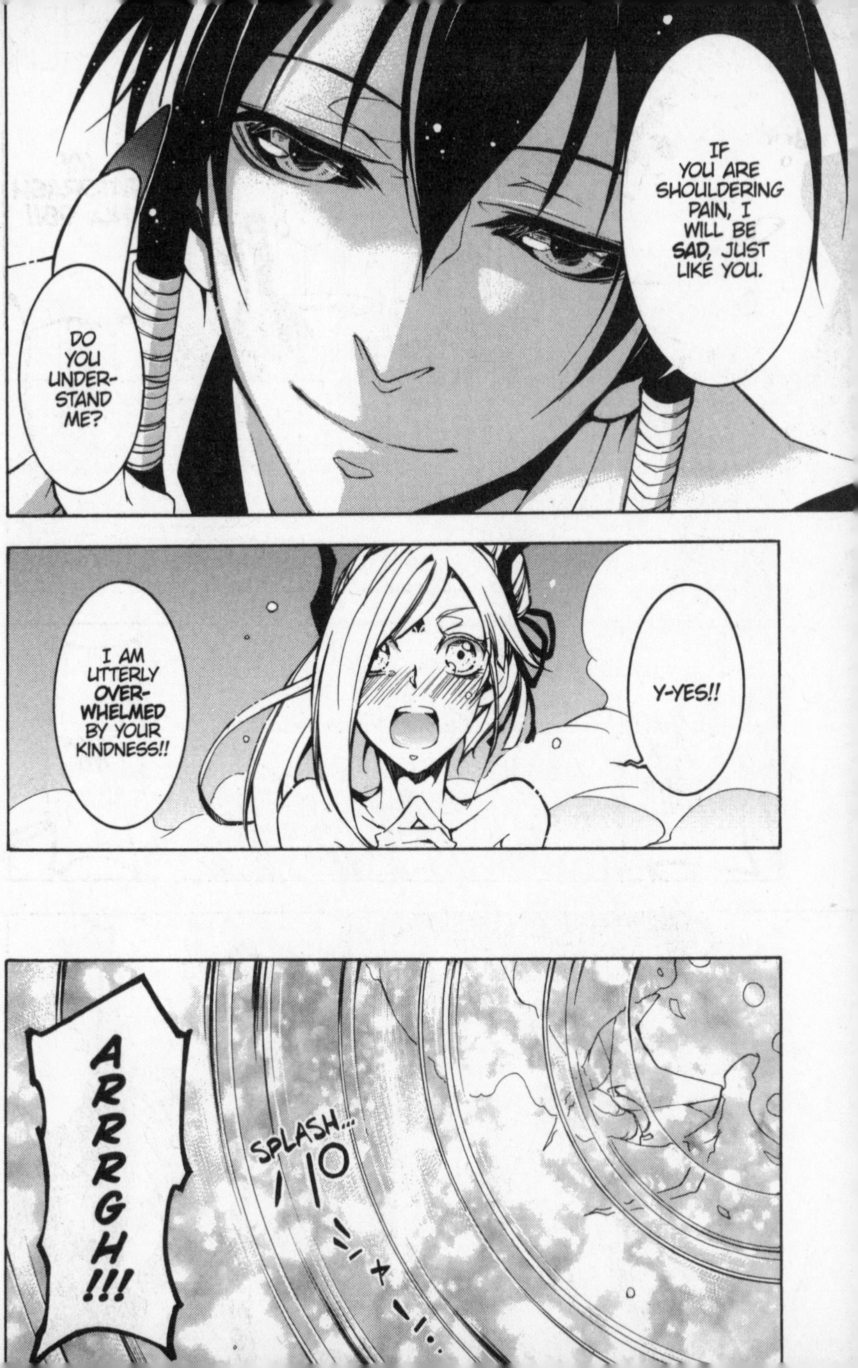
IF YOU ARE SHOULDERING PAIN, I WILL BE SAD, JUST LIKE YOU.
DO YOU UNDERSTAND ME?
Y-YES!!
I AM UTTERLY OVERWHELMED BY YOUR KINDNESS!!
SPLASH...
ARRRGH!!!

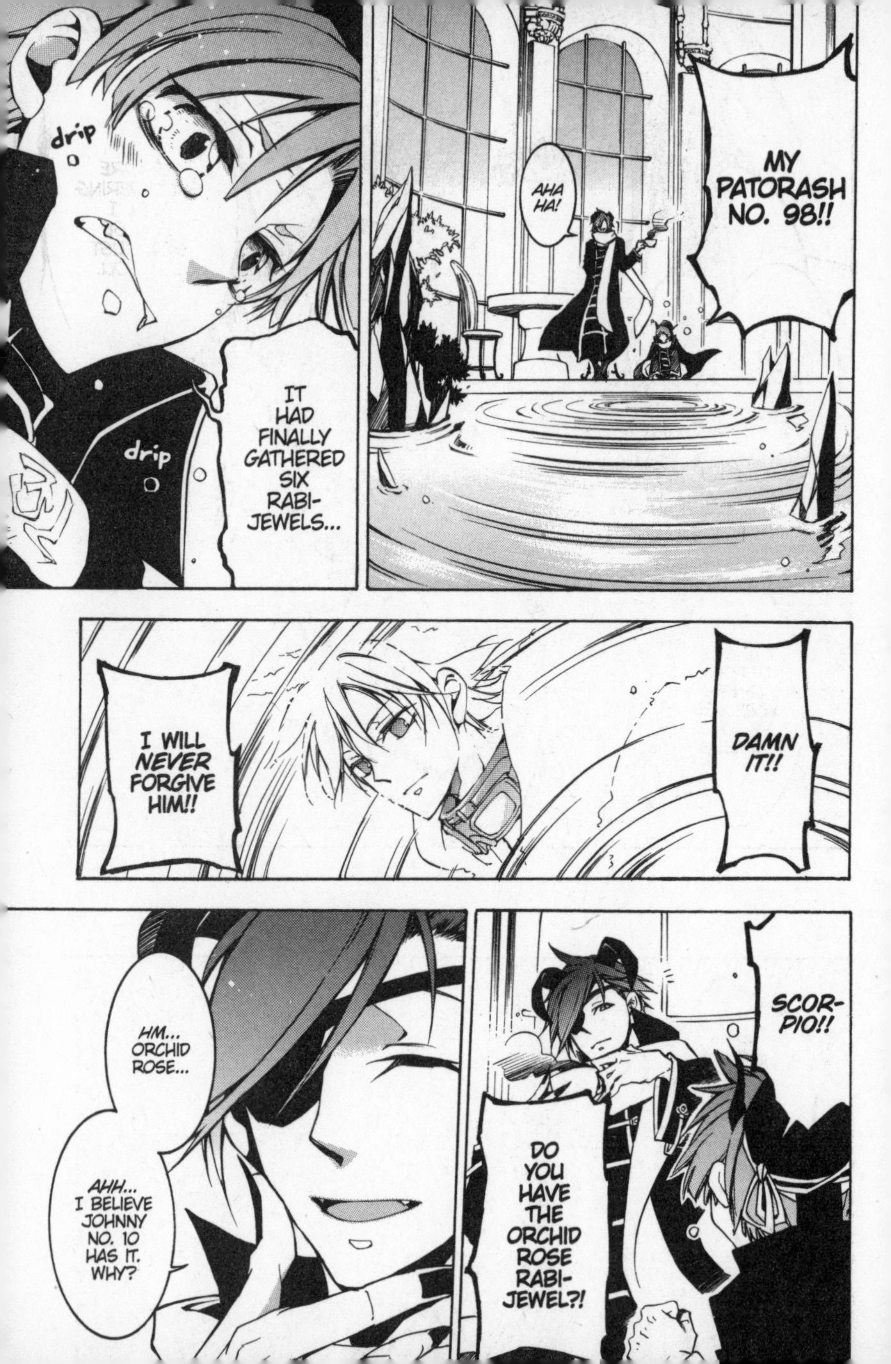
MY PATORASH NO. 98!!
AHA HA!
drip
IT HAD FINALLY GATHERED SIX RABI-JEWELS...
drip
DAMN IT!!
I WILL NEVER FORGIVE HIM!!
SCORPIO!!
DO YOU HAVE THE ORCHID ROSE RABI-JEWEL?!
HM... ORCHID ROSE...
AHH... I BELIEVE JOHNNY NO. 10 HAS IT. WHY?

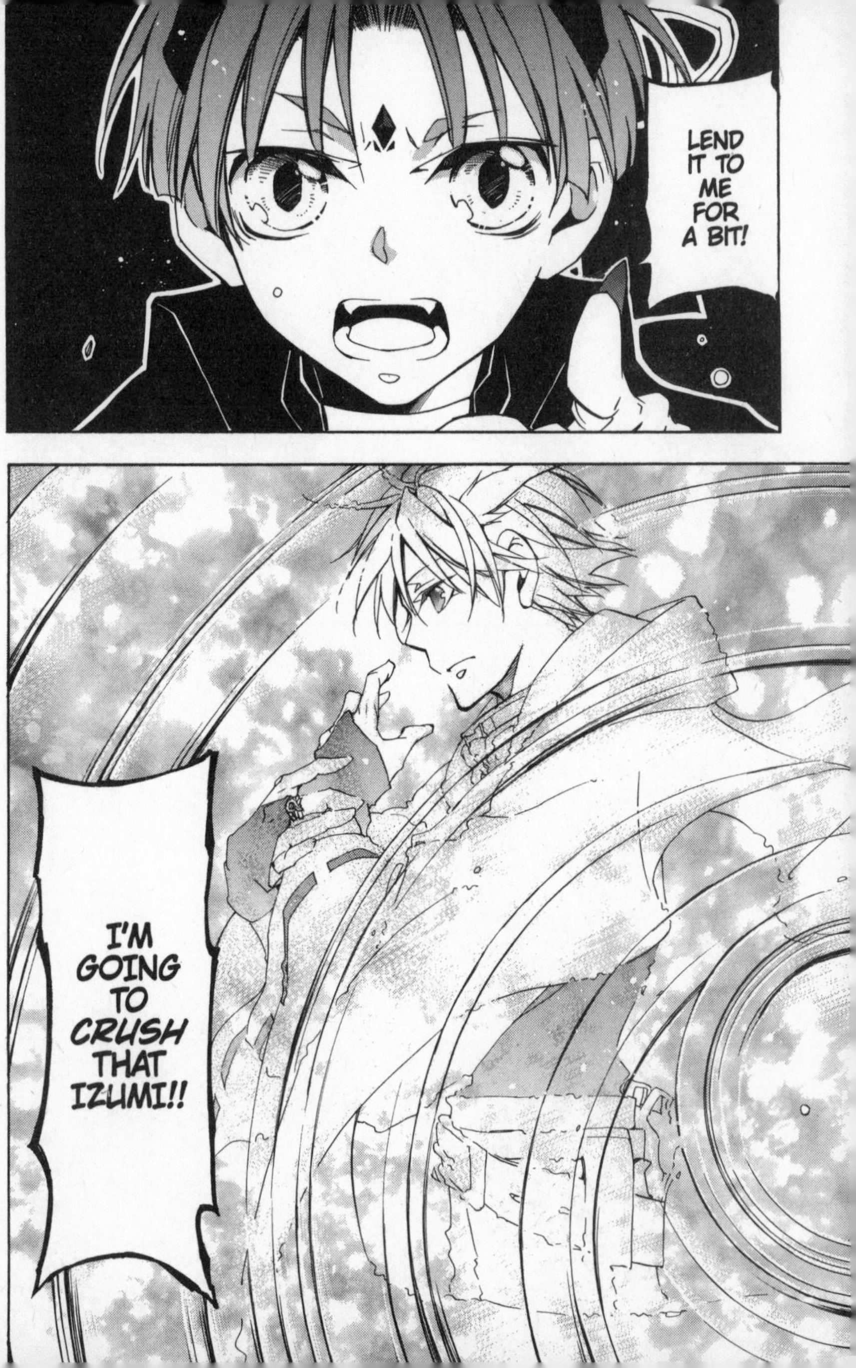
LEND IT TO ME FOR A BIT!
I'M GOING TO CRUSH THAT IZUMI!!

BATTLE
RABBITS
バトラビッツ

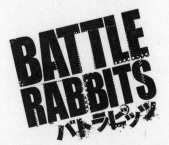

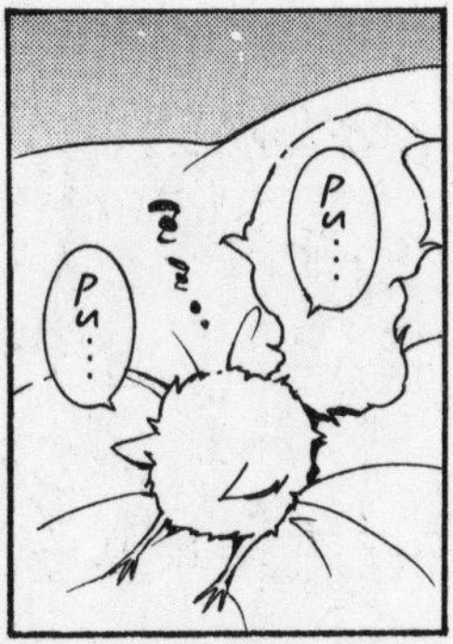
Pu...
Pu...

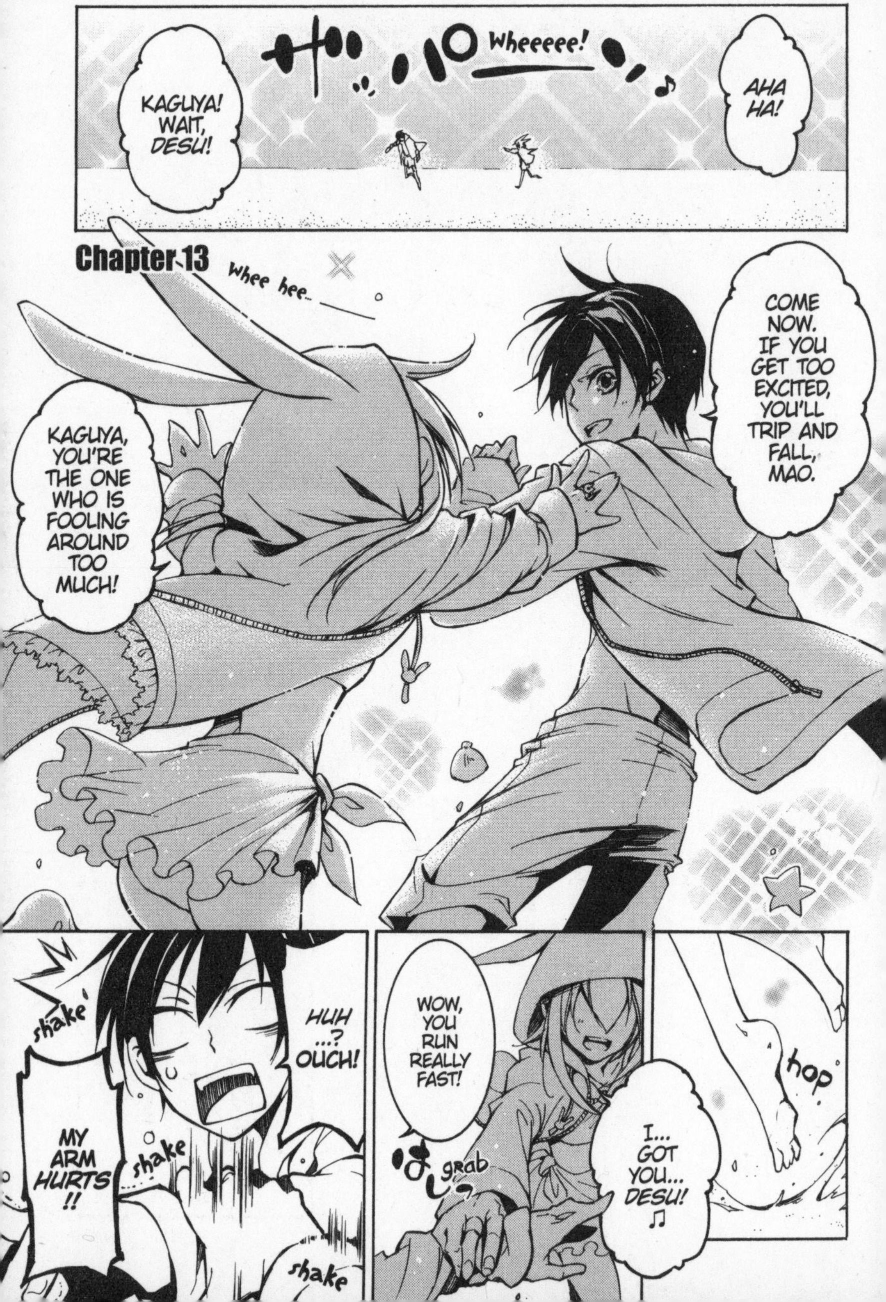
AHA HA!
Wheeeee!
KAGUYA! WAIT, DESU!
Chapter 13
COME NOW. IF YOU GET TOO EXCITED, YOU'LL TRIP AND FALL, MAO.
Whee hee...
KAGUYA, YOU'RE THE ONE WHO IS FOOLING AROUND TOO MUCH!
hop
I... GOT YOU... DESU! ♫
WOW, YOU RUN REALLY FAST!
grab
HUH ...? OUCH!
shake
MY ARM HURTS!!
shake
shake

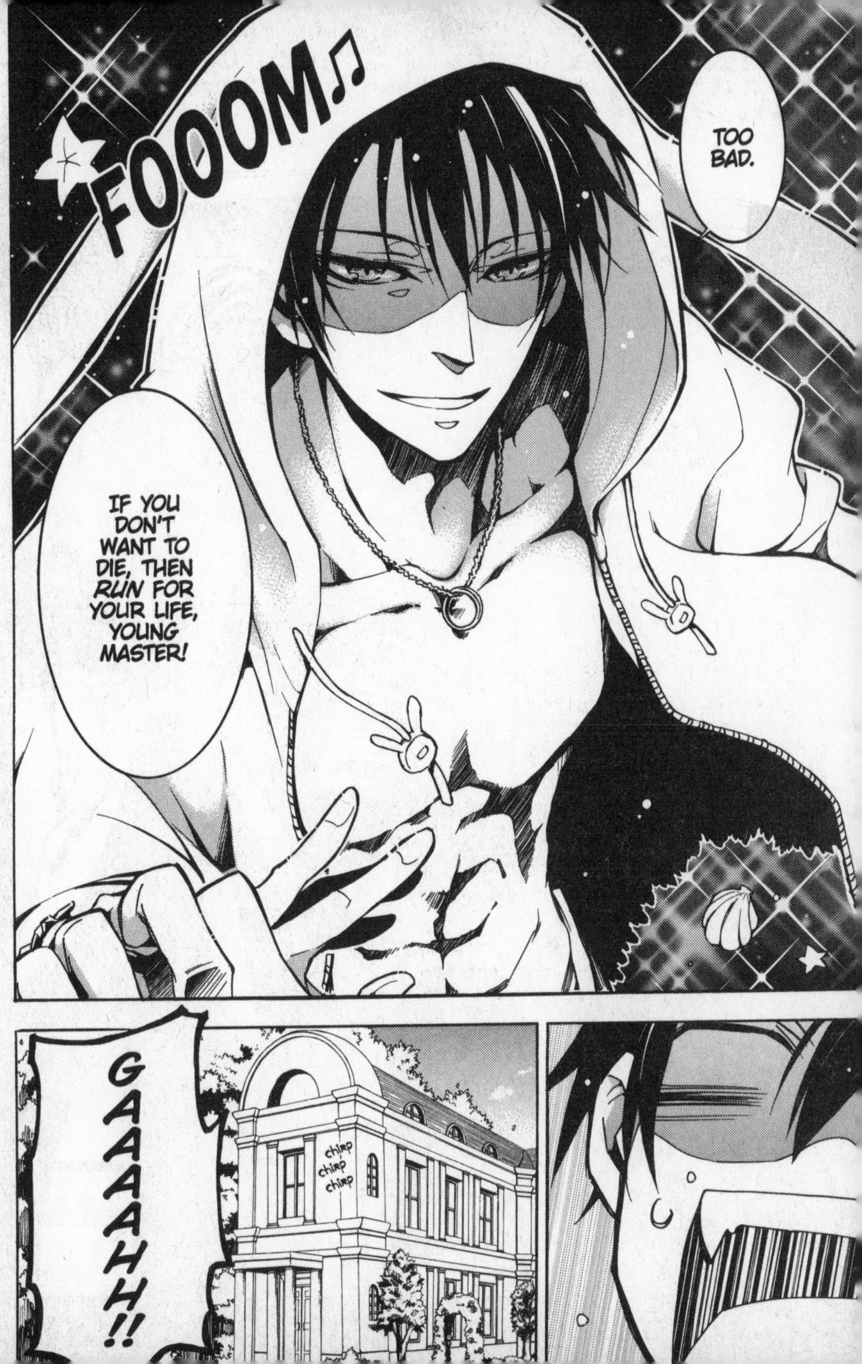
TOO BAD.
FOOOM♫
IF YOU DON'T WANT TO DIE, THEN *RUN* FOR YOUR LIFE, YOUNG MASTER!
chirp chirp chirp
GAAAAHH!!

Chapter 13

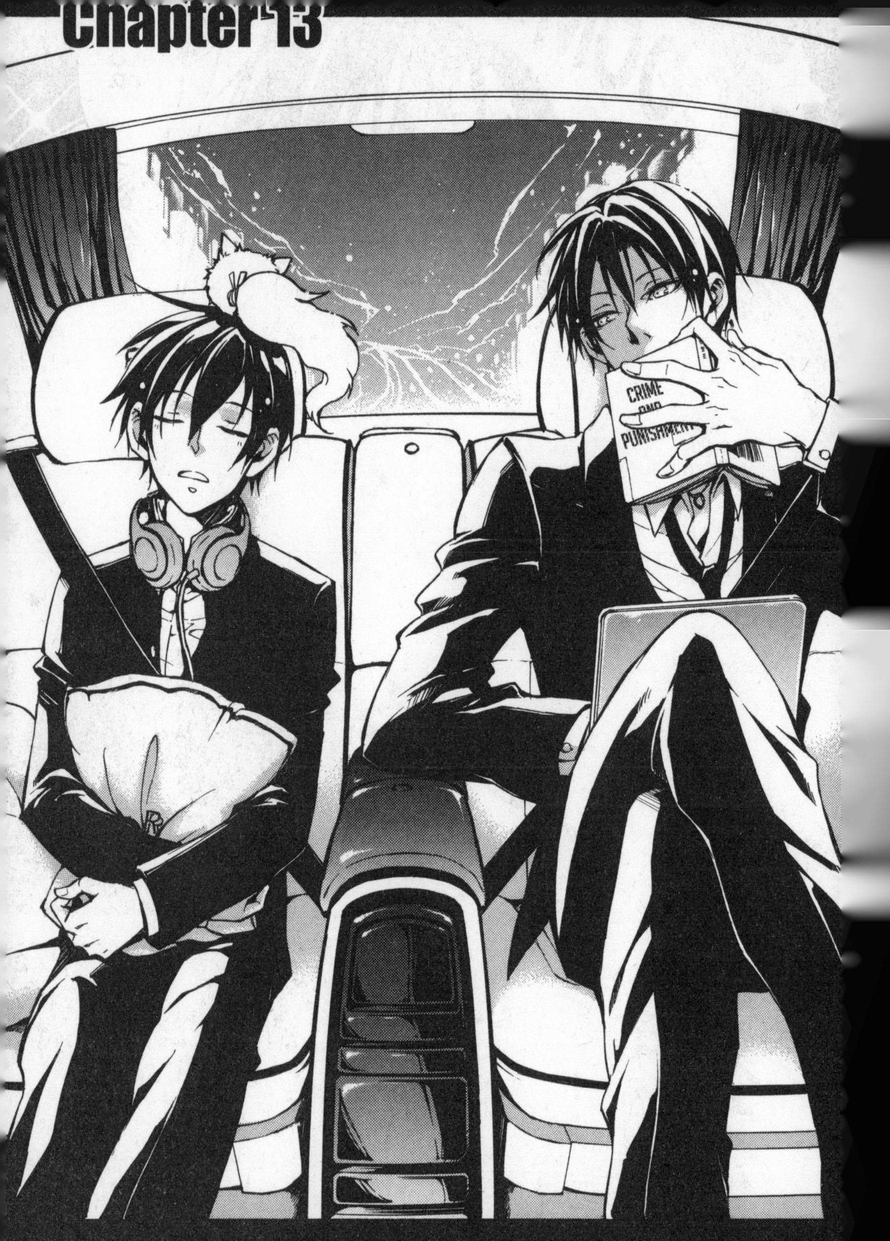
CRIME AND PUNISHMENT

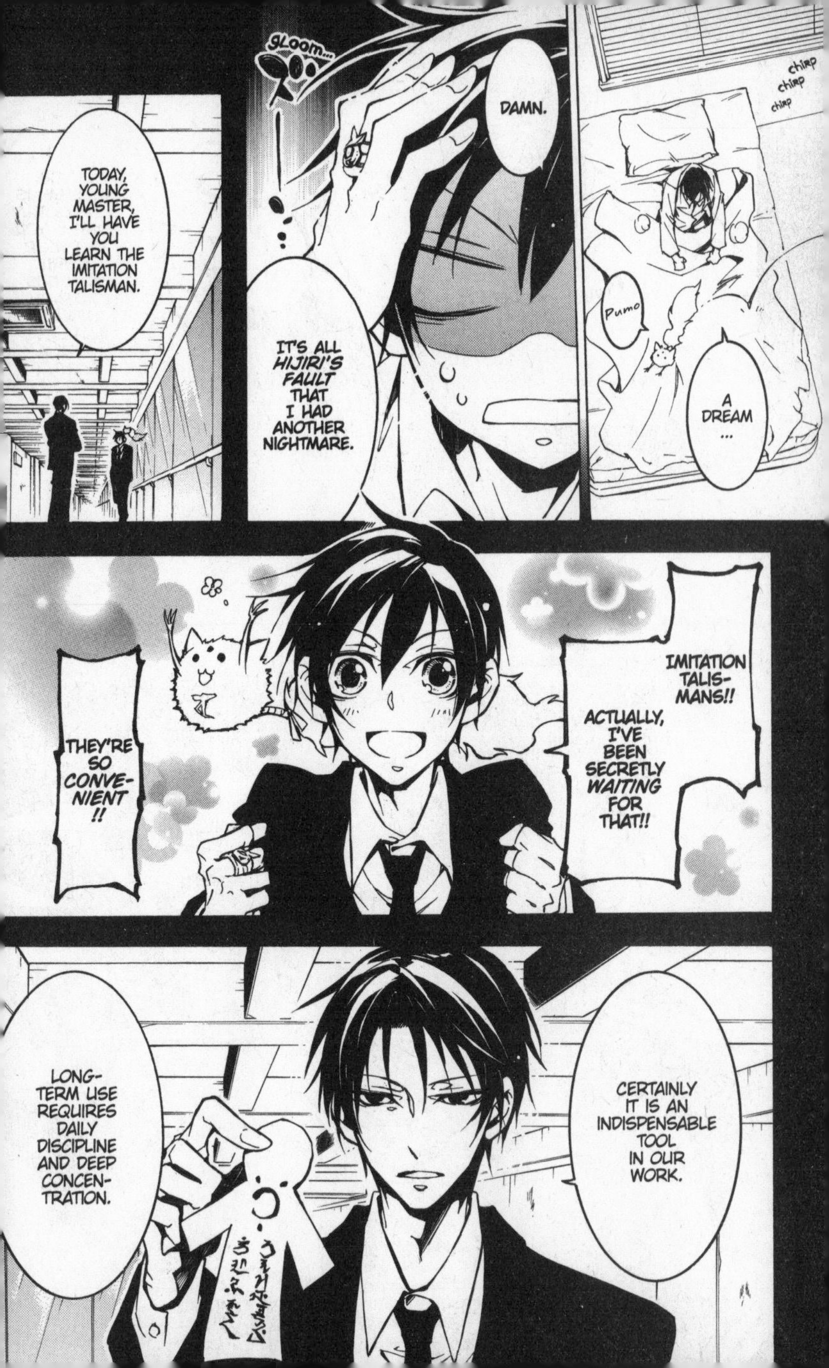
chirp
chirp
chirp
Pumo
A DREAM ...
gLOOM...
DAMN.
IT'S ALL HIJIRI'S FAULT THAT I HAD ANOTHER NIGHTMARE.
TODAY, YOUNG MASTER, I'LL HAVE YOU LEARN THE IMITATION TALISMAN.
IMITATION TALIS-MANS!!
ACTUALLY, I'VE BEEN SECRETLY WAITING FOR THAT!!
THEY'RE SO CONVE-NIENT !!
CERTAINLY IT IS AN INDISPENSABLE TOOL IN OUR WORK.
LONG-TERM USE REQUIRES DAILY DISCIPLINE AND DEEP CONCEN-TRATION.

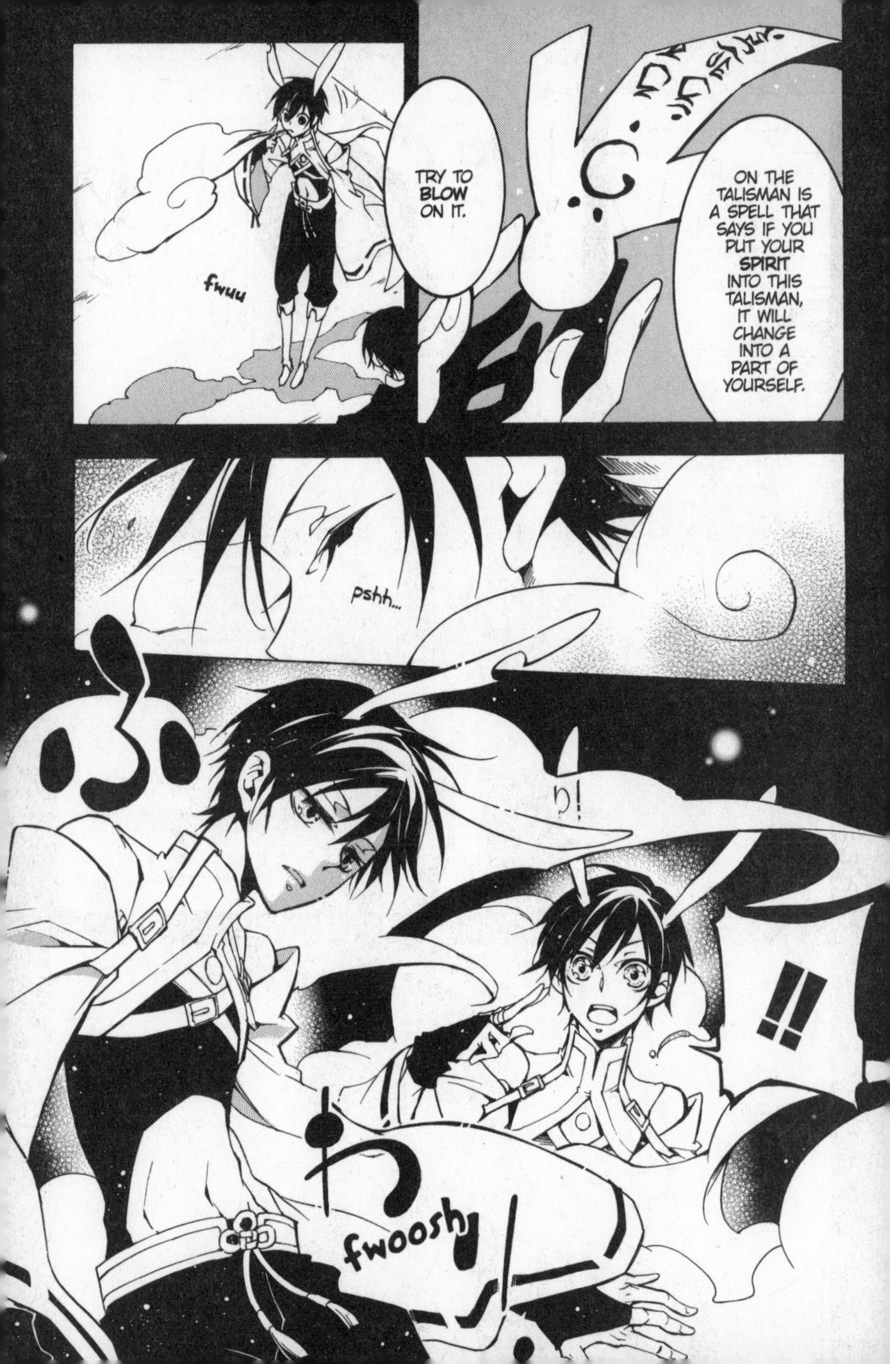
ON THE TALISMAN IS A SPELL THAT SAYS IF YOU PUT YOUR **SPIRIT** INTO THIS TALISMAN, IT WILL CHANGE INTO A PART OF YOURSELF.
TRY TO **BLOW** ON IT.
fwuu
pshh...
!!
fwoosh

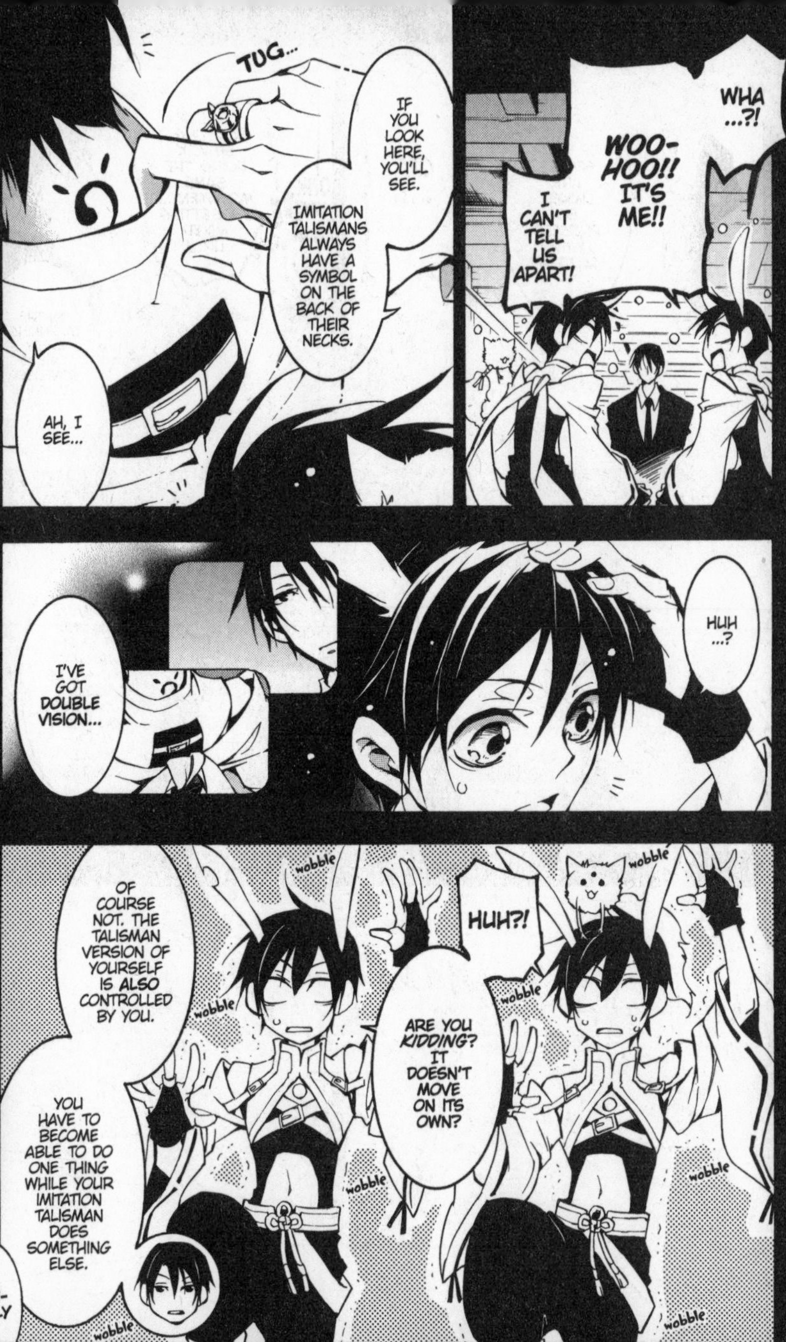
WHA ...?!
WOO-HOO!! IT'S ME!!
I CAN'T TELL US APART!
TUG...
IF YOU LOOK HERE, YOU'LL SEE.
IMITATION TALISMANS ALWAYS HAVE A SYMBOL ON THE BACK OF THEIR NECKS.
AH, I SEE...
HUH ...?
I'VE GOT DOUBLE VISION...
wobble
HUH?!
wobble
wobble
ARE YOU *KIDDING*? IT DOESN'T MOVE ON ITS OWN?
wobble
wobble
OF COURSE NOT. THE TALISMAN VERSION OF YOURSELF IS ALSO CONTROLLED BY YOU.
wobble
YOU HAVE TO BECOME ABLE TO DO ONE THING WHILE YOUR IMITATION TALISMAN DOES SOMETHING ELSE.
wobble
SERI-OUSLY ?!
wobble

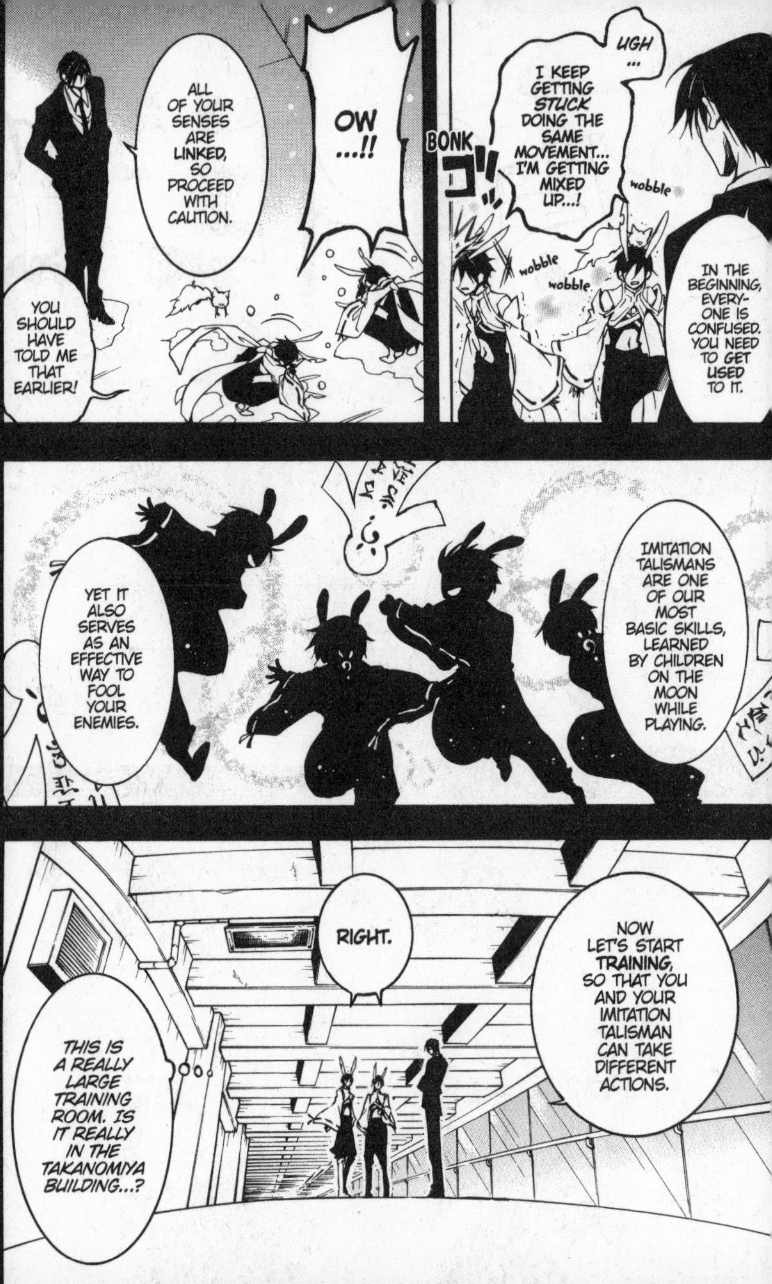
UGH ...
I KEEP GETTING STUCK DOING THE SAME MOVEMENT... I'M GETTING MIXED UP...!
BONK
wobble
wobble
wobble
IN THE BEGINNING, EVERY-ONE IS CONFUSED. YOU NEED TO GET USED TO IT.
OW ...!!
ALL OF YOUR SENSES ARE LINKED, SO PROCEED WITH CAUTION.
YOU SHOULD HAVE TOLD ME THAT EARLIER!
IMITATION TALISMANS ARE ONE OF OUR MOST BASIC SKILLS, LEARNED BY CHILDREN ON THE MOON WHILE PLAYING.
YET IT ALSO SERVES AS AN EFFECTIVE WAY TO FOOL YOUR ENEMIES.
NOW LET'S START TRAINING, SO THAT YOU AND YOUR IMITATION TALISMAN CAN TAKE DIFFERENT ACTIONS.
RIGHT.
THIS IS A REALLY LARGE TRAINING ROOM. IS IT REALLY IN THE TAKANOMIYA BUILDING...?

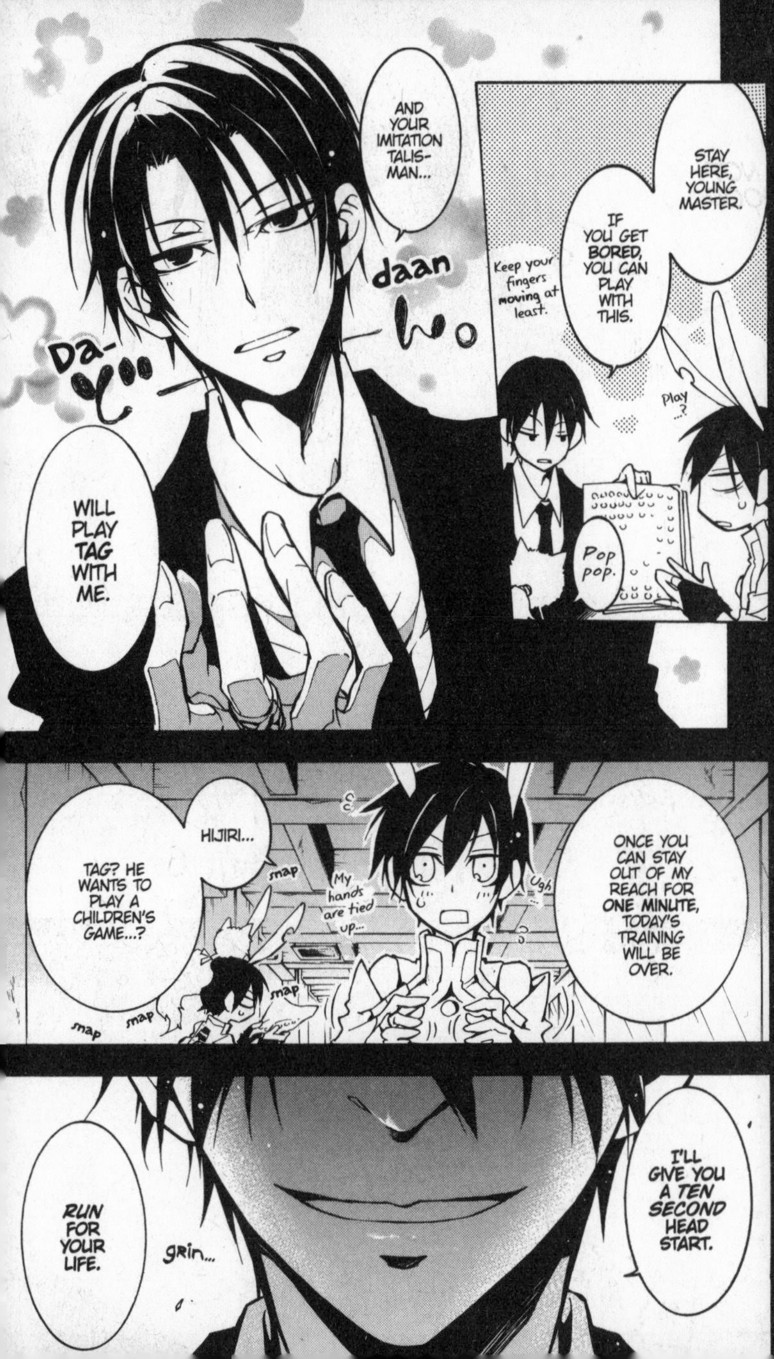
STAY HERE, YOUNG MASTER.
IF YOU GET BORED, YOU CAN PLAY WITH THIS.
Keep your fingers moving at least.
Play ...?
Pop pop.
AND YOUR IMITATION TALIS-MAN...
daan
Da-
WILL PLAY TAG WITH ME.
ONCE YOU CAN STAY OUT OF MY REACH FOR ONE MINUTE, TODAY'S TRAINING WILL BE OVER.
Ugh...
My hands are tied up...
HIJIRI...
TAG? HE WANTS TO PLAY A CHILDREN'S GAME...?
snap
snap
snap
snap
I'LL GIVE YOU A *TEN SECOND* HEAD START.
grin...
RUN FOR YOUR LIFE.

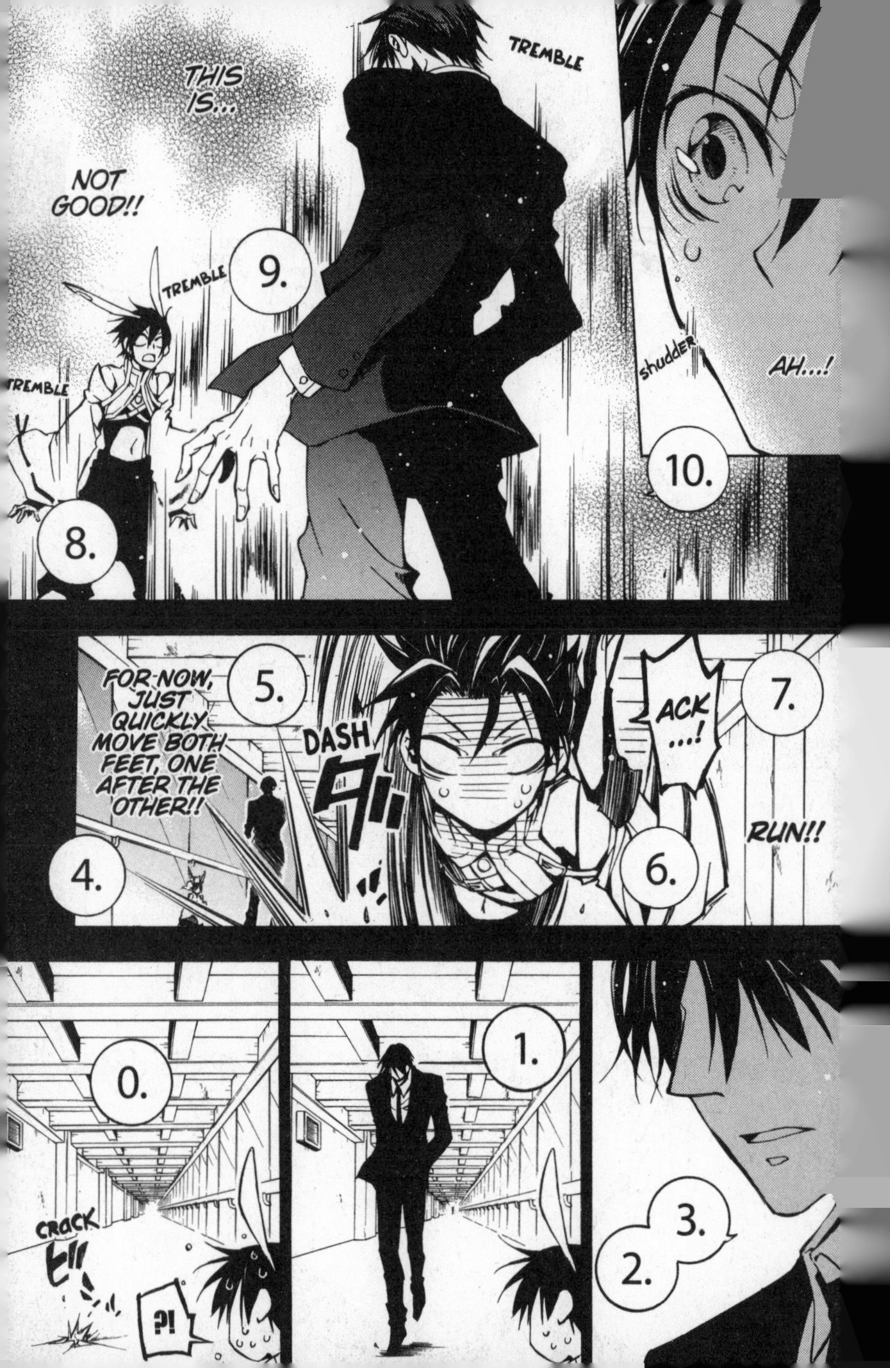
0.
CRACK
?!
CRACK
1.
2.
3.
4.
FOR NOW, JUST QUICKLY MOVE BOTH FEET, ONE AFTER THE OTHER!!
5.
DASH
6.
ACK ...!
7.
RUN!!
8.
TREMBLE
NOT GOOD!!
THIS IS...
TREMBLE
9.
TREMBLE
shudder
10.
AH...!

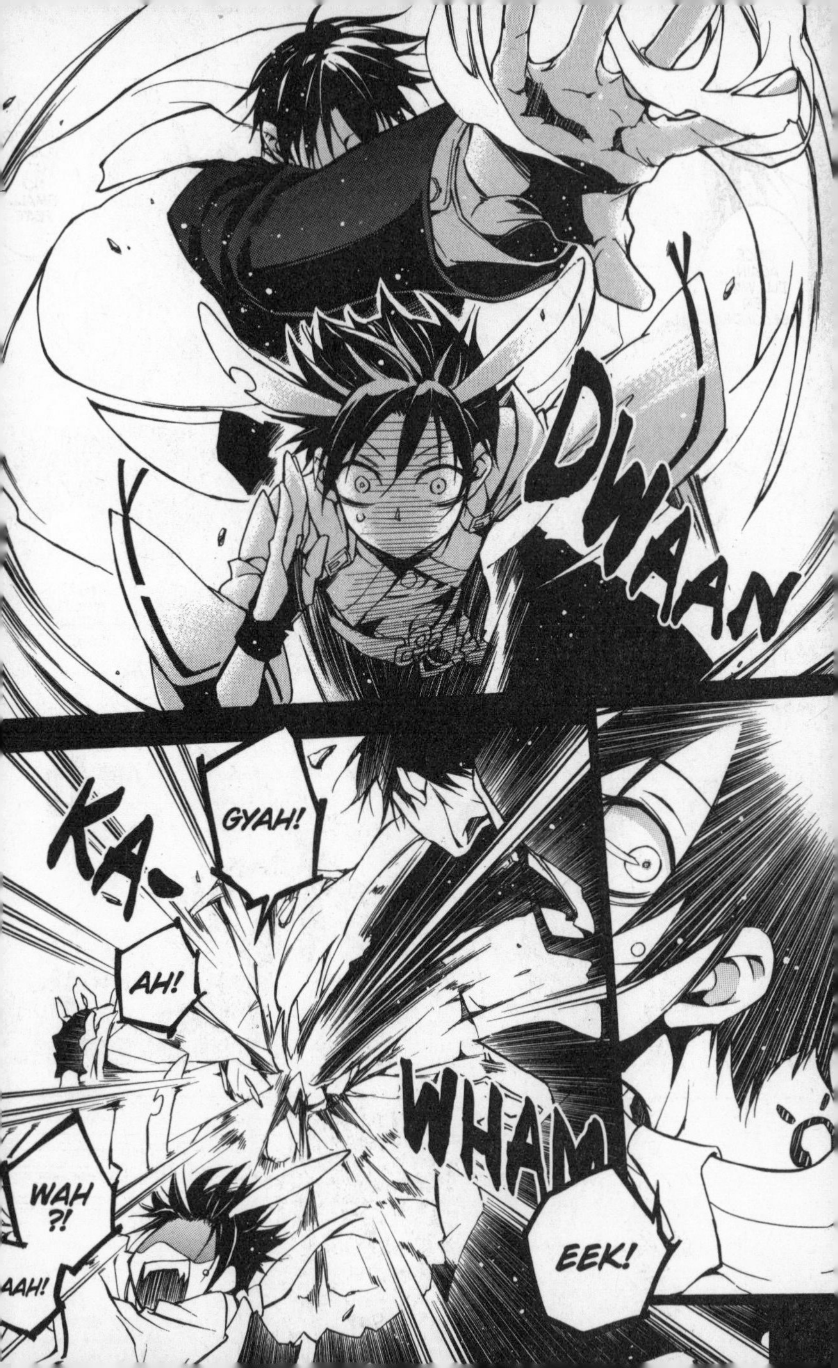
DWAAN
EEK!
GYAH!
KA-
AH!
WHAM
WAH ?!
AAH!

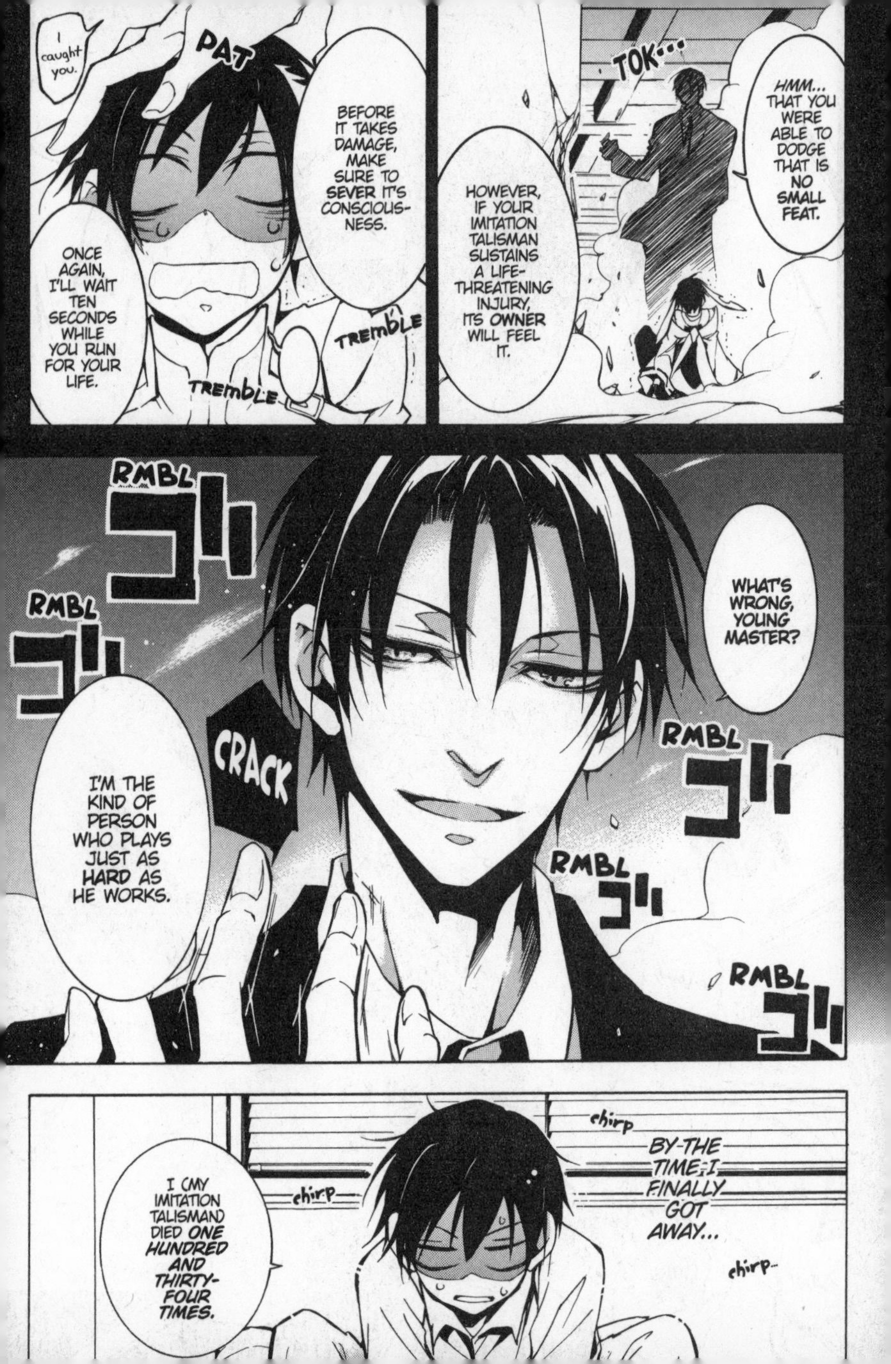
HMM... THAT YOU WERE ABLE TO DODGE THAT IS NO SMALL FEAT.
TOK...
HOWEVER, IF YOUR IMITATION TALISMAN SUSTAINS A LIFE-THREATENING INJURY, ITS OWNER WILL FEEL IT.
BEFORE IT TAKES DAMAGE, MAKE SURE TO SEVER IT'S CONSCIOUSNESS.
PAT
I caught you.
ONCE AGAIN, I'LL WAIT TEN SECONDS WHILE YOU RUN FOR YOUR LIFE.
TREMBLE
TREMBLE
WHAT'S WRONG, YOUNG MASTER?
RMBL ゴ
RMBL ゴ
RMBL ゴ
RMBL ゴ
CRACK
I'M THE KIND OF PERSON WHO PLAYS JUST AS HARD AS HE WORKS.
RMBL ゴ
RMBL ゴ
chirp
BY THE TIME I FINALLY GOT AWAY...
chirp
chirp
I (MY IMITATION TALISMAN) DIED ONE HUNDRED AND THIRTY-FOUR TIMES.

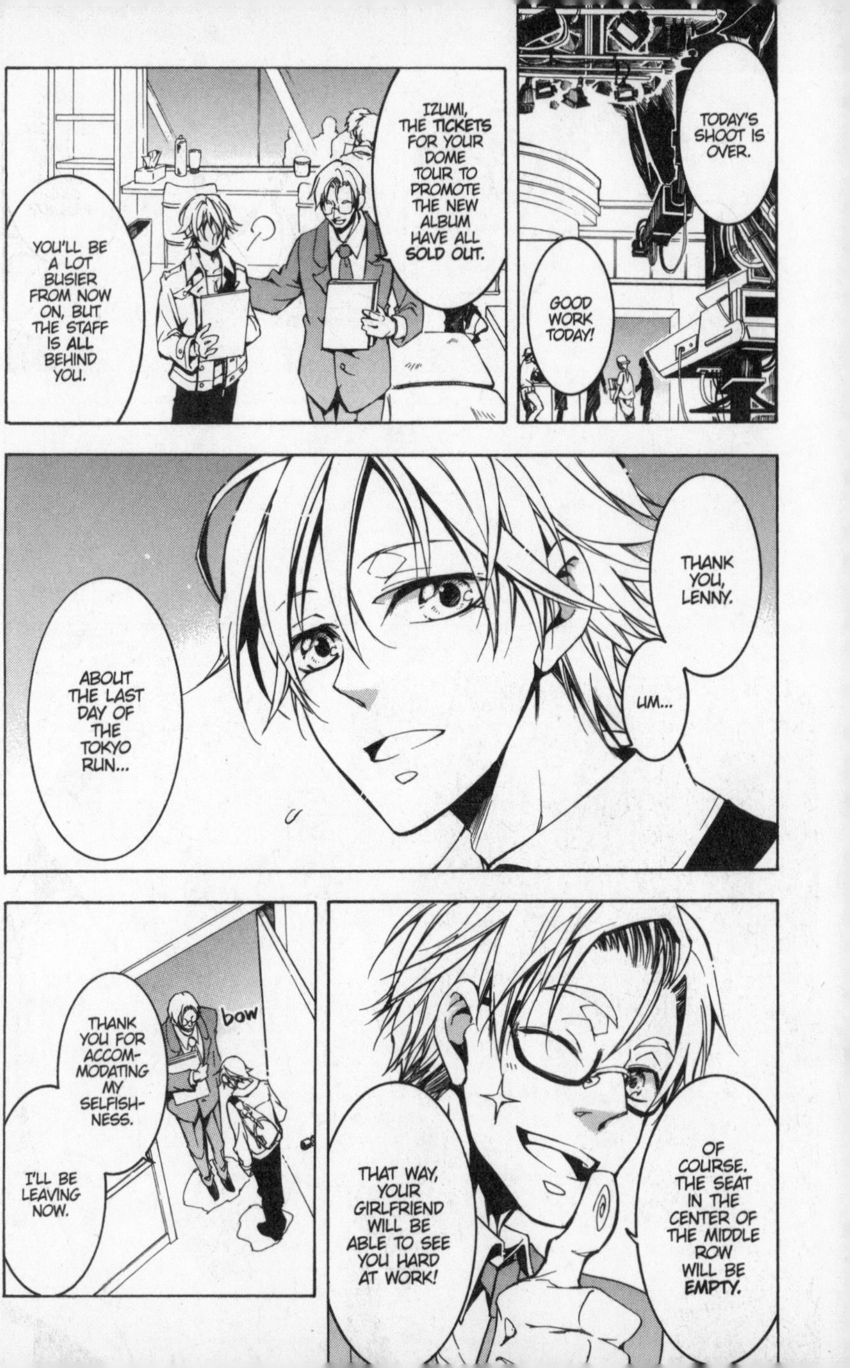
TODAY'S SHOOT IS OVER.
GOOD WORK TODAY!
IZUMI, THE TICKETS FOR YOUR DOME TOUR TO PROMOTE THE NEW ALBUM HAVE ALL SOLD OUT.
YOU'LL BE A LOT BUSIER FROM NOW ON, BUT THE STAFF IS ALL BEHIND YOU.
THANK YOU, LENNY.
UM...
ABOUT THE LAST DAY OF THE TOKYO RUN...
OF COURSE. THE SEAT IN THE CENTER OF THE MIDDLE ROW WILL BE EMPTY.
THAT WAY, YOUR GIRLFRIEND WILL BE ABLE TO SEE YOU HARD AT WORK!
THANK YOU FOR ACCOM-MODATING MY SELFISH-NESS.
bow
I'LL BE LEAVING NOW.

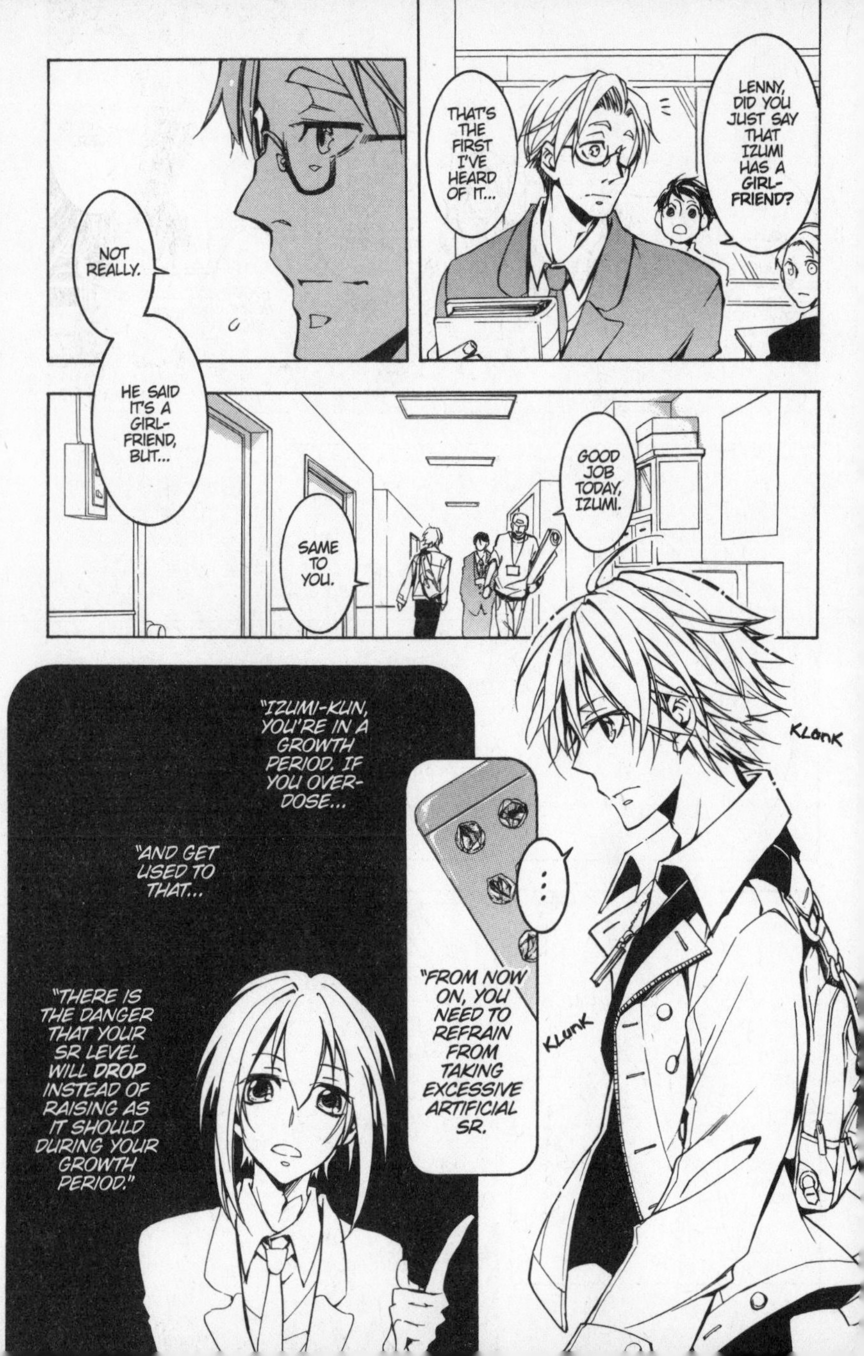
LENNY, DID YOU JUST SAY THAT IZUMI HAS A GIRL-FRIEND?
THAT'S THE FIRST I'VE HEARD OF IT...
NOT REALLY.
HE SAID IT'S A GIRL-FRIEND, BUT...
GOOD JOB TODAY, IZUMI.
SAME TO YOU.
KLonK
"IZUMI-KUN, YOU'RE IN A GROWTH PERIOD. IF YOU OVER-DOSE...
...
"AND GET USED TO THAT...
KLunK
"THERE IS THE DANGER THAT YOUR SR LEVEL WILL DROP INSTEAD OF RAISING AS IT SHOULD DURING YOUR GROWTH PERIOD."
"FROM NOW ON, YOU NEED TO REFRAIN FROM TAKING EXCESSIVE ARTIFICIAL SR.

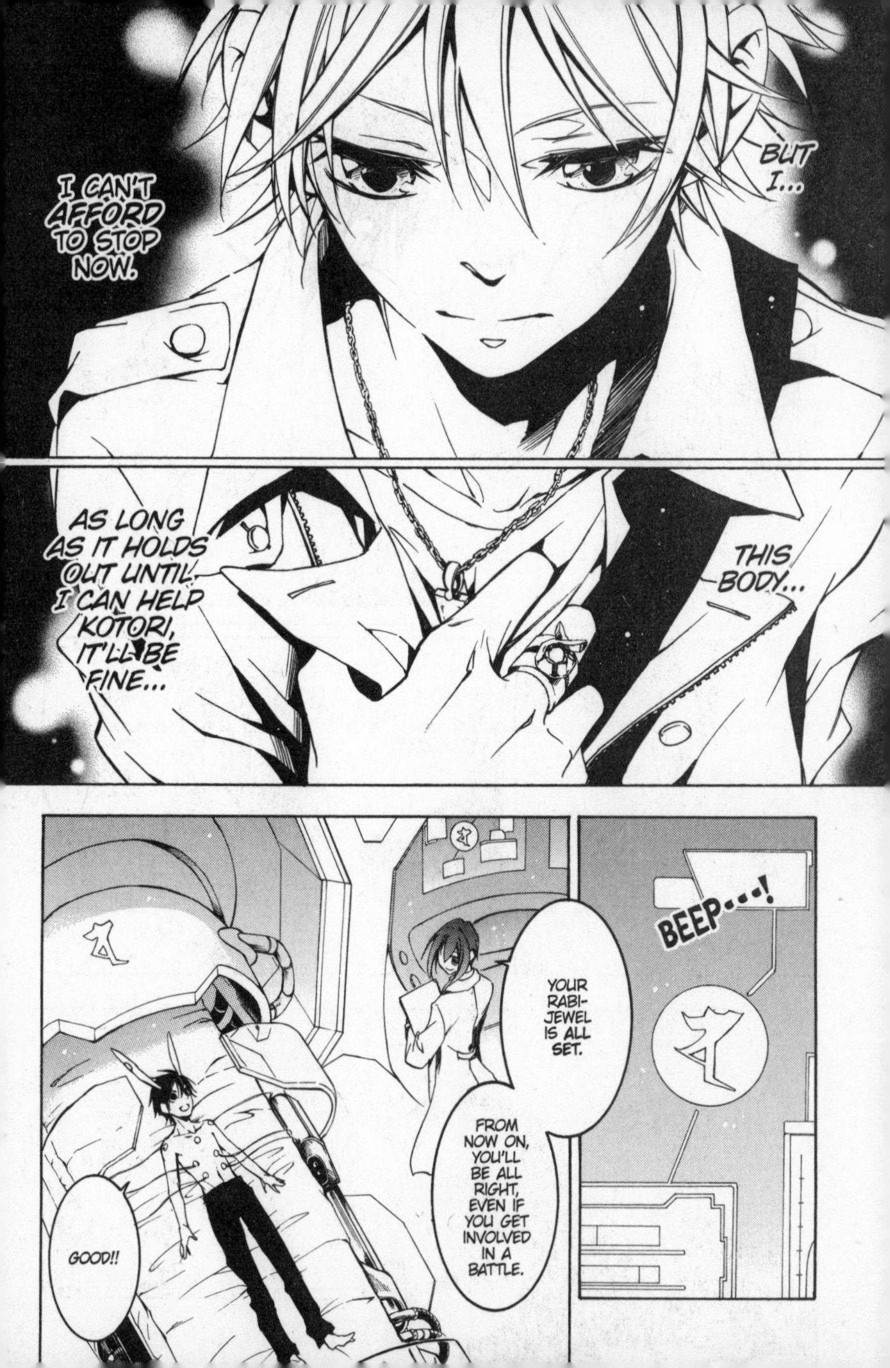
BUT I...
I CAN'T AFFORD TO STOP NOW.
THIS BODY...
AS LONG AS IT HOLDS OUT UNTIL I CAN HELP KOTORI, IT'LL BE FINE...
BEEP...!
YOUR RABI-JEWEL IS ALL SET.
FROM NOW ON, YOU'LL BE ALL RIGHT, EVEN IF YOU GET INVOLVED IN A BATTLE.
GOOD!!

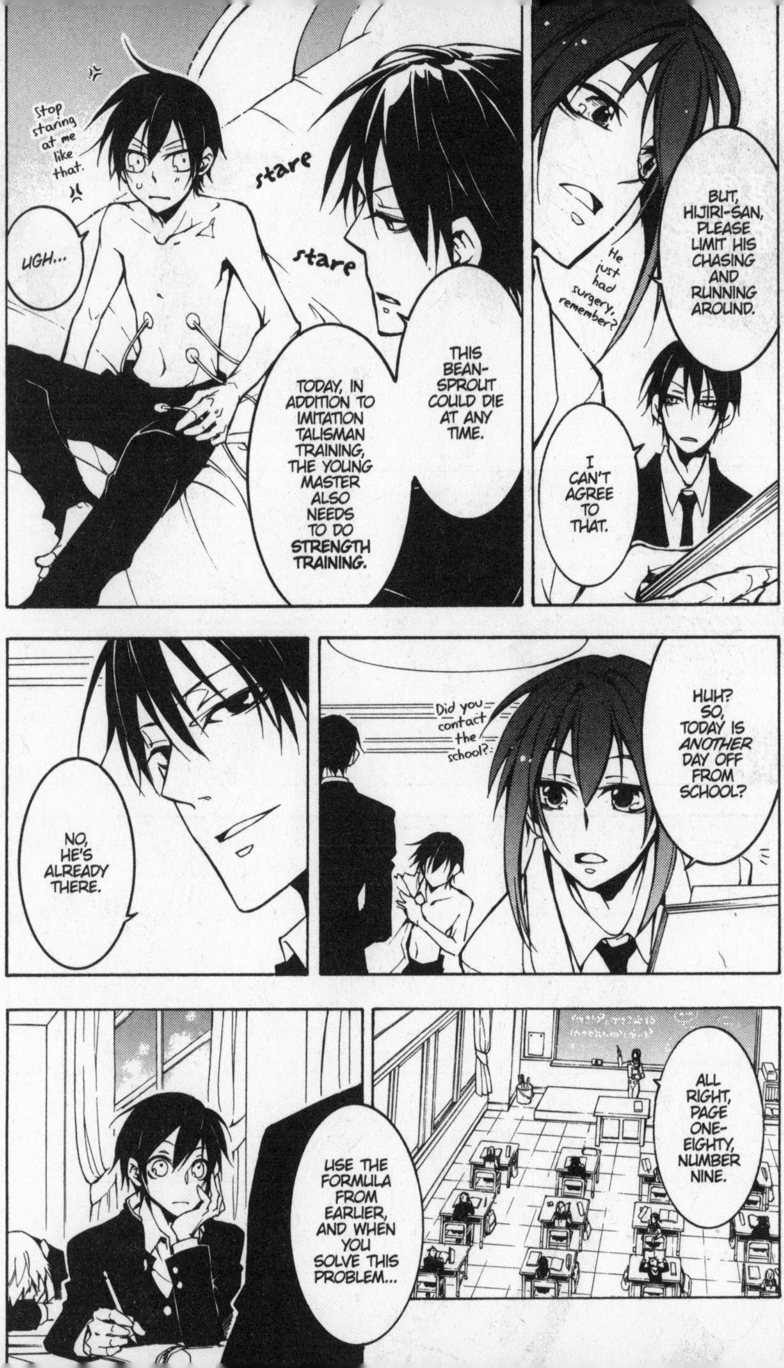
BUT, HIJIRI-SAN, PLEASE LIMIT HIS CHASING AND RUNNING AROUND.
He just had surgery, remember?
I CAN'T AGREE TO THAT.
THIS BEAN-SPROUT COULD DIE AT ANY TIME.
TODAY, IN ADDITION TO IMITATION TALISMAN TRAINING, THE YOUNG MASTER ALSO NEEDS TO DO STRENGTH TRAINING.
stare
stare
Stop staring at me like that.
UGH...
HUH? SO, TODAY IS *ANOTHER* DAY OFF FROM SCHOOL?
Did you contact the school?
NO, HE'S ALREADY THERE.
ALL RIGHT, PAGE ONE-EIGHTY, NUMBER NINE.
USE THE FORMULA FROM EARLIER, AND WHEN YOU SOLVE THIS PROBLEM...

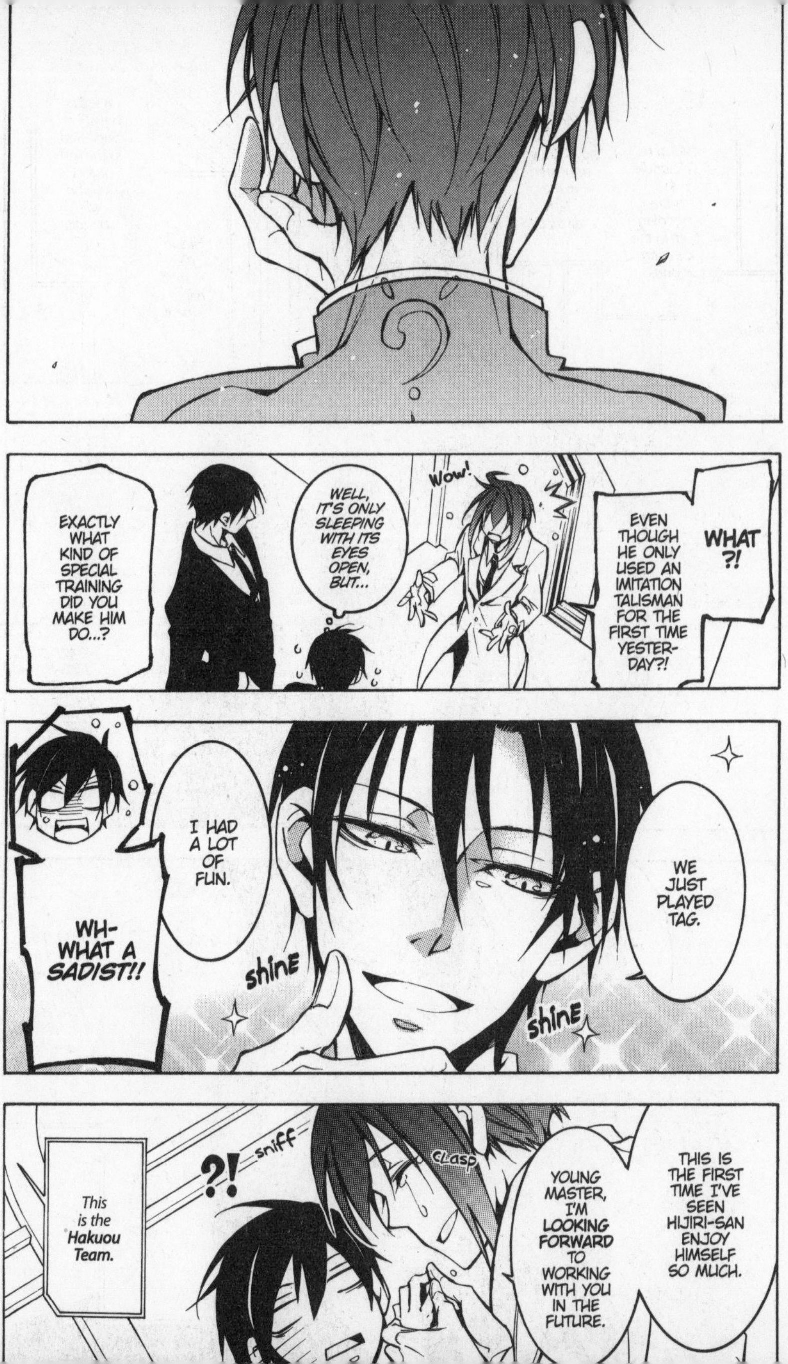
WHAT?!
EVEN THOUGH HE ONLY USED AN IMITATION TALISMAN FOR THE FIRST TIME YESTERDAY?!
Wow!
WELL, IT'S ONLY SLEEPING WITH ITS EYES OPEN, BUT...
EXACTLY WHAT KIND OF SPECIAL TRAINING DID YOU MAKE HIM DO...?
WE JUST PLAYED TAG.
shine
shine
I HAD A LOT OF FUN.
WH-WHAT A SADIST!!
THIS IS THE FIRST TIME I'VE SEEN HIJIRI-SAN ENJOY HIMSELF SO MUCH.
YOUNG MASTER, I'M LOOKING FORWARD TO WORKING WITH YOU IN THE FUTURE.
Clasp
sniff
?!
This is the Hakuou Team.

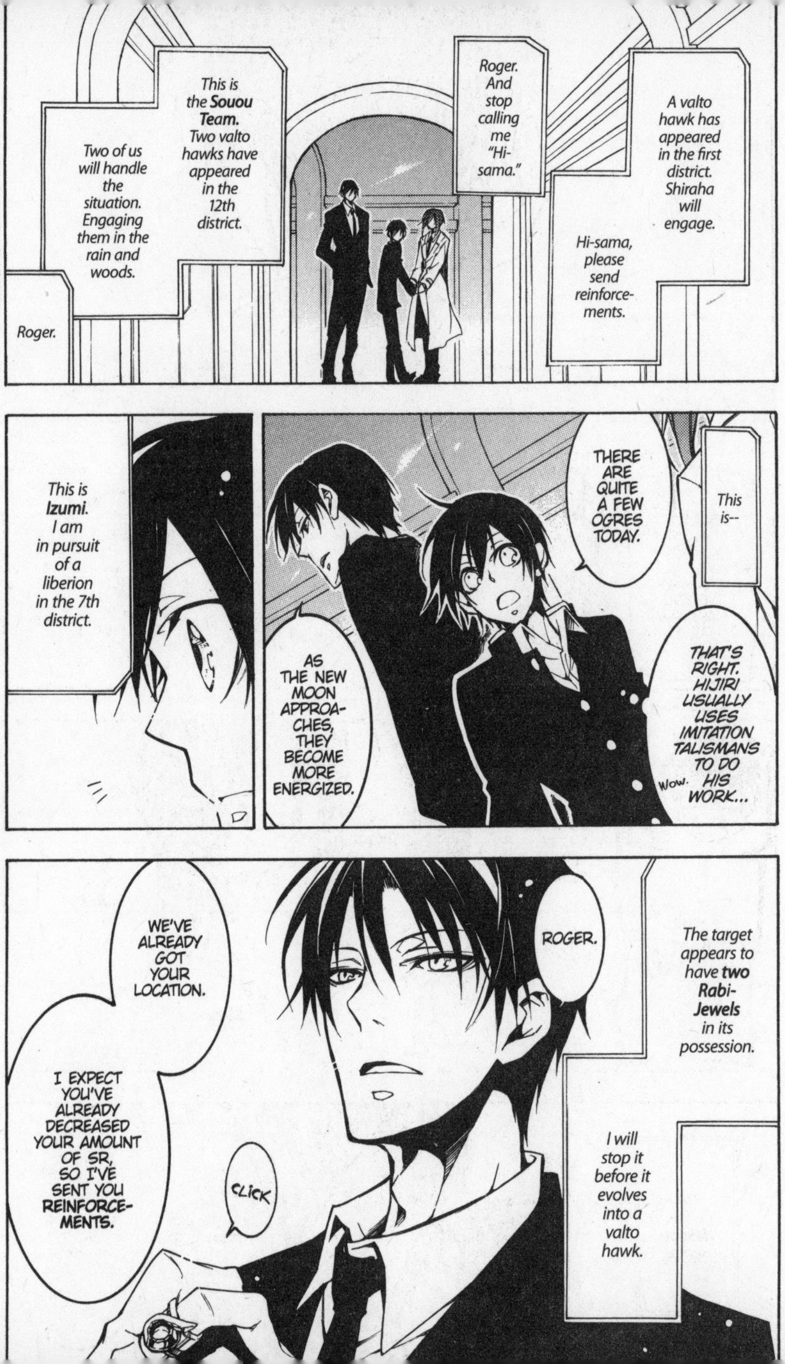
A valto hawk has appeared in the first district. Shiraha will engage.
Hi-sama, please send reinforce-ments.
Roger. And stop calling me "Hi-sama."
This is the **Souou Team.** Two valto hawks have appeared in the 12th district.
Two of us will handle the situation. Engaging them in the rain and woods.
Roger.
This is--
THERE ARE QUITE A FEW OGRES TODAY.
THAT'S RIGHT. HIJIRI USUALLY USES IMITATION TALISMANS TO DO HIS WORK...
Wow.
AS THE NEW MOON APPROACHES, THEY BECOME MORE ENERGIZED.
This is **Izumi**. I am in pursuit of a liberion in the 7th district.
The target appears to have **two Rabi-Jewels** in its possession.
I will stop it before it evolves into a valto hawk.
ROGER.
WE'VE ALREADY GOT YOUR LOCATION.
I EXPECT YOU'VE ALREADY DECREASED YOUR AMOUNT OF SR, SO I'VE SENT YOU **REINFORCE-MENTS.**
CLICK

Kiiiin

but...
SKSH
SKSH...

Reinforce-
ments...?
There's
no
need...

SKSH
SKSH...

WHAT IS
THIS...? I'VE
GOT A BAD
FEELING...

IZUMI...!!

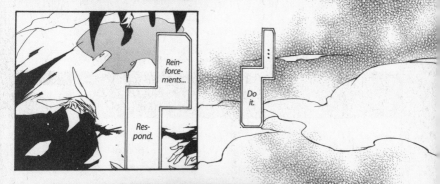

Rein-
force-
ments...

....

Res-
pond.

Do
it.

smirk

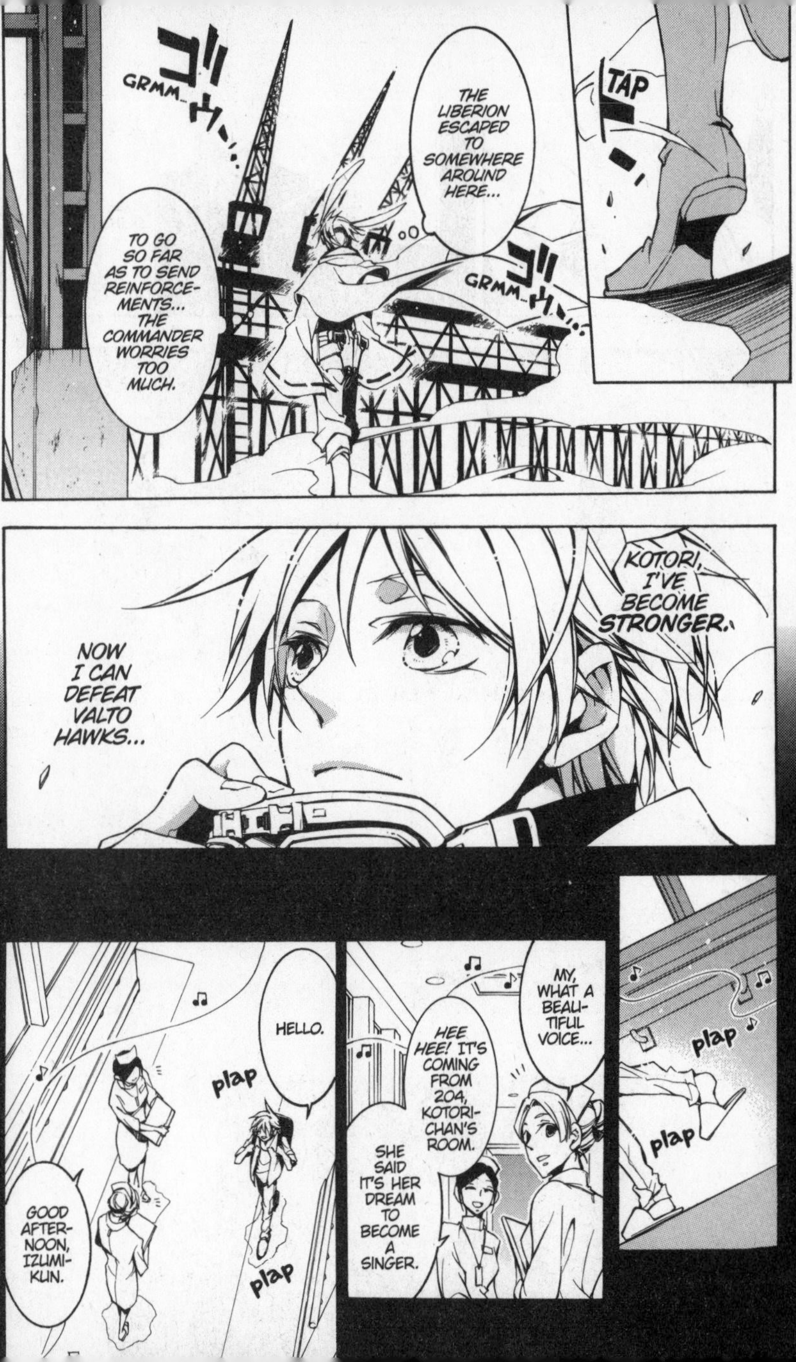
TAP
THE LIBERION ESCAPED TO SOMEWHERE AROUND HERE...
GRMM...
GRMM...
TO GO SO FAR AS TO SEND REINFORCE-MENTS... THE COMMANDER WORRIES TOO MUCH.
KOTORI, I'VE BECOME STRONGER.
NOW I CAN DEFEAT VALTO HAWKS...
plap
plap
MY, WHAT A BEAU-TIFUL VOICE...
HEE HEE! IT'S COMING FROM 204, KOTORI-CHAN'S ROOM.
SHE SAID IT'S HER DREAM TO BECOME A SINGER.
HELLO.
plap
GOOD AFTER-NOON, IZUMI-KUN.
plap

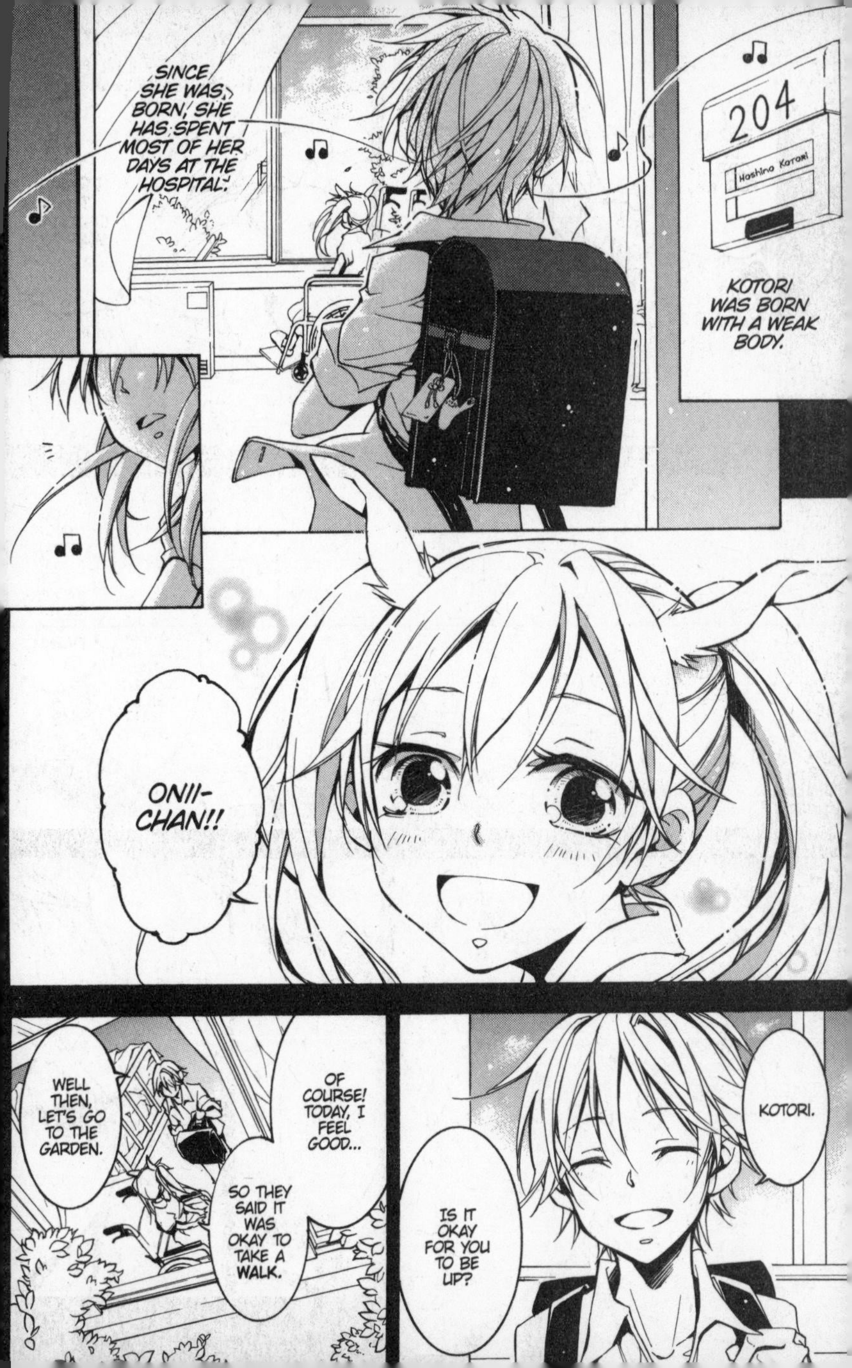
204
Hoshino Kotori
KOTORI WAS BORN WITH A WEAK BODY.
SINCE SHE WAS BORN, SHE HAS SPENT MOST OF HER DAYS AT THE HOSPITAL.
ONII-CHAN!!
KOTORI.
IS IT OKAY FOR YOU TO BE UP?
OF COURSE! TODAY, I FEEL GOOD...
SO THEY SAID IT WAS OKAY TO TAKE A WALK.
WELL THEN, LET'S GO TO THE GARDEN.

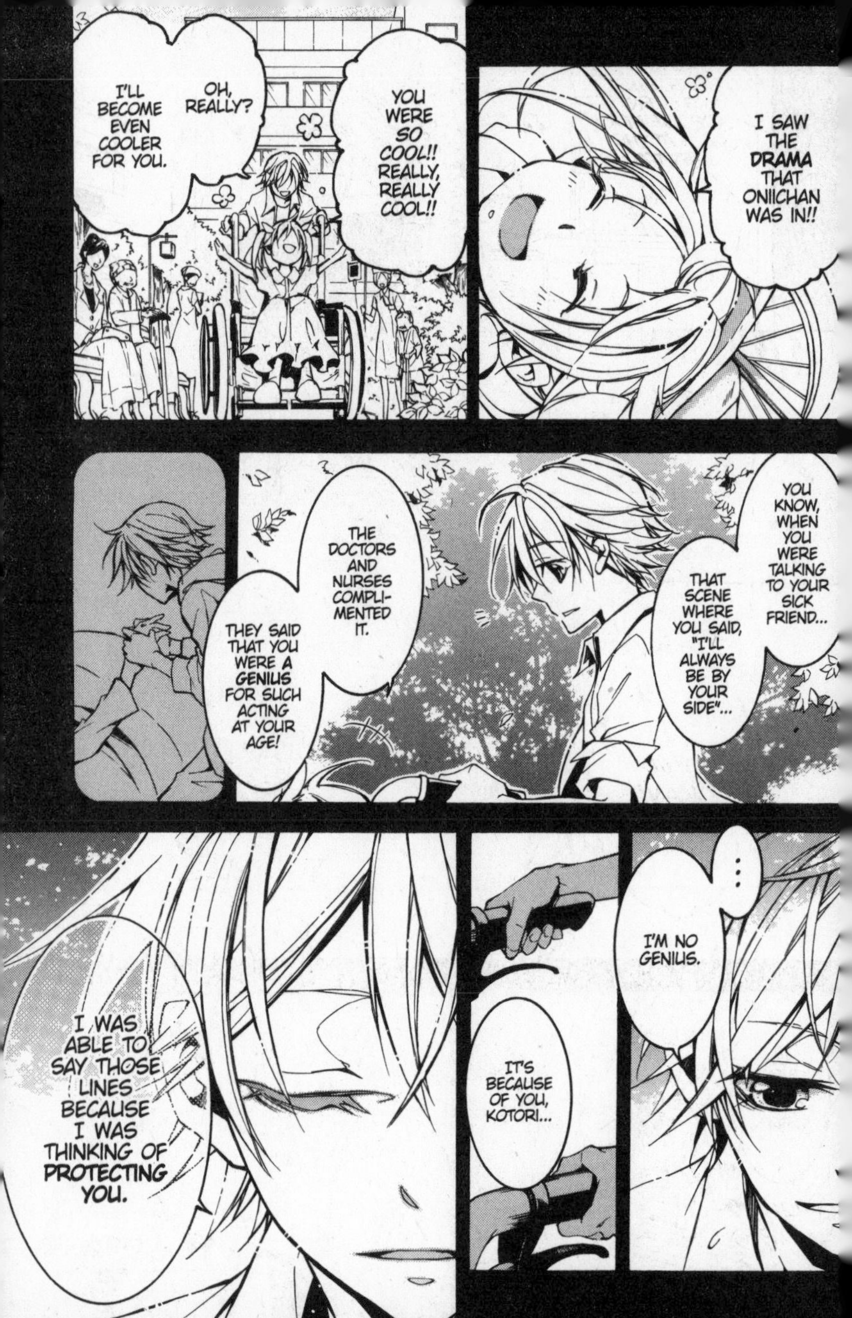
I SAW THE DRAMA THAT ONIICHAN WAS IN!!
YOU WERE SO COOL!! REALLY, REALLY COOL!!
OH, REALLY?
I'LL BECOME EVEN COOLER FOR YOU.
YOU KNOW, WHEN YOU WERE TALKING TO YOUR SICK FRIEND...
THAT SCENE WHERE YOU SAID, "I'LL ALWAYS BE BY YOUR SIDE"...
THE DOCTORS AND NURSES COMPLIMENTED IT.
THEY SAID THAT YOU WERE A GENIUS FOR SUCH ACTING AT YOUR AGE!
...
I'M NO GENIUS.
IT'S BECAUSE OF YOU, KOTORI...
I WAS ABLE TO SAY THOSE LINES BECAUSE I WAS THINKING OF PROTECTING YOU.

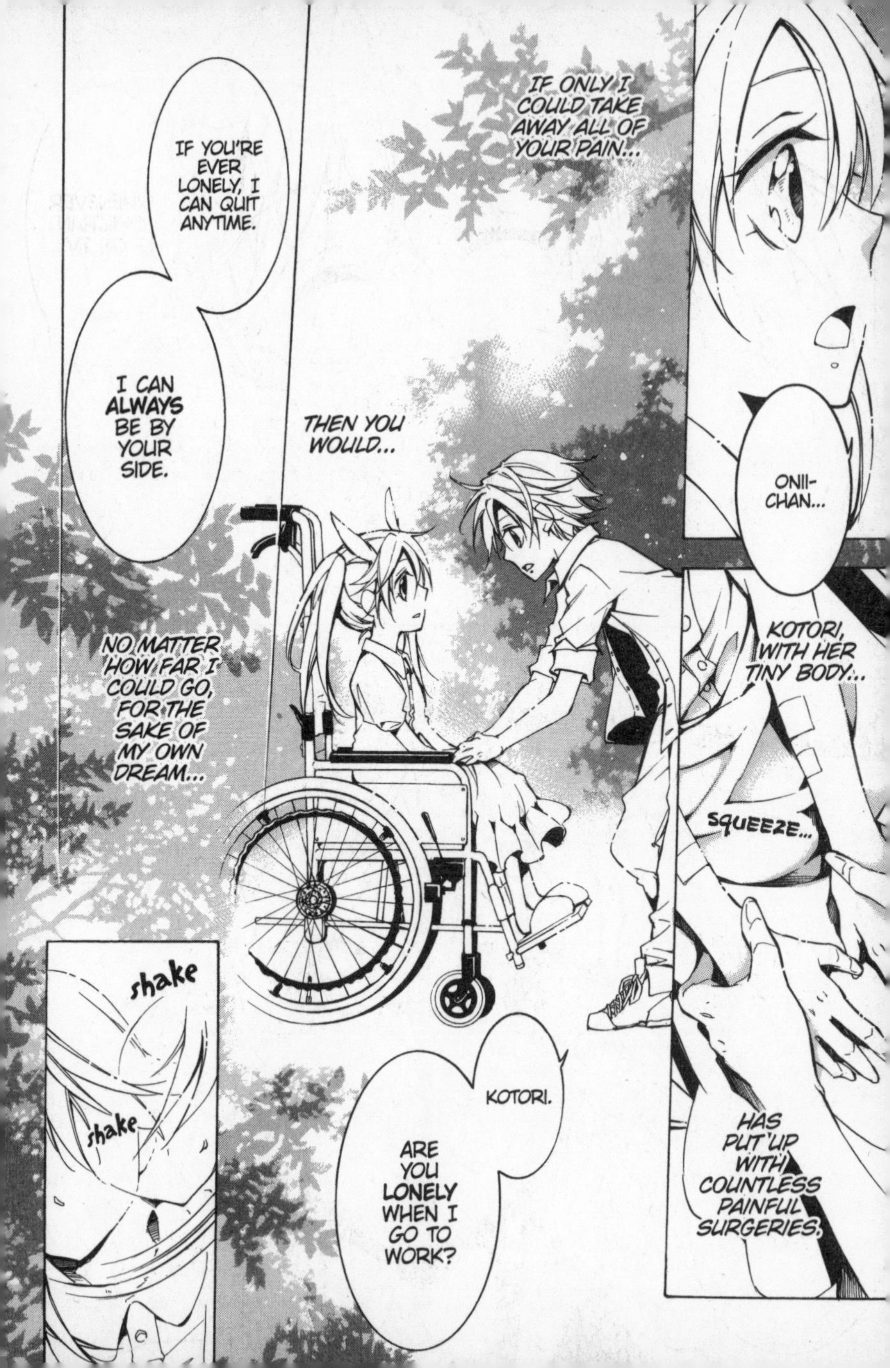
ONII-CHAN...
KOTORI, WITH HER TINY BODY...
SQUEEZE...
HAS PUT UP WITH COUNTLESS PAINFUL SURGERIES.
IF ONLY I COULD TAKE AWAY ALL OF YOUR PAIN...
THEN YOU WOULD...
NO MATTER HOW FAR I COULD GO, FOR THE SAKE OF MY OWN DREAM...
KOTORI.
ARE YOU LONELY WHEN I GO TO WORK?
IF YOU'RE EVER LONELY, I CAN QUIT ANYTIME.
I CAN ALWAYS BE BY YOUR SIDE.
shake
shake

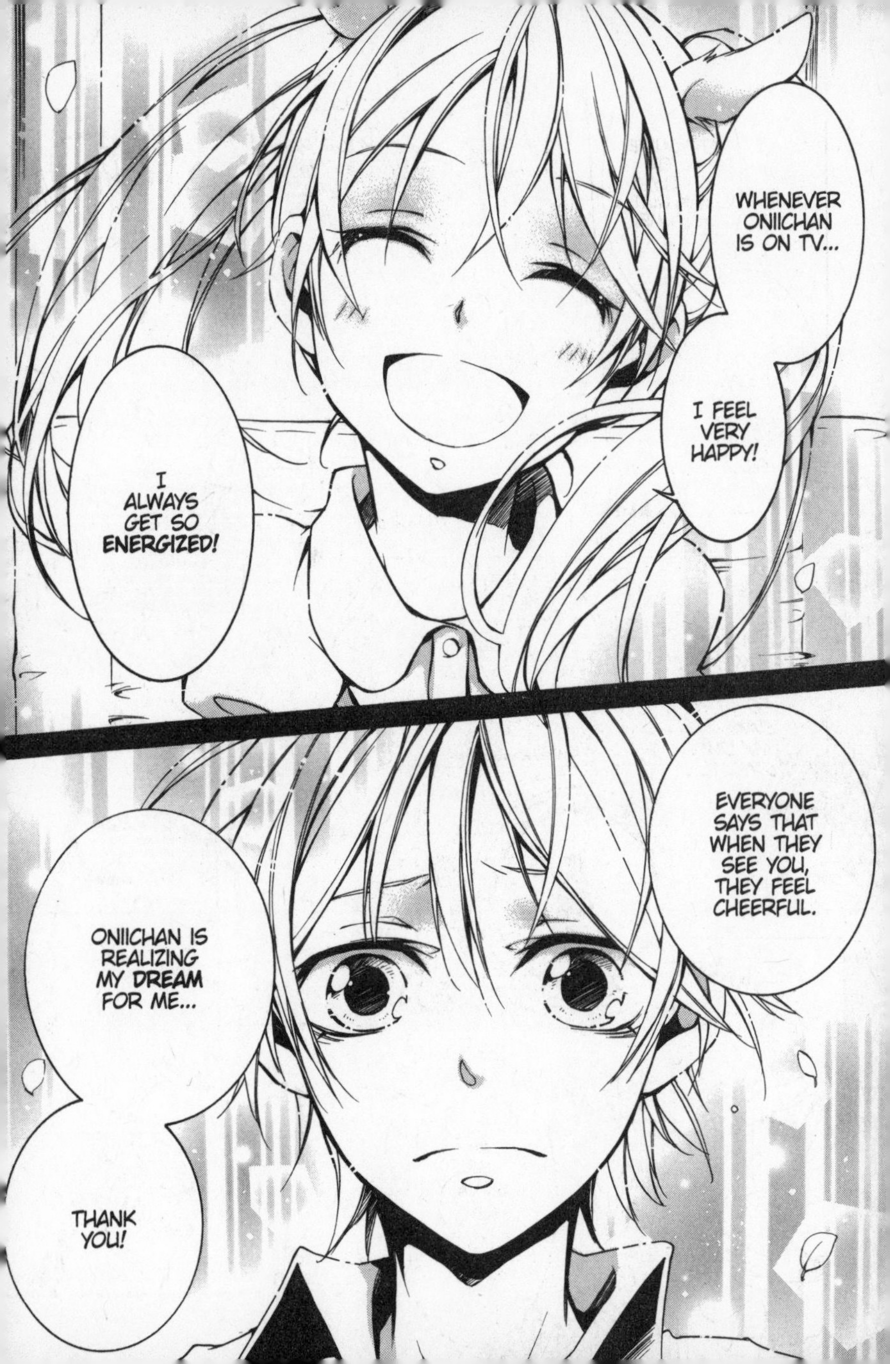
WHENEVER ONIICHAN IS ON TV...
I FEEL VERY HAPPY!
I ALWAYS GET SO ENERGIZED!
EVERYONE SAYS THAT WHEN THEY SEE YOU, THEY FEEL CHEERFUL.
ONIICHAN IS REALIZING MY DREAM FOR ME...
THANK YOU!

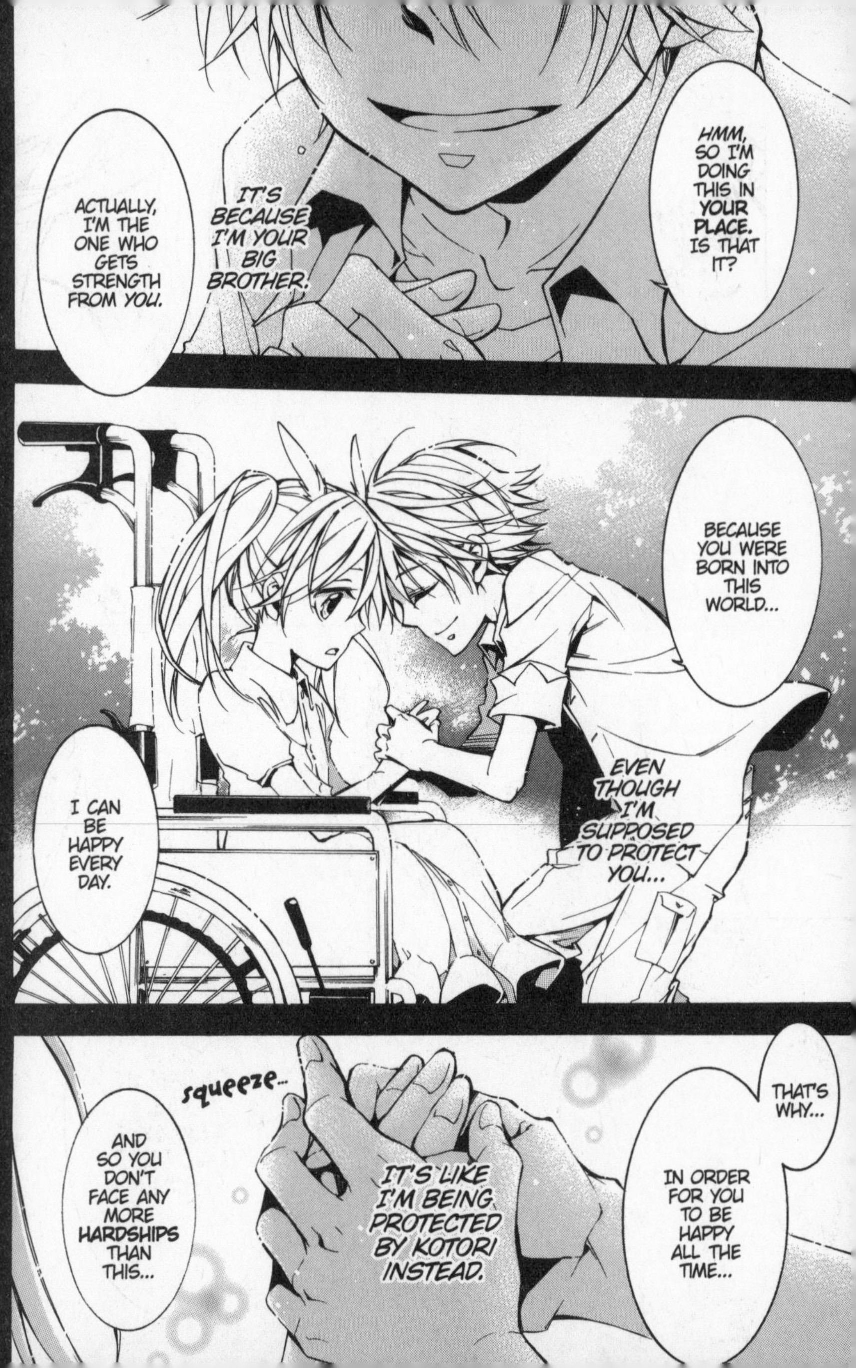
HMM, SO I'M DOING THIS IN **YOUR PLACE.** IS THAT IT?
IT'S BECAUSE I'M YOUR BIG BROTHER.
ACTUALLY, I'M THE ONE WHO GETS STRENGTH FROM YOU.
BECAUSE YOU WERE BORN INTO THIS WORLD...
EVEN THOUGH I'M SUPPOSED TO PROTECT YOU...
I CAN BE HAPPY EVERY DAY.
THAT'S WHY...
IN ORDER FOR YOU TO BE HAPPY ALL THE TIME...
squeeze...
IT'S LIKE I'M BEING PROTECTED BY KOTORI INSTEAD.
AND SO YOU DON'T FACE ANY MORE **HARDSHIPS** THAN THIS...

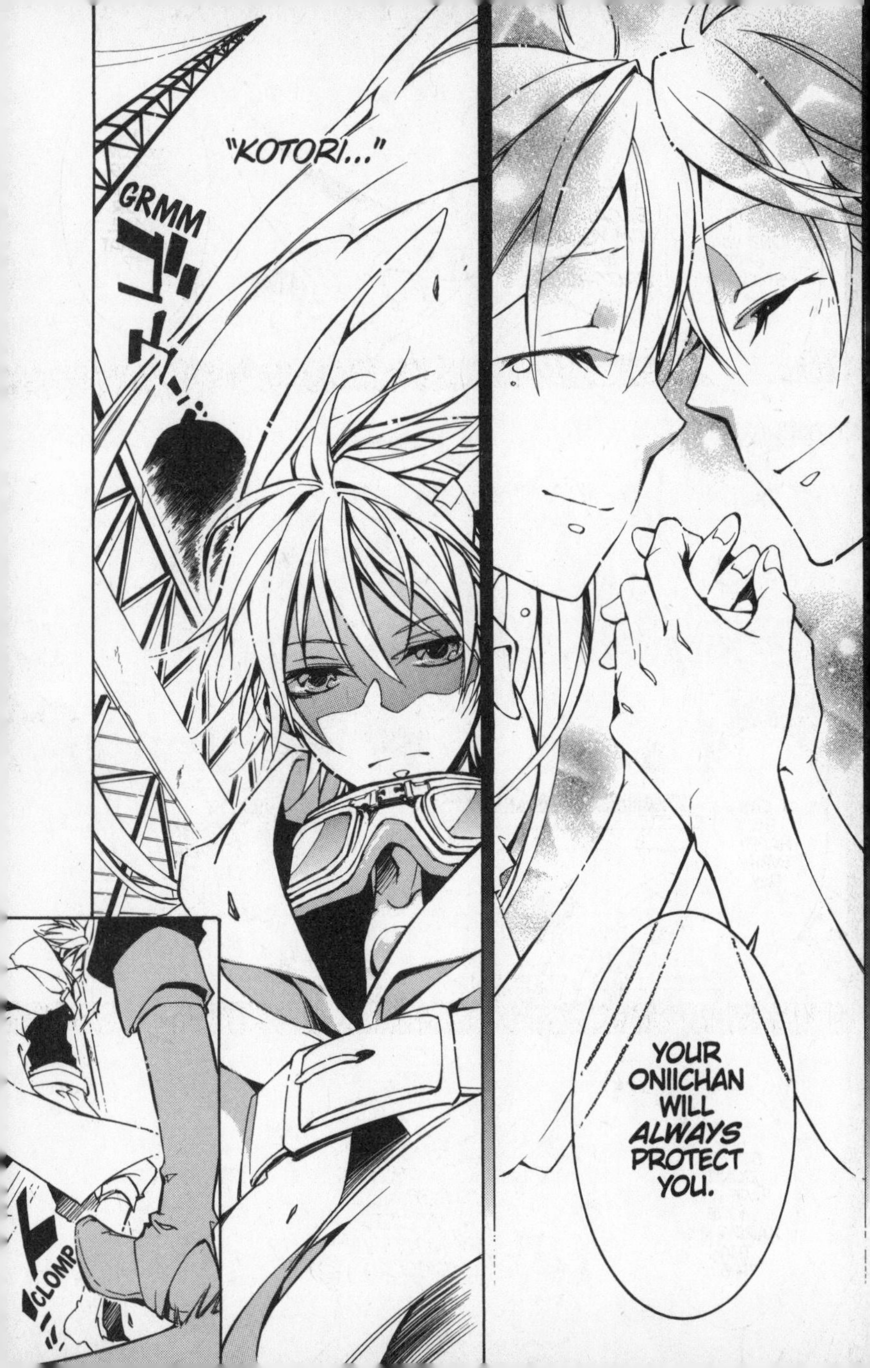
YOUR ONIICHAN WILL ALWAYS PROTECT YOU.
"KOTORI..."
GRMM
CLOMP

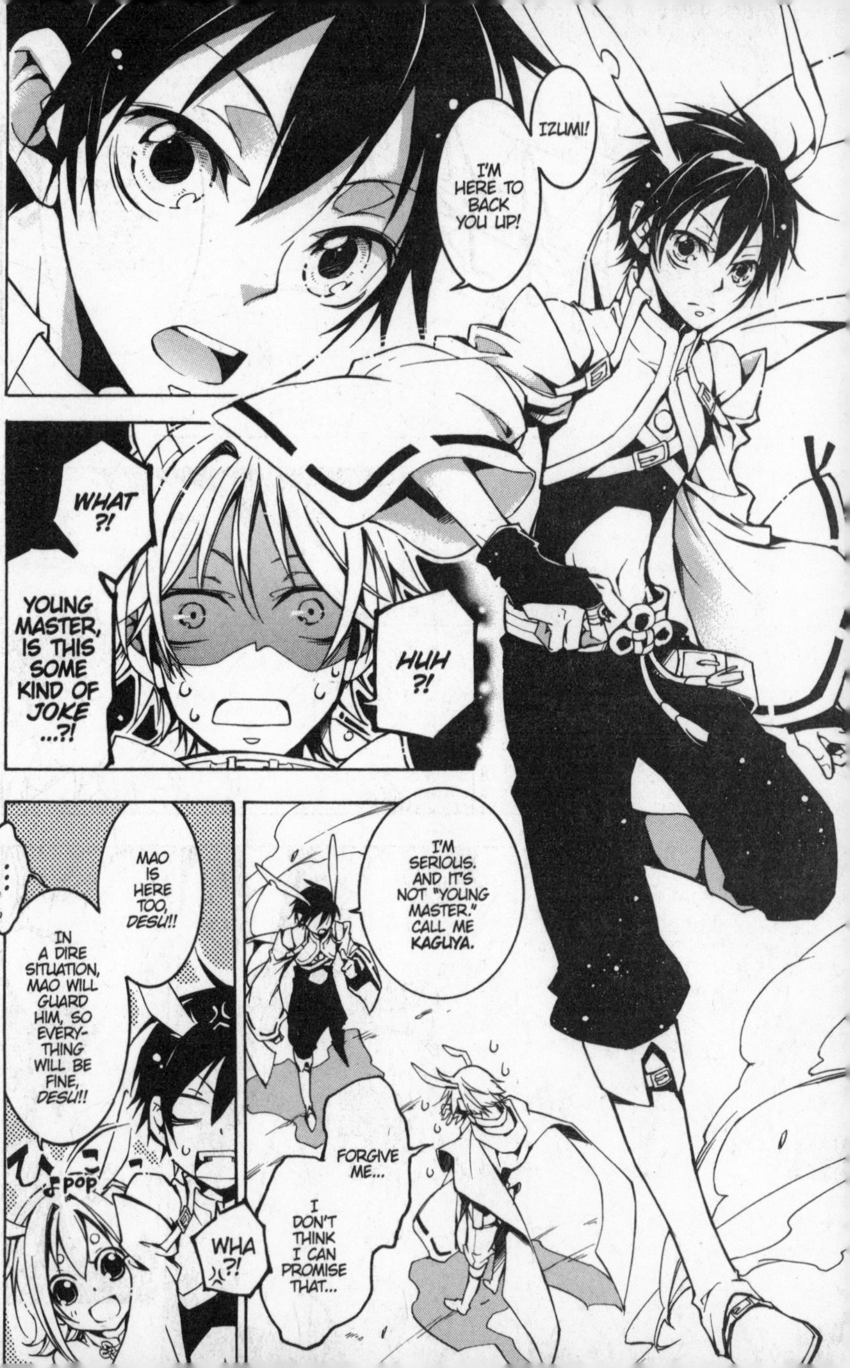
IZUMI!
I'M HERE TO BACK YOU UP!
HUH ?!
WHAT ?!
YOUNG MASTER, IS THIS SOME KIND OF JOKE ...?!
I'M SERIOUS. AND IT'S NOT "YOUNG MASTER." CALL ME KAGUYA.
FORGIVE ME...
I DON'T THINK I CAN PROMISE THAT...
MAO IS HERE TOO, DESU!!
IN A DIRE SITUATION, MAO WILL GUARD HIM, SO EVERYTHING WILL BE FINE, DESU!!
...
POP
WHA ?!

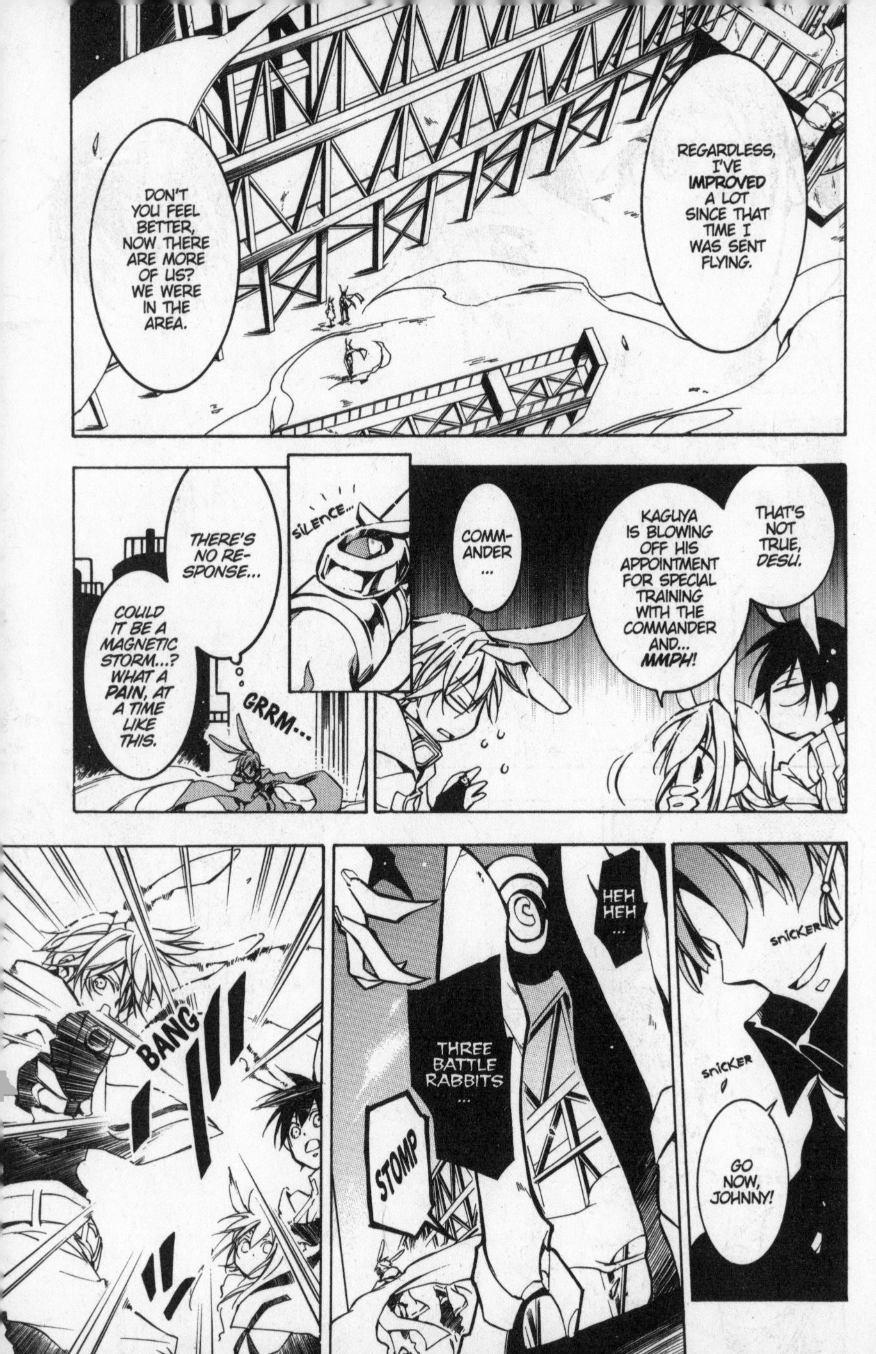
REGARDLESS, I'VE IMPROVED A LOT SINCE THAT TIME I WAS SENT FLYING.
DON'T YOU FEEL BETTER, NOW THERE ARE MORE OF US? WE WERE IN THE AREA.
THAT'S NOT TRUE, DESU.
KAGUYA IS BLOWING OFF HIS APPOINTMENT FOR SPECIAL TRAINING WITH THE COMMANDER AND... MMPH!
COMMANDER ...
SILENCE...
THERE'S NO RESPONSE...
COULD IT BE A MAGNETIC STORM...? WHAT A PAIN, AT A TIME LIKE THIS.
GRRM...
SNICKER
SNICKER
GO NOW, JOHNNY!
HEH HEH ...
THREE BATTLE RABBITS ...
STOMP
BANG

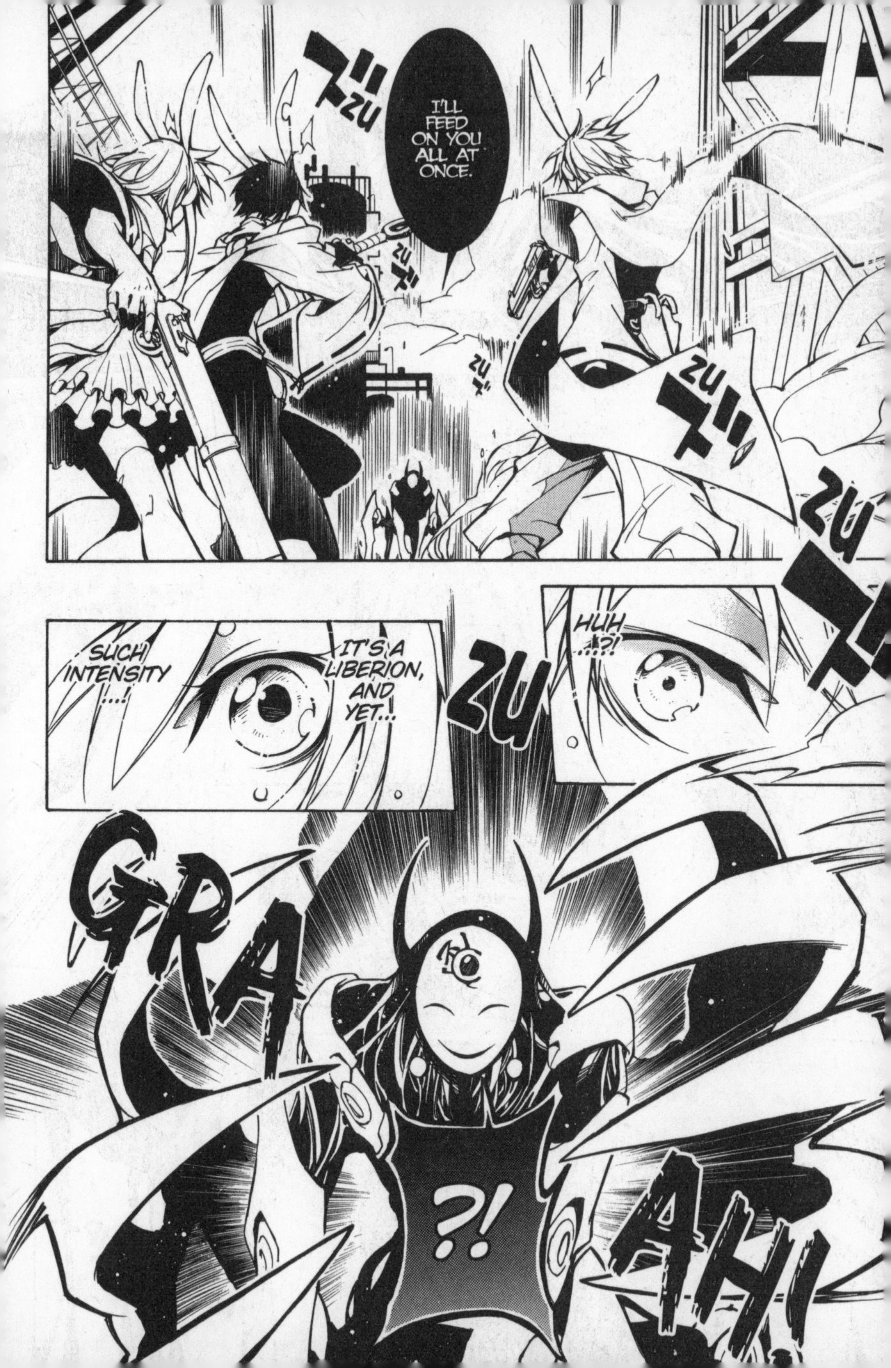
ZU
I'LL FEED ON YOU ALL AT ONCE.
ZU
ZU
ZU
ZU
ZU
HUH ...?!
ZU
IT'S A LIBERION, AND YET...!
SUCH INTENSITY ...!
AH!
?!
GRA

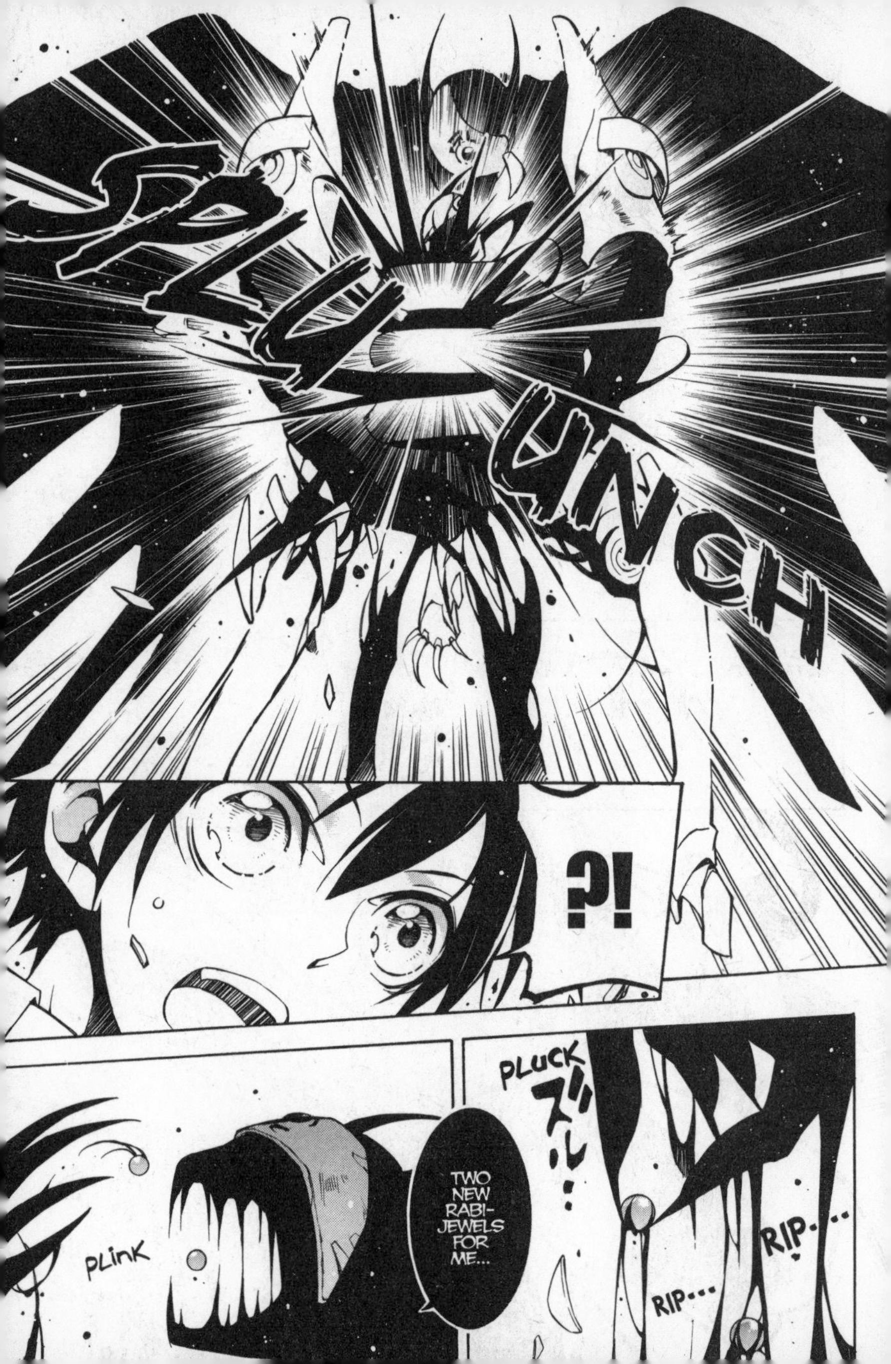
UNCH
?!
PLUCK
ズル!!
RIP...
RIP...
TWO NEW RABI-JEWELS FOR ME...
PLINK

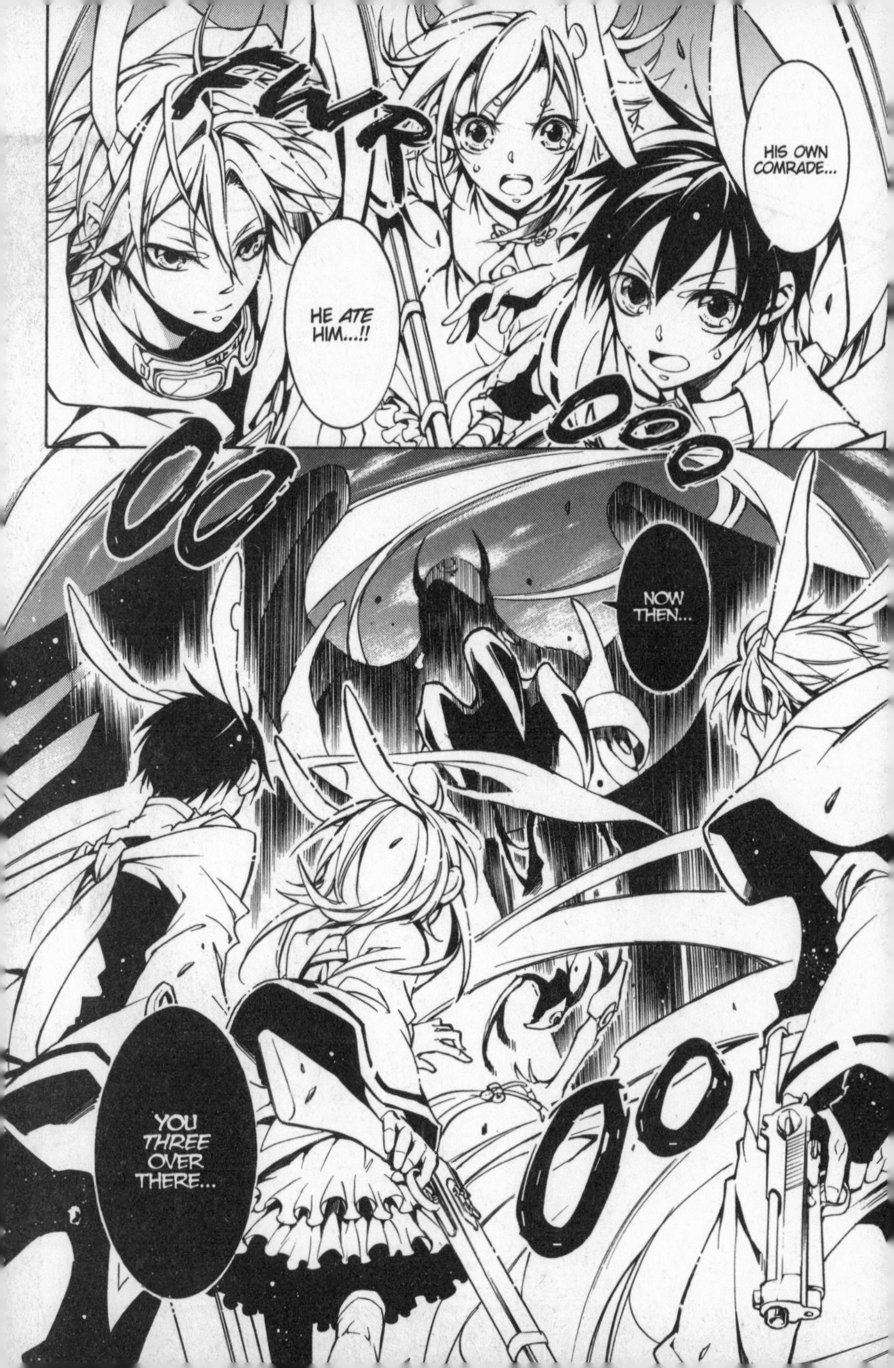
HIS OWN COMRADE...
HE ATE HIM...!!
NOW THEN...
YOU THREE OVER THERE...

Chapter 14

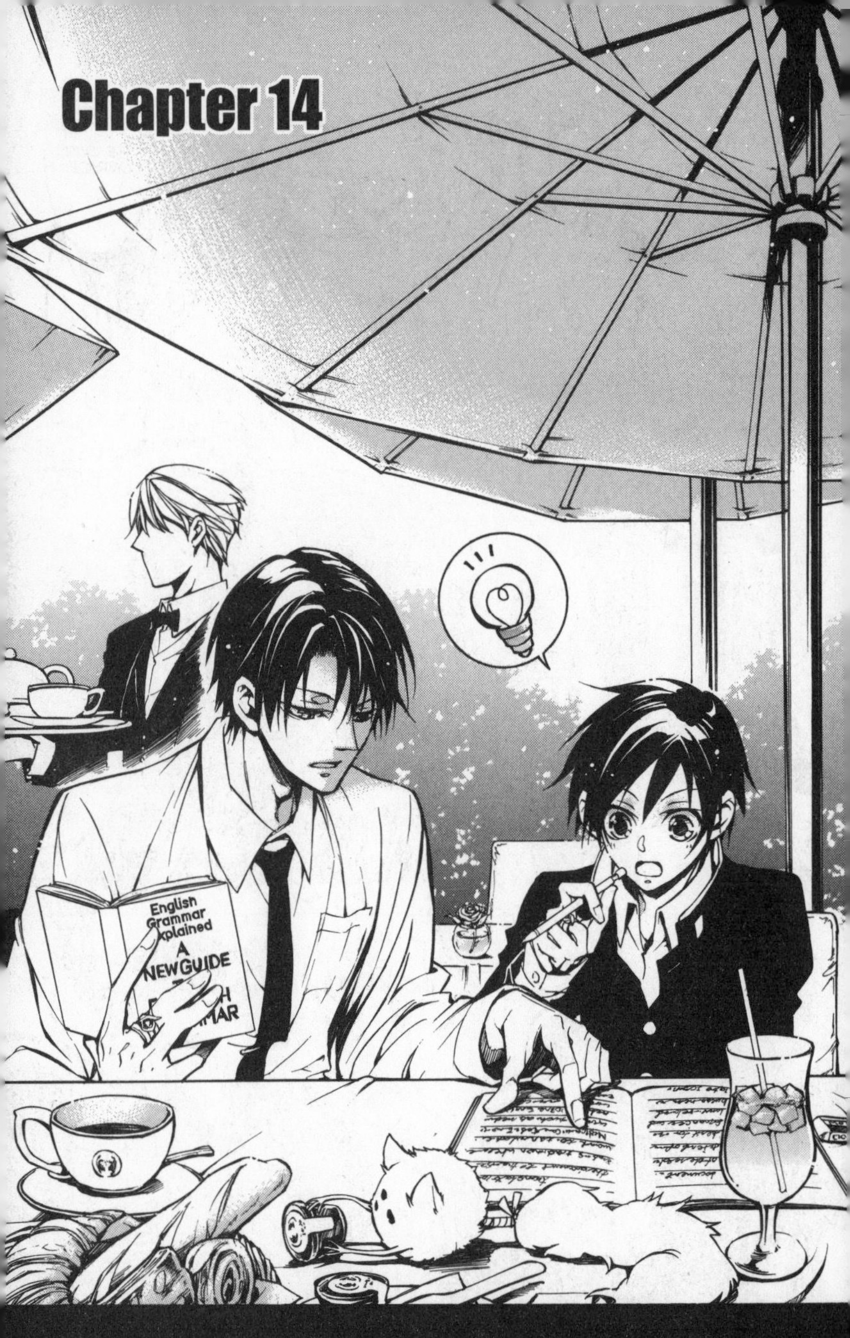
English
Grammar
A
NEW GUIDE

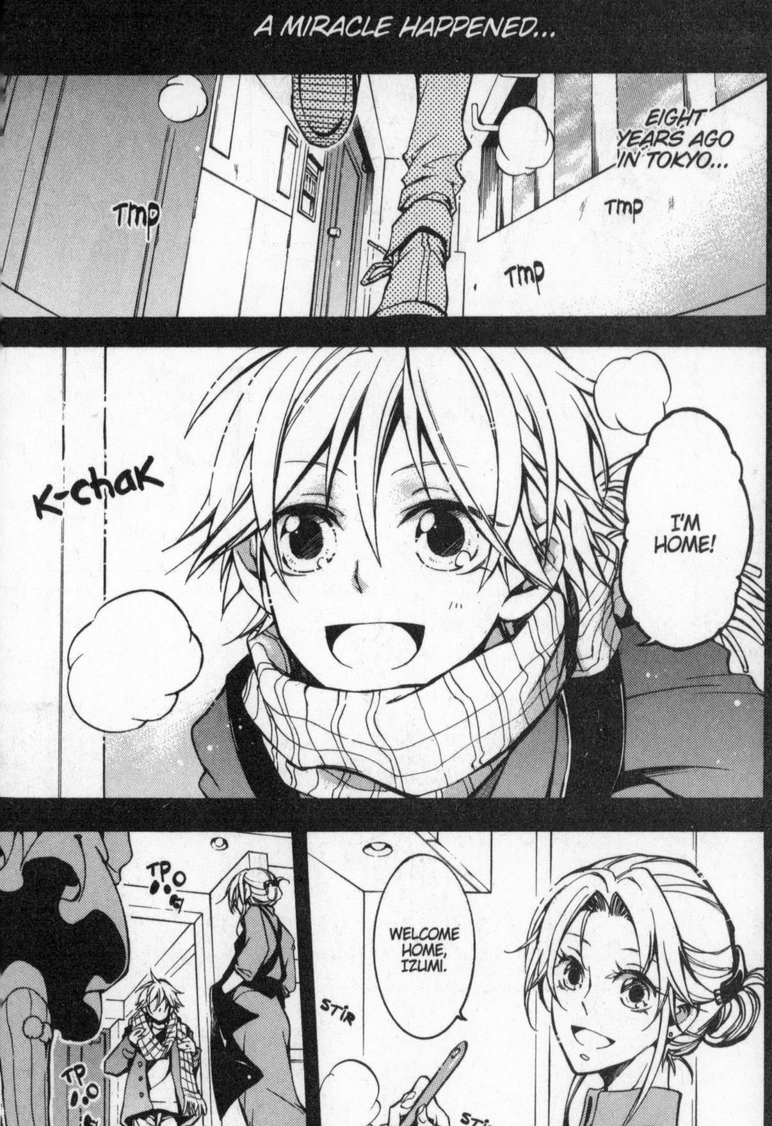
A MIRACLE HAPPENED...
EIGHT YEARS AGO IN TOKYO...
TMP
TMP
TMP
I'M HOME!
K-CHAK
WELCOME HOME, IZUMI.
STIR
STIR
STIR
TP
TP

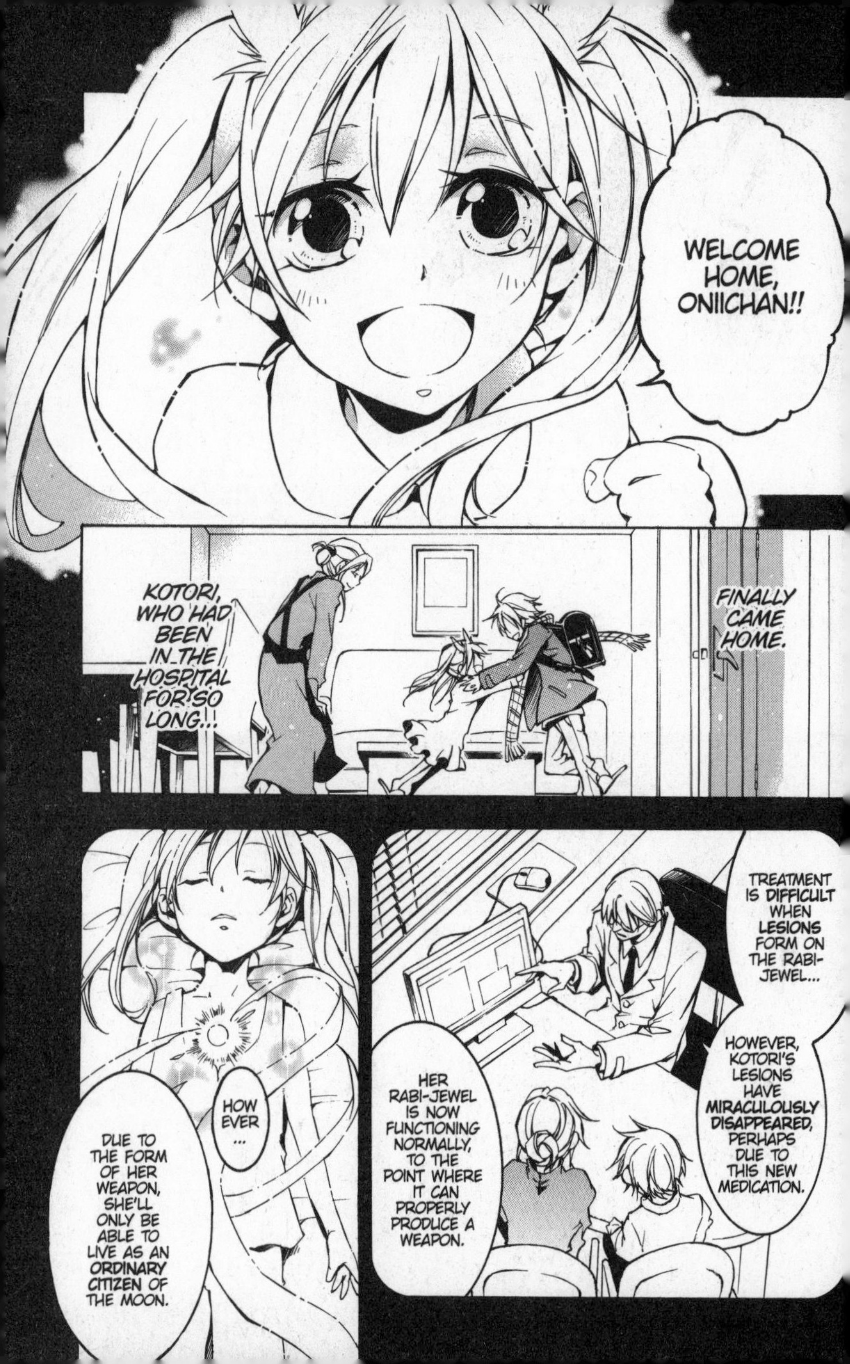
WELCOME HOME, ONIICHAN!!
KOTORI, WHO HAD BEEN IN THE HOSPITAL FOR SO LONG...
FINALLY CAME HOME.
TREATMENT IS DIFFICULT WHEN LESIONS FORM ON THE RABI-JEWEL...
HOWEVER, KOTORI'S LESIONS HAVE MIRACULOUSLY DISAPPEARED, PERHAPS DUE TO THIS NEW MEDICATION.
HER RABI-JEWEL IS NOW FUNCTIONING NORMALLY, TO THE POINT WHERE IT CAN PROPERLY PRODUCE A WEAPON.
HOW EVER ...
DUE TO THE FORM OF HER WEAPON, SHE'LL ONLY BE ABLE TO LIVE AS AN ORDINARY CITIZEN OF THE MOON.

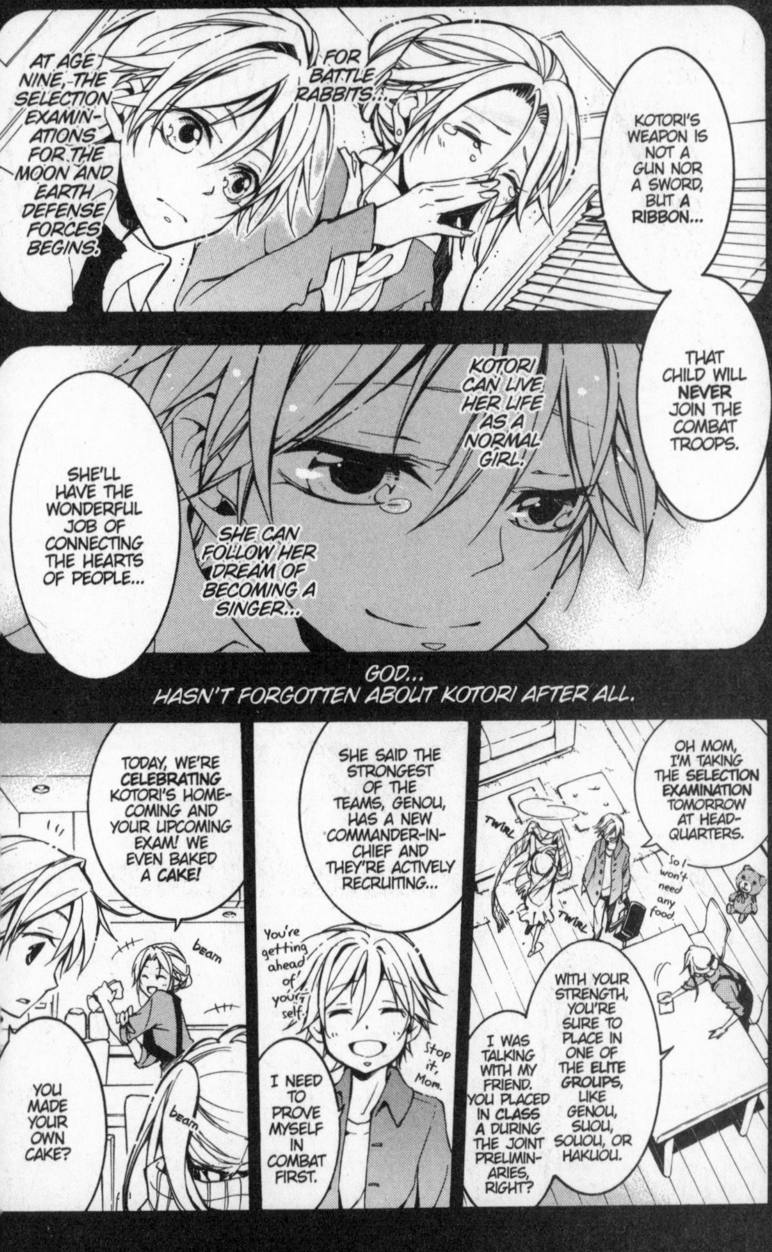
KOTORI'S WEAPON IS NOT A GUN NOR A SWORD, BUT A RIBBON...
FOR BATTLE RABBITS...
AT AGE NINE, THE SELECTION EXAMINATIONS FOR THE MOON AND EARTH DEFENSE FORCES BEGINS.
THAT CHILD WILL NEVER JOIN THE COMBAT TROOPS.
KOTORI CAN LIVE HER LIFE AS A NORMAL GIRL!
SHE CAN FOLLOW HER DREAM OF BECOMING A SINGER...
SHE'LL HAVE THE WONDERFUL JOB OF CONNECTING THE HEARTS OF PEOPLE...
GOD... HASN'T FORGOTTEN ABOUT KOTORI AFTER ALL.
OH MOM, I'M TAKING THE SELECTION EXAMINATION TOMORROW AT HEADQUARTERS.
So I won't need any food.
TWIRL
TWIRL
WITH YOUR STRENGTH, YOU'RE SURE TO PLACE IN ONE OF THE ELITE GROUPS, LIKE GENOU, SUOU, SOUOU, OR HAKUOU.
I WAS TALKING WITH MY FRIEND. YOU PLACED IN CLASS A DURING THE JOINT PRELIMINARIES, RIGHT?
SHE SAID THE STRONGEST OF THE TEAMS, GENOU, HAS A NEW COMMANDER-IN-CHIEF AND THEY'RE ACTIVELY RECRUITING...
Stop it, Mom.
You're getting ahead of yourself.
I NEED TO PROVE MYSELF IN COMBAT FIRST.
TODAY, WE'RE CELEBRATING KOTORI'S HOMECOMING AND YOUR UPCOMING EXAM! WE EVEN BAKED A CAKE!
beam
beam
YOU MADE YOUR OWN CAKE?

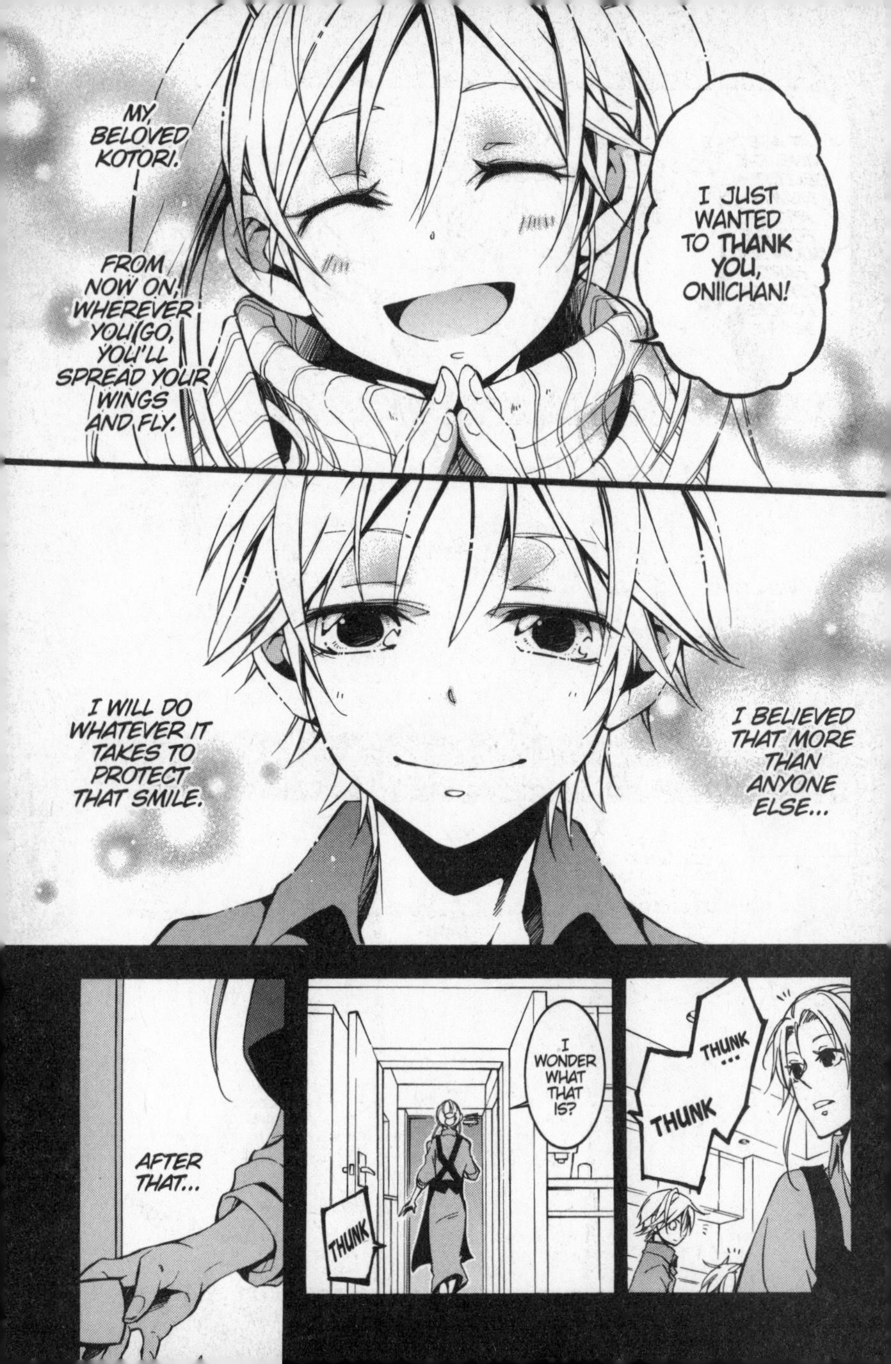
I JUST WANTED TO THANK YOU, ONIICHAN!
MY, BELOVED KOTORI.
FROM NOW ON, WHEREVER YOU GO, YOU'LL SPREAD YOUR WINGS AND FLY.
I BELIEVED THAT MORE THAN ANYONE ELSE...
I WILL DO WHATEVER IT TAKES TO PROTECT THAT SMILE.
THUNK...
THUNK
I WONDER WHAT THAT IS?
THUNK
AFTER THAT...

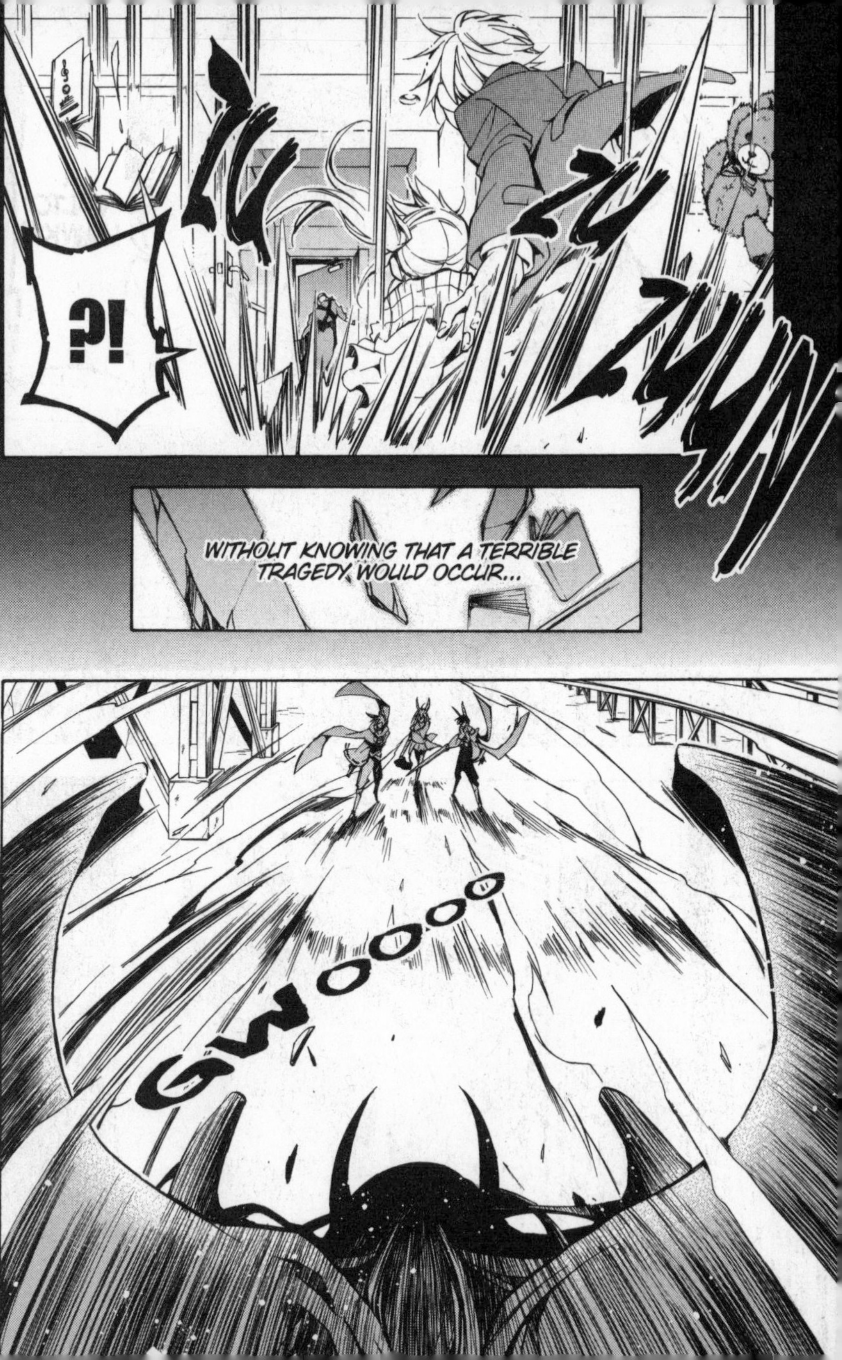
?!
WITHOUT KNOWING THAT A TERRIBLE TRAGEDY WOULD OCCUR...
GWOOOOO

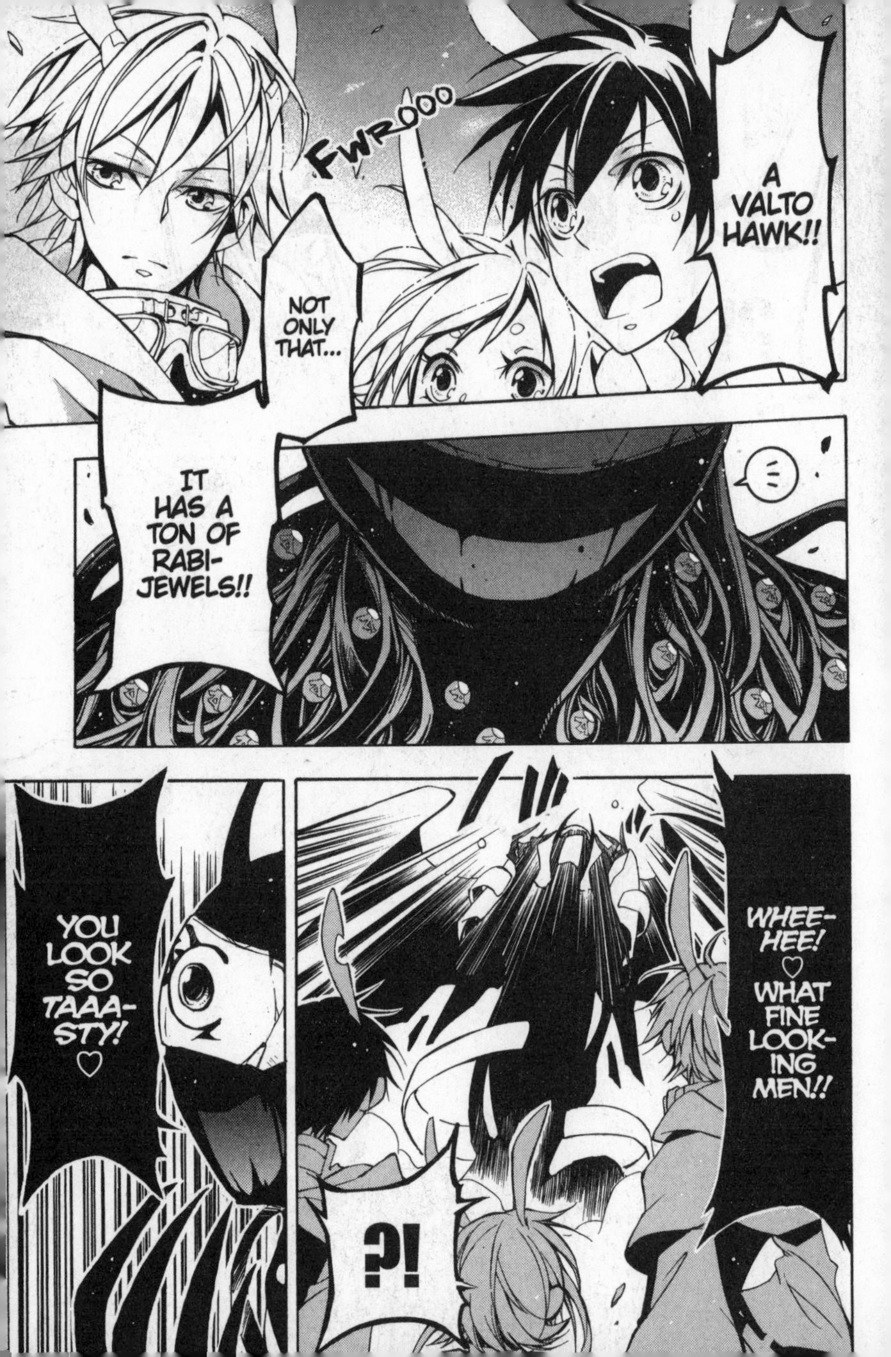
A VALTO HAWK!!
FWROOO
NOT ONLY THAT...
IT HAS A TON OF RABI-JEWELS!!
WHEE-HEE! ♡ WHAT FINE LOOKING MEN!!
?!
YOU LOOK SO TAAAASTY! ♡

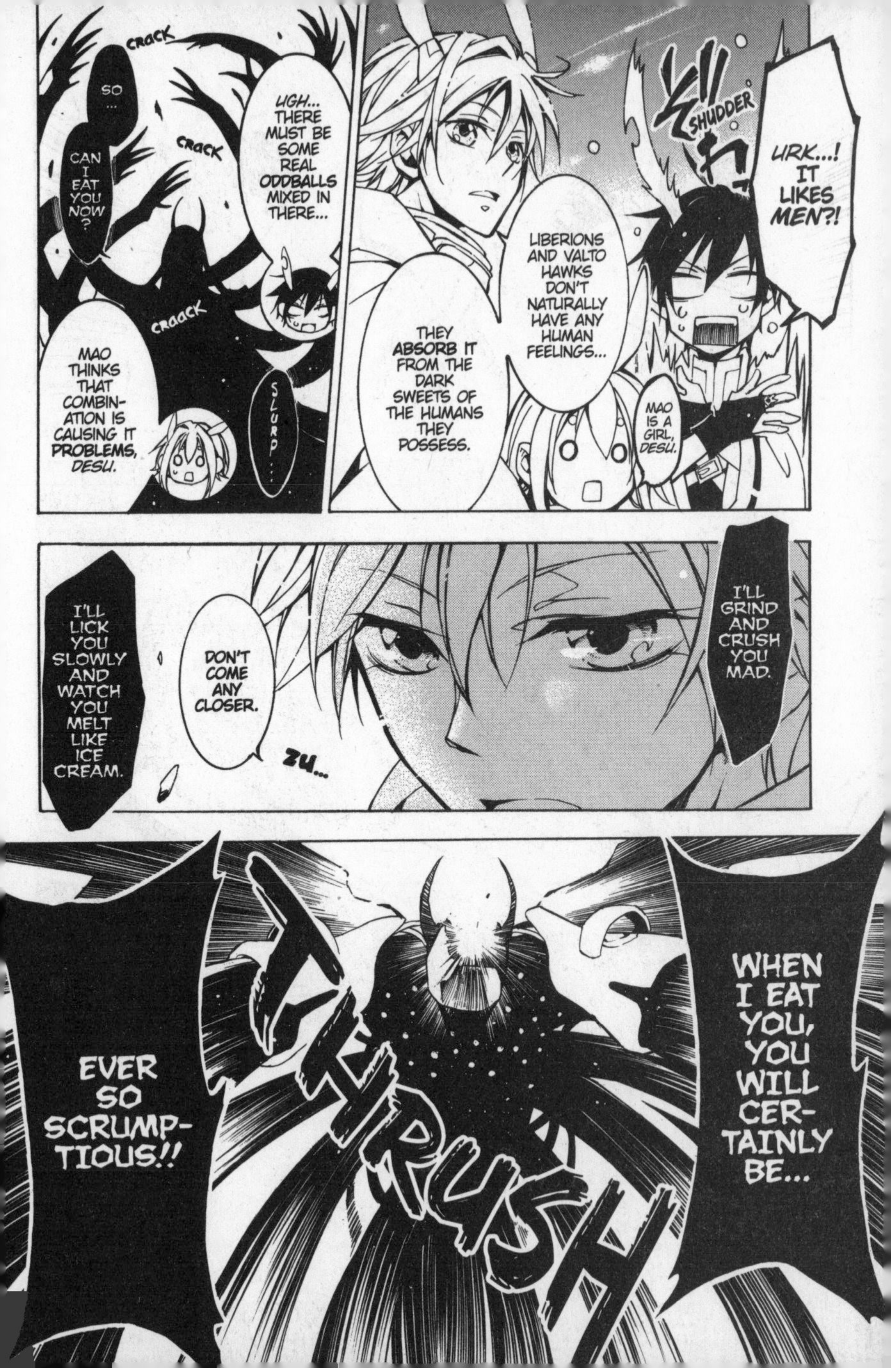
URK...! IT LIKES MEN?!
SHUDDER
LIBERIONS AND VALTO HAWKS DON'T NATURALLY HAVE ANY HUMAN FEELINGS...
MAO IS A GIRL, DESU.
THEY ABSORB IT FROM THE DARK SWEETS OF THE HUMANS THEY POSSESS.
UGH... THERE MUST BE SOME REAL ODDBALLS MIXED IN THERE...
CRACK
SO... CAN I EAT YOU NOW?
CRACK
CRAACK
SLURP...
MAO THINKS THAT COMBINATION IS CAUSING IT PROBLEMS, DESU.
I'LL GRIND AND CRUSH YOU MAD.
DON'T COME ANY CLOSER.
ZU...
I'LL LICK YOU SLOWLY AND WATCH YOU MELT LIKE ICE CREAM.
WHEN I EAT YOU, YOU WILL CER-TAINLY BE...
THRUSH
EVER SO SCRUMP-TIOUS!!

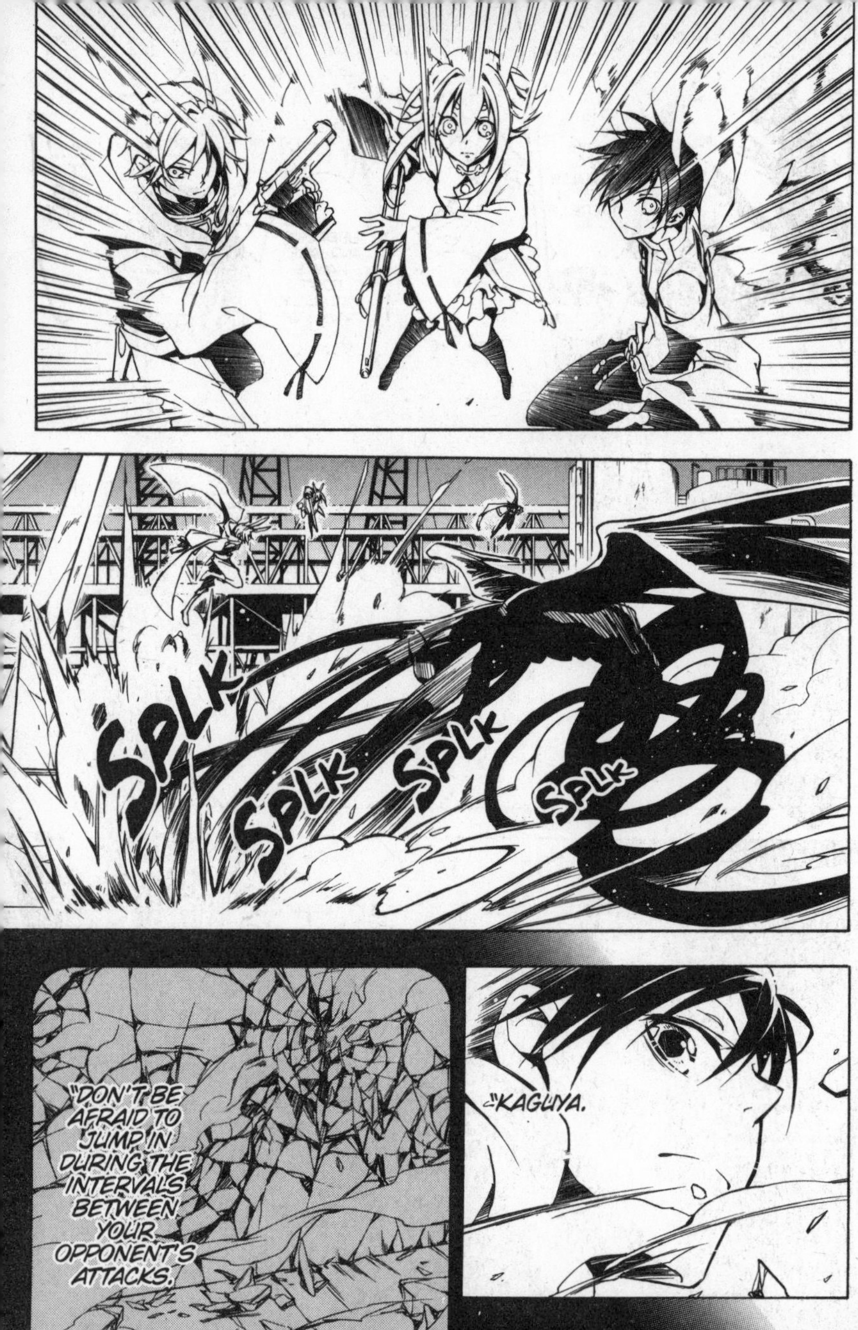
SPLK
SPLK
SPLK
SPLK
...KAGUYA.
"DON'T BE AFRAID TO JUMP IN DURING THE INTERVALS BETWEEN YOUR OPPONENT'S ATTACKS.

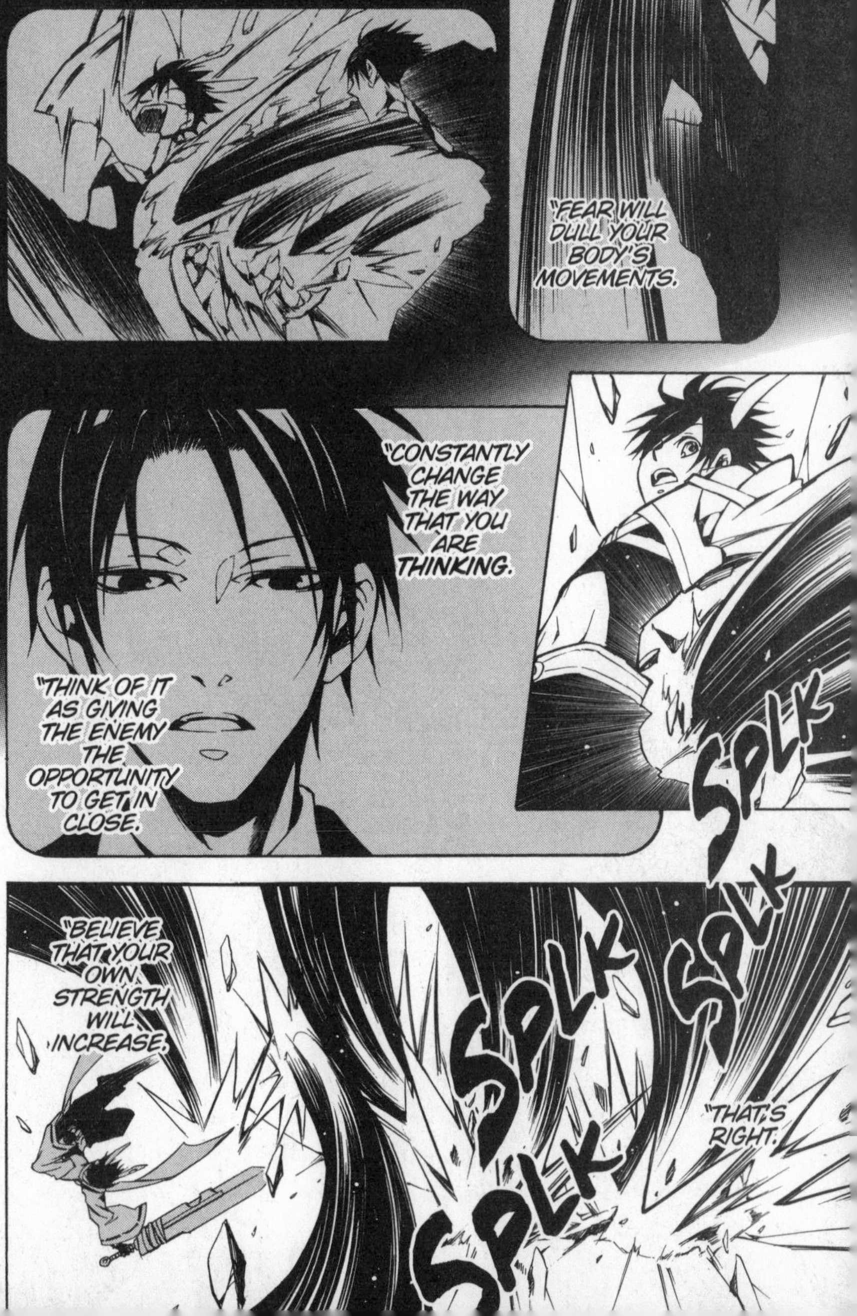
"FEAR WILL DULL YOUR BODY'S MOVEMENTS.
SPLK
SPLK
"CONSTANTLY CHANGE THE WAY THAT YOU ARE THINKING.
"THINK OF IT AS GIVING THE ENEMY THE OPPORTUNITY TO GET IN CLOSE.
SPLK
"THAT'S RIGHT.
SPLK
SPLK
"BELIEVE THAT YOUR OWN STRENGTH WILL INCREASE.

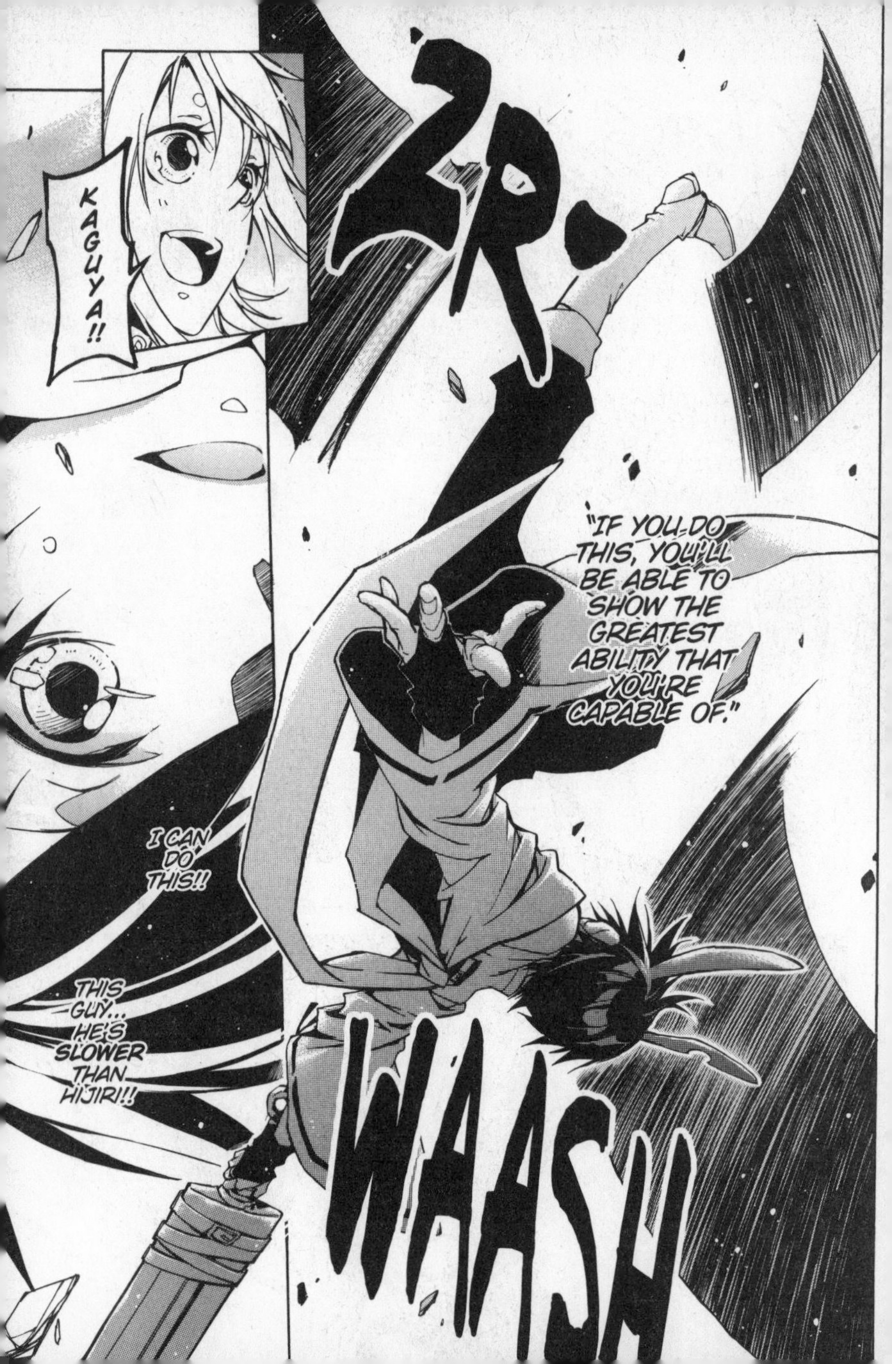
"IF YOU DO THIS, YOU'LL BE ABLE TO SHOW THE GREATEST ABILITY THAT YOU'RE CAPABLE OF."
WAASH
KAGUYA!!
I CAN DO THIS!!
THIS GUY... HE'S SLOWER THAN HIJIRI!!

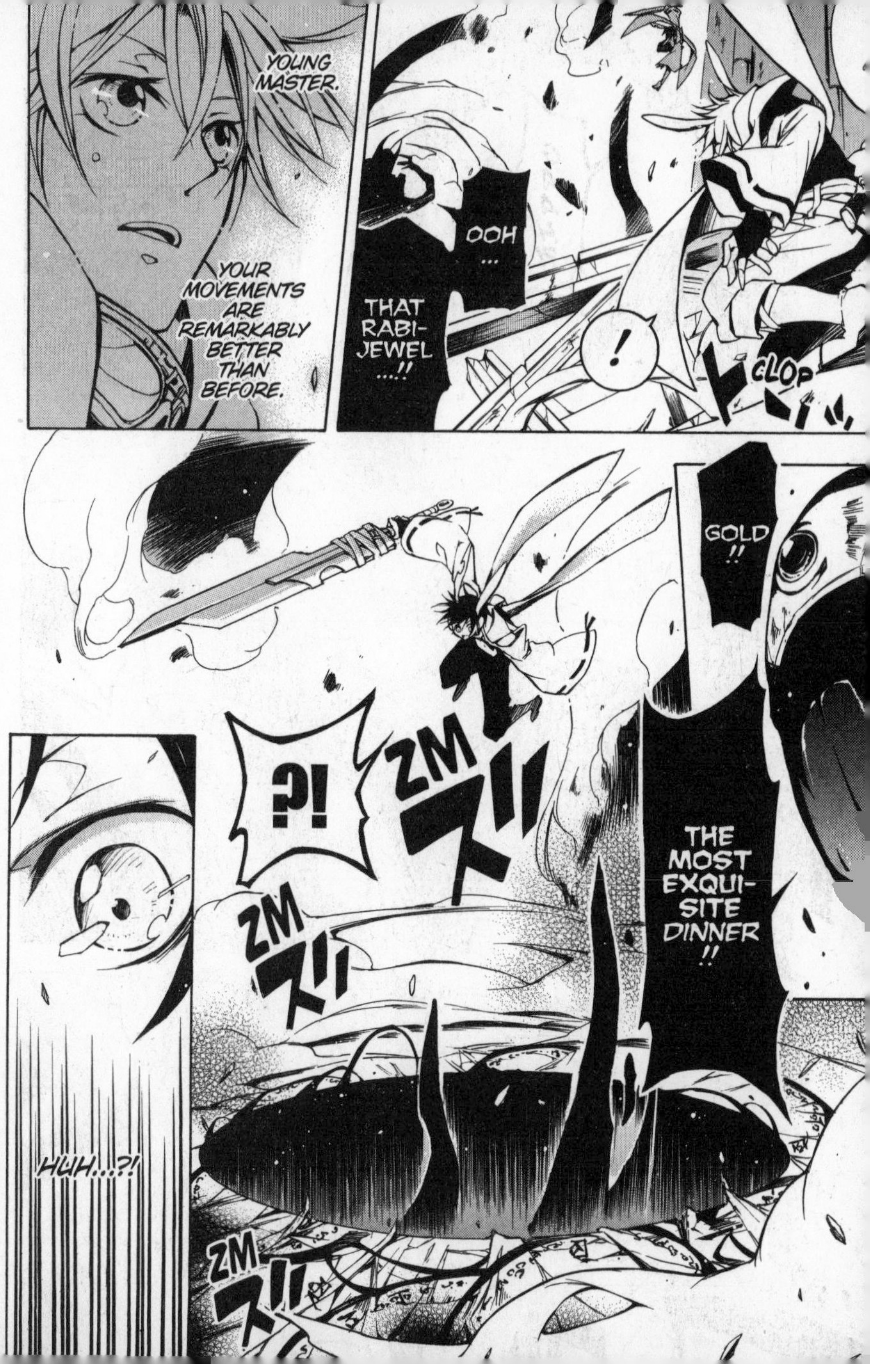

!
CLOP
OOH ...
THAT RABI-JEWEL ....!!
YOUNG MASTER.
YOUR MOVEMENTS ARE REMARKABLY BETTER THAN BEFORE.
GOLD!!
THE MOST EXQUISITE DINNER!!
?!
ZM
ZM
ZM
HUH...?!

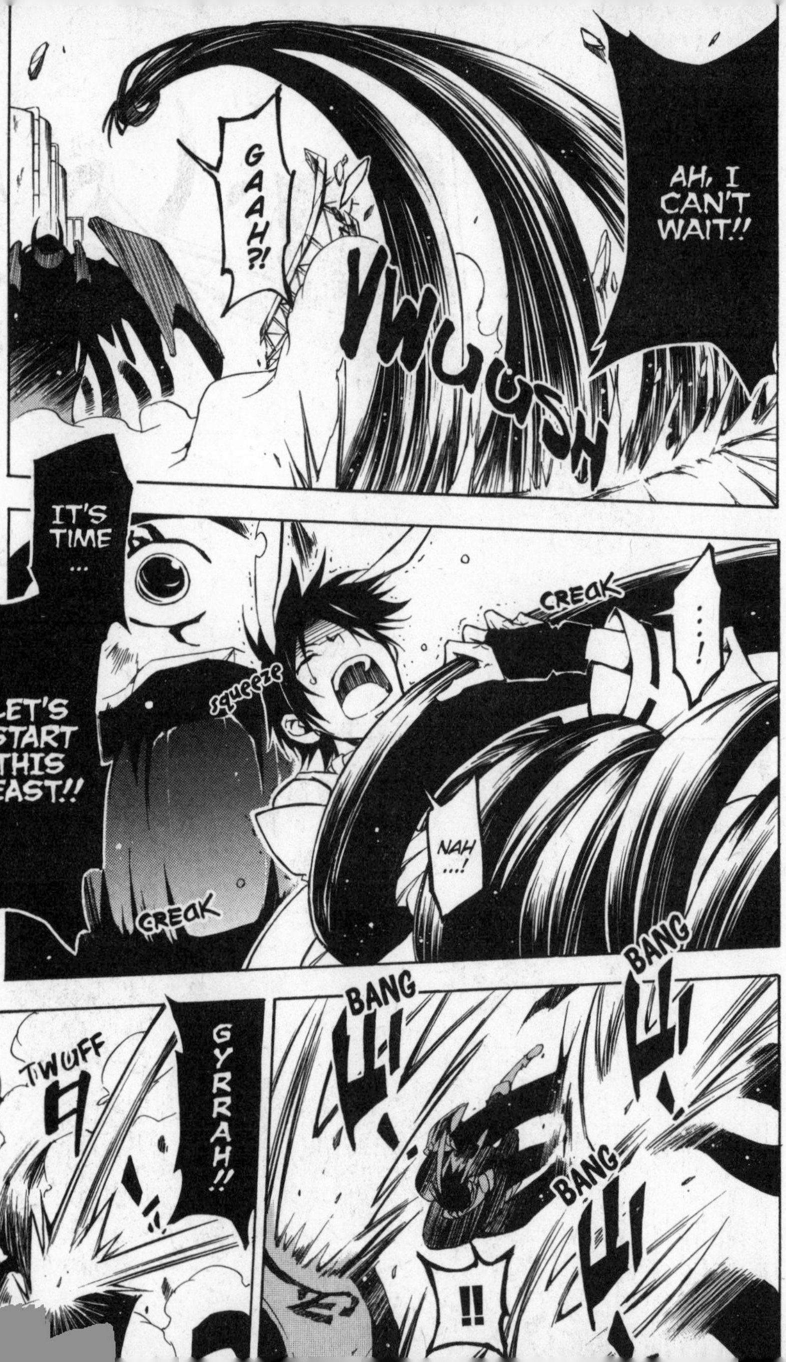
AH, I CAN'T WAIT!!
GAAH?!
VWUUSH
CREAK
...!
IT'S TIME ...
squeeze
LET'S START THIS FEAST!!
NAH ...!
CREAK
BANG
BANG
BANG
!!
GYRRAH!!
TWUFF

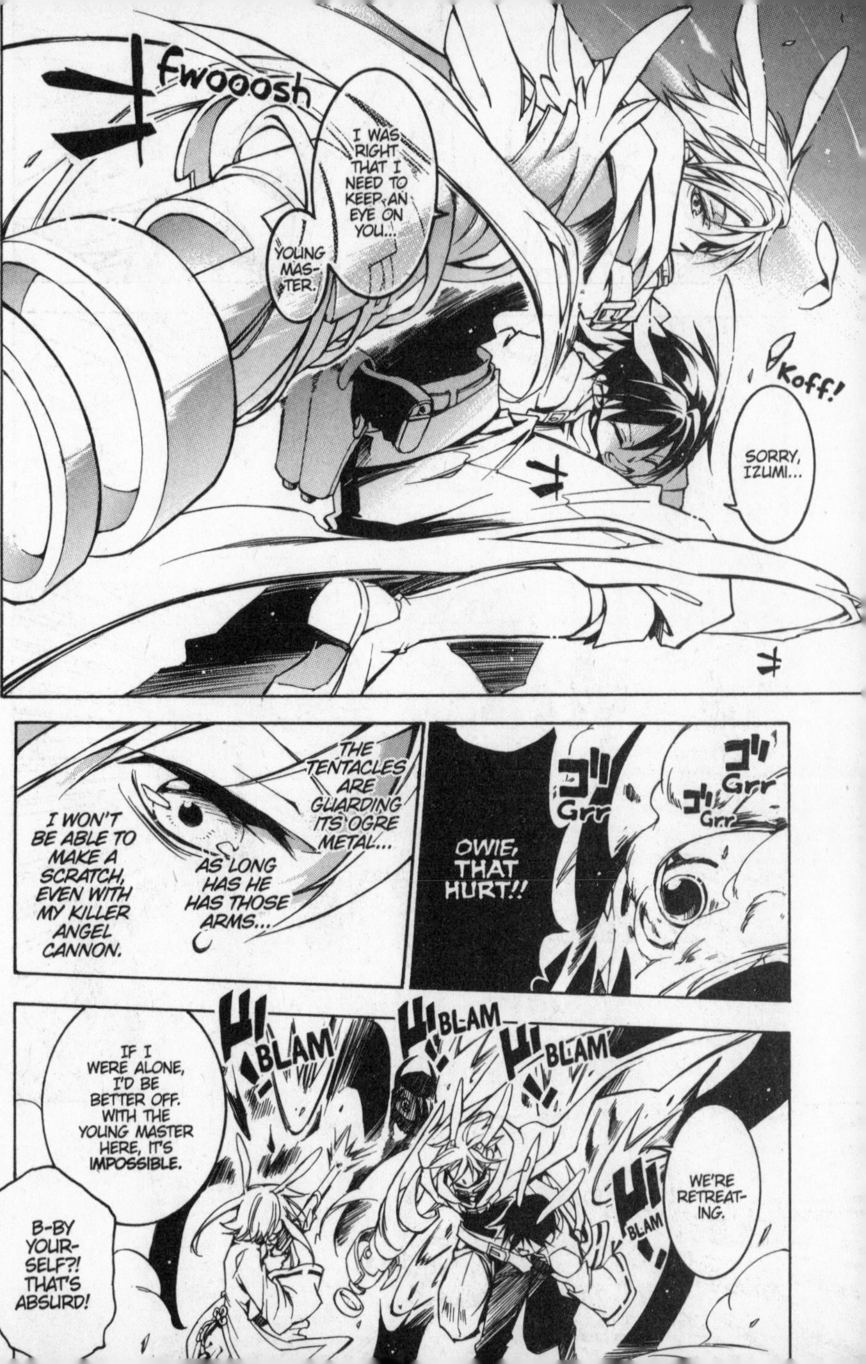
Koff!
SORRY, IZUMI...
I WAS RIGHT THAT I NEED TO KEEP AN EYE ON YOU...
YOUNG MASTER.
fwoooosh
Grr
Grr
Grr
OWIE, THAT HURT!!
THE TENTACLES ARE GUARDING ITS OGRE METAL...
AS LONG HAS HE HAS THOSE ARMS...
I WON'T BE ABLE TO MAKE A SCRATCH, EVEN WITH MY KILLER ANGEL CANNON.
WE'RE RETREATING.
BLAM
BLAM
BLAM
BLAM
BLAM
IF I WERE ALONE, I'D BE BETTER OFF. WITH THE YOUNG MASTER HERE, IT'S IMPOSSIBLE.
B-BY YOURSELF?! THAT'S ABSURD!

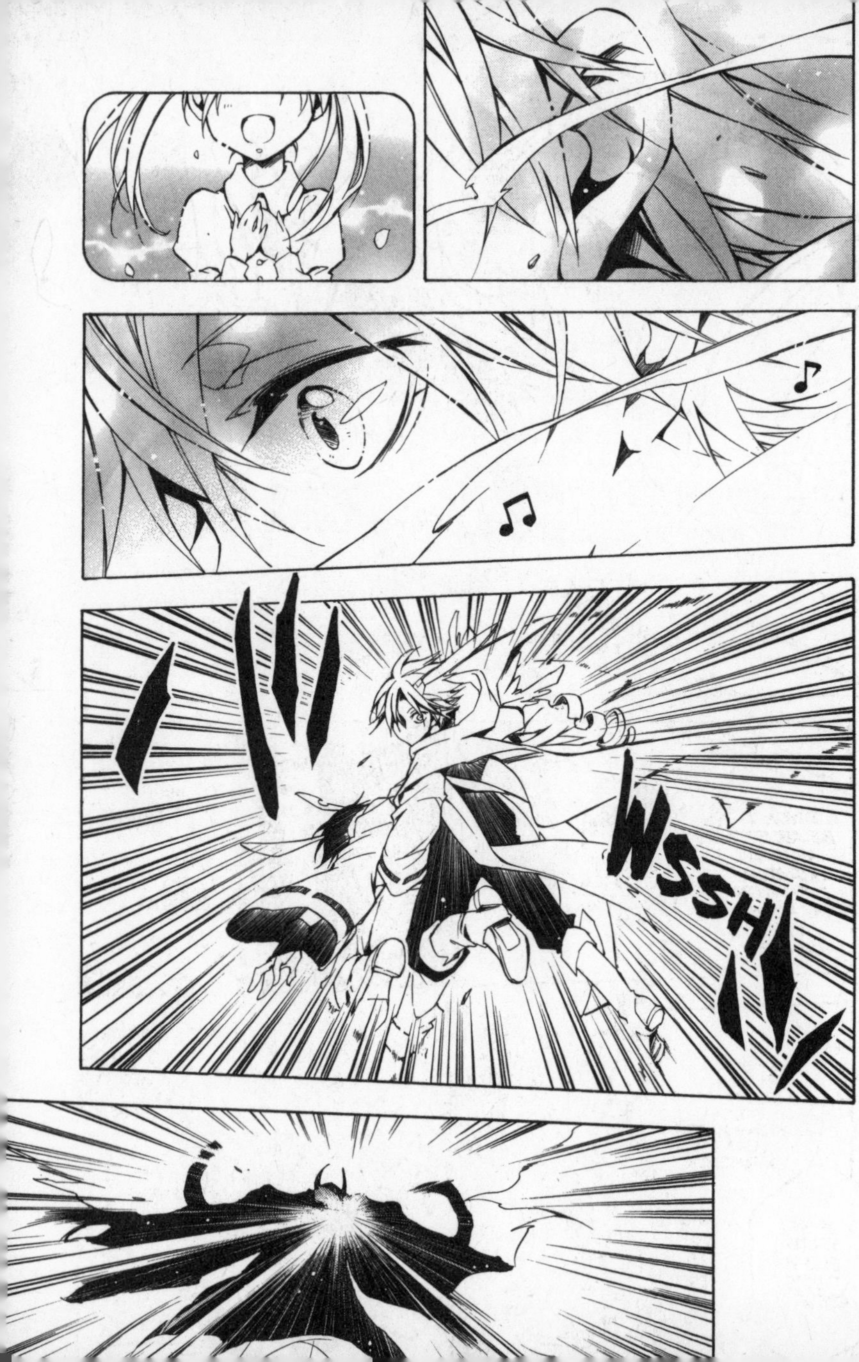
WSSH!!

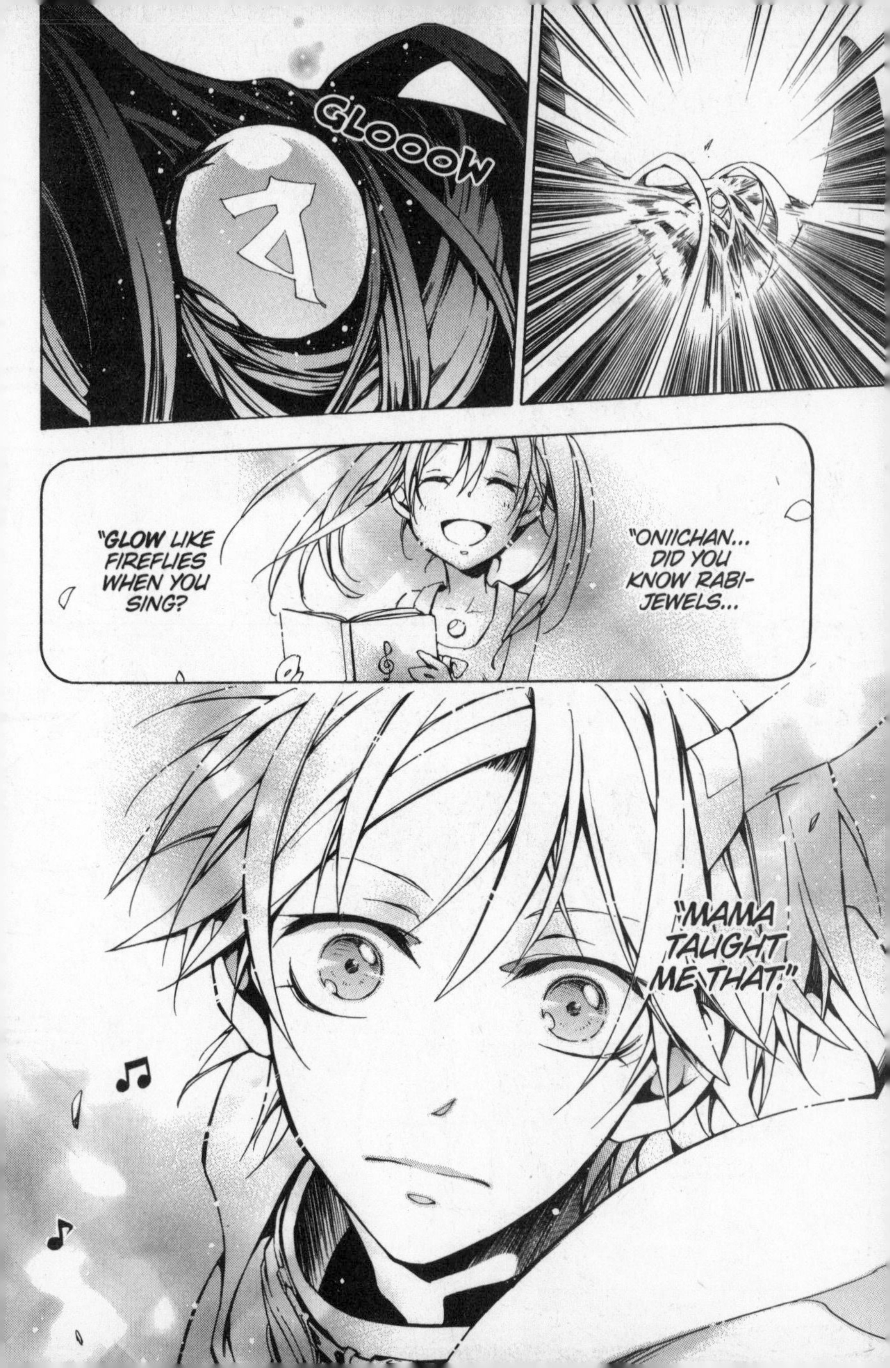
GLOOOW
"ONIICHAN... DID YOU KNOW RABI-JEWELS...
"GLOW LIKE FIREFLIES WHEN YOU SING?
"MAMA TAUGHT ME THAT!"

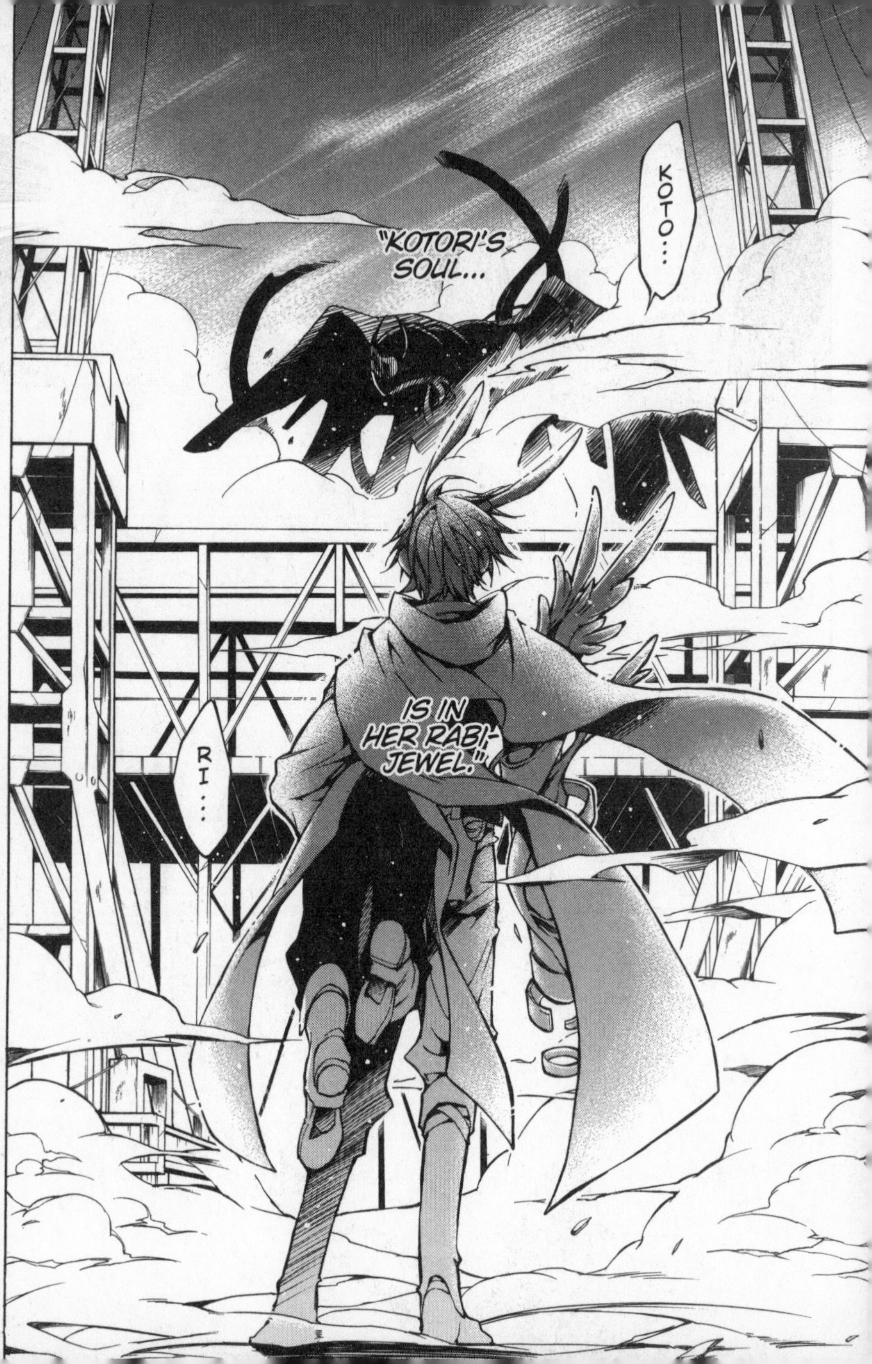
KOTO...
"KOTORI'S SOUL...
IS IN HER RABI-JEWEL."
RI...

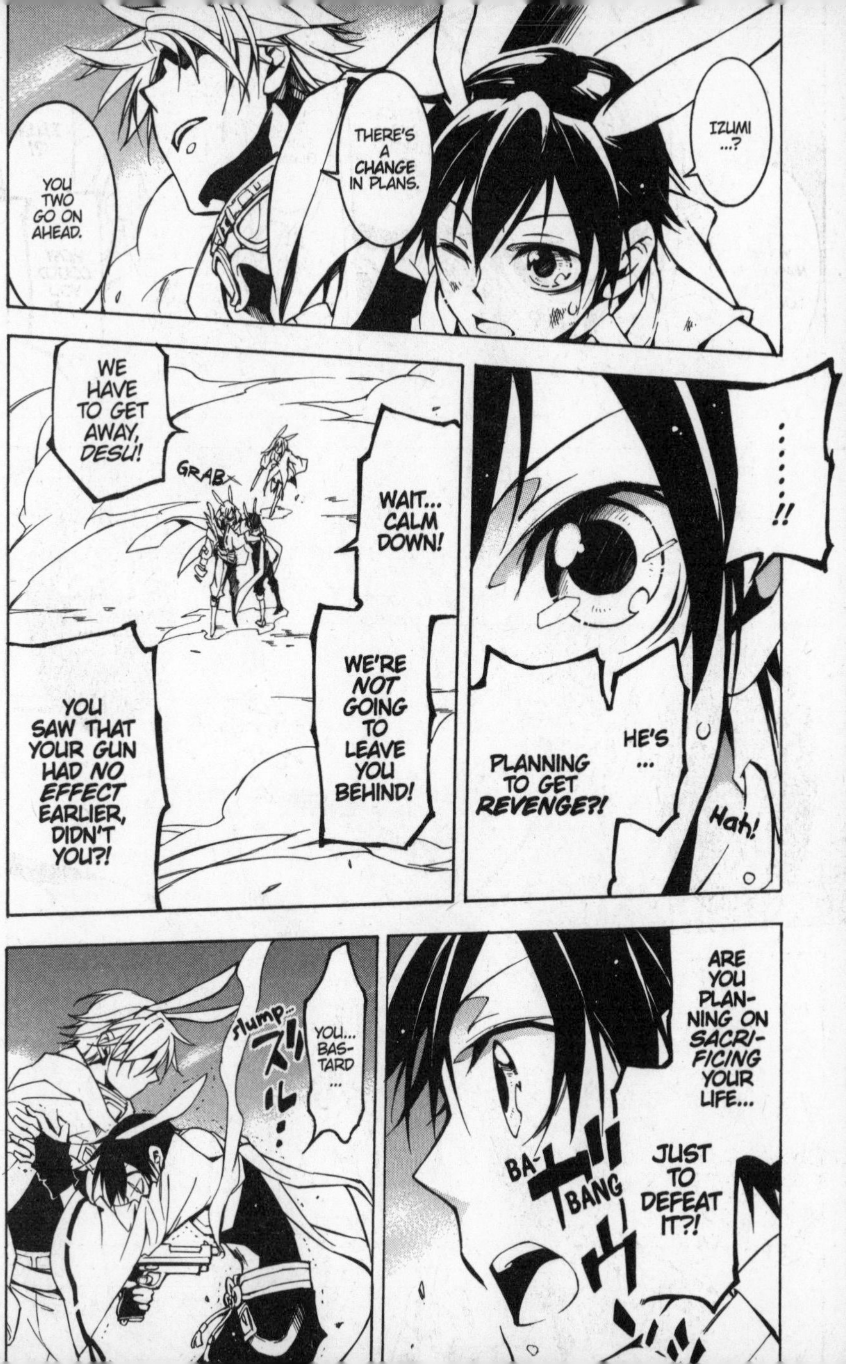
IZUMI ...?
THERE'S A CHANGE IN PLANS.
YOU TWO GO ON AHEAD.
......!!
HE'S ... PLANNING TO GET REVENGE?!
Hah!
WAIT... CALM DOWN!
WE HAVE TO GET AWAY, DESU!
GRAB
WE'RE NOT GOING TO LEAVE YOU BEHIND!
YOU SAW THAT YOUR GUN HAD NO EFFECT EARLIER, DIDN'T YOU?!
ARE YOU PLANNING ON SACRIFICING YOUR LIFE...
BA-BANG
JUST TO DEFEAT IT?!
YOU... BASTARD ...
slump..

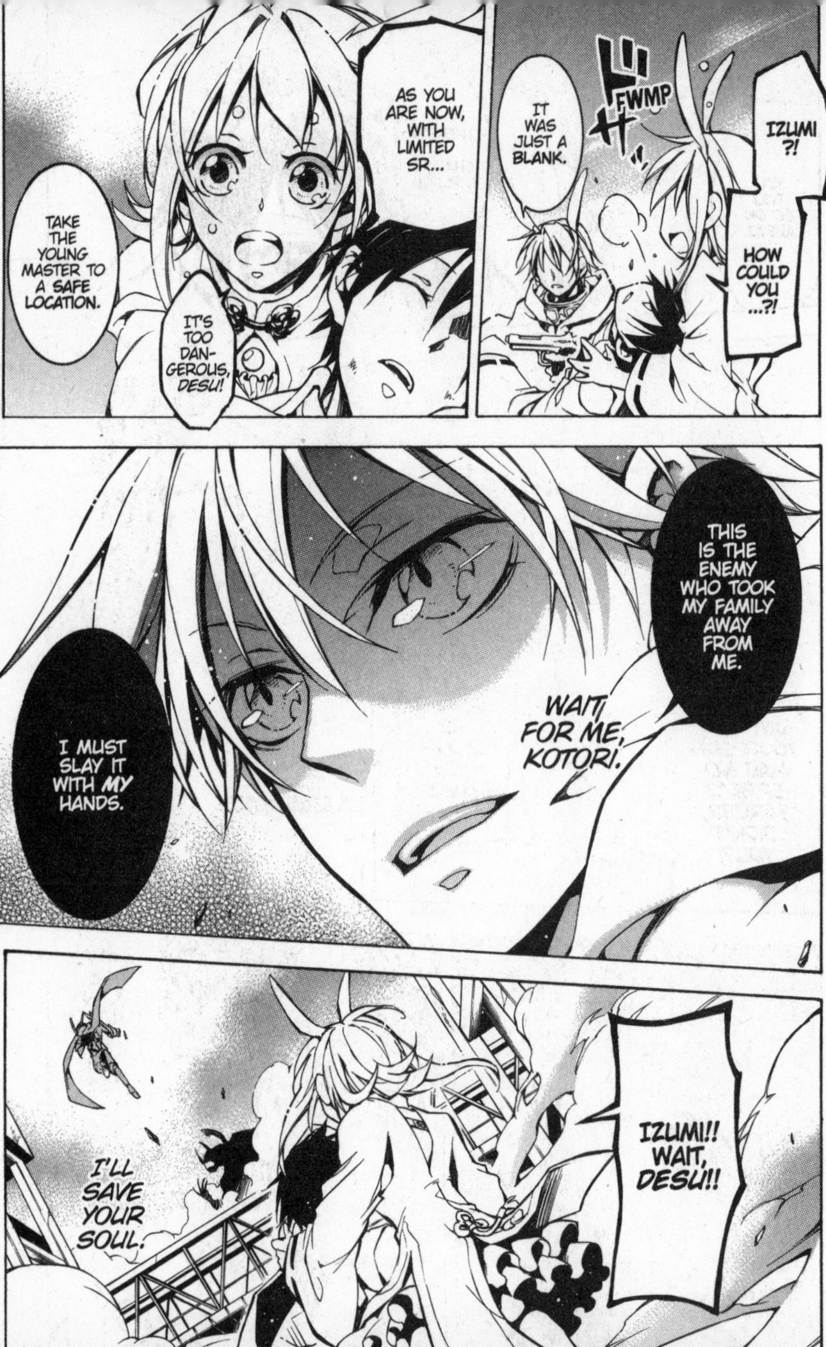
IZUMI ?!
FWMP
IT WAS JUST A BLANK.
HOW COULD YOU ...?!
AS YOU ARE NOW, WITH LIMITED SR...
TAKE THE YOUNG MASTER TO A SAFE LOCATION.
IT'S TOO DANGEROUS, DESU!
THIS IS THE ENEMY WHO TOOK MY FAMILY AWAY FROM ME.
WAIT FOR ME, KOTORI.
I MUST SLAY IT WITH MY HANDS.
IZUMI!! WAIT, DESU!!
I'LL SAVE YOUR SOUL.

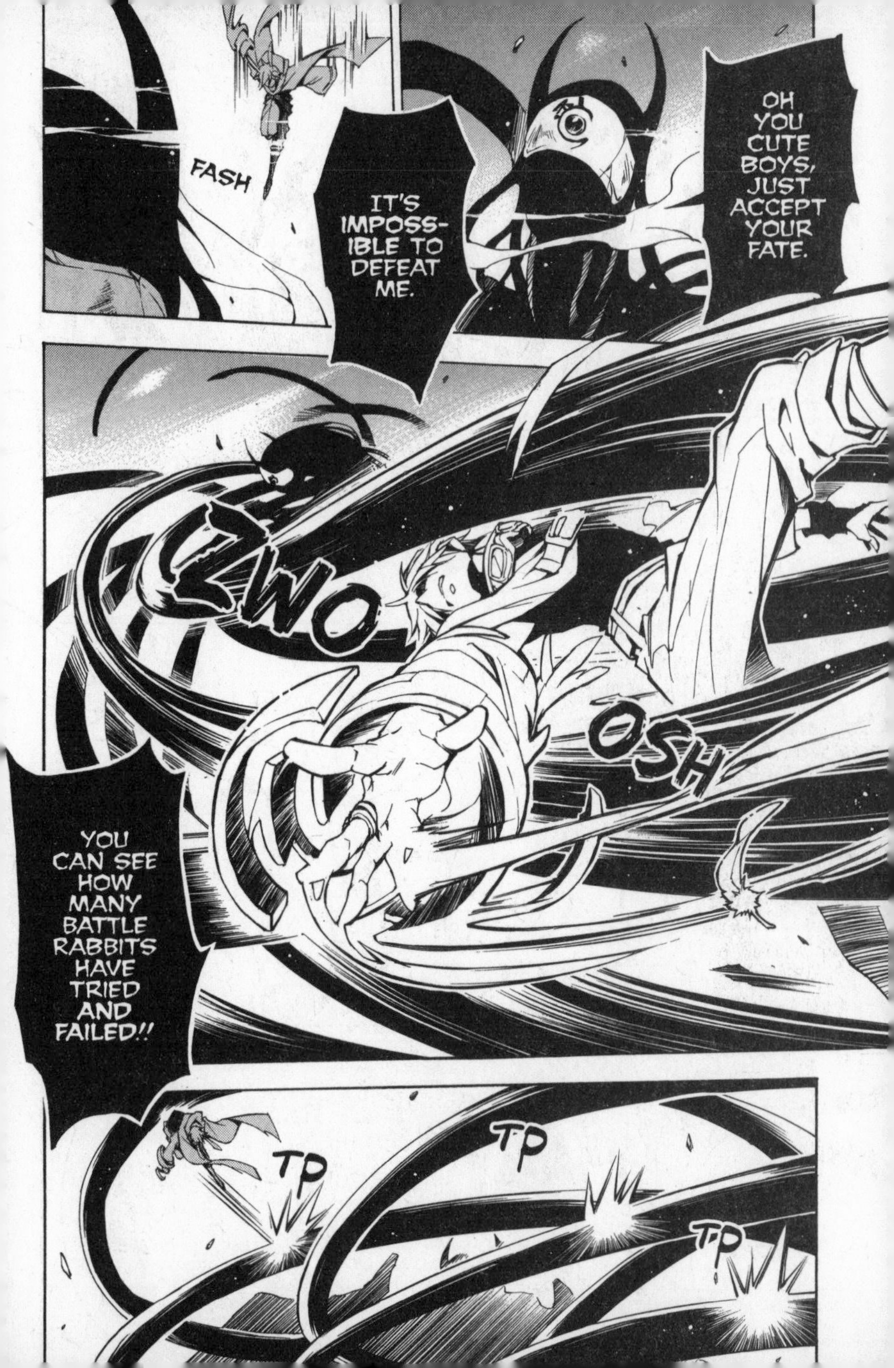
OH YOU CUTE BOYS, JUST ACCEPT YOUR FATE.
IT'S IMPOSS-IBLE TO DEFEAT ME.
FASH
ZWO
OSH
YOU CAN SEE HOW MANY BATTLE RABBITS HAVE TRIED AND FAILED!!
TP
TP
TP

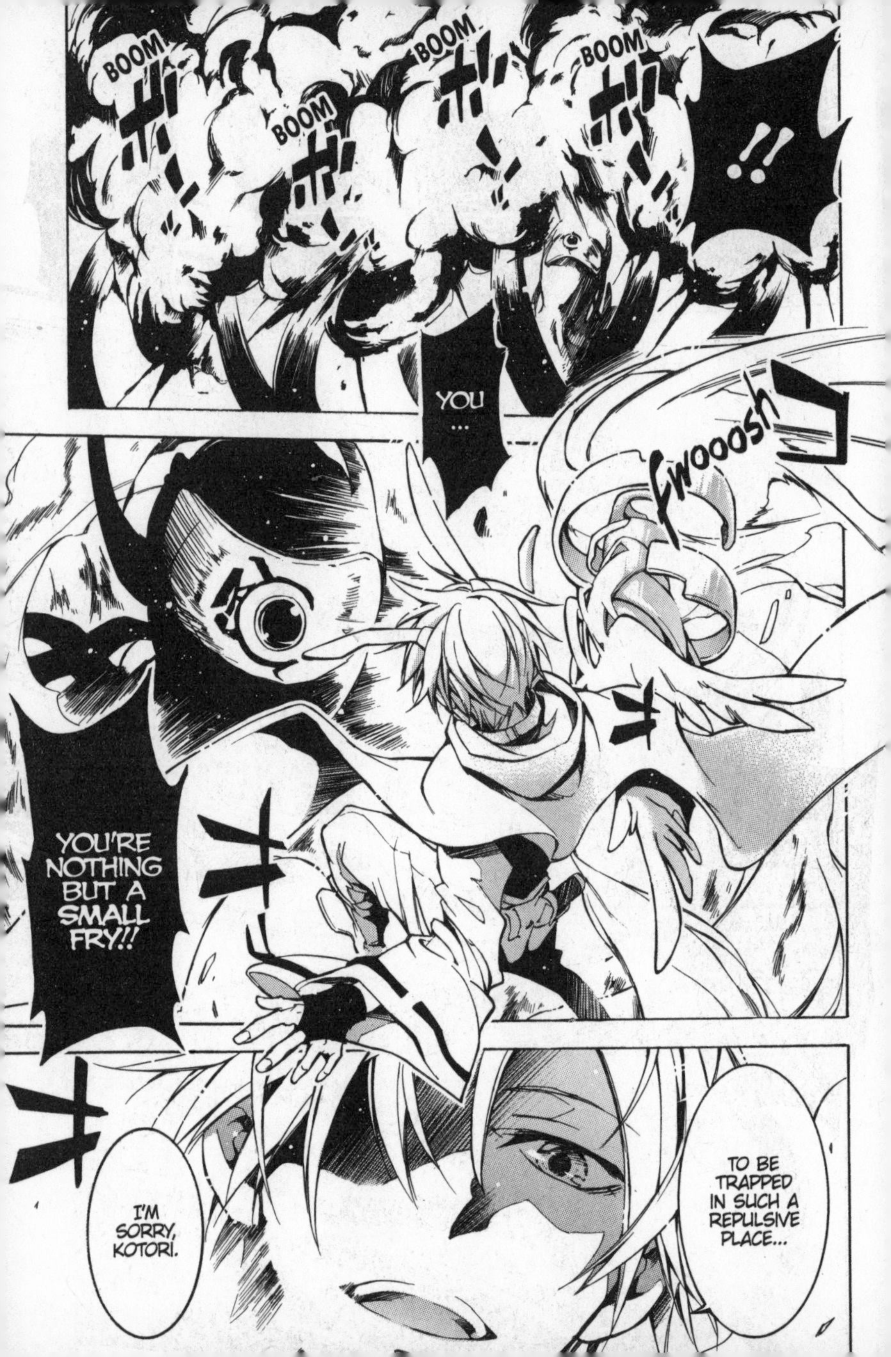
!!
BOOM
BOOM
BOOM
BOOM
YOU ...
fwooosh
YOU'RE NOTHING BUT A SMALL FRY!!
TO BE TRAPPED IN SUCH A REPULSIVE PLACE...
I'M SORRY, KOTORI.

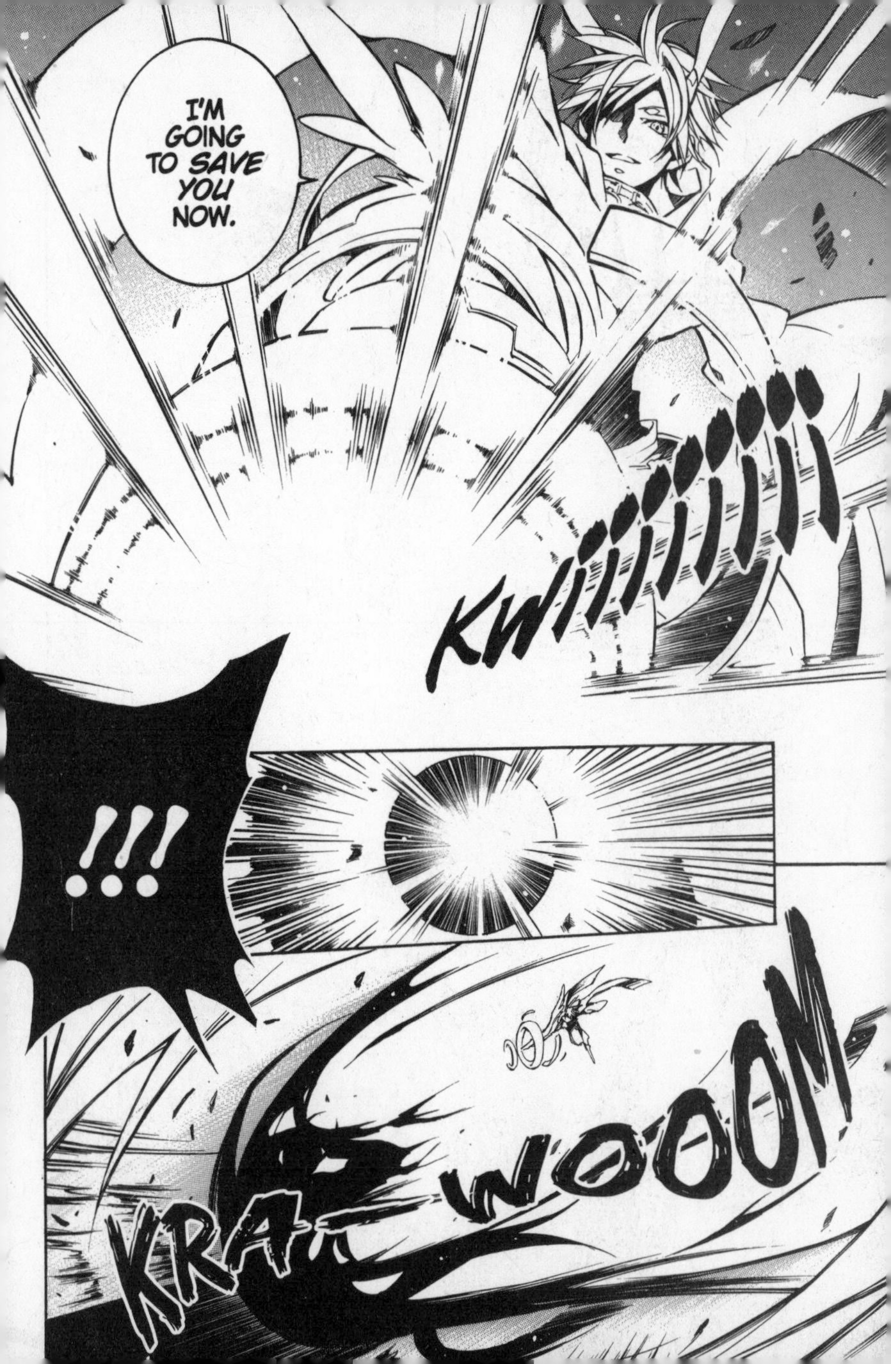
I'M GOING TO SAVE YOU NOW.
KWIIIIIIII
!!!
KRA-WOOOM

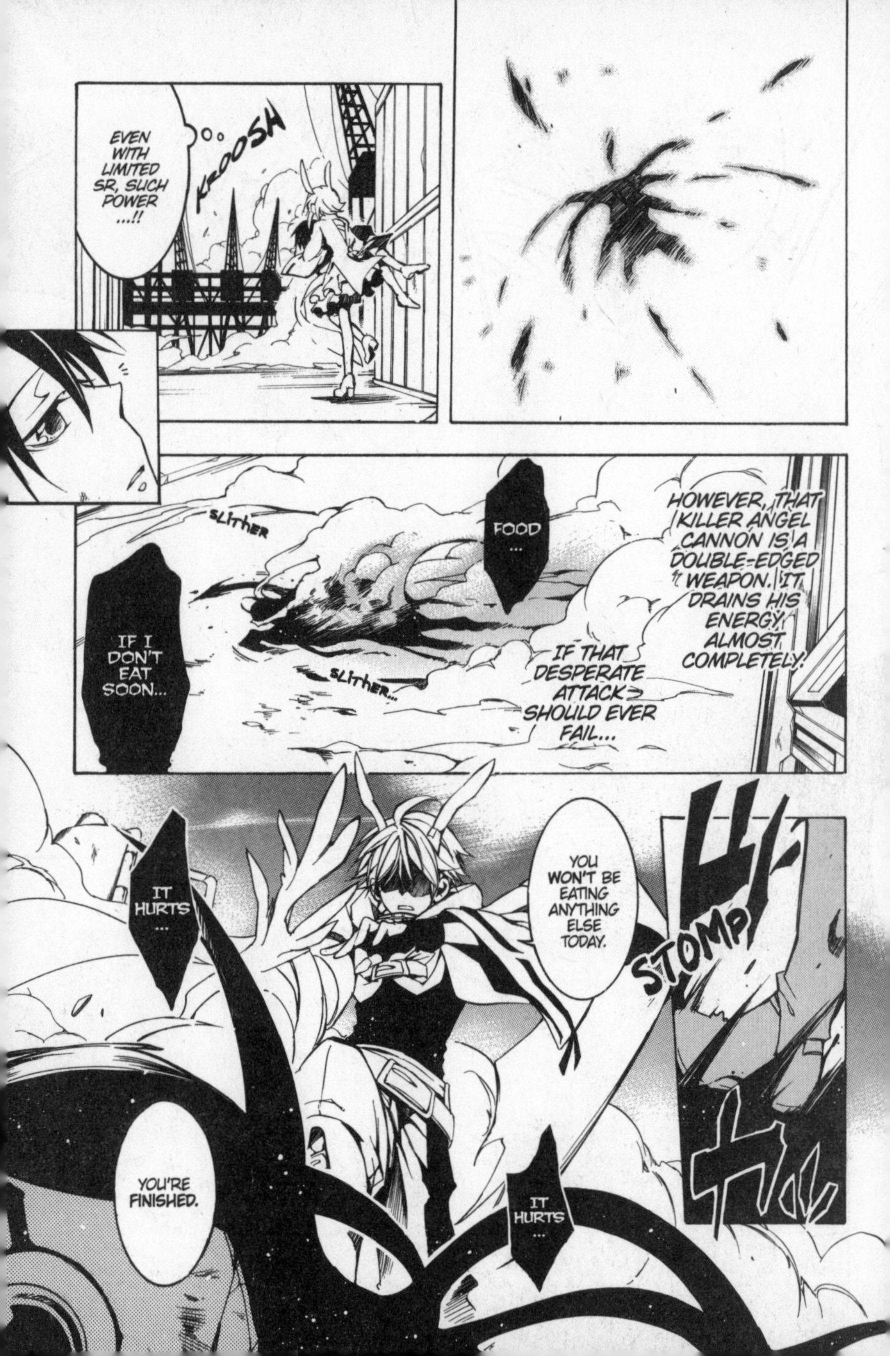
EVEN WITH LIMITED SR, SUCH POWER ...!!
KROOSH
HOWEVER, THAT KILLER ANGEL CANNON IS A DOUBLE-EDGED WEAPON. IT DRAINS HIS ENERGY ALMOST COMPLETELY.
IF THAT DESPERATE ATTACK SHOULD EVER FAIL...
FOOD ...
SLITHER
IF I DON'T EAT SOON...
SLITHER...
STOMP
YOU WON'T BE EATING ANYTHING ELSE TODAY.
IT HURTS ...
IT HURTS ...
YOU'RE FINISHED.

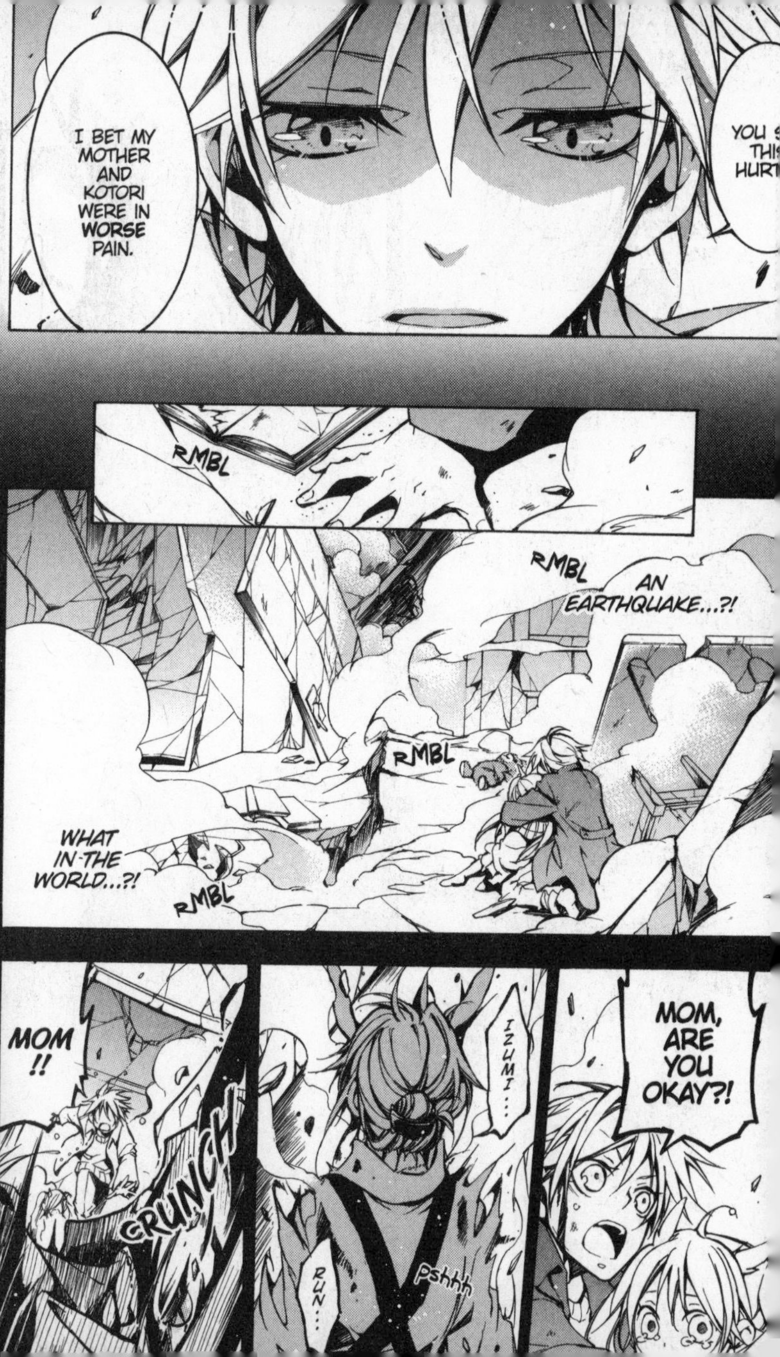
YOU S THIS HURT
I BET MY MOTHER AND KOTORI WERE IN WORSE PAIN.
RMBL
RMBL
AN EARTHQUAKE...?!
RMBL
WHAT IN THE WORLD...?!
RMBL
MOM, ARE YOU OKAY?!
IZUMI...
pshhh
RUN...
MOM!!
CRUNCH

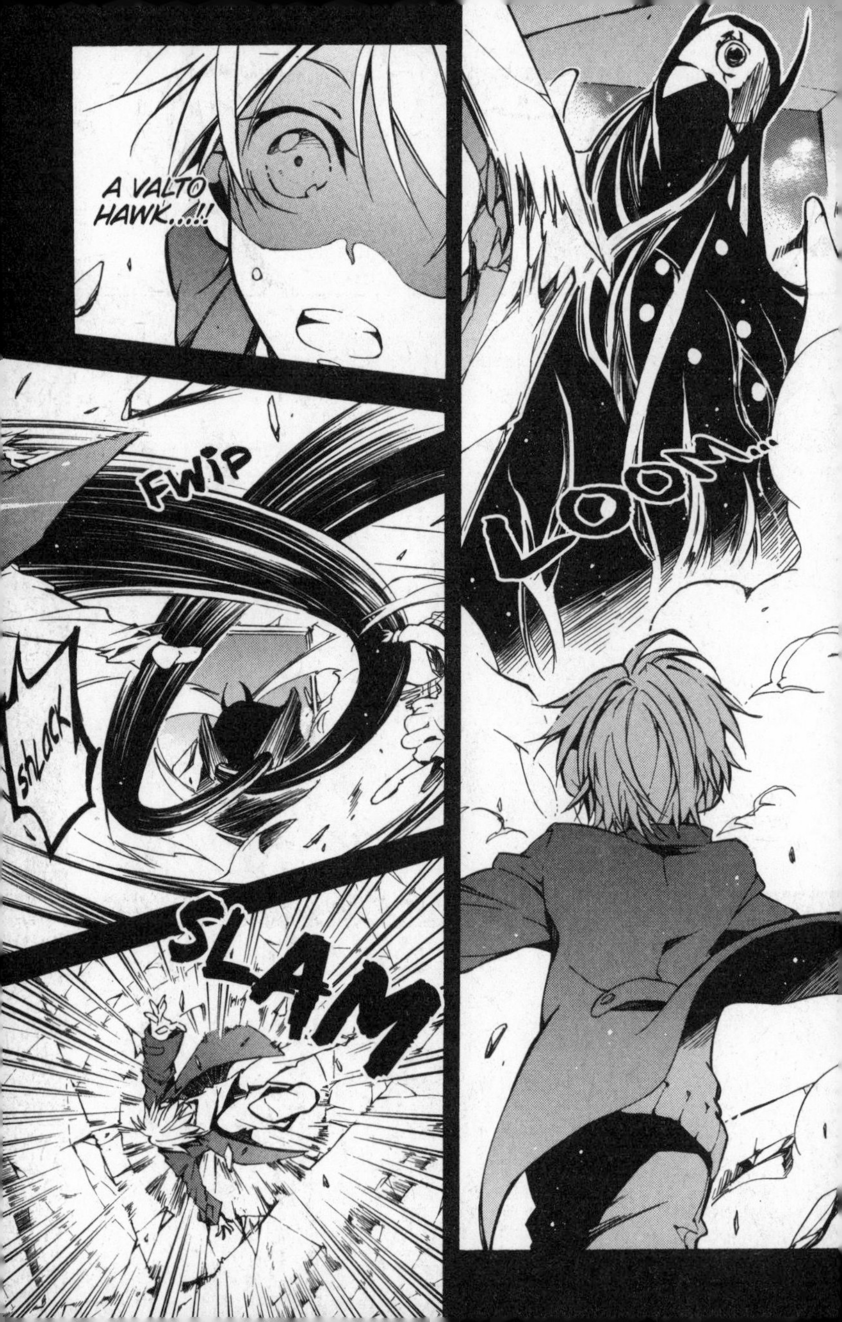
LOOOM...
A VALTO HAWK...!!
FWIP
shLACK
SLAM

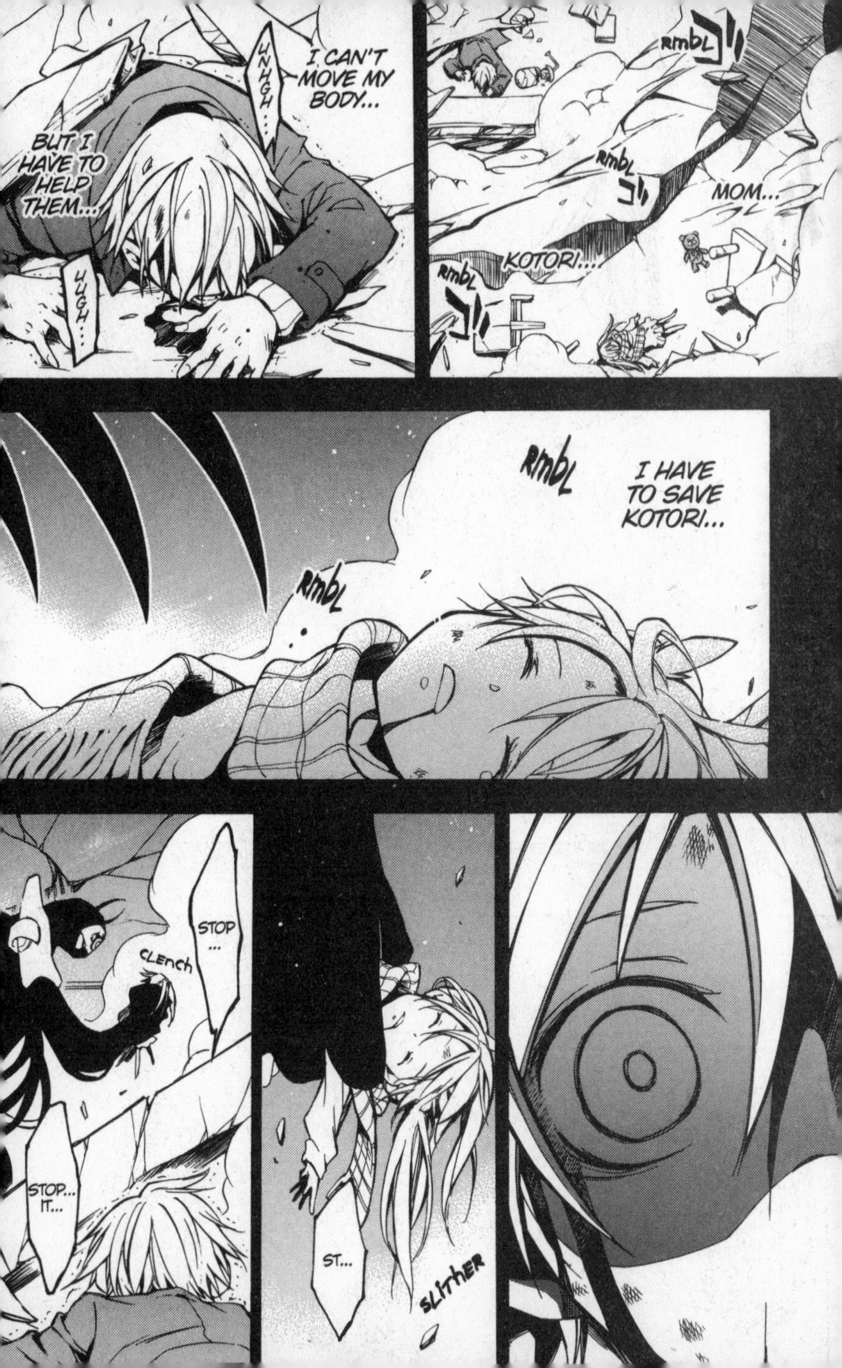
RMBL
RMBL
MOM...
KOTORI...
RMBL
I CAN'T MOVE MY BODY...
UNHGH...
BUT I HAVE TO HELP THEM...
UUGH...
RMBL
I HAVE TO SAVE KOTORI...
RMBL
ST...
SLITHER
STOP...
CLENCH
STOP... IT...

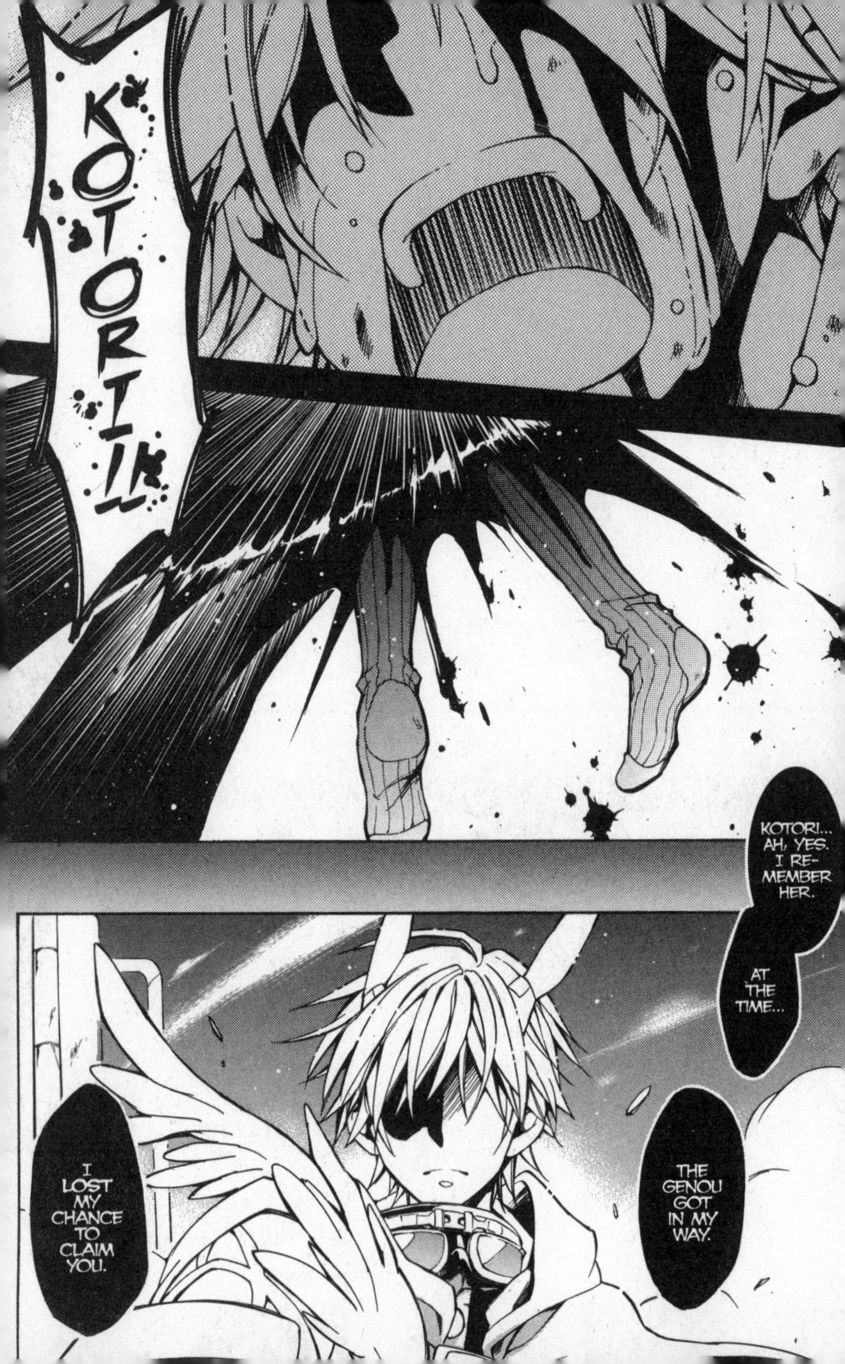
KOTORIII!!
KOTORI... AH, YES. I RE-MEMBER HER.
AT THE TIME...
THE GENOU GOT IN MY WAY.
I LOST MY CHANCE TO CLAIM YOU.

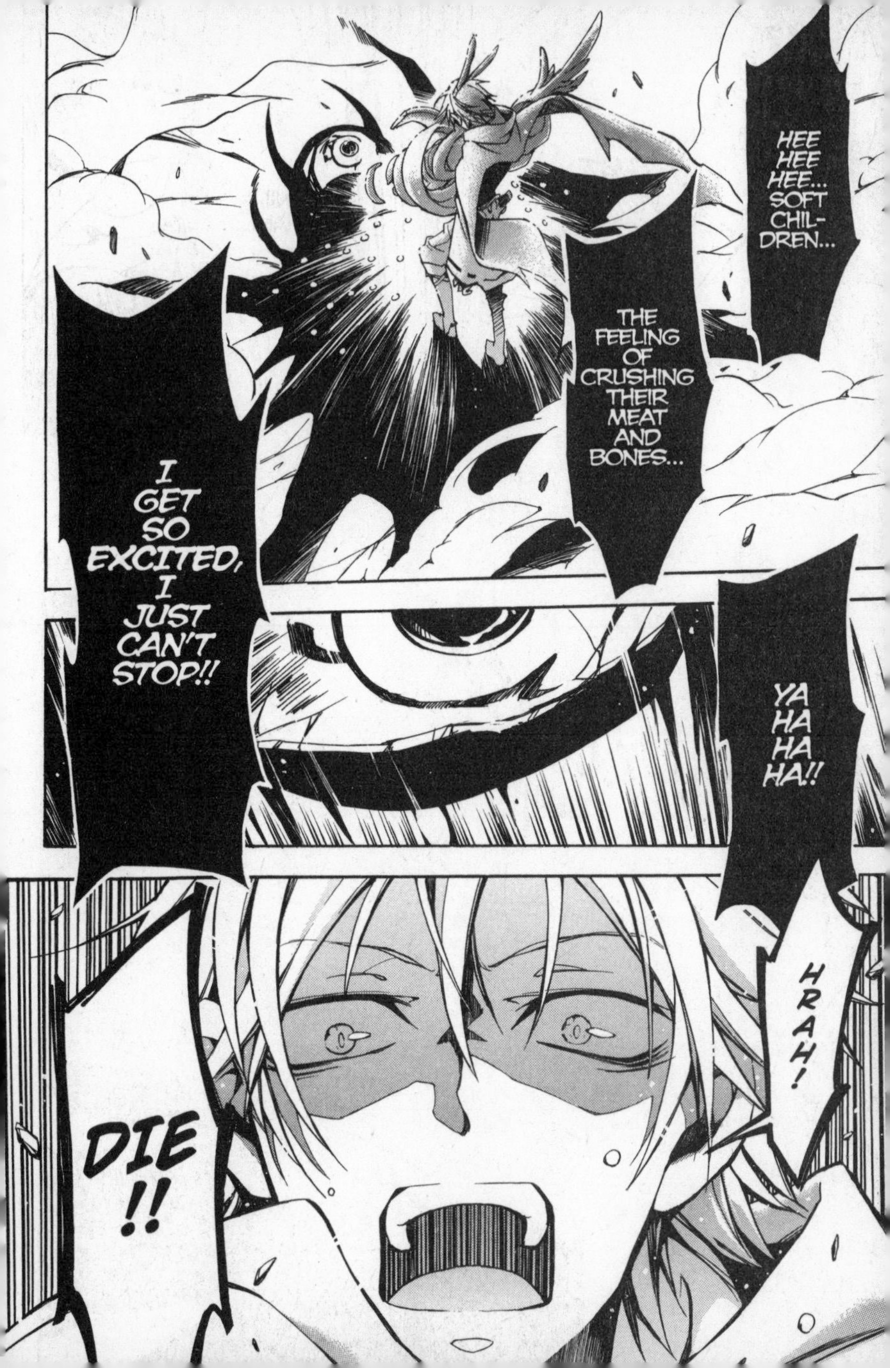
HEE HEE HEE... SOFT CHIL-DREN...
THE FEELING OF CRUSHING THEIR MEAT AND BONES...
I GET SO EXCITED, I JUST CAN'T STOP!!
YA HA HA HA!!
HRAH!
DIE!!

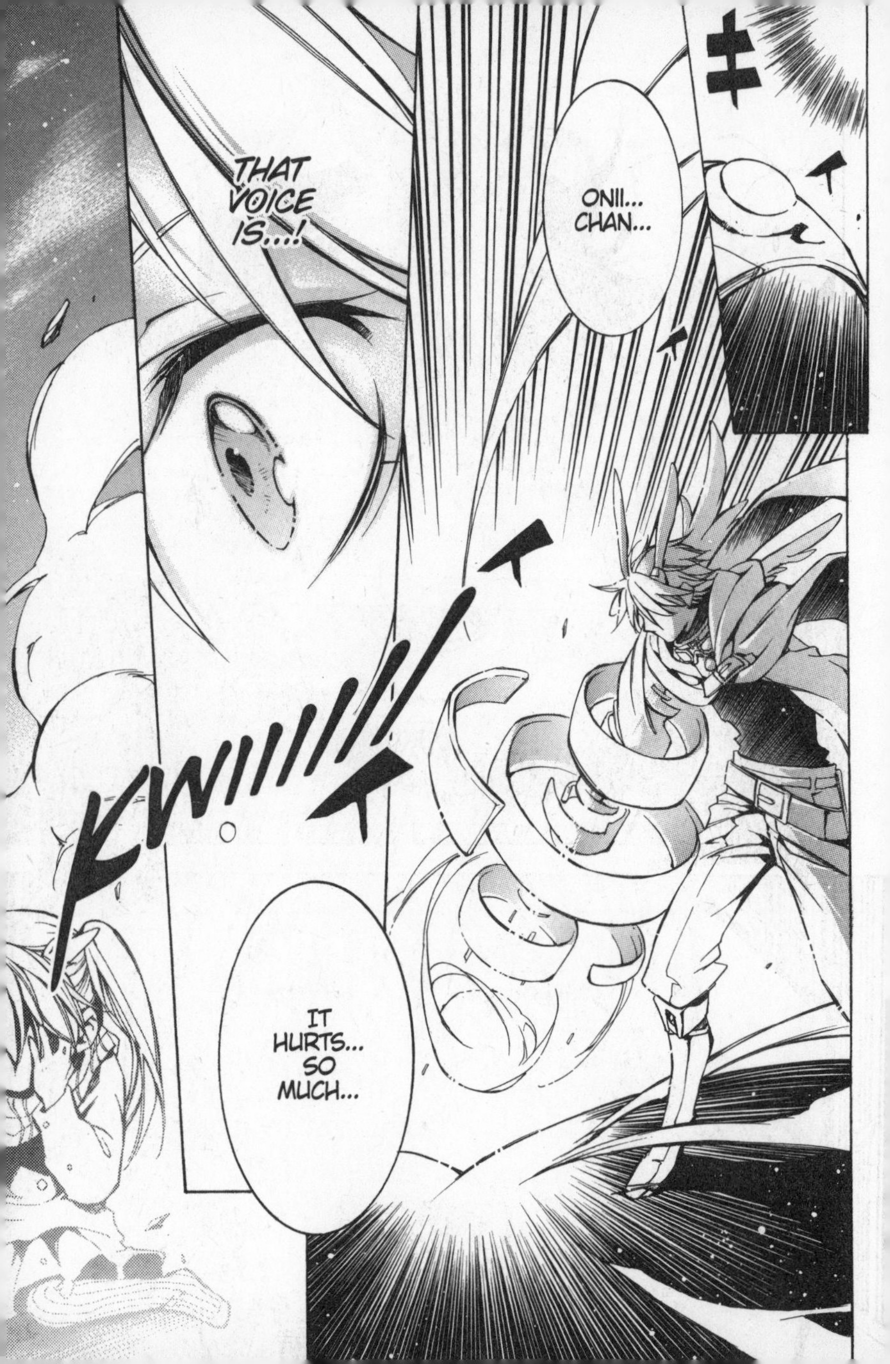
ONII... CHAN...
THAT VOICE IS...!
KWIIIII
IT HURTS... SO MUCH...

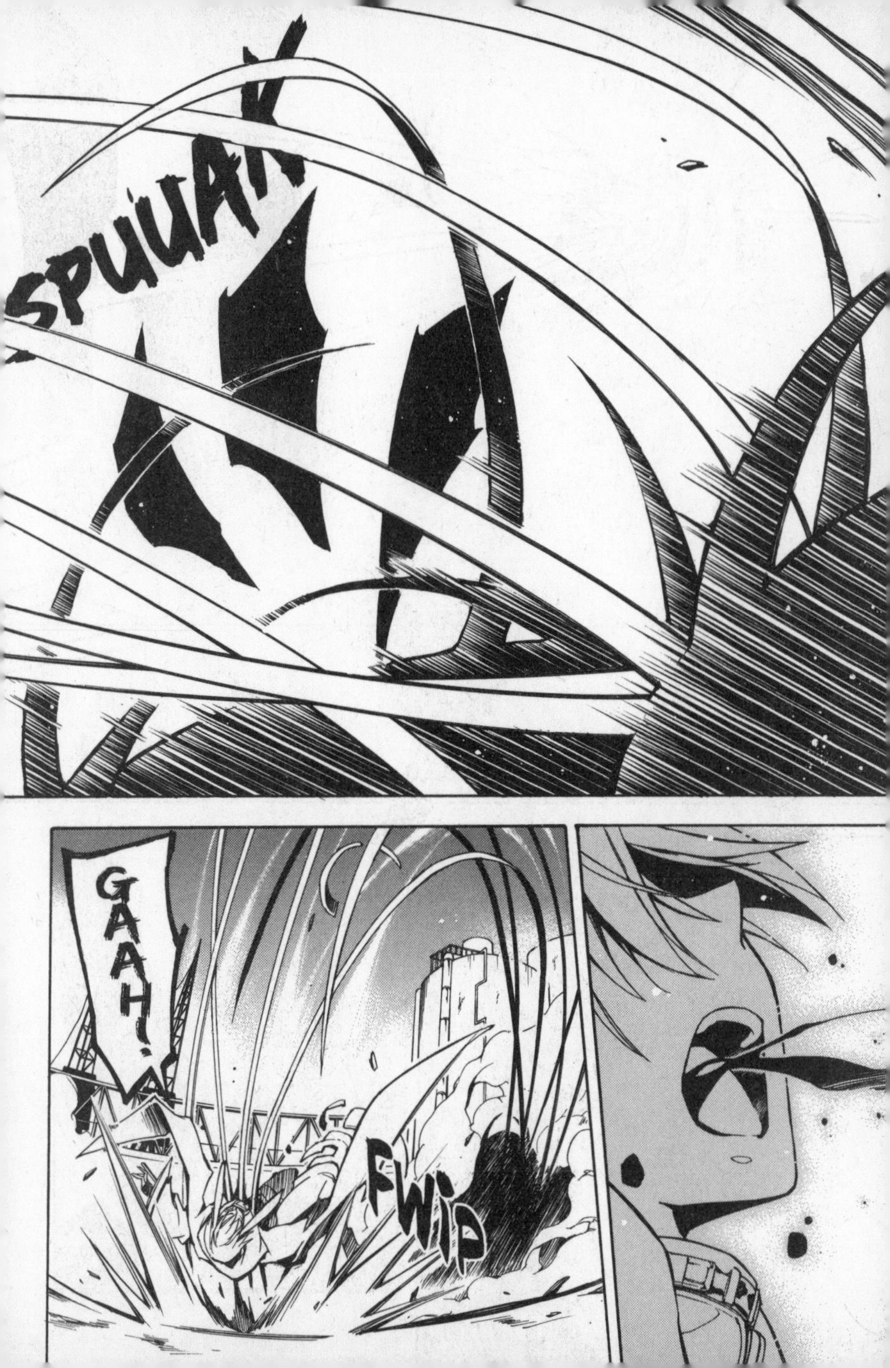
SPUUAK
GAAH!
FWIP

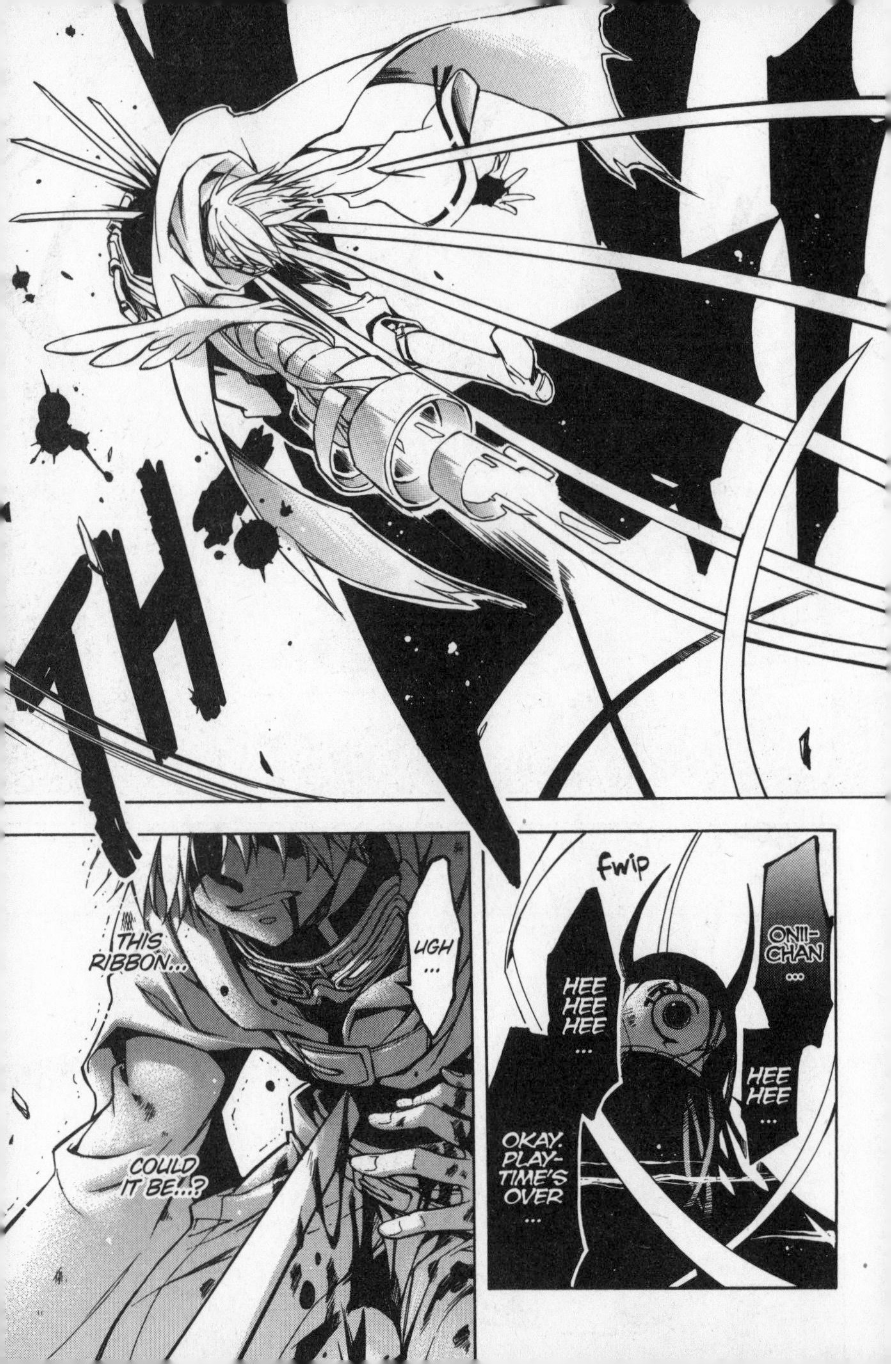
fwip
ONII-CHAN...
HEE HEE HEE...
HEE HEE...
OKAY. PLAY-TIME'S OVER...
UGH...
THIS RIBBON...
COULD IT BE...?

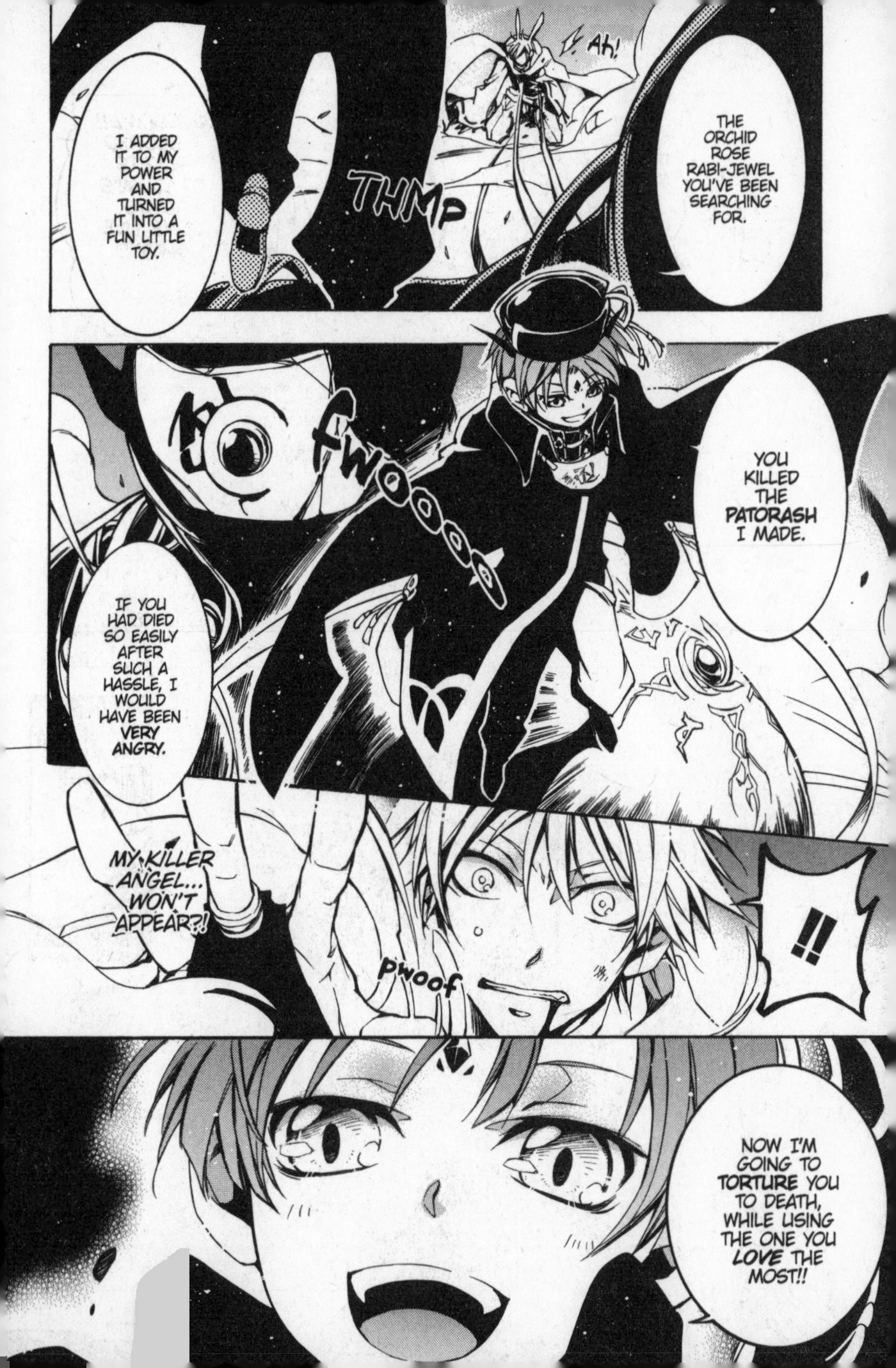
Ah!
THE ORCHID ROSE RABI-JEWEL YOU'VE BEEN SEARCHING FOR.
THMP
I ADDED IT TO MY POWER AND TURNED IT INTO A FUN LITTLE TOY.
YOU KILLED THE **PATORASH** I MADE.
fwoooo
IF YOU HAD DIED SO EASILY AFTER SUCH A HASSLE, I WOULD HAVE BEEN **VERY** ANGRY.
!!
pwoof
MY KILLER ANGEL... WON'T APPEAR?!
NOW I'M GOING TO **TORTURE** YOU TO DEATH, WHILE USING THE ONE YOU ***LOVE*** THE MOST!!

Chapter 15

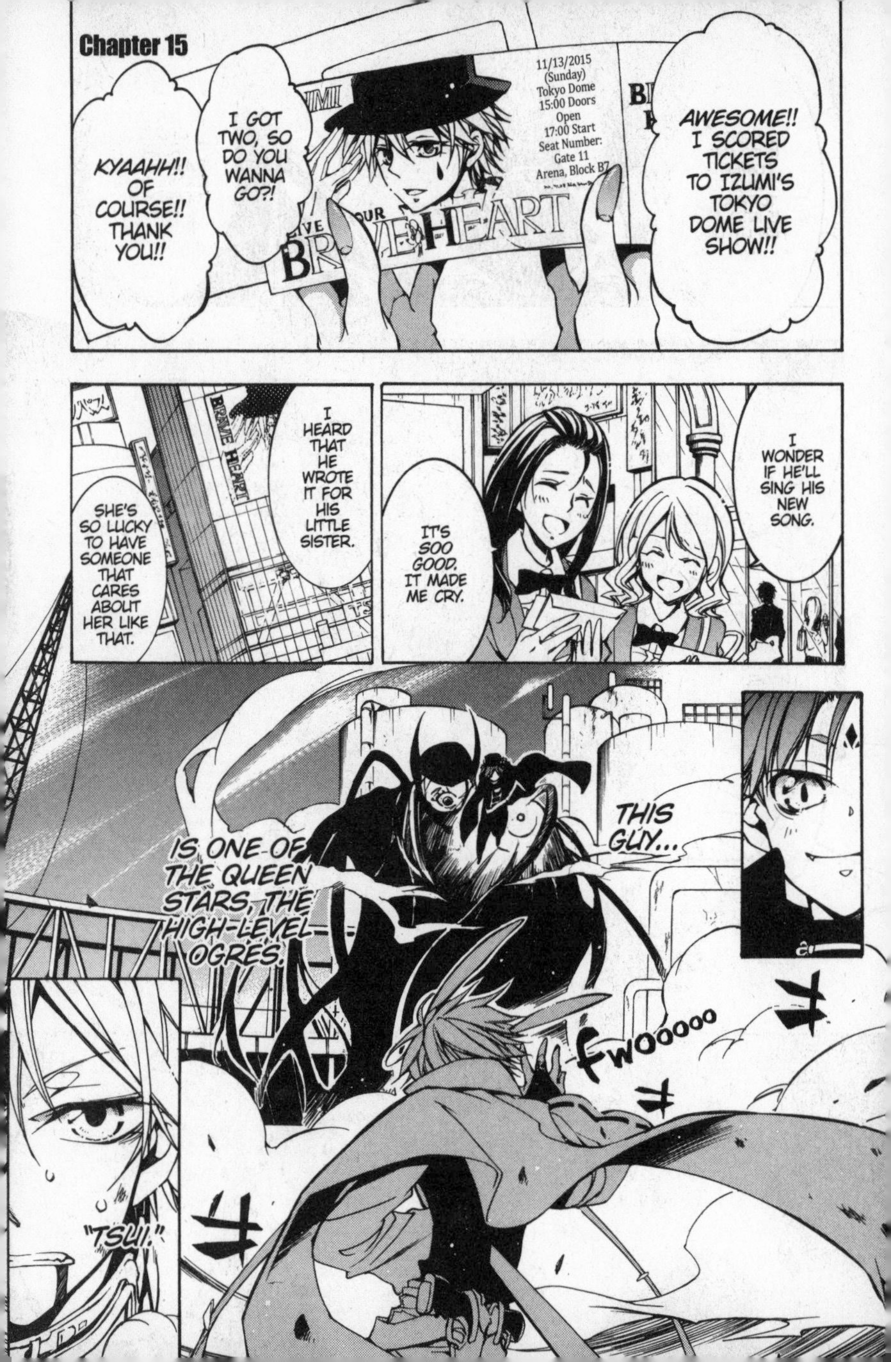
AWESOME!! I SCORED TICKETS TO IZUMI'S TOKYO DOME LIVE SHOW!!
11/13/2015 (Sunday) Tokyo Dome 15:00 Doors Open 17:00 Start Seat Number: Gate 11 Arena, Block B7
BRAVE HEART
I GOT TWO, SO DO YOU WANNA GO?!
KYAAHH!! OF COURSE!! THANK YOU!!
I WONDER IF HE'LL SING HIS NEW SONG.
IT'S SOO GOOD. IT MADE ME CRY.
I HEARD THAT HE WROTE IT FOR HIS LITTLE SISTER.
SHE'S SO LUCKY TO HAVE SOMEONE THAT CARES ABOUT HER LIKE THAT.
BRAVE HEART
THIS GUY...
IS ONE OF THE QUEEN STARS, THE HIGH-LEVEL OGRES.
FWOOOOO
"TSU!"

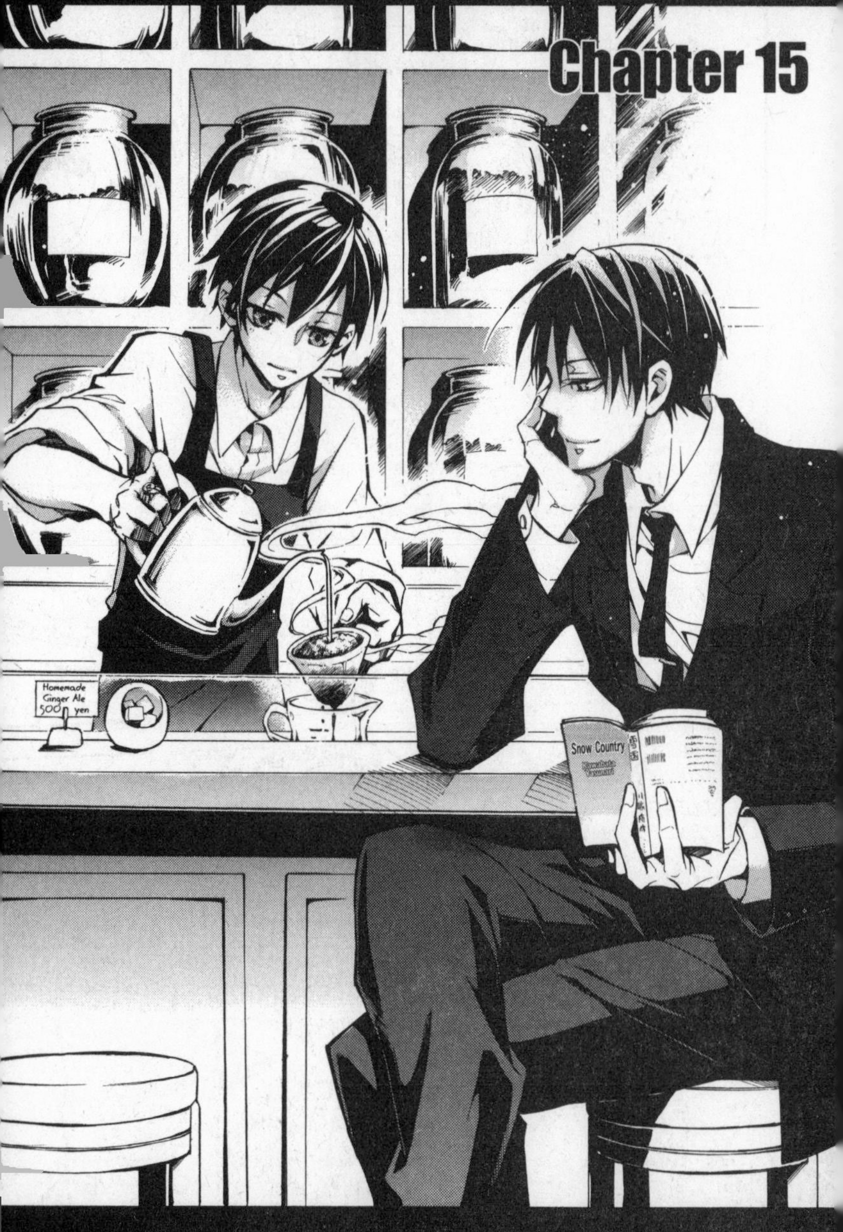
Chapter 15
Homemade
Ginger Ale
500 yen
Snow Country

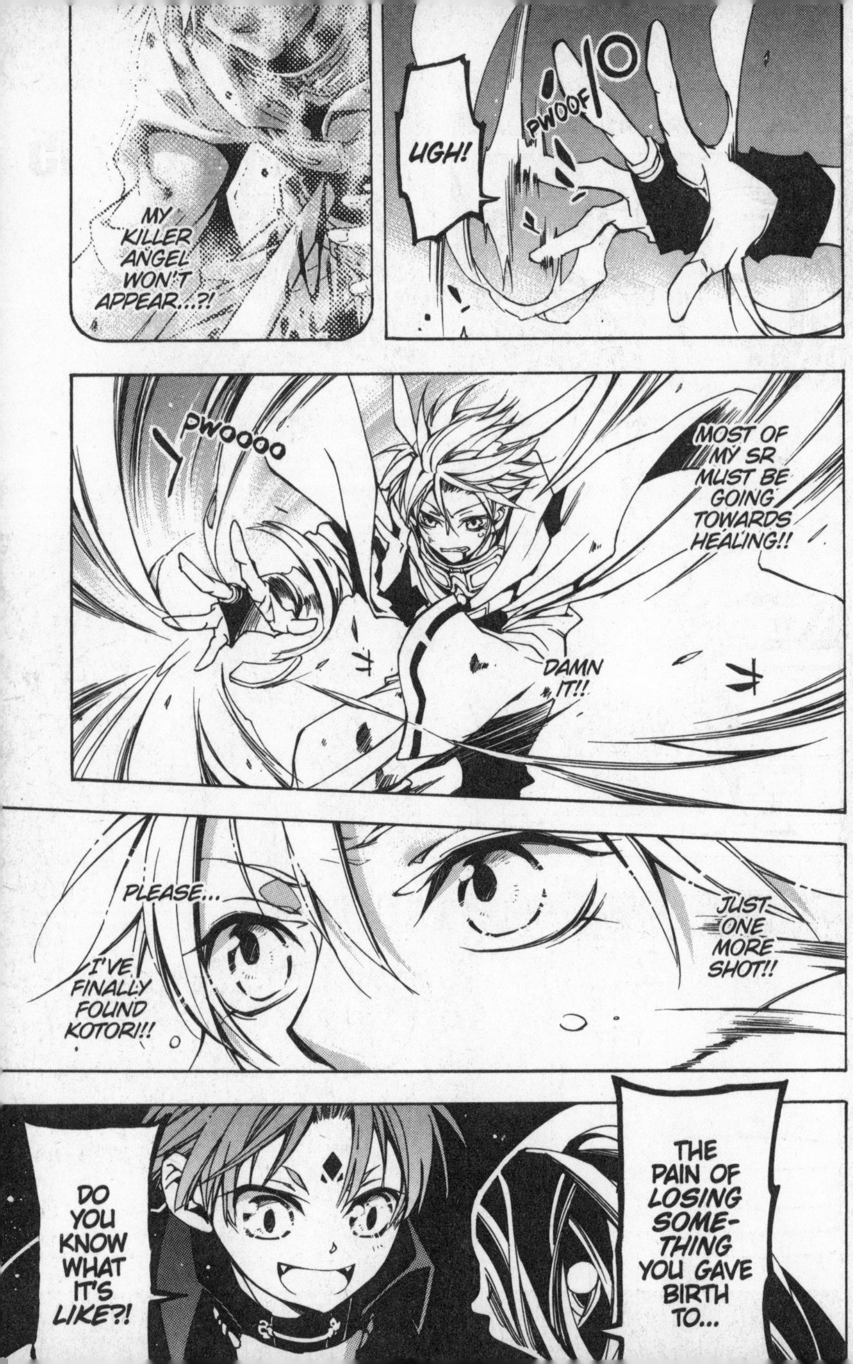
UGH!
PWOOF
MY KILLER ANGEL WON'T APPEAR...?!
MOST OF MY SR MUST BE GOING TOWARDS HEALING!!
PWOOOOO
DAMN IT!!
JUST ONE MORE SHOT!!
PLEASE...
I'VE FINALLY FOUND KOTORI!!
THE PAIN OF LOSING SOME-THING YOU GAVE BIRTH TO...
DO YOU KNOW WHAT IT'S LIKE?!

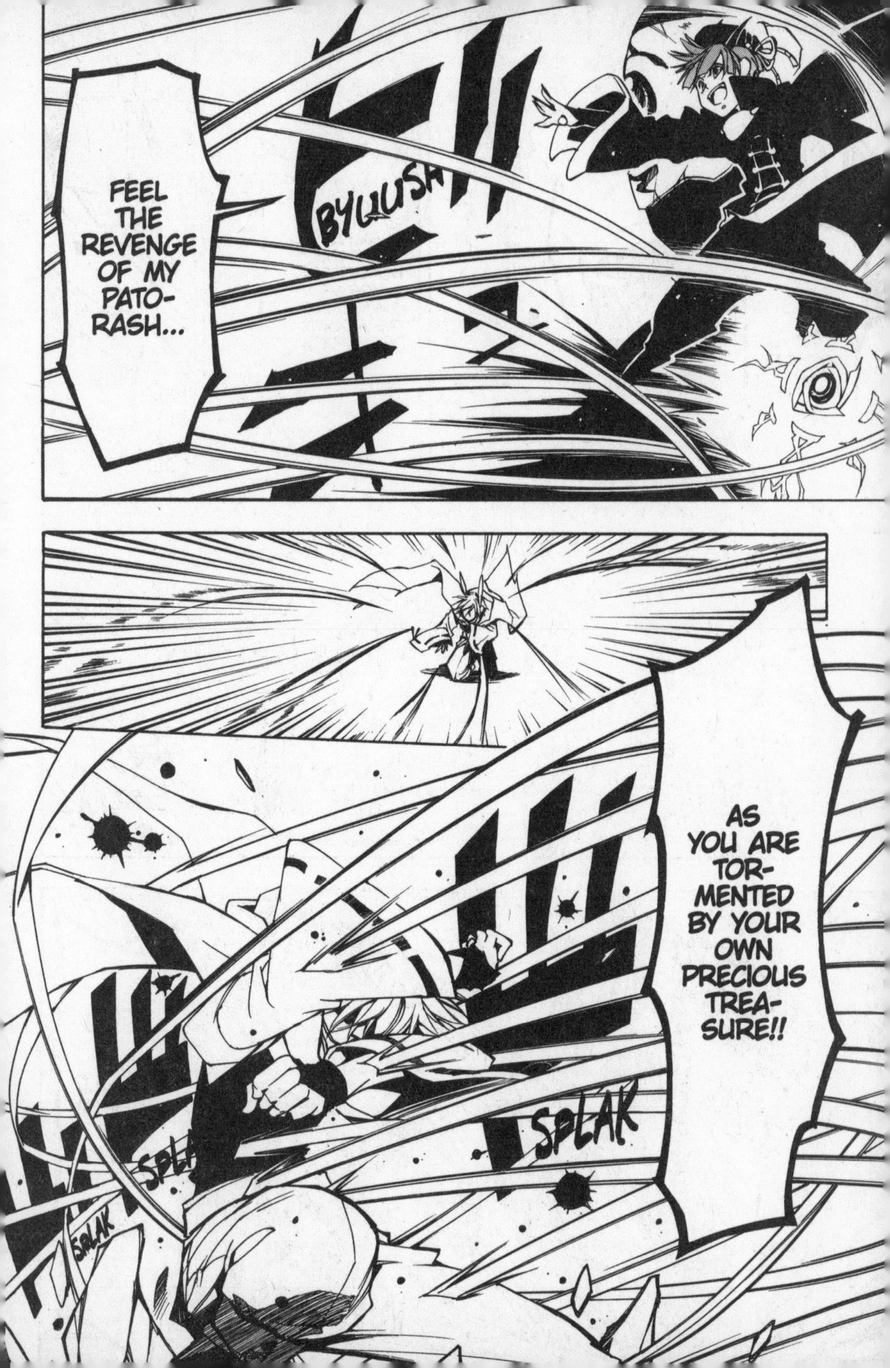

FEEL THE REVENGE OF MY PATO-RASH...
BYUUSH
AS YOU ARE TOR-MENTED BY YOUR OWN PRECIOUS TREA-SURE!!
SPLAK
SPLA
SPLAK

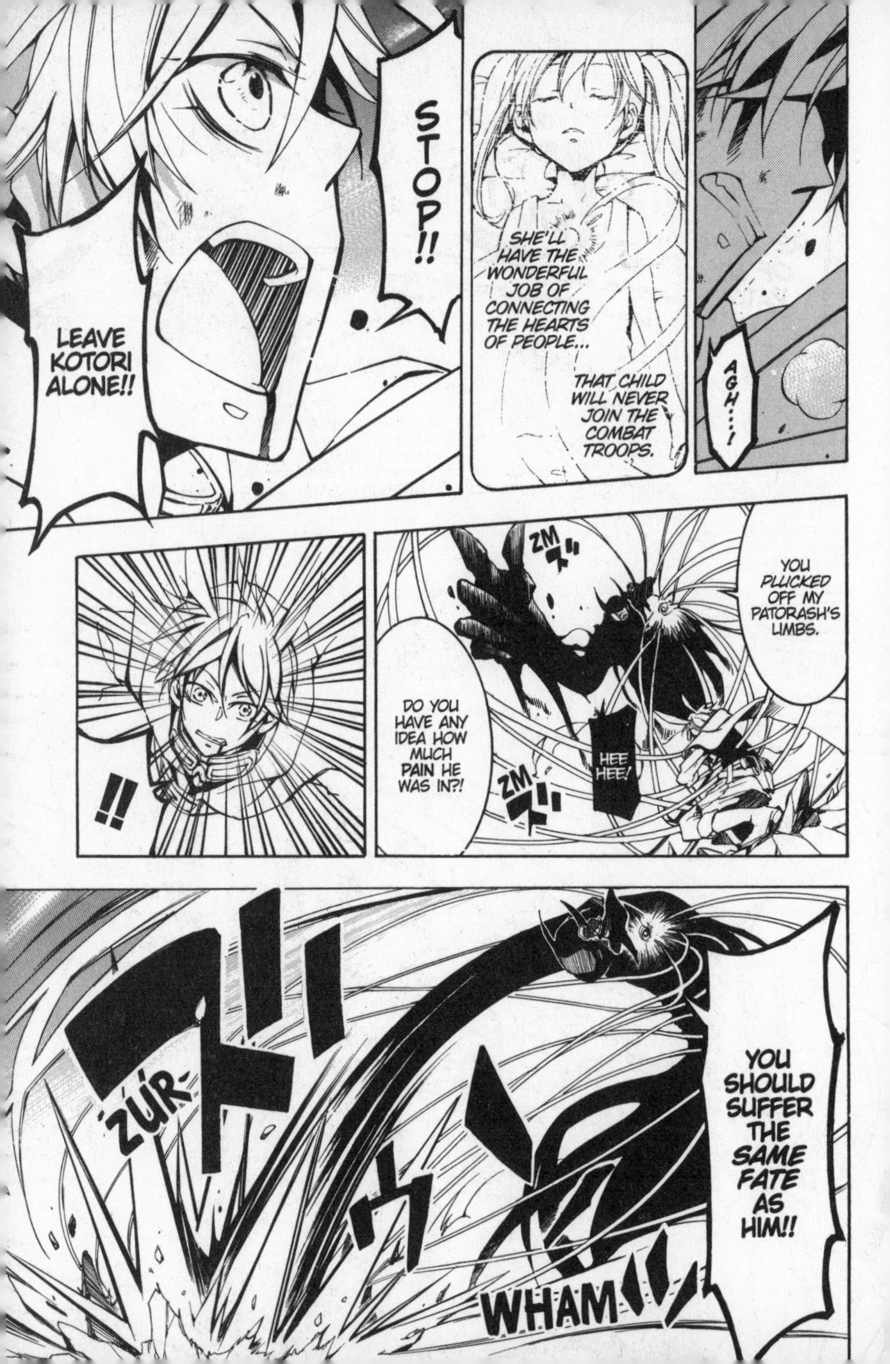
AGH...!
SHE'LL HAVE THE WONDERFUL JOB OF CONNECTING THE HEARTS OF PEOPLE...
THAT CHILD WILL NEVER JOIN THE COMBAT TROOPS.
STOP!!
LEAVE KOTORI ALONE!!
YOU PLUCKED OFF MY PATORASH'S LIMBS.
ZM
DO YOU HAVE ANY IDEA HOW MUCH PAIN HE WAS IN?!
HEE HEE!
ZM
!!
YOU SHOULD SUFFER THE SAME FATE AS HIM!!
ZUR-
WHAM

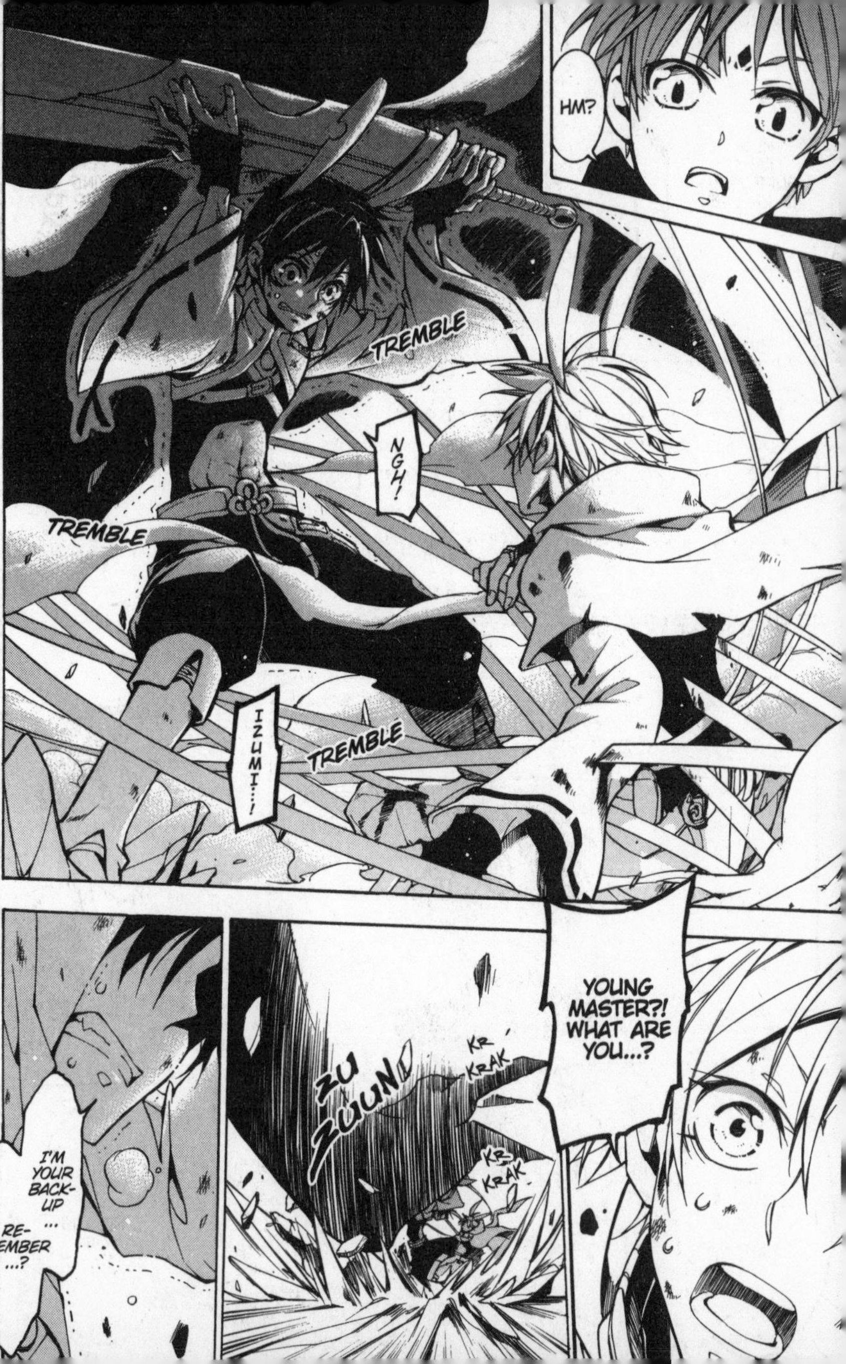
HM?
TREMBLE
NGH!
TREMBLE
IZUMI...!
TREMBLE
YOUNG MASTER?! WHAT ARE YOU...?
KR KRAK
ZU ZUUN
KR KRAK
I'M YOUR BACK-UP ... RE-MEMBER ...?

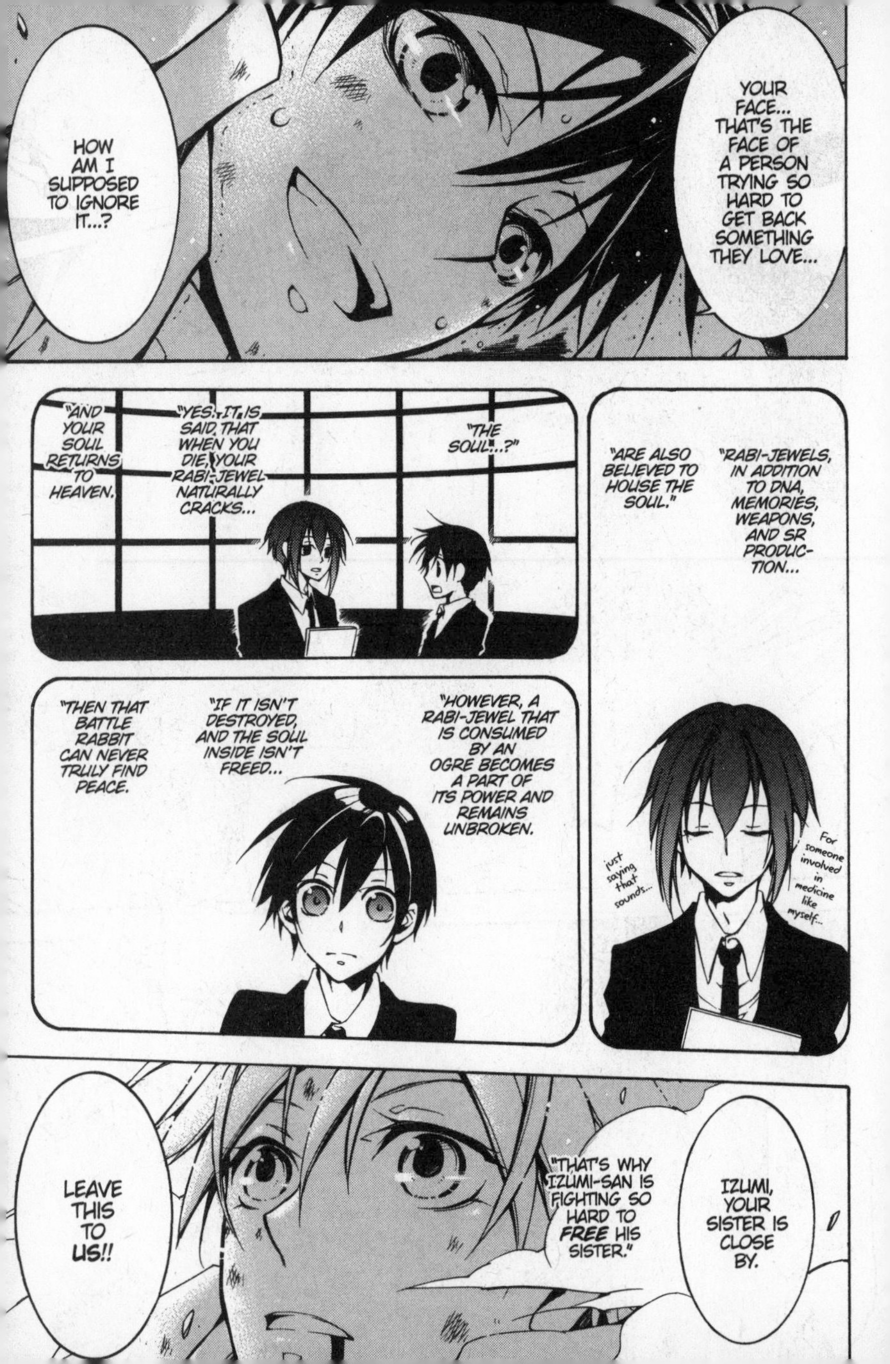
YOUR FACE... THAT'S THE FACE OF A PERSON TRYING SO HARD TO GET BACK SOMETHING THEY LOVE...
HOW AM I SUPPOSED TO IGNORE IT...?
"RABI-JEWELS, IN ADDITION TO DNA, MEMORIES, WEAPONS, AND SR PRODUCTION...
"ARE ALSO BELIEVED TO HOUSE THE SOUL."
For someone involved in medicine like myself...
just saying that sounds...
"THE SOUL...?"
"YES. IT IS SAID THAT WHEN YOU DIE, YOUR RABI-JEWEL NATURALLY CRACKS...
"AND YOUR SOUL RETURNS TO HEAVEN.
"HOWEVER, A RABI-JEWEL THAT IS CONSUMED BY AN OGRE BECOMES A PART OF ITS POWER AND REMAINS UNBROKEN.
"IF IT ISN'T DESTROYED, AND THE SOUL INSIDE ISN'T FREED...
"THEN THAT BATTLE RABBIT CAN NEVER TRULY FIND PEACE.
IZUMI, YOUR SISTER IS CLOSE BY.
"THAT'S WHY IZUMI-SAN IS FIGHTING SO HARD TO FREE HIS SISTER."
LEAVE THIS TO US!!

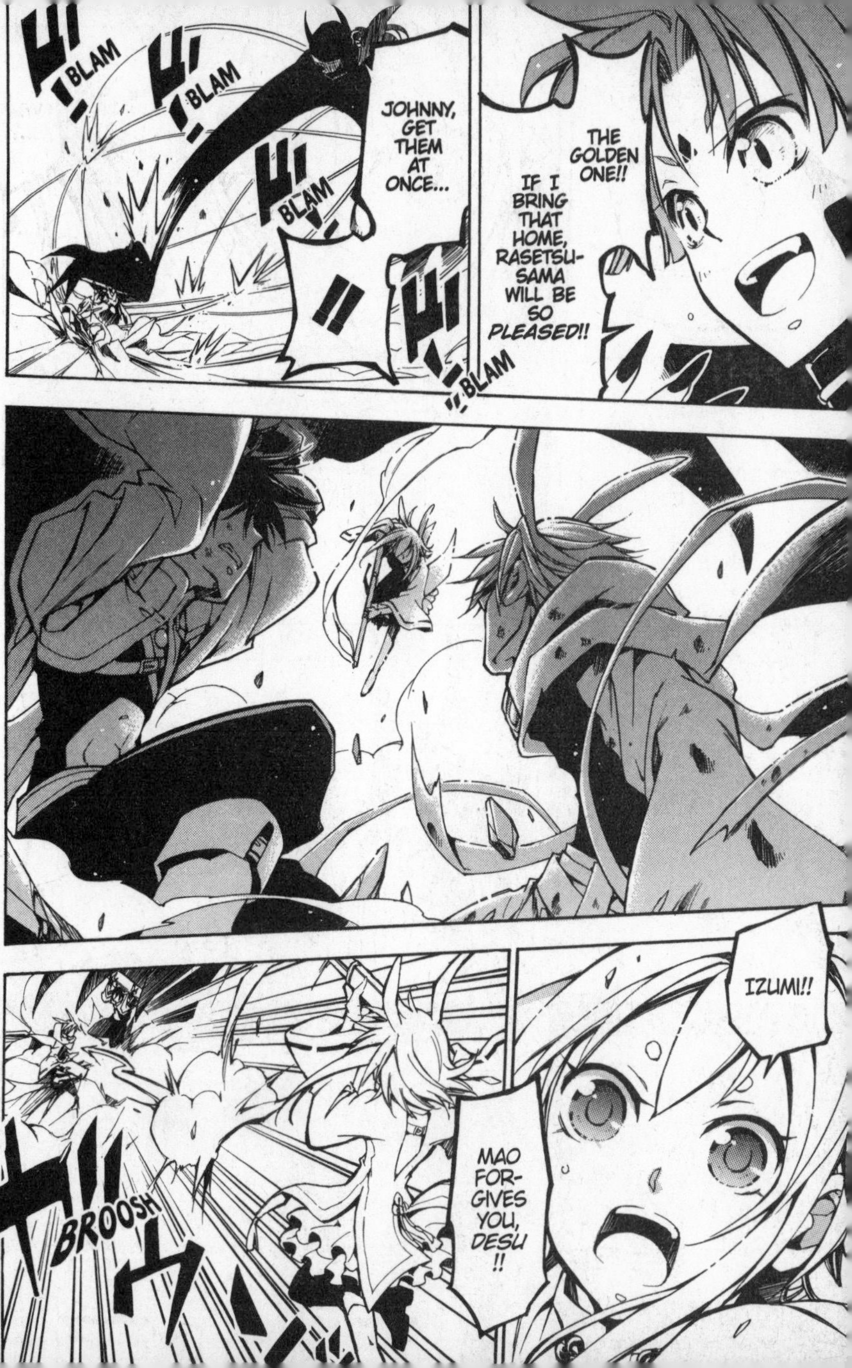
THE GOLDEN ONE!!
IF I BRING THAT HOME, RASETSU-SAMA WILL BE SO PLEASED!!
BLAM
JOHNNY, GET THEM AT ONCE...
BLAM
BLAM
BLAM
IZUMI!!
MAO FORGIVES YOU, DESU!!
BROOSH

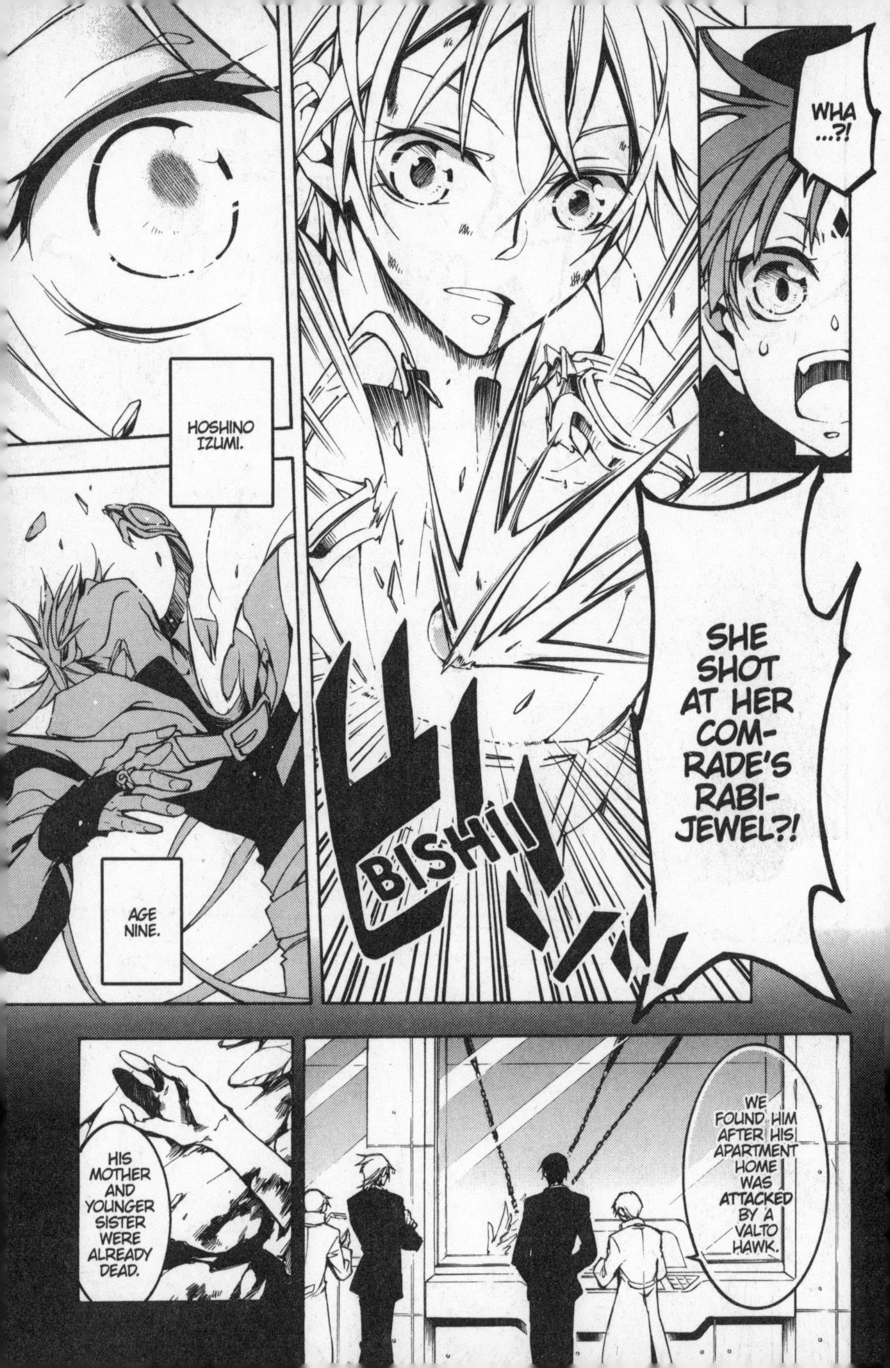
WHA ...?!
SHE SHOT AT HER COM-RADE'S RABI-JEWEL?!
BISHI!
HOSHINO IZUMI.
AGE NINE.
WE FOUND HIM AFTER HIS APARTMENT HOME WAS ATTACKED BY A VALTO HAWK.
HIS MOTHER AND YOUNGER SISTER WERE ALREADY DEAD.

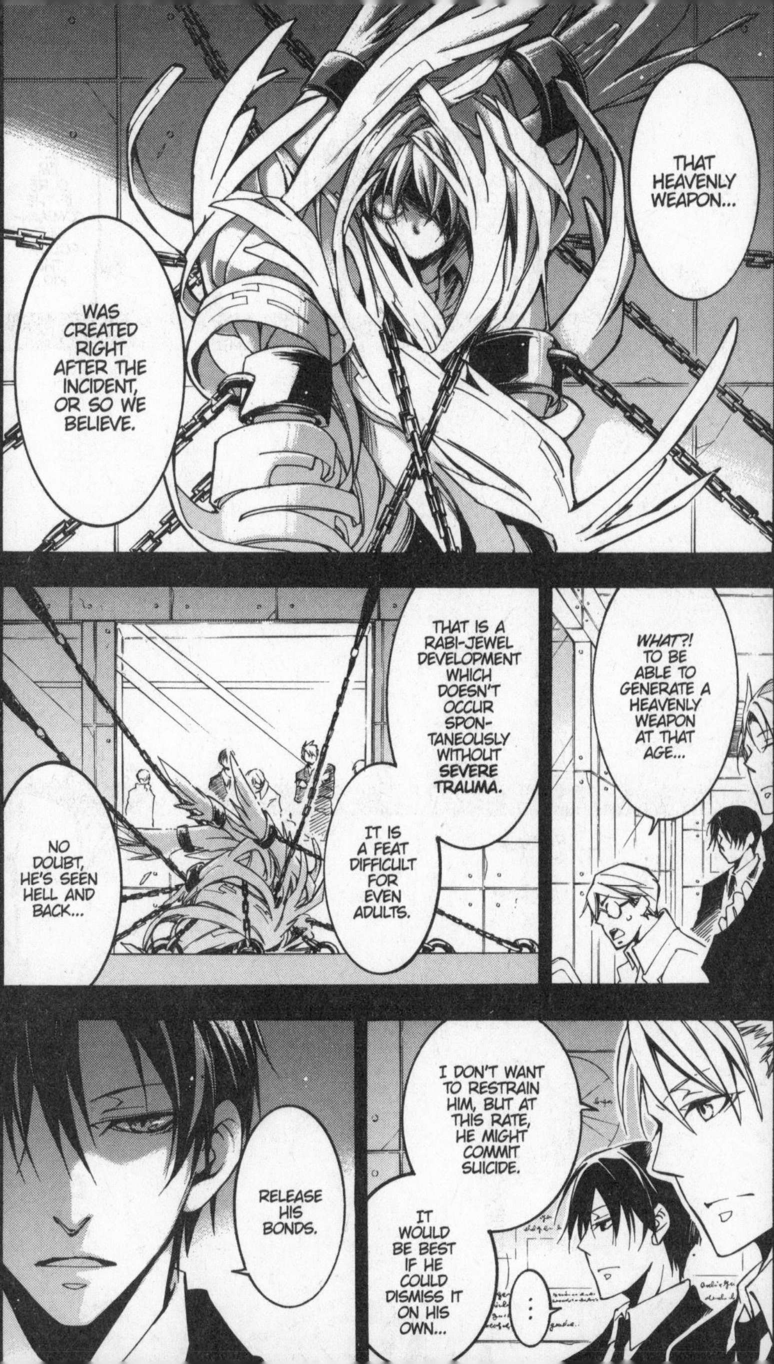
THAT HEAVENLY WEAPON...
WAS CREATED RIGHT AFTER THE INCIDENT, OR SO WE BELIEVE.
WHAT?! TO BE ABLE TO GENERATE A HEAVENLY WEAPON AT THAT AGE...
THAT IS A RABI-JEWEL DEVELOPMENT WHICH DOESN'T OCCUR SPONTANEOUSLY WITHOUT **SEVERE TRAUMA.**
IT IS A FEAT DIFFICULT FOR EVEN ADULTS.
NO DOUBT, HE'S SEEN HELL AND BACK...
I DON'T WANT TO RESTRAIN HIM, BUT AT THIS RATE, HE MIGHT COMMIT SUICIDE.
IT WOULD BE BEST IF HE COULD DISMISS IT ON HIS OWN...
...
RELEASE HIS BONDS.

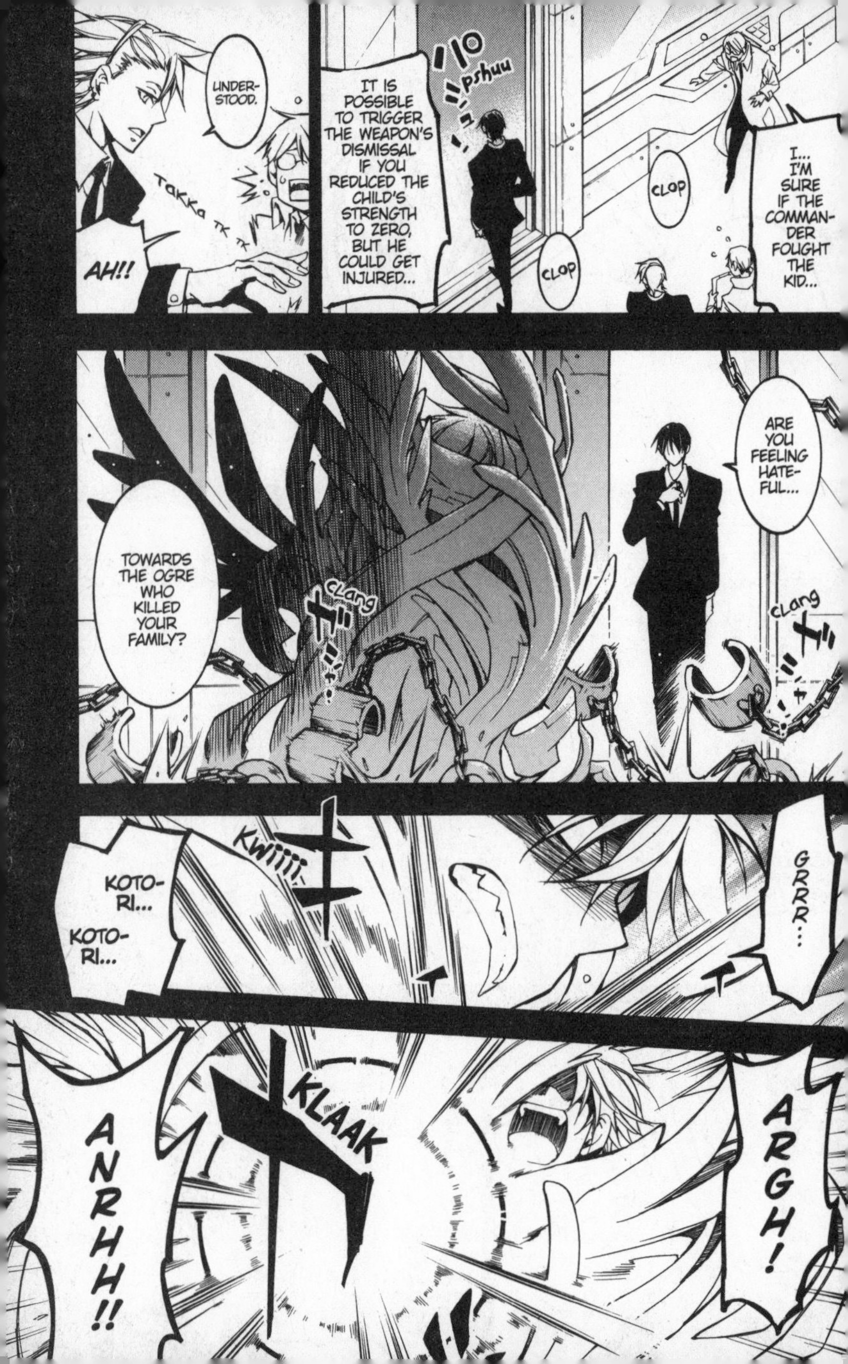
I... I'M SURE IF THE COMMAN-DER FOUGHT THE KID...
CLOP
CLOP
pshuu
IT IS POSSIBLE TO TRIGGER THE WEAPON'S DISMISSAL IF YOU REDUCED THE CHILD'S STRENGTH TO ZERO, BUT HE COULD GET INJURED...
UNDER-STOOD.
TaKKa TK TK
AH!!
ARE YOU FEELING HATE-FUL...
clang
clang
TOWARDS THE OGRE WHO KILLED YOUR FAMILY?
GRRR...
Kwiiiii
KOTO-RI...
KOTO-RI...
ARGH!
KLAAK
ANRHH!!

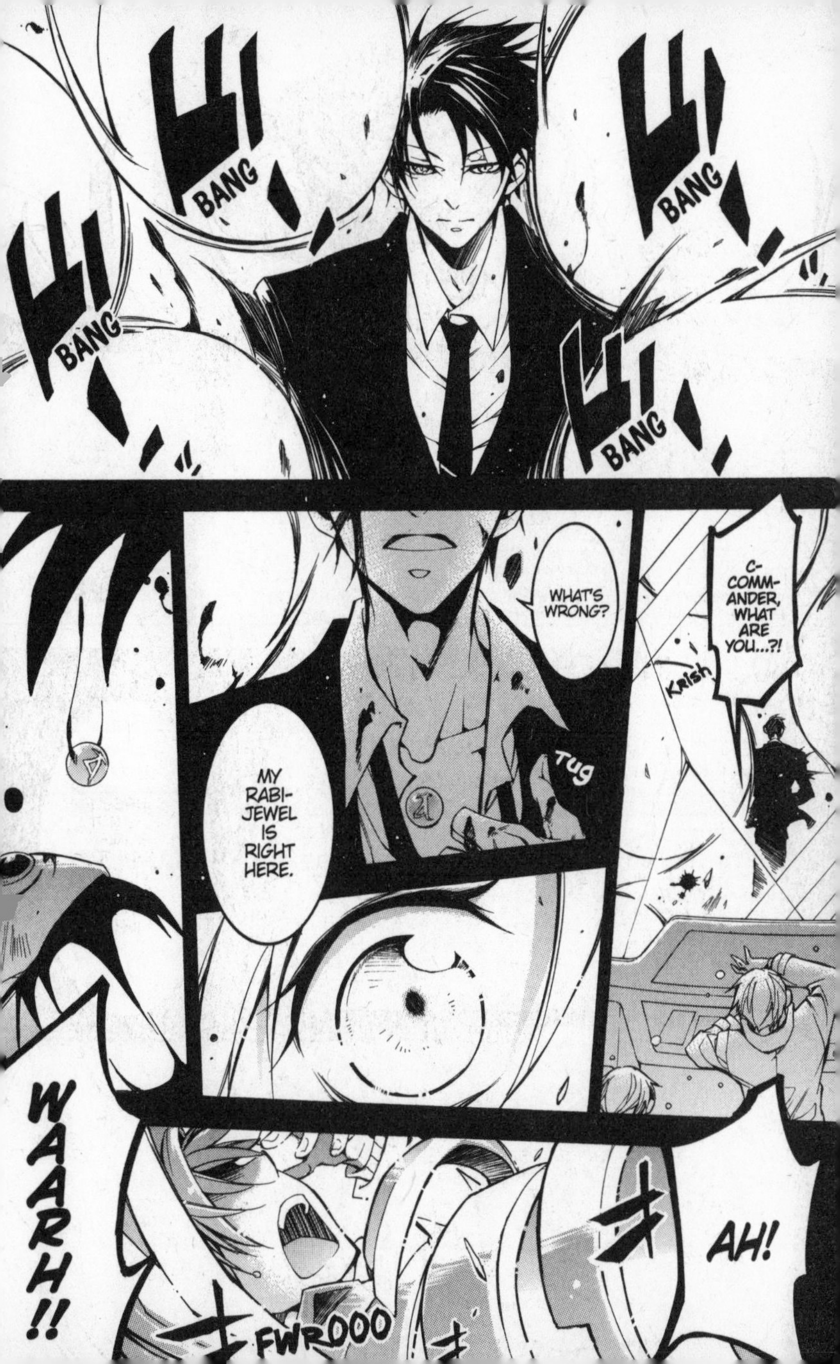
BANG
BANG
BANG
BANG
C-COMMANDER, WHAT ARE YOU...?!
Krish
WHAT'S WRONG?
Tug
MY RABI-JEWEL IS RIGHT HERE.
AH!
WAARRH!!
FWROOO

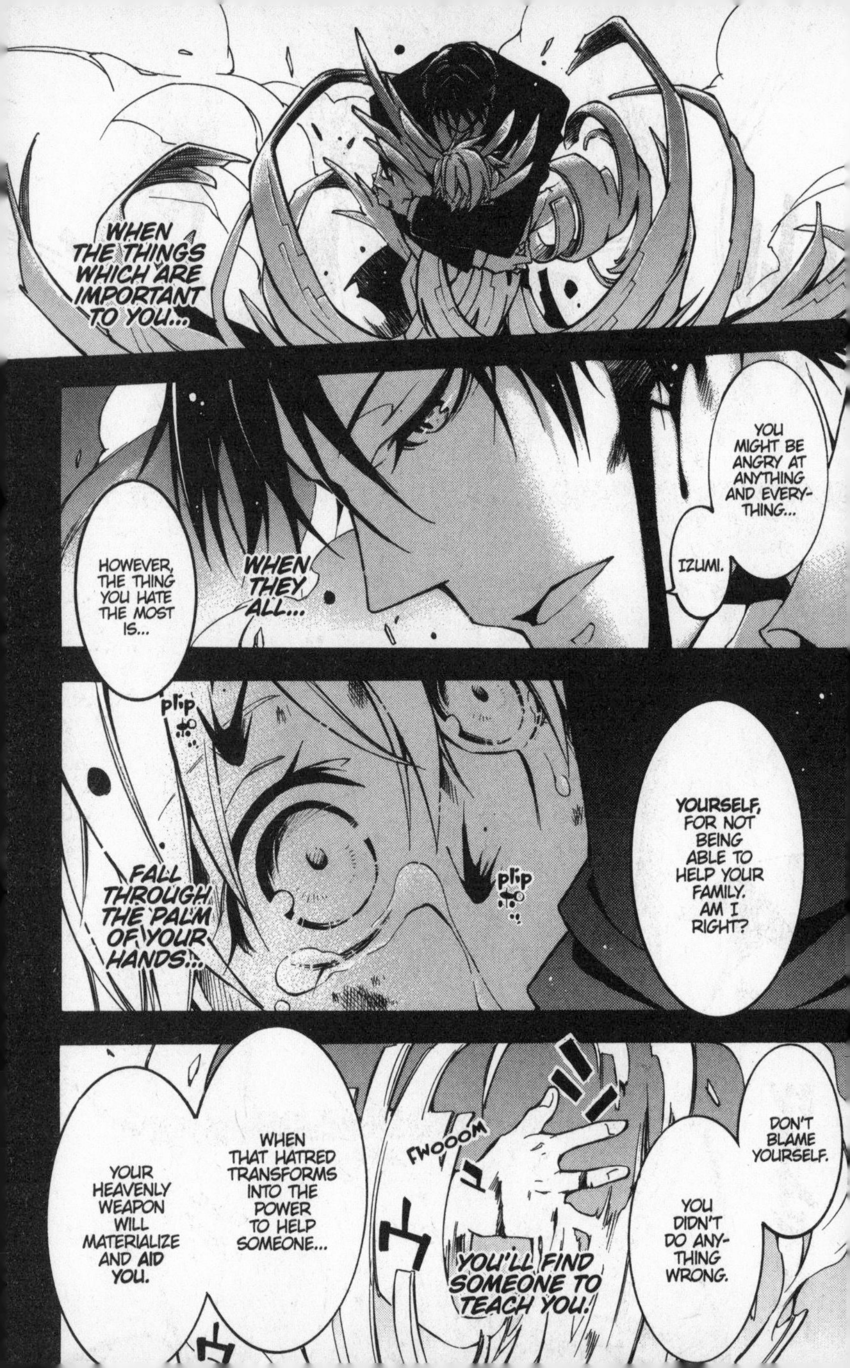
WHEN THE THINGS WHICH ARE IMPORTANT TO YOU...
YOU MIGHT BE ANGRY AT ANYTHING AND EVERY-THING...
IZUMI.
WHEN THEY ALL...
HOWEVER, THE THING YOU HATE THE MOST IS...
YOURSELF, FOR NOT BEING ABLE TO HELP YOUR FAMILY. AM I RIGHT?
plip
FALL THROUGH THE PALM OF YOUR HANDS...
plip
DON'T BLAME YOURSELF.
YOU DIDN'T DO ANY-THING WRONG.
FWOOOM
YOU'LL FIND SOMEONE TO TEACH YOU.
WHEN THAT HATRED TRANSFORMS INTO THE POWER TO HELP SOMEONE...
YOUR HEAVENLY WEAPON WILL MATERIALIZE AND AID YOU.

EVEN IF YOU LOSE EVERYTHING AND MORE...
YOU HAVE THE POWER TO LOVE PEOPLE.
KOTORI...
JOIN GENOU.
I WILL TEACH YOU HOW TO DEFEAT OGRES.
THEY WILL TEACH YOU THE VALUE OF LIVING ON.

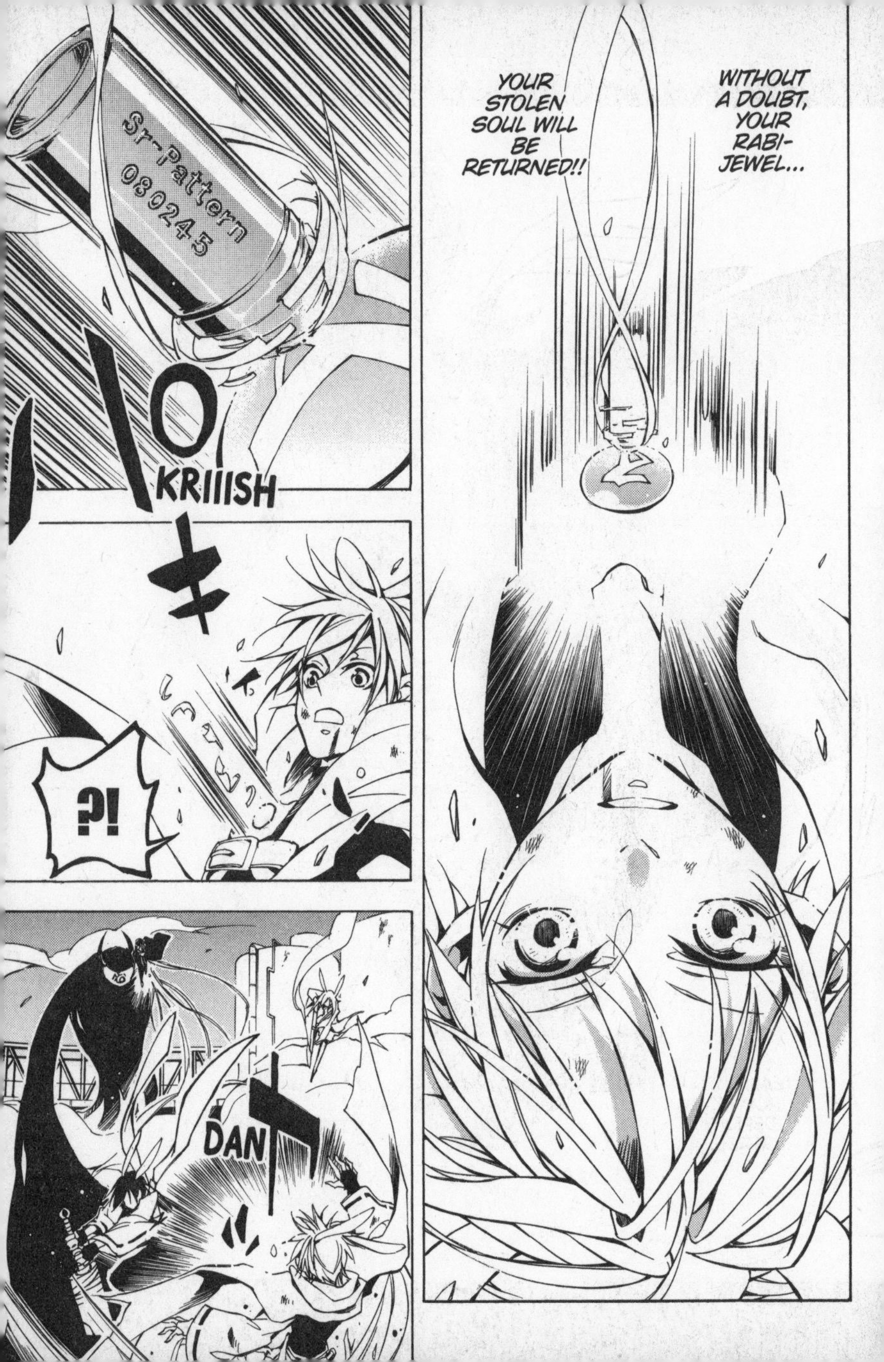
WITHOUT A DOUBT, YOUR RABI-JEWEL...
YOUR STOLEN SOUL WILL BE RETURNED!!
Sr-Pattern 080245
KRIIISH
?!
DANT

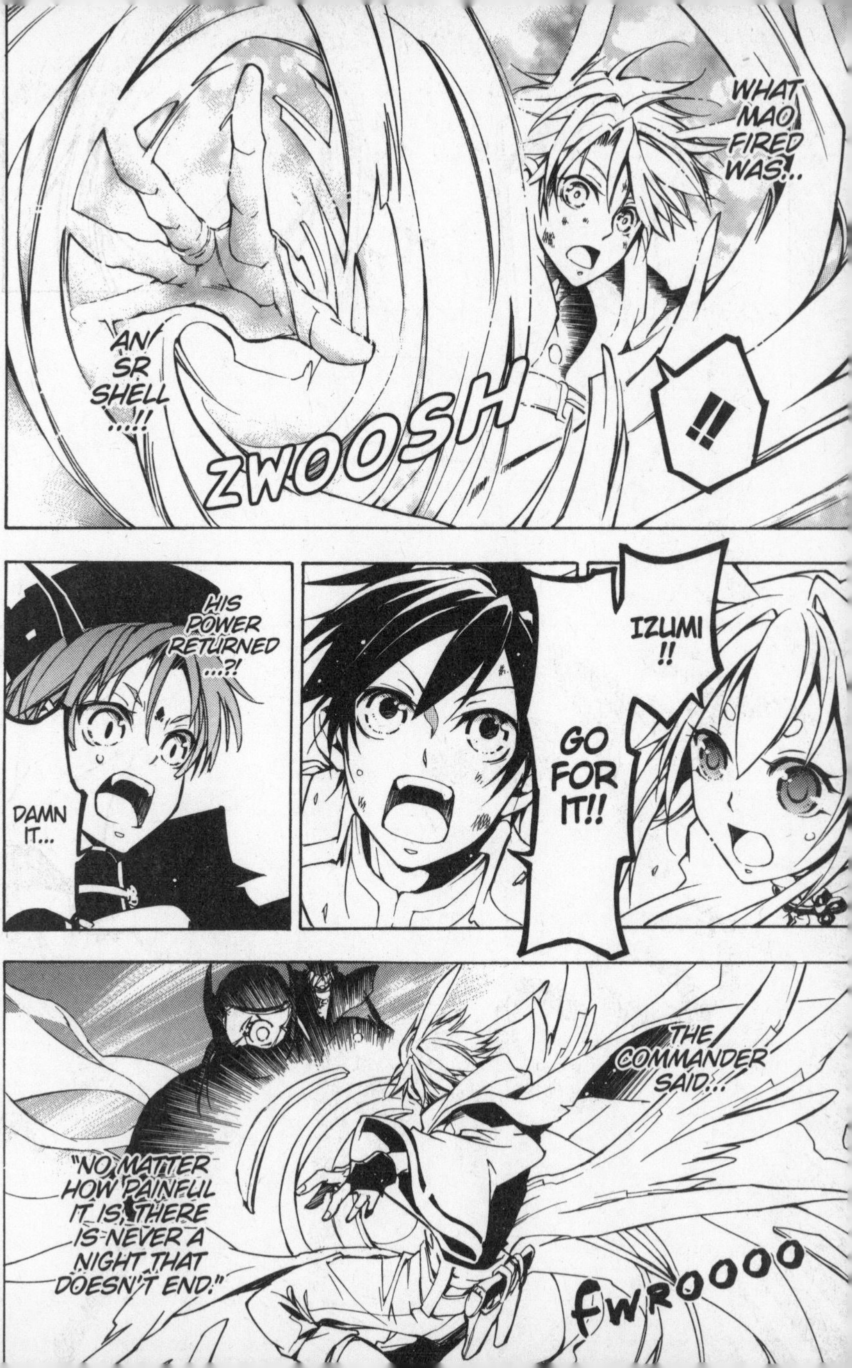

WHAT MAO FIRED WAS...
!!
AN SR SHELL...!!
ZWOOSH
IZUMI!!
GO FOR IT!!
HIS POWER RETURNED...?!
DAMN IT...
THE COMMANDER SAID...
"NO MATTER HOW PAINFUL IT IS, THERE IS NEVER A NIGHT THAT DOESN'T END."
FWROOOO

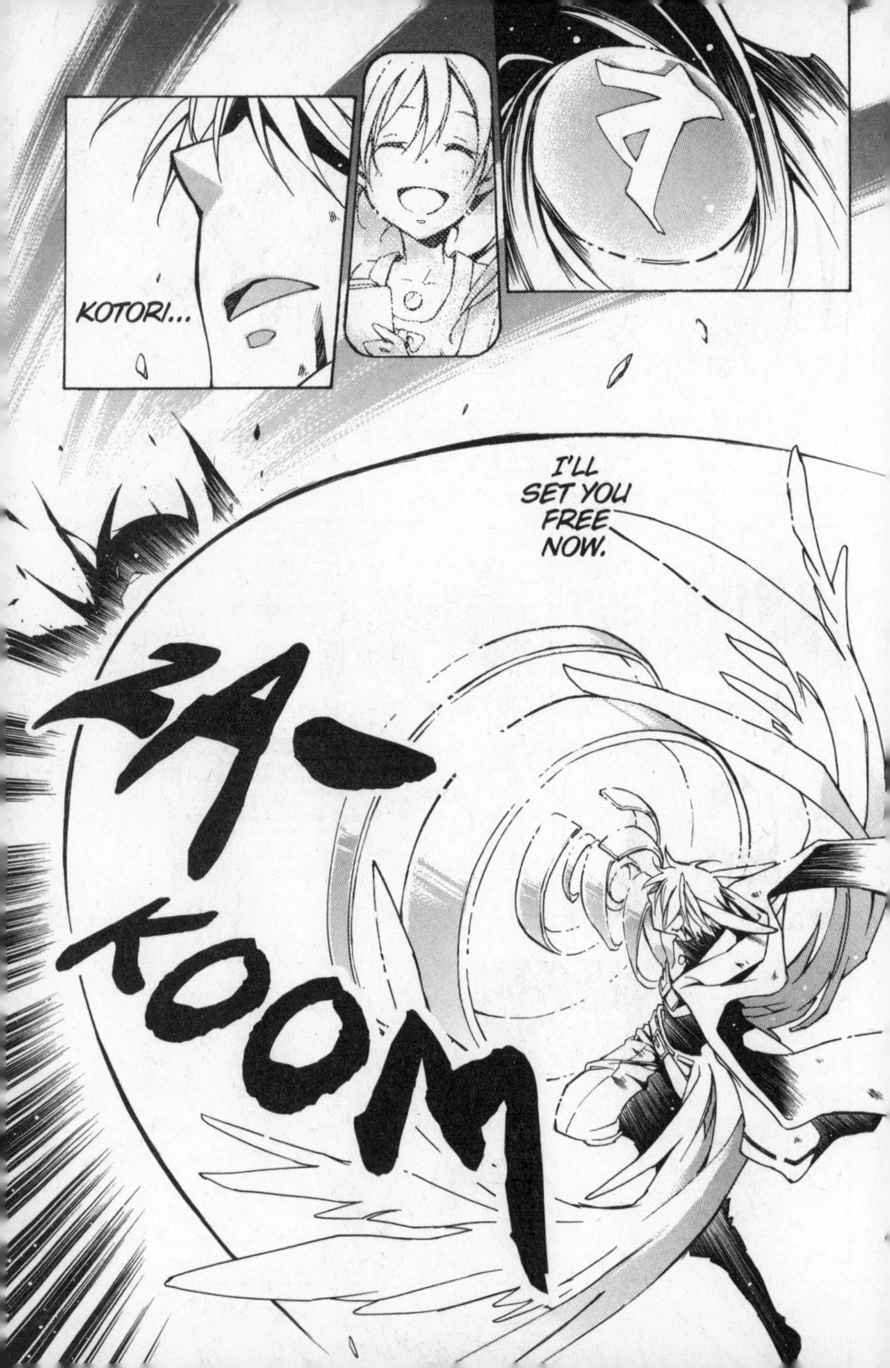
KOTORI...
I'LL SET YOU FREE NOW.
ZA-KOOM

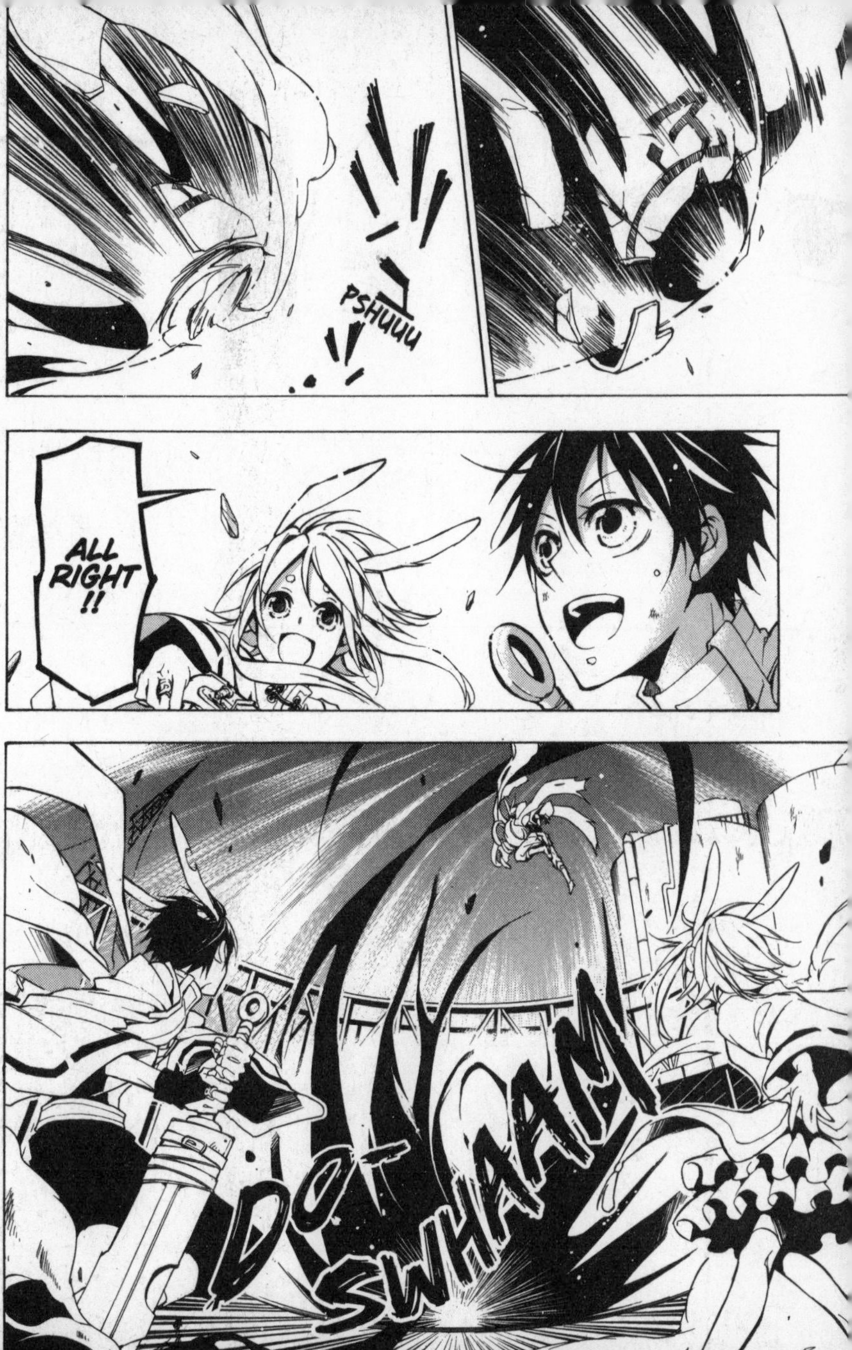
PSHUUU
ALL RIGHT!!
DO-SWHAAM

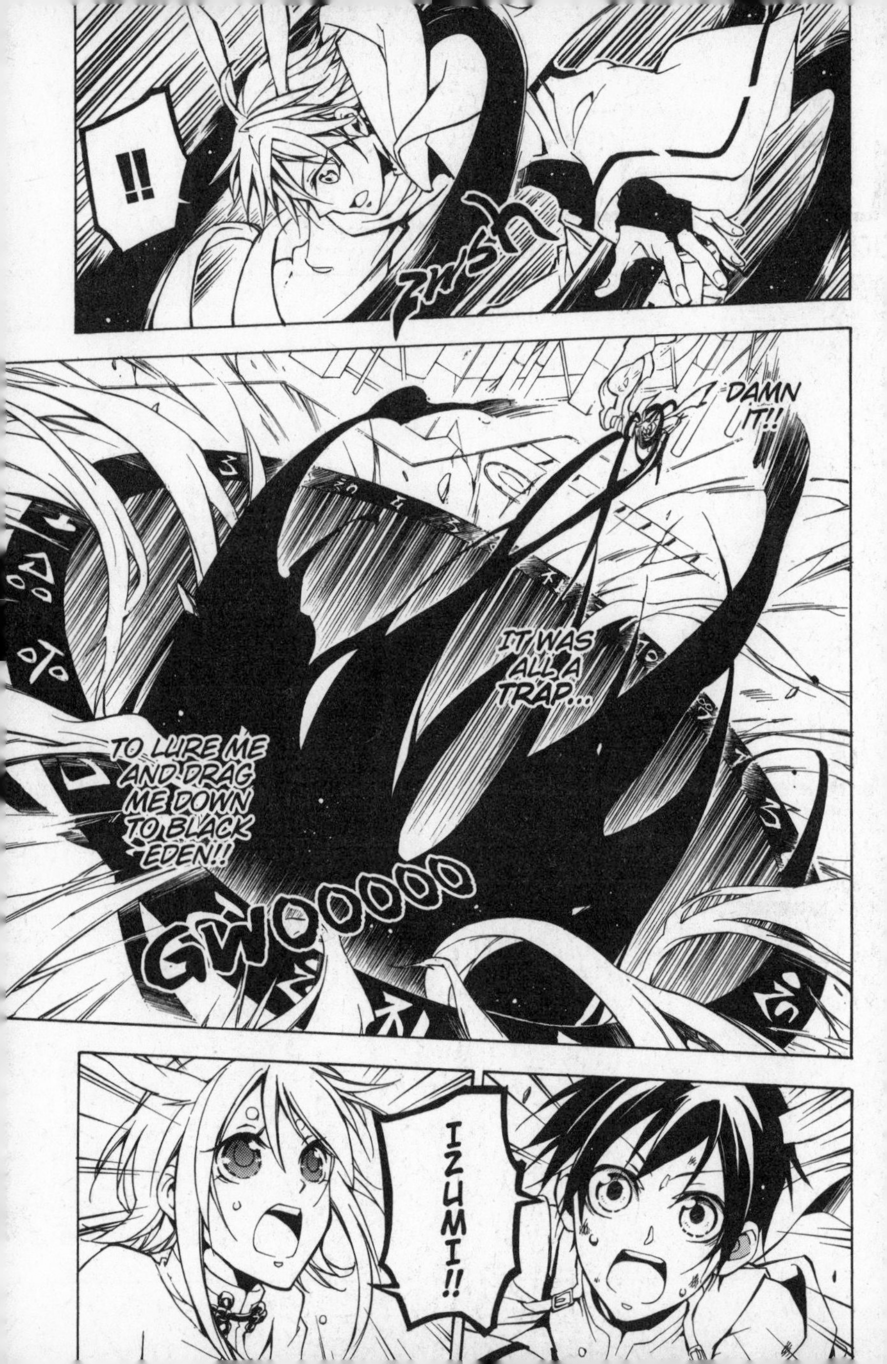
!!
DAMN IT!!
IT WAS ALL A TRAP...
TO LURE ME AND DRAG ME DOWN TO BLACK EDEN!!
GWOOOOO
IZUMI!!

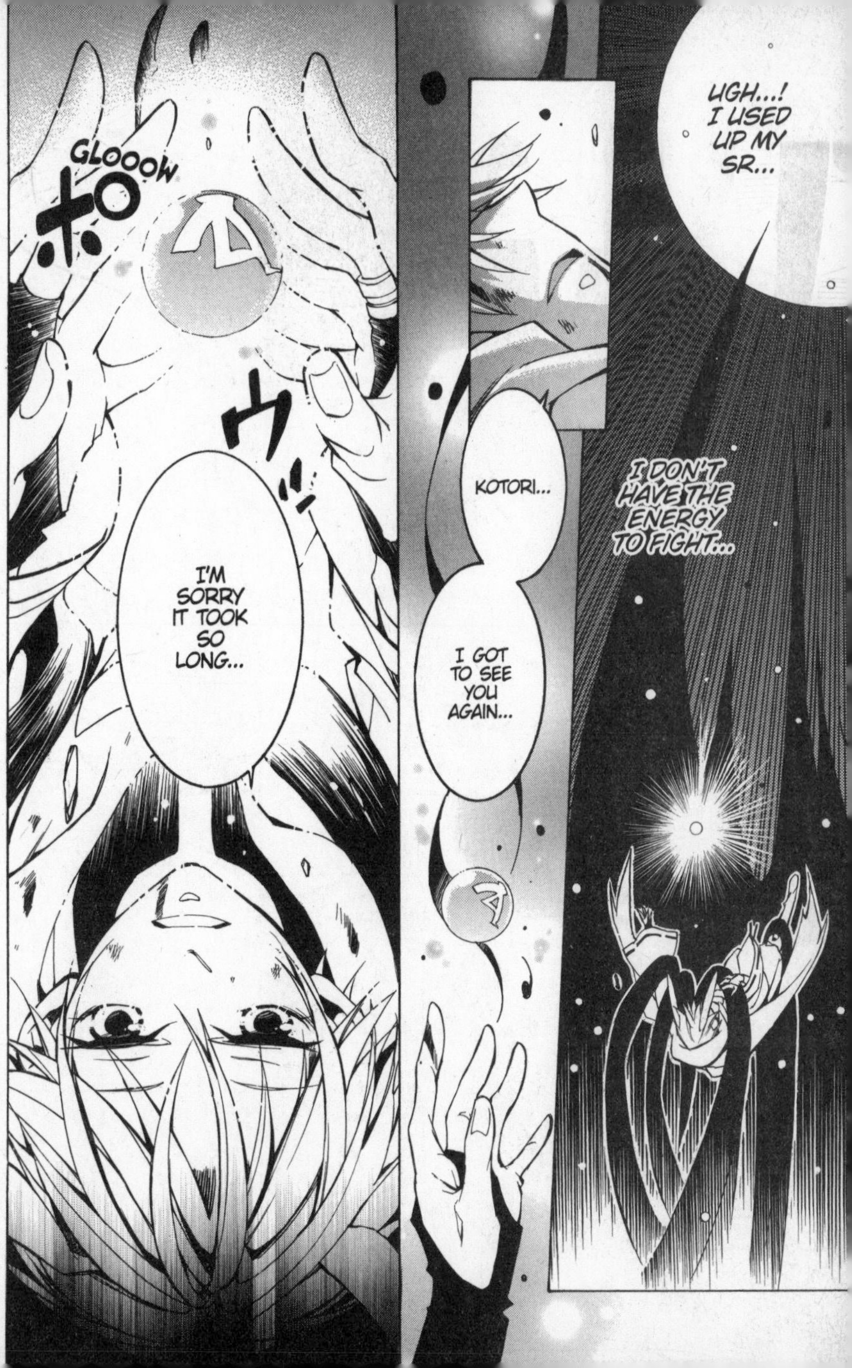
UGH...! I USED UP MY SR...
I DON'T HAVE THE ENERGY TO FIGHT...
KOTORI...
I GOT TO SEE YOU AGAIN...
GLOOOW
I'M SORRY IT TOOK SO LONG...

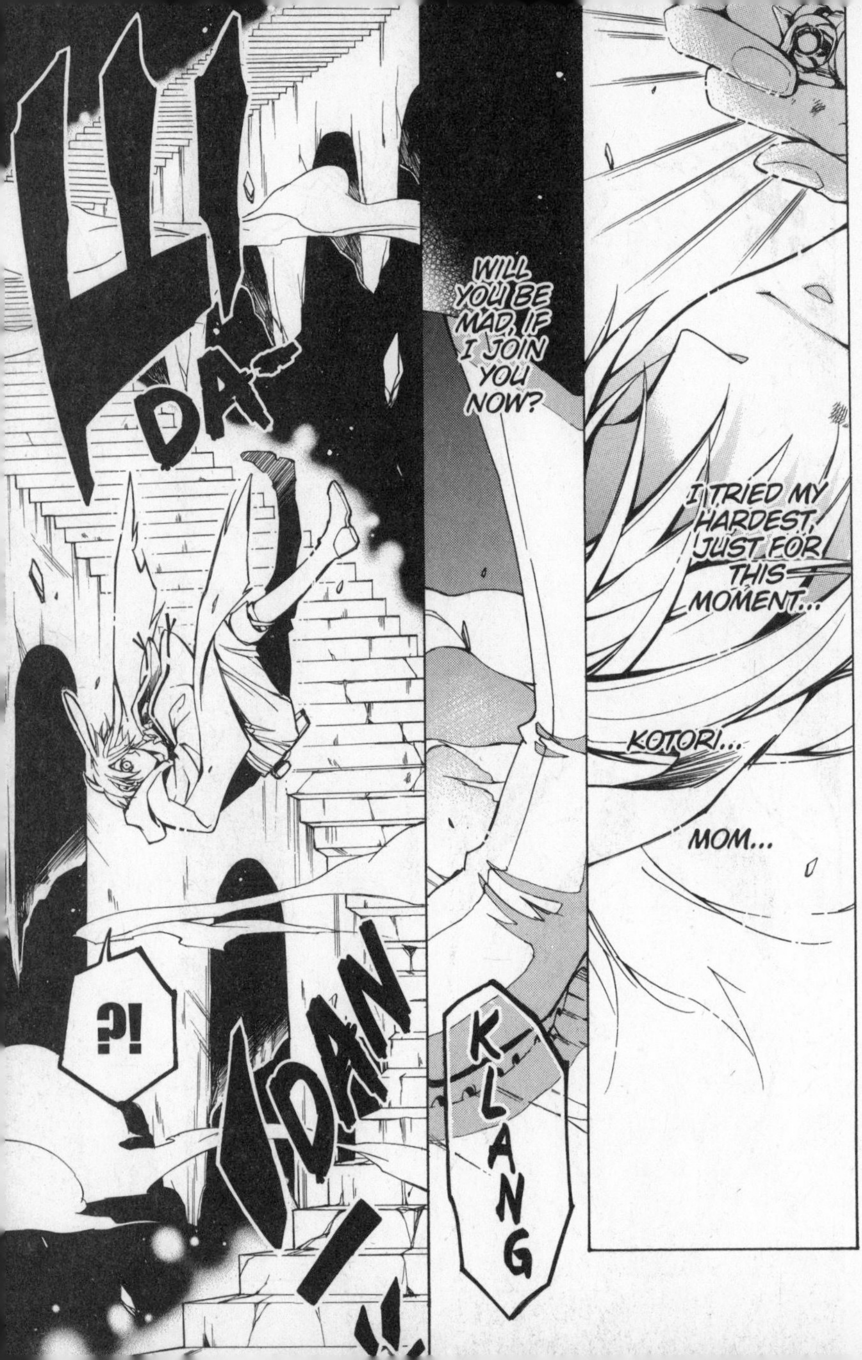
I TRIED MY HARDEST, JUST FOR THIS MOMENT...
KOTORI...
MOM...
WILL YOU BE MAD, IF I JOIN YOU NOW?
KLANG
DA
?!
DAN

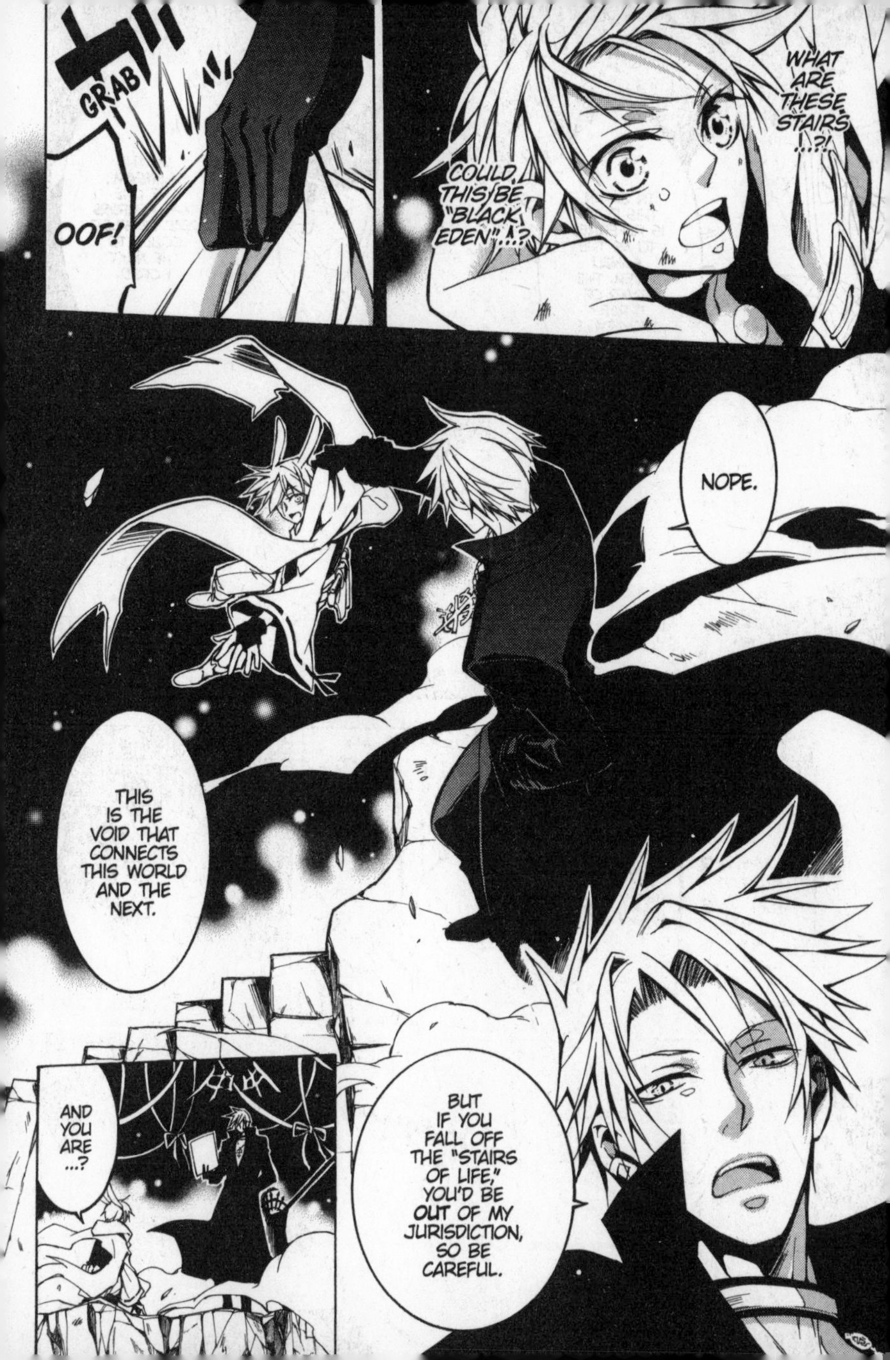
WHAT ARE THESE STAIRS ...?!
COULD THIS BE "BLACK EDEN"...?
GRAB
OOF!
NOPE.
THIS IS THE VOID THAT CONNECTS THIS WORLD AND THE NEXT.
BUT IF YOU FALL OFF THE "STAIRS OF LIFE," YOU'D BE OUT OF MY JURISDICTION, SO BE CAREFUL.
AND YOU ARE ...?

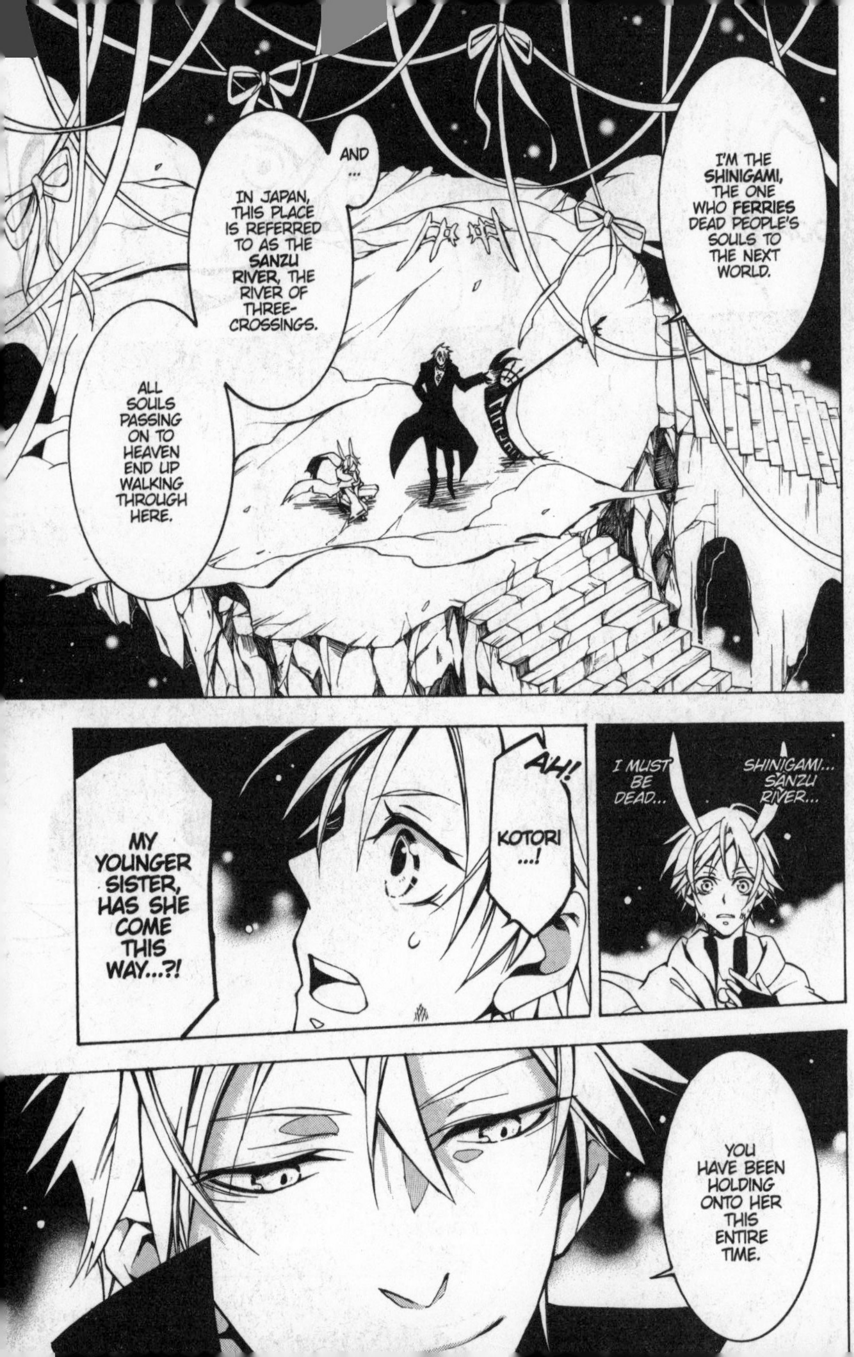
I'M THE SHINIGAMI, THE ONE WHO FERRIES DEAD PEOPLE'S SOULS TO THE NEXT WORLD.
AND ...
IN JAPAN, THIS PLACE IS REFERRED TO AS THE SANZU RIVER, THE RIVER OF THREE-CROSSINGS.
ALL SOULS PASSING ON TO HEAVEN END UP WALKING THROUGH HERE.
SHINIGAMI... SANZU RIVER...
I MUST BE DEAD...
AH!
KOTORI ...!
MY YOUNGER SISTER, HAS SHE COME THIS WAY...?!
YOU HAVE BEEN HOLDING ONTO HER THIS ENTIRE TIME.

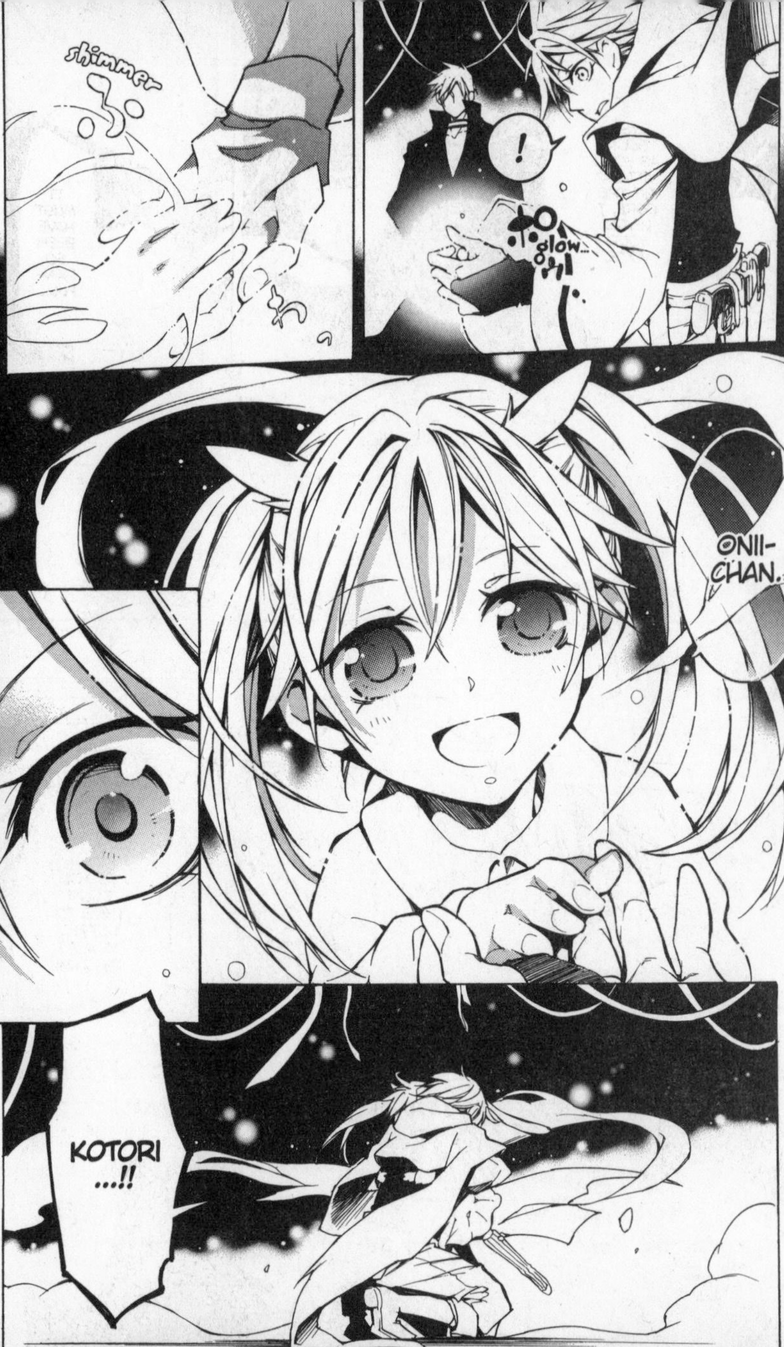
!
glow...
shimmer
ONII-CHAN...
KOTORI ...!!

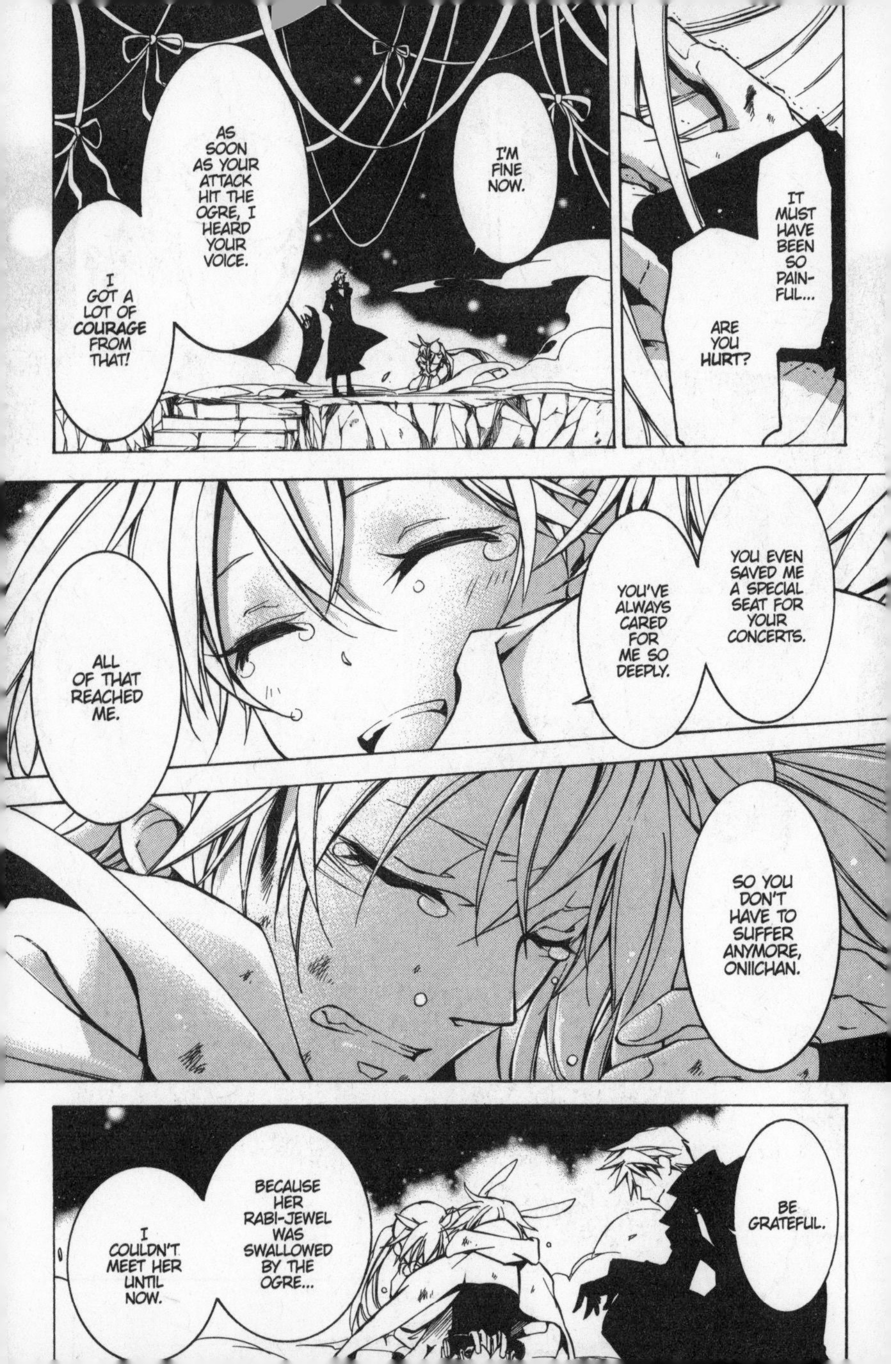
IT MUST HAVE BEEN SO PAINFUL...
ARE YOU HURT?
I'M FINE NOW.
AS SOON AS YOUR ATTACK HIT THE OGRE, I HEARD YOUR VOICE.
I GOT A LOT OF COURAGE FROM THAT!
YOU EVEN SAVED ME A SPECIAL SEAT FOR YOUR CONCERTS.
YOU'VE ALWAYS CARED FOR ME SO DEEPLY.
ALL OF THAT REACHED ME.
SO YOU DON'T HAVE TO SUFFER ANYMORE, ONIICHAN.
BE GRATEFUL.
BECAUSE HER RABI-JEWEL WAS SWALLOWED BY THE OGRE...
I COULDN'T MEET HER UNTIL NOW.

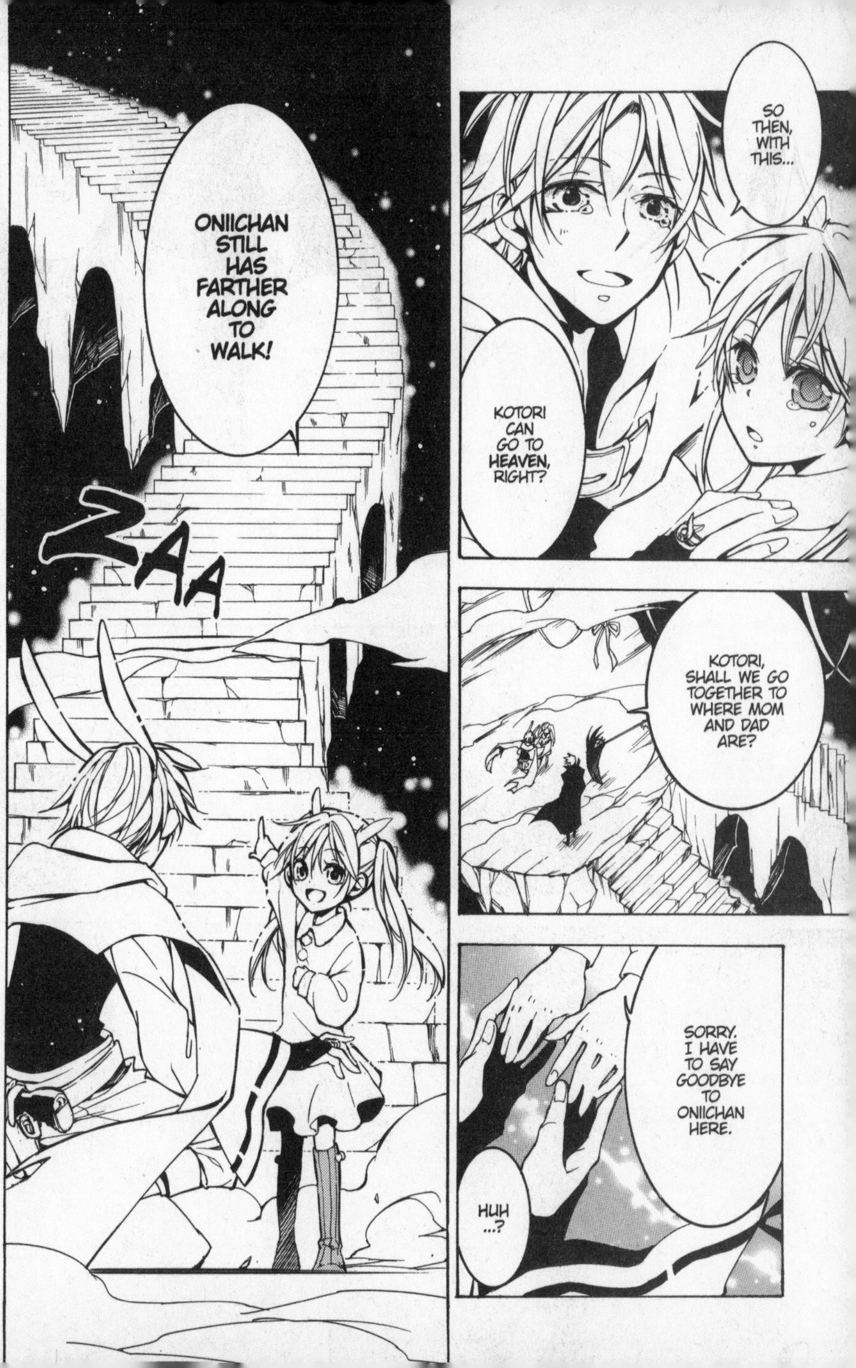
SO THEN, WITH THIS...
KOTORI CAN GO TO HEAVEN, RIGHT?
KOTORI, SHALL WE GO TOGETHER TO WHERE MOM AND DAD ARE?
SORRY. I HAVE TO SAY GOODBYE TO ONIICHAN HERE.
HUH ...?
ONIICHAN STILL HAS FARTHER ALONG TO WALK!
ZAA

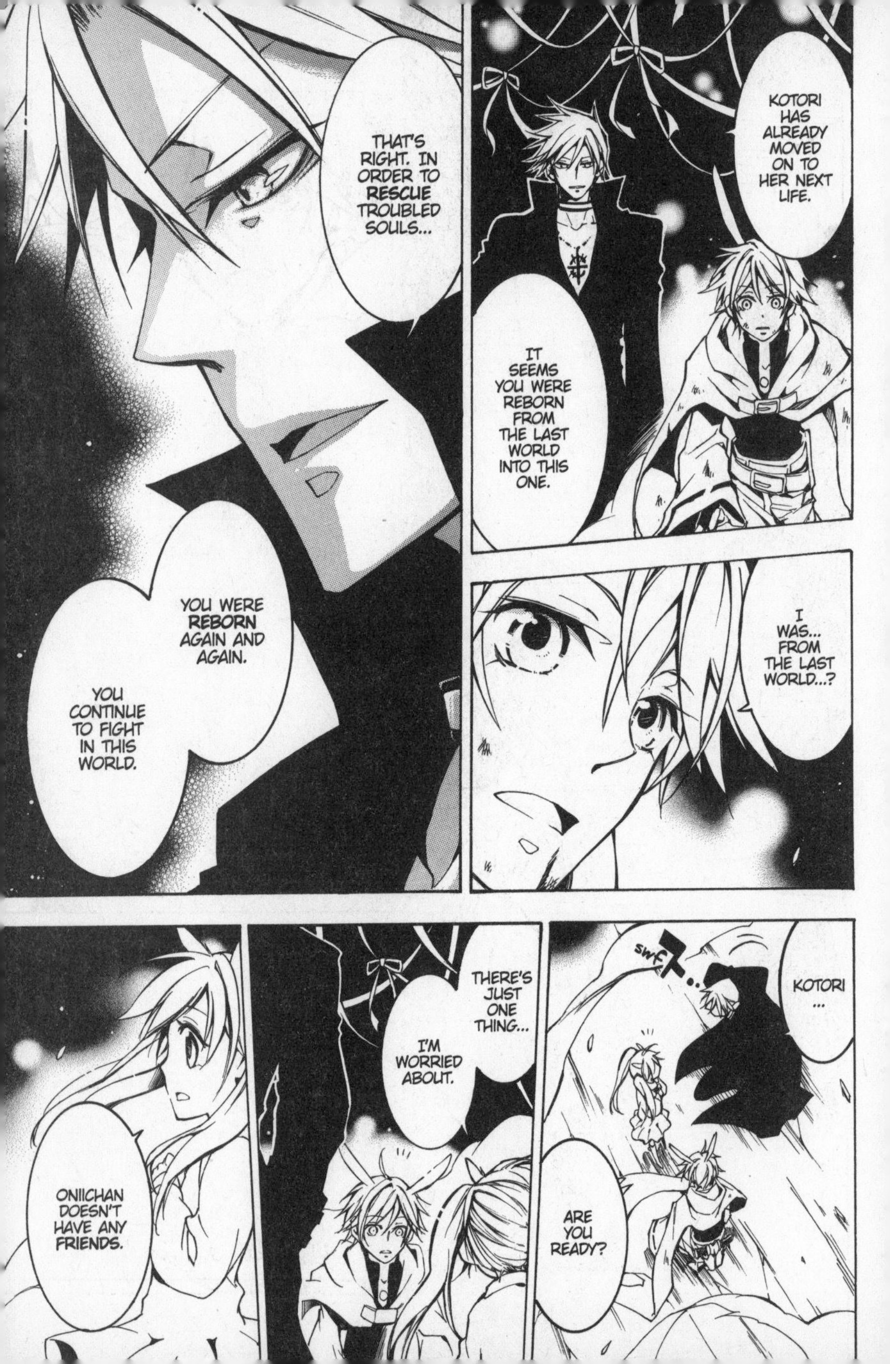
KOTORI HAS ALREADY MOVED ON TO HER NEXT LIFE.
IT SEEMS YOU WERE REBORN FROM THE LAST WORLD INTO THIS ONE.
I WAS... FROM THE LAST WORLD...?
THAT'S RIGHT. IN ORDER TO RESCUE TROUBLED SOULS...
YOU WERE REBORN AGAIN AND AGAIN.
YOU CONTINUE TO FIGHT IN THIS WORLD.
KOTORI ...
swf
ARE YOU READY?
THERE'S JUST ONE THING...
I'M WORRIED ABOUT.
ONIICHAN DOESN'T HAVE ANY FRIENDS.

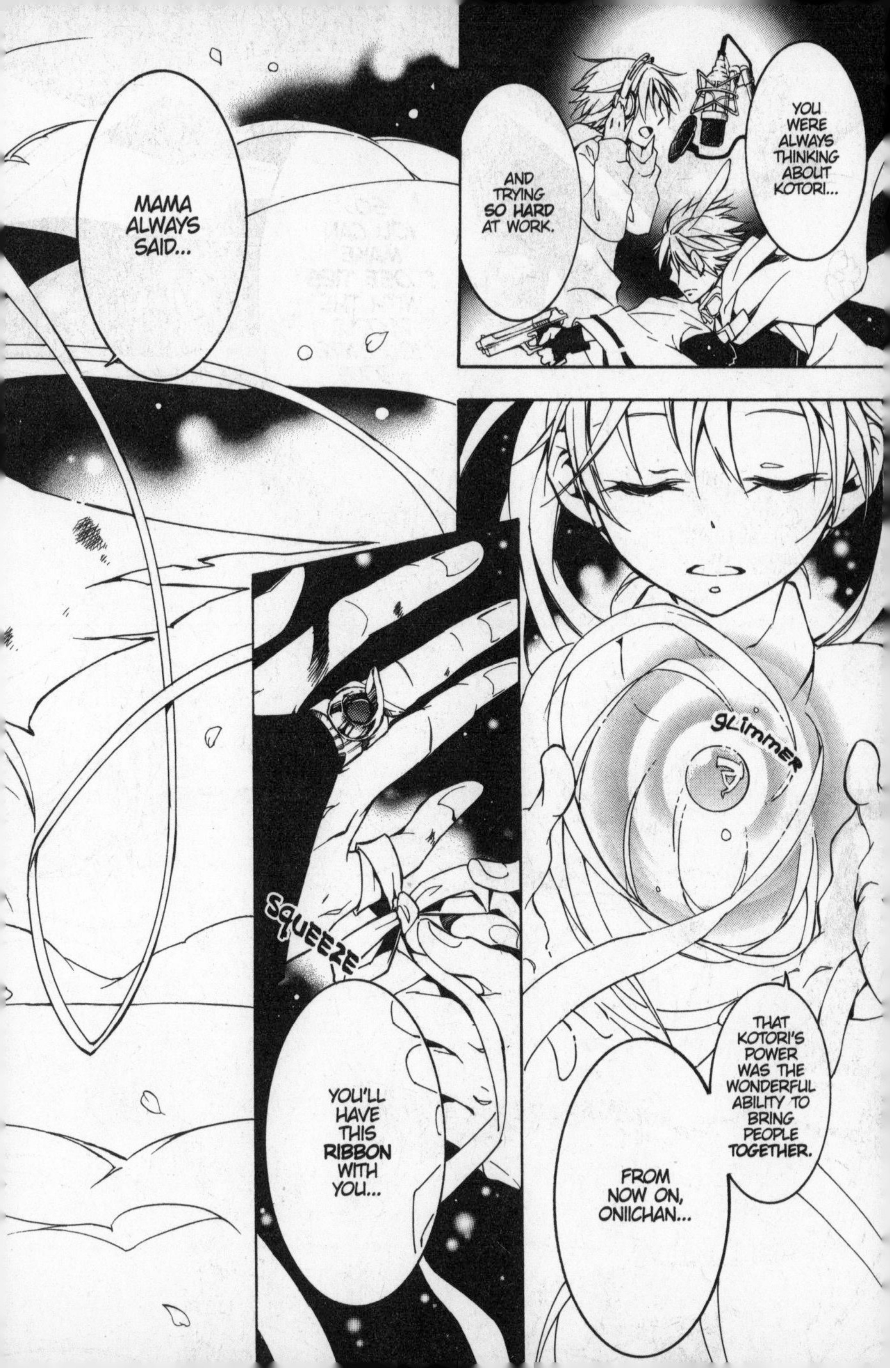
YOU WERE ALWAYS THINKING ABOUT KOTORI...
AND TRYING SO HARD AT WORK.
MAMA ALWAYS SAID...
GLIMMER
THAT KOTORI'S POWER WAS THE WONDERFUL ABILITY TO BRING PEOPLE TOGETHER.
FROM NOW ON, ONIICHAN...
SQUEEZE
YOU'LL HAVE THIS RIBBON WITH YOU...

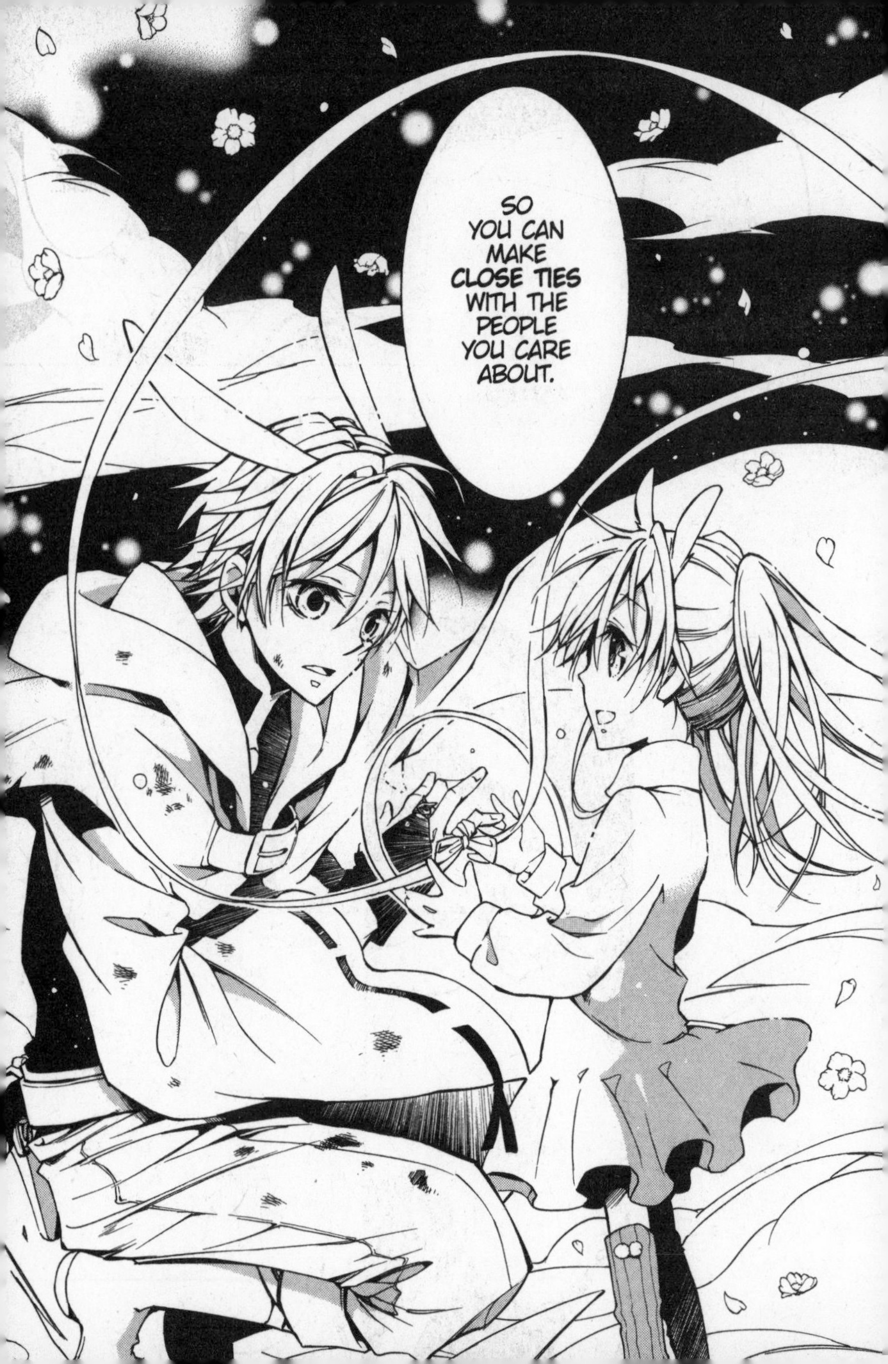
SO YOU CAN MAKE CLOSE TIES WITH THE PEOPLE YOU CARE ABOUT.

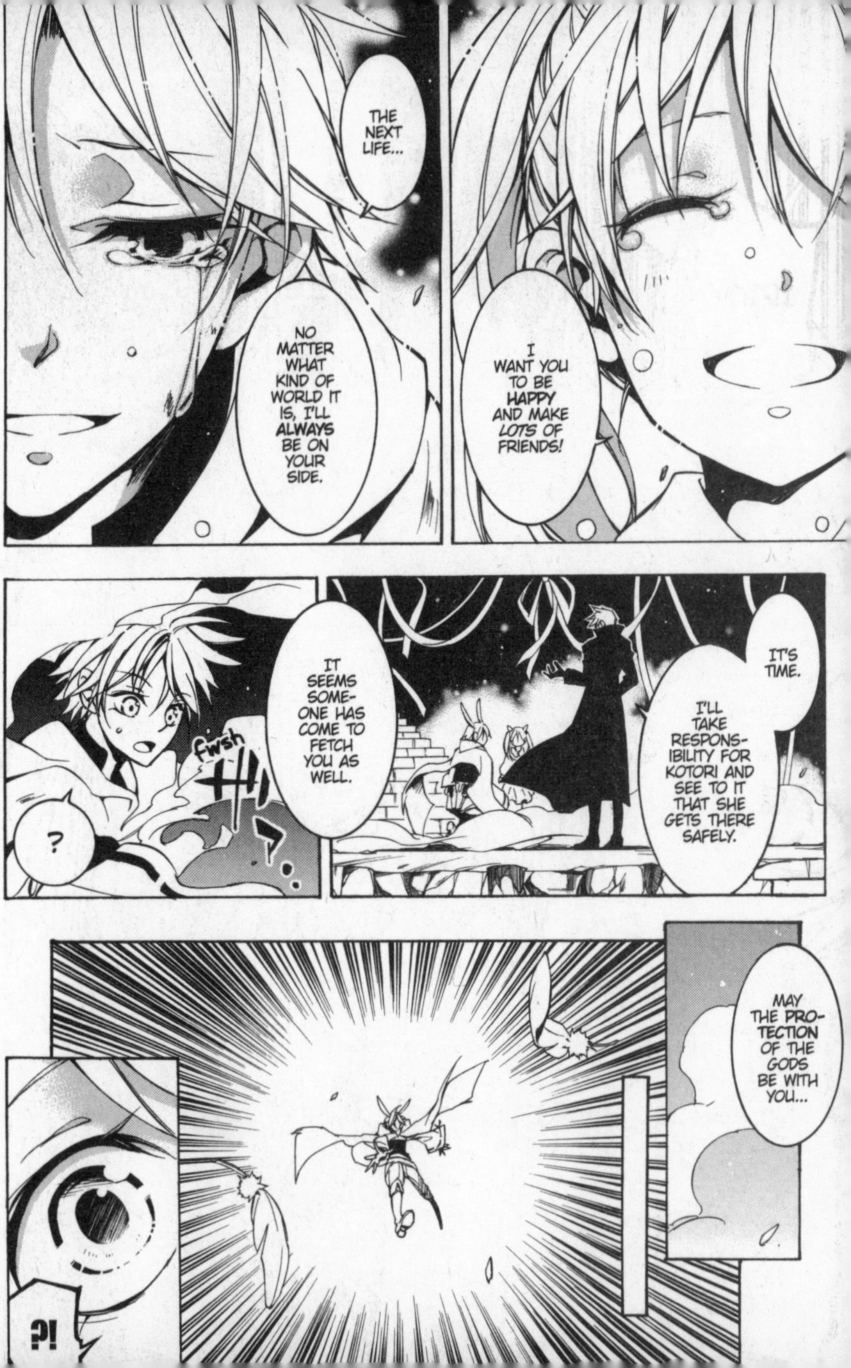

I WANT YOU TO BE HAPPY AND MAKE LOTS OF FRIENDS!
THE NEXT LIFE...
NO MATTER WHAT KIND OF WORLD IT IS, I'LL ALWAYS BE ON YOUR SIDE.
IT'S TIME.
I'LL TAKE RESPONSIBILITY FOR KOTORI AND SEE TO IT THAT SHE GETS THERE SAFELY.
IT SEEMS SOMEONE HAS COME TO FETCH YOU AS WELL.
fwsh
?
MAY THE PROTECTION OF THE GODS BE WITH YOU...
?!

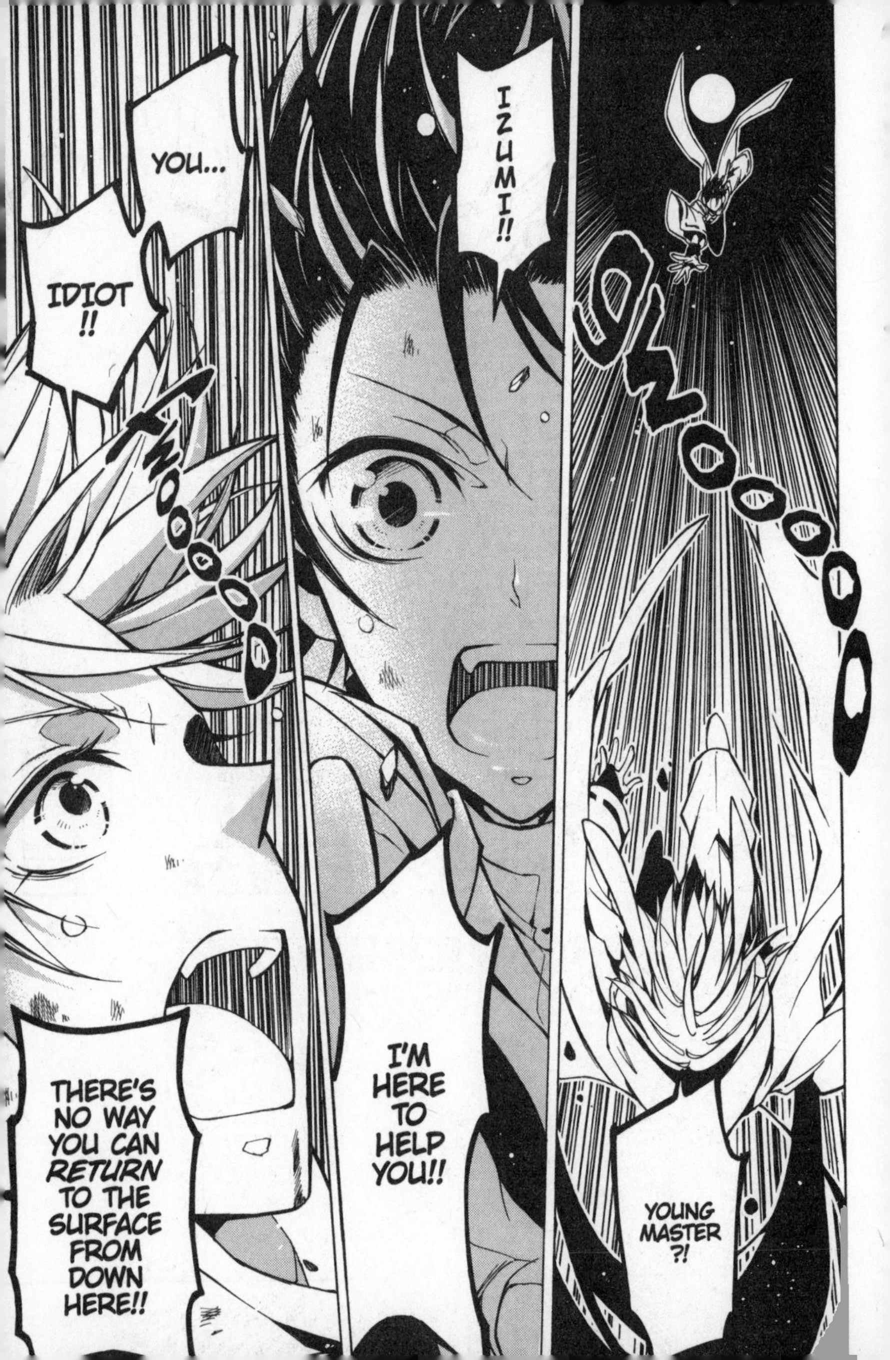
YOUNG MASTER?!
IZUMI!!
I'M HERE TO HELP YOU!!
YOU...
IDIOT!!
THERE'S NO WAY YOU CAN *RETURN* TO THE SURFACE FROM DOWN HERE!!

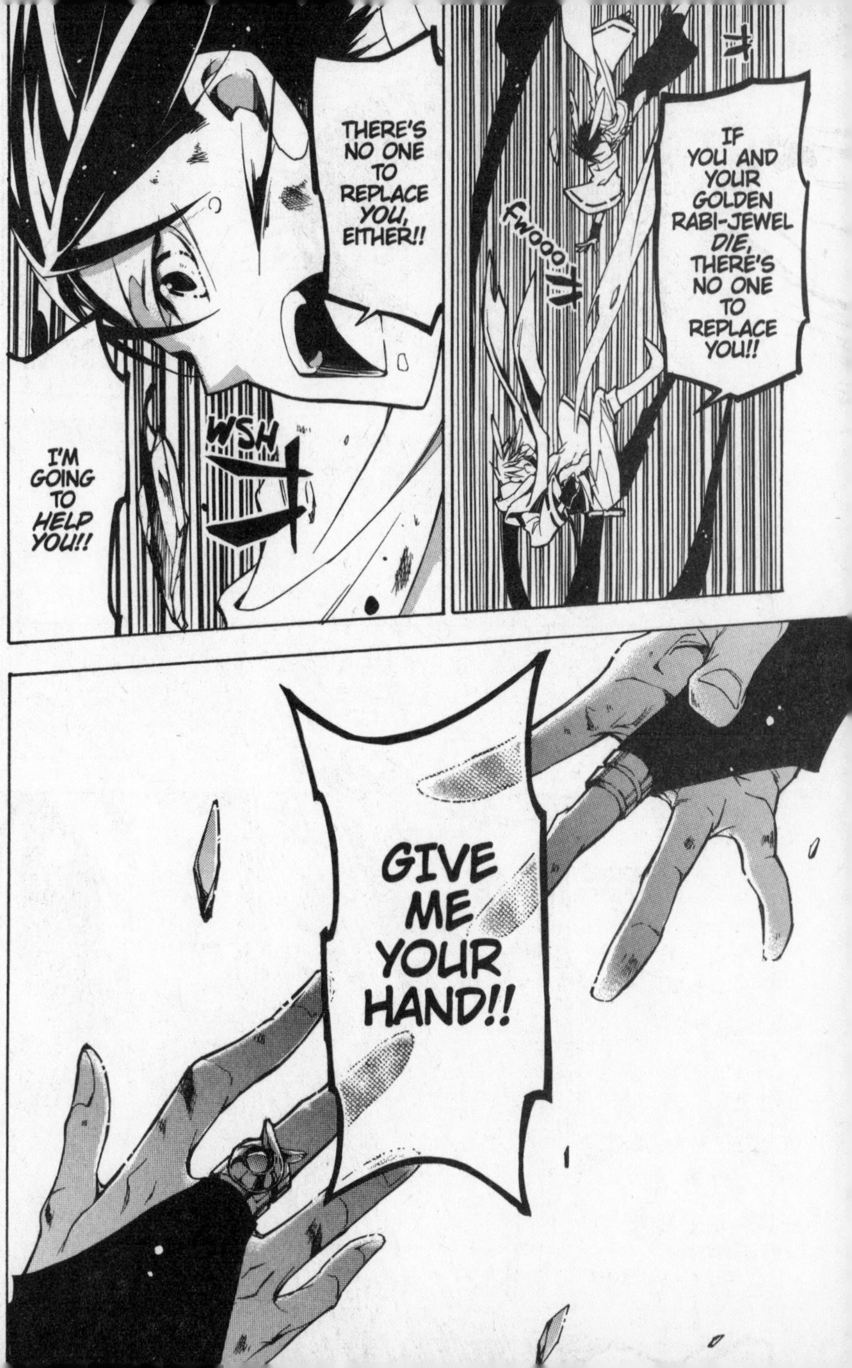
IF YOU AND YOUR GOLDEN RABI-JEWEL DIE, THERE'S NO ONE TO REPLACE YOU!!
fwooo
THERE'S NO ONE TO REPLACE YOU, EITHER!!
WSH
I'M GOING TO HELP YOU!!
GIVE ME YOUR HAND!!

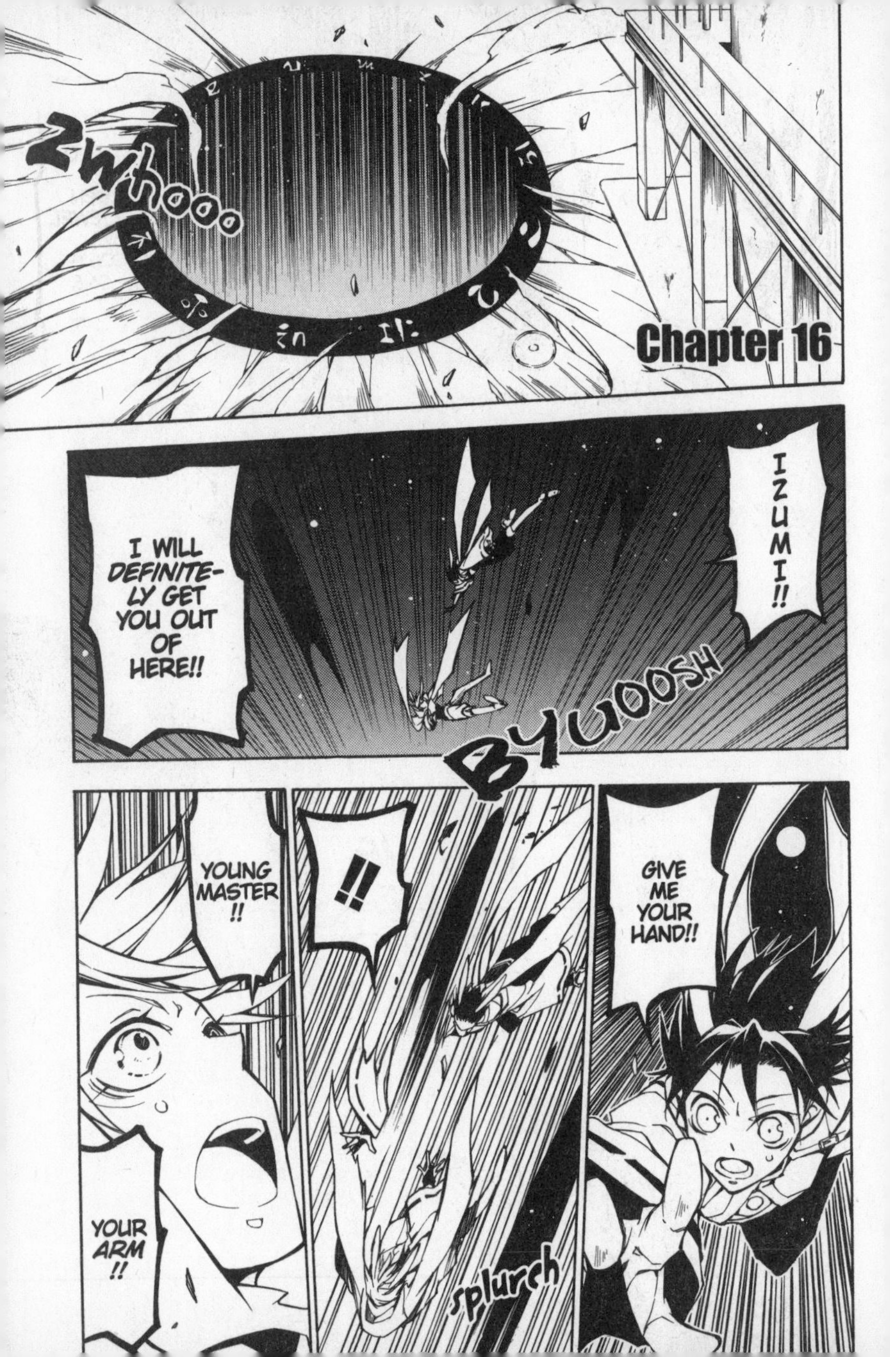
Chapter 16
Zwhooo
IZUMI!!
BYUOOSH
I WILL DEFINITE-LY GET YOU OUT OF HERE!!
GIVE ME YOUR HAND!!
!!
splurch
YOUNG MASTER!!
YOUR ARM!!

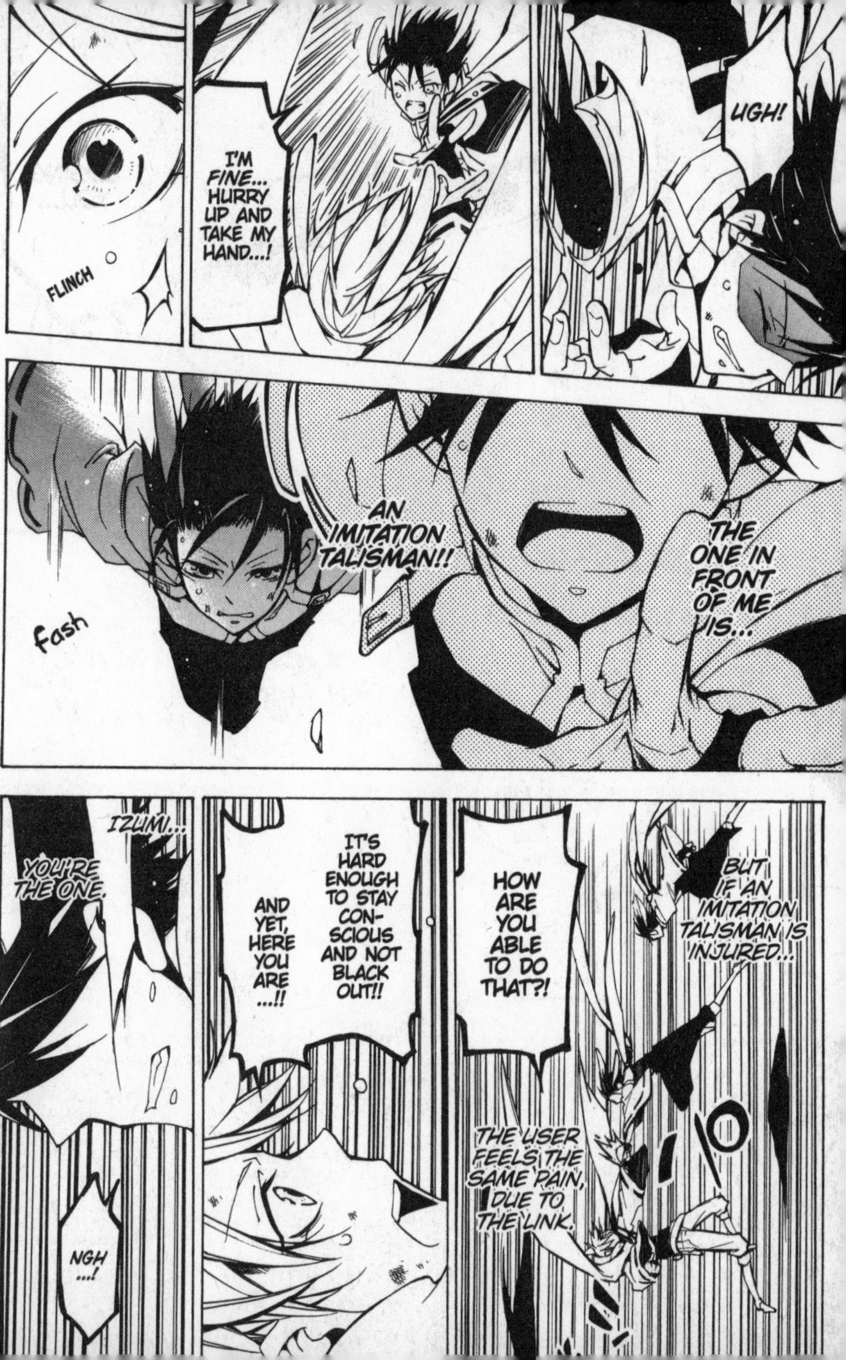
UGH!
I'M FINE... HURRY UP AND TAKE MY HAND...!
FLINCH
THE ONE IN FRONT OF ME IS...
AN IMITATION TALISMAN!!
fash
BUT IF AN IMITATION TALISMAN IS INJURED...
THE USER FEELS THE SAME PAIN, DUE TO THE LINK.
HOW ARE YOU ABLE TO DO THAT?!
IT'S HARD ENOUGH TO STAY CON-SCIOUS AND NOT BLACK OUT!!
AND YET, HERE YOU ARE...!!
IZUMI...
YOU'RE THE ONE.
NGH...!

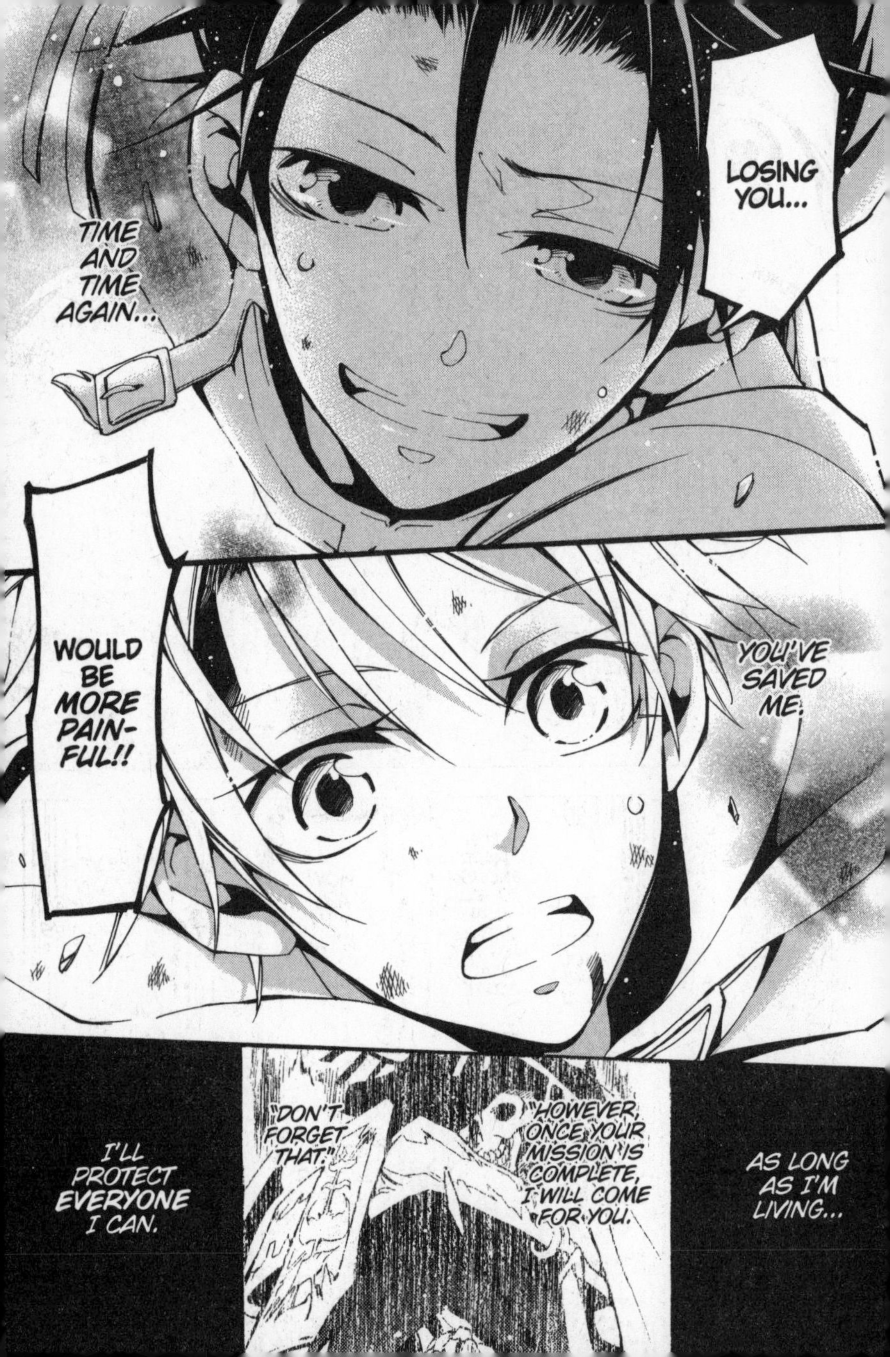
LOSING YOU...
TIME AND TIME AGAIN...
YOU'VE SAVED ME.
WOULD BE MORE PAIN-FUL!!
AS LONG AS I'M LIVING...
"HOWEVER, ONCE YOUR MISSION IS COMPLETE, I WILL COME FOR YOU.
"DON'T FORGET THAT."
I'LL PROTECT EVERYONE I CAN.

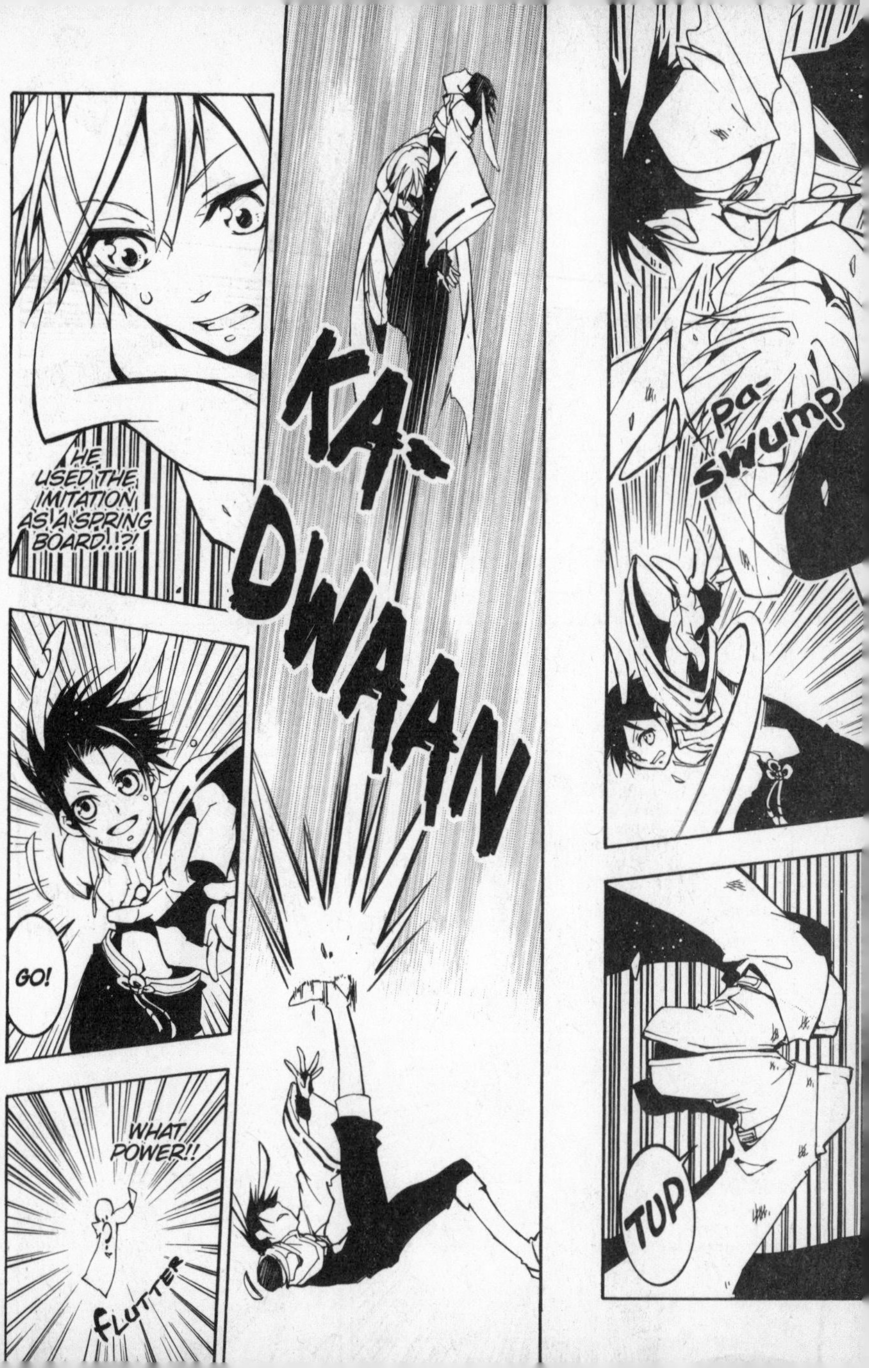

Pa-swump
TUP
KA-DWAAN
HE USED THE IMITATION AS A SPRING BOARD!..?!
GO!
WHAT POWER!!
FLUTTER

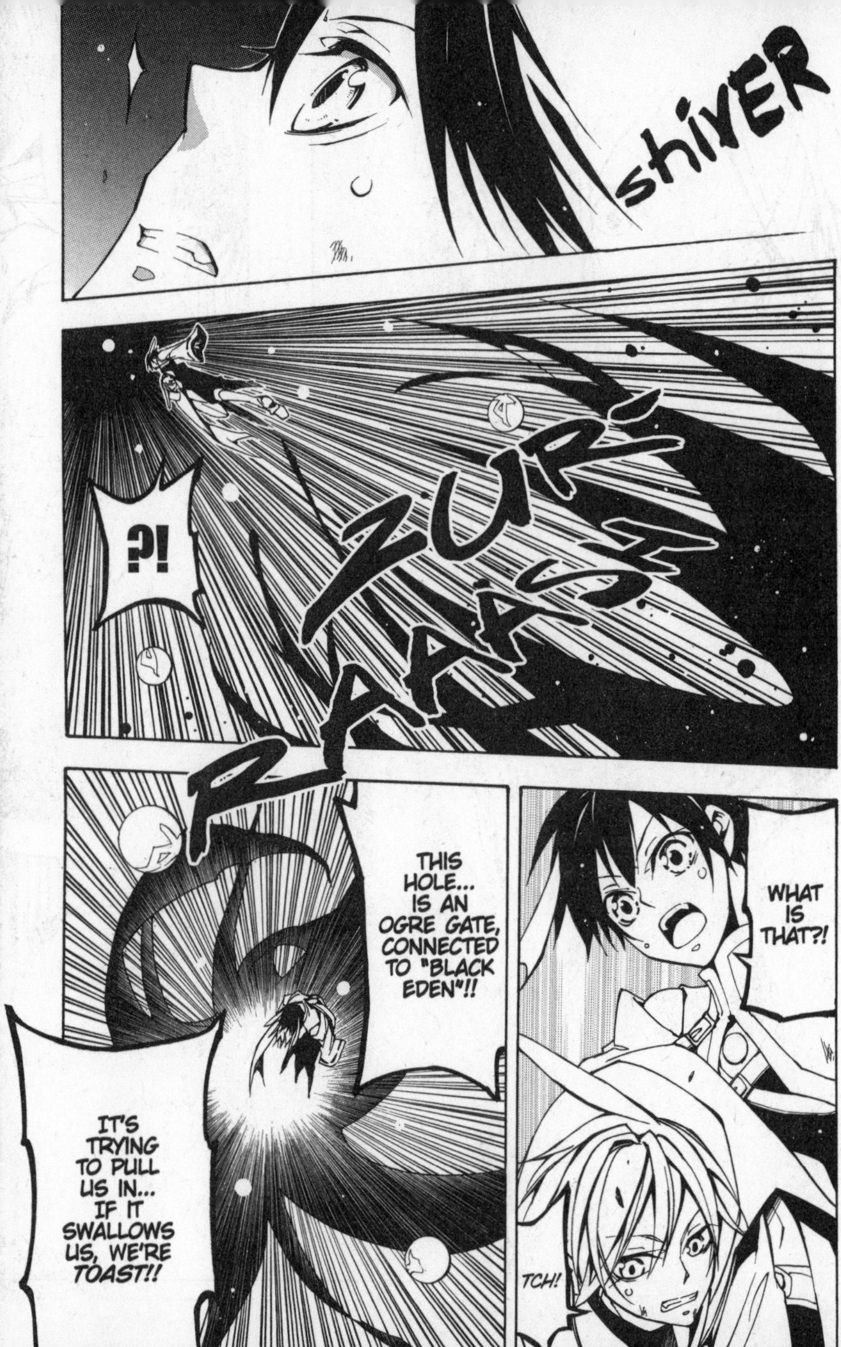
shiver
?!
ZURI
ZAAAS
WHAT IS THAT?!
TCH!
THIS HOLE... IS AN OGRE GATE, CONNECTED TO "BLACK EDEN"!!
IT'S TRYING TO PULL US IN... IF IT SWALLOWS US, WE'RE *TOAST*!!

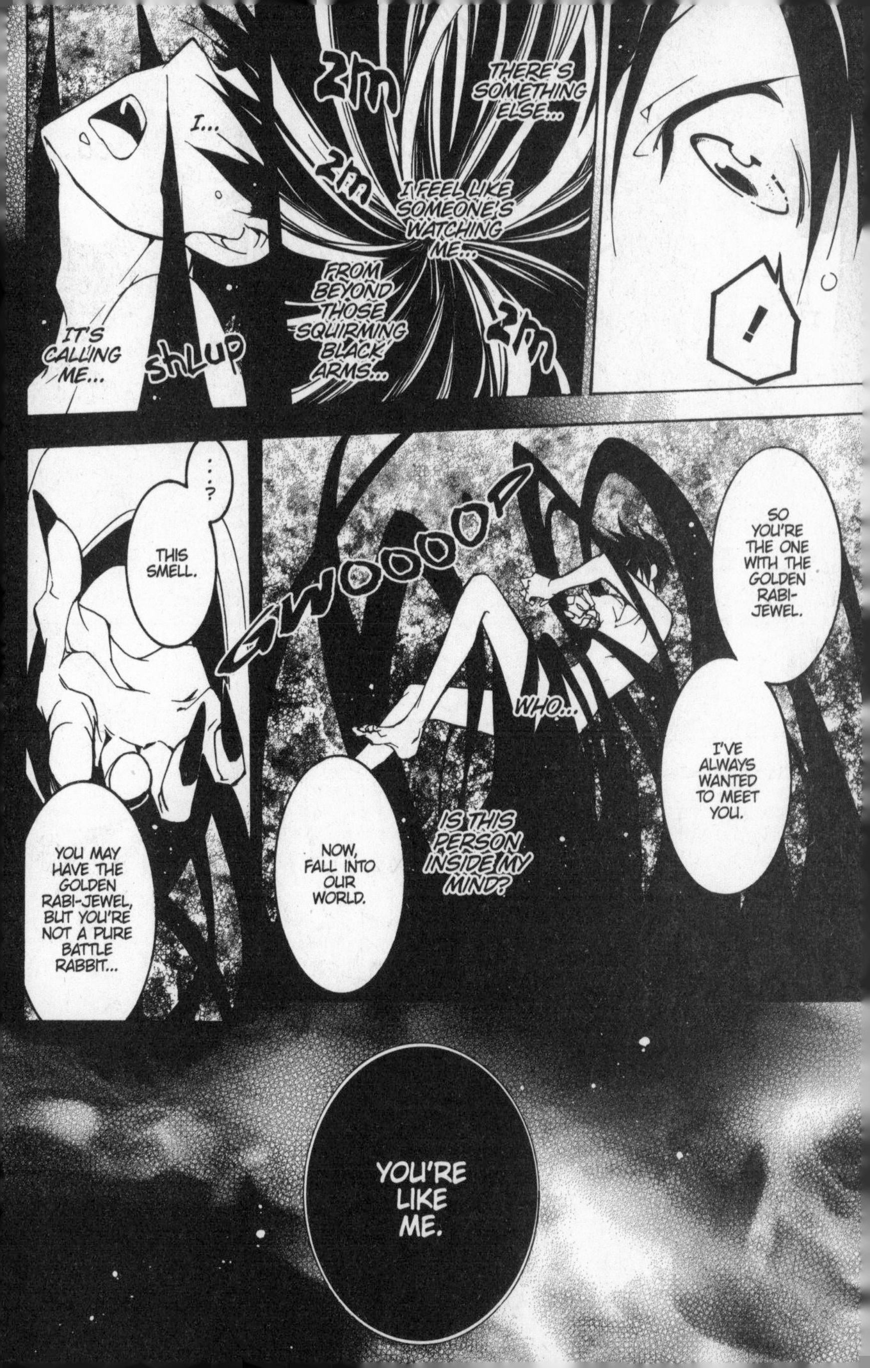
!
THERE'S SOMETHING ELSE...
zm
zm
I FEEL LIKE SOMEONE'S WATCHING ME...
FROM BEYOND THOSE SQUIRMING BLACK ARMS...
zm
I...
IT'S CALLING ME...
shLUP
SO YOU'RE THE ONE WITH THE GOLDEN RABI-JEWEL.
I'VE ALWAYS WANTED TO MEET YOU.
WHO...
IS THIS PERSON INSIDE MY MIND?
SWOOOOP
NOW, FALL INTO OUR WORLD.
...?
THIS SMELL.
YOU MAY HAVE THE GOLDEN RABI-JEWEL, BUT YOU'RE NOT A PURE BATTLE RABBIT...
YOU'RE LIKE ME.

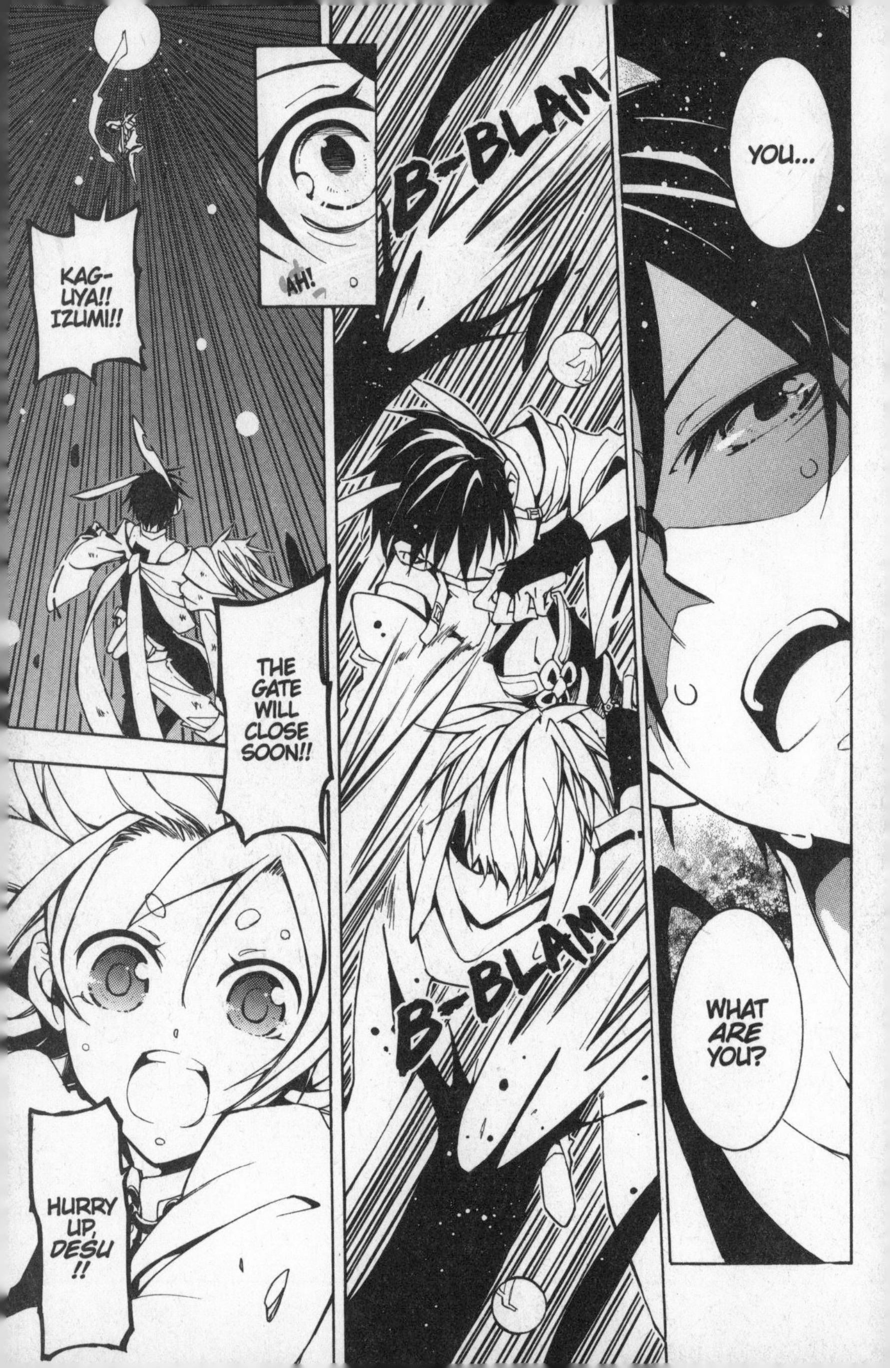
YOU...
WHAT ARE YOU?
B-BLAM
B-BLAM
AH!
KAG-UYA!! IZUMI!!
THE GATE WILL CLOSE SOON!!
HURRY UP, DESU!!

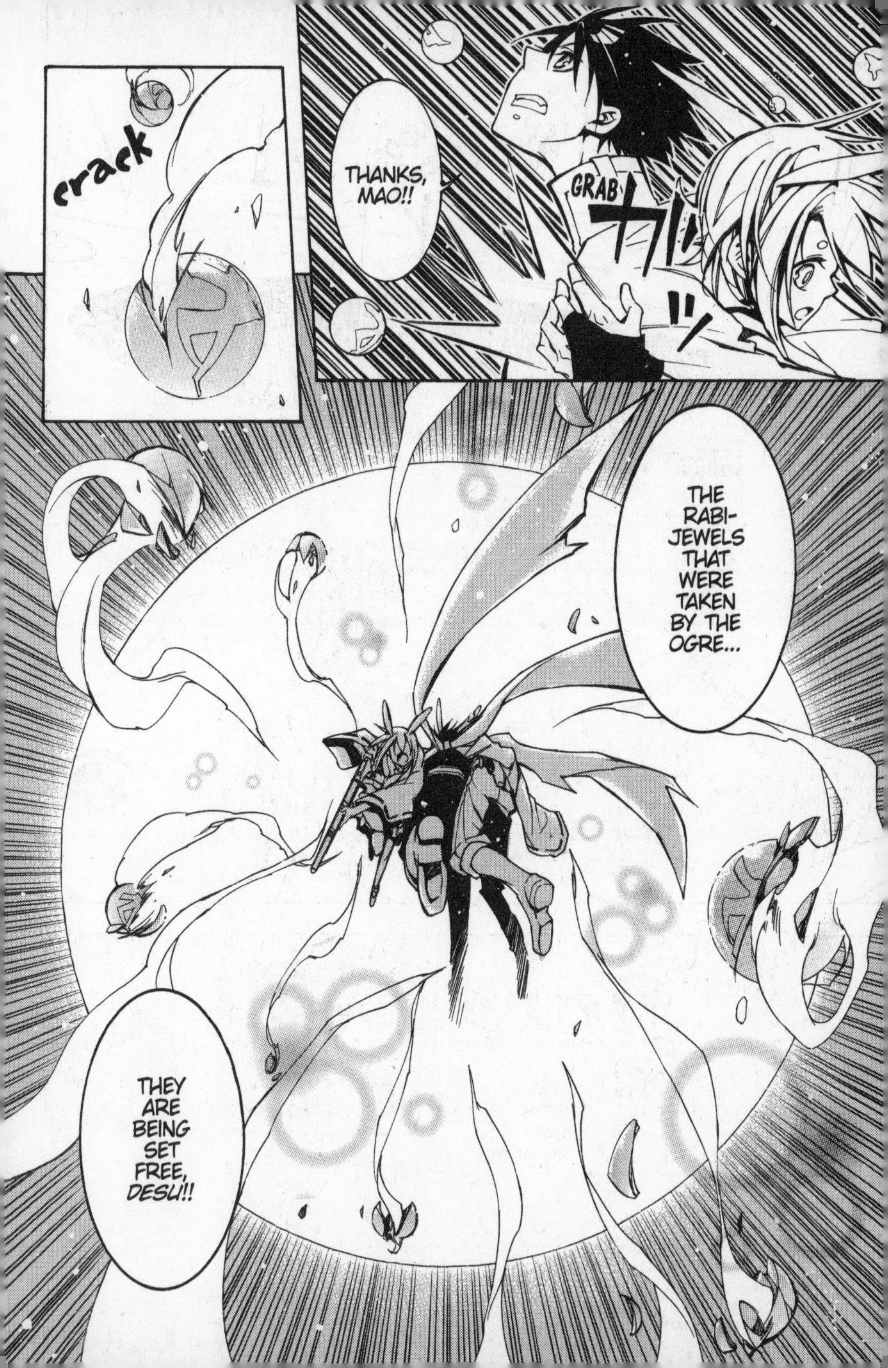
THANKS, MAO!!
GRAB
crack
THE RABI-JEWELS THAT WERE TAKEN BY THE OGRE...
THEY ARE BEING SET FREE, DESU!!

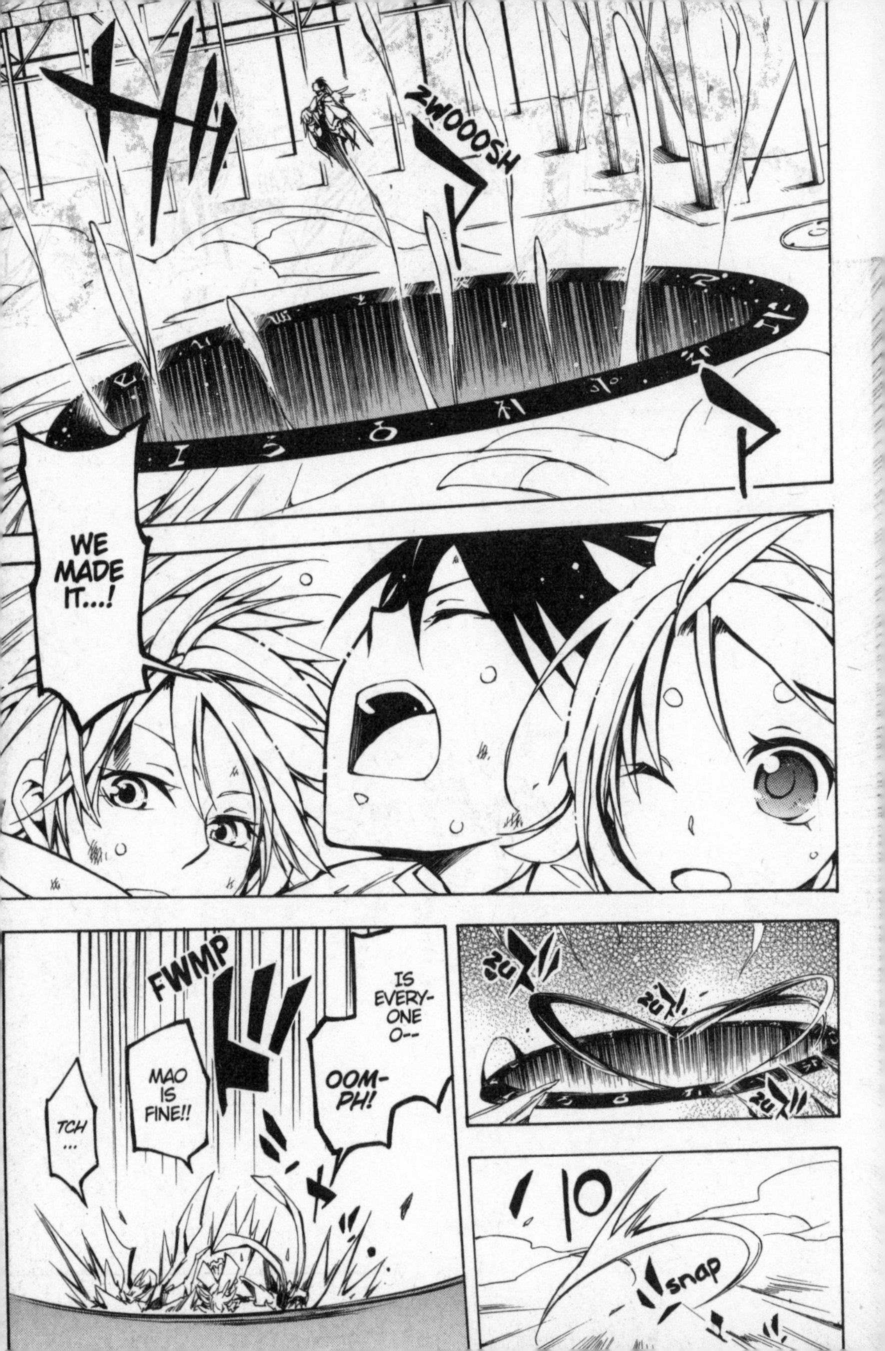
ZWOOOSH
WE MADE IT...!
ZU
ZU
ZU
snap
IS EVERY-ONE O--
OOMPH!
FWMP
MAO IS FINE!!
TCH ...

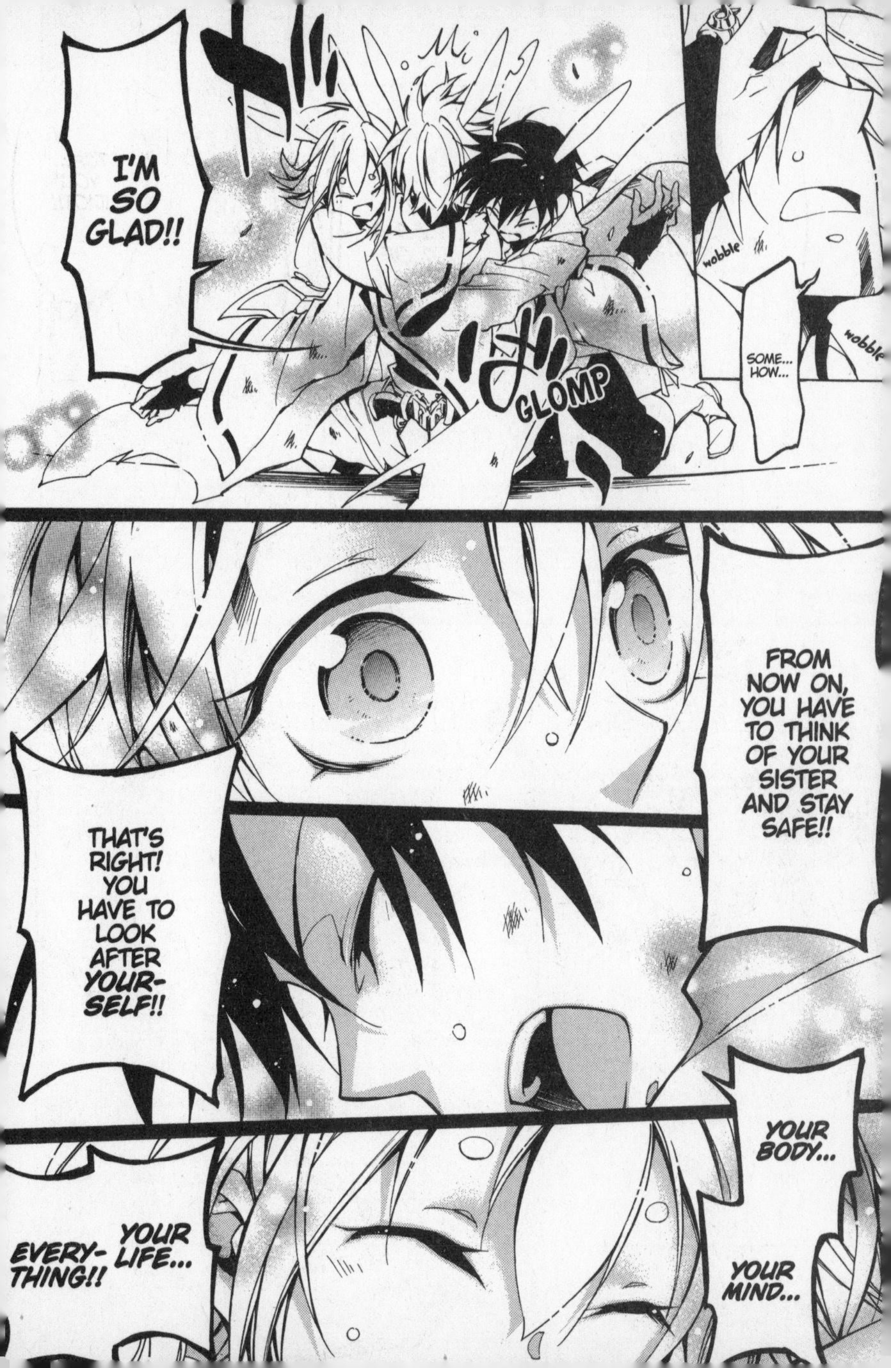
wobble
SOME... HOW...
wobble
I'M SO GLAD!!
GLOMP
FROM NOW ON, YOU HAVE TO THINK OF YOUR SISTER AND STAY SAFE!!
THAT'S RIGHT! YOU HAVE TO LOOK AFTER YOURSELF!!
YOUR BODY...
YOUR MIND...
YOUR LIFE...
EVERYTHING!!

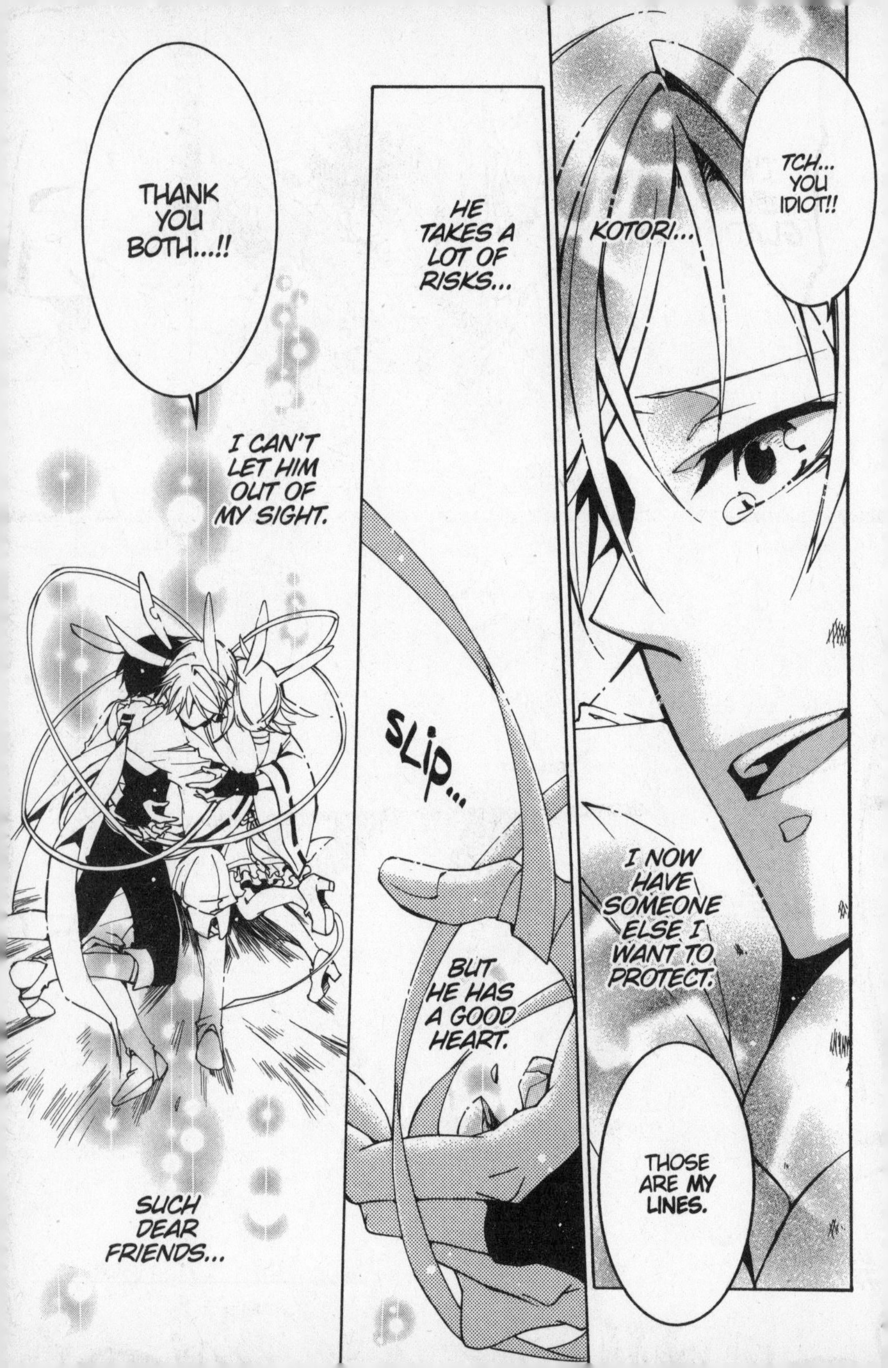
TCH... YOU IDIOT!!
KOTORI...
I NOW HAVE SOMEONE ELSE I WANT TO PROTECT.
THOSE ARE MY LINES.
HE TAKES A LOT OF RISKS...
SLIP...
BUT HE HAS A GOOD HEART.
THANK YOU BOTH...!!
I CAN'T LET HIM OUT OF MY SIGHT.
SUCH DEAR FRIENDS...

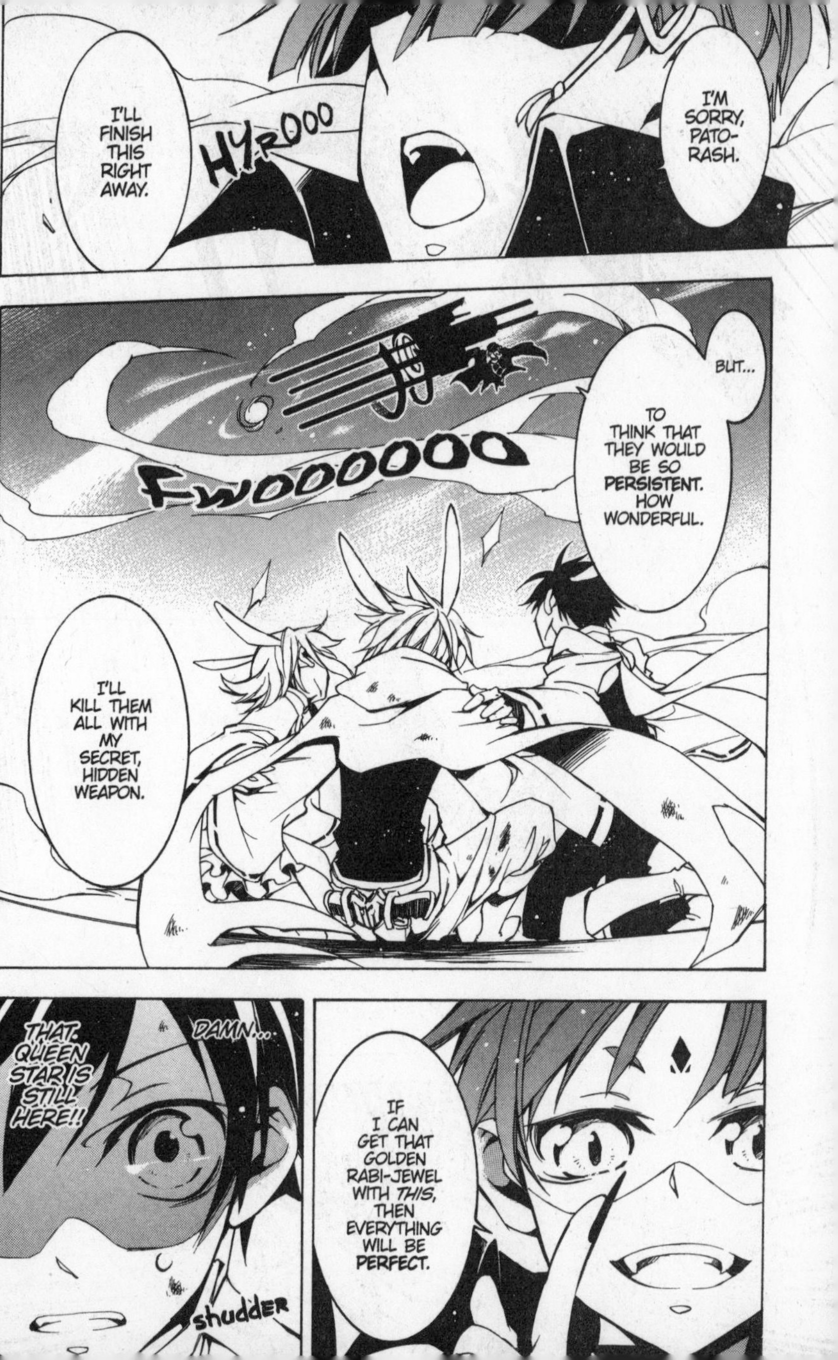
I'M SORRY, PATO-RASH.
HYROOO
I'LL FINISH THIS RIGHT AWAY.
BUT...
TO THINK THAT THEY WOULD BE SO PERSISTENT. HOW WONDERFUL.
FWOOOOOO
I'LL KILL THEM ALL WITH MY SECRET, HIDDEN WEAPON.
IF I CAN GET THAT GOLDEN RABI-JEWEL WITH *THIS*, THEN EVERYTHING WILL BE PERFECT.
DAMN...
THAT QUEEN STAR IS STILL HERE!!
shudder

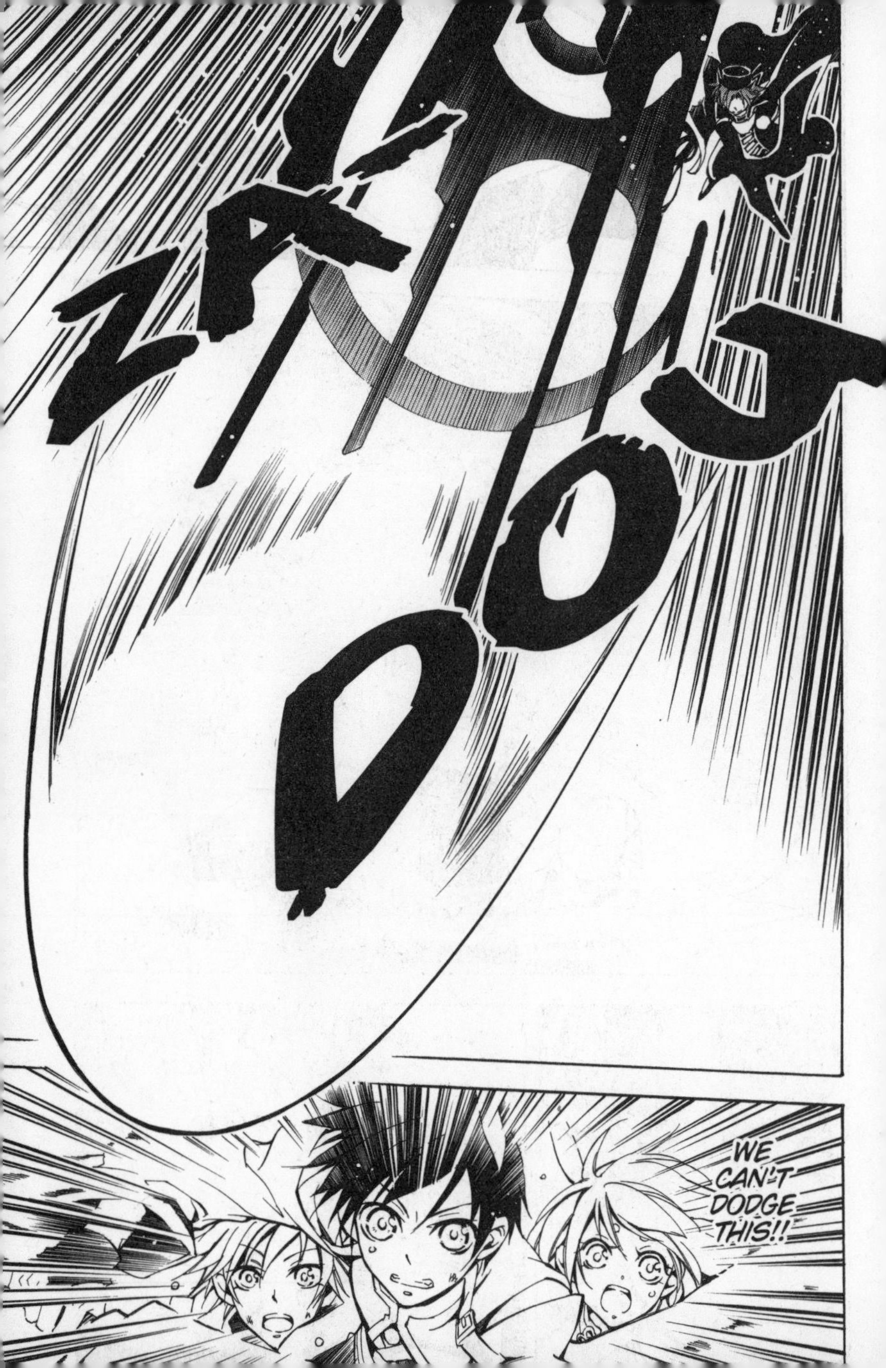
ZAP
DOOM
WE CAN'T DODGE THIS!!

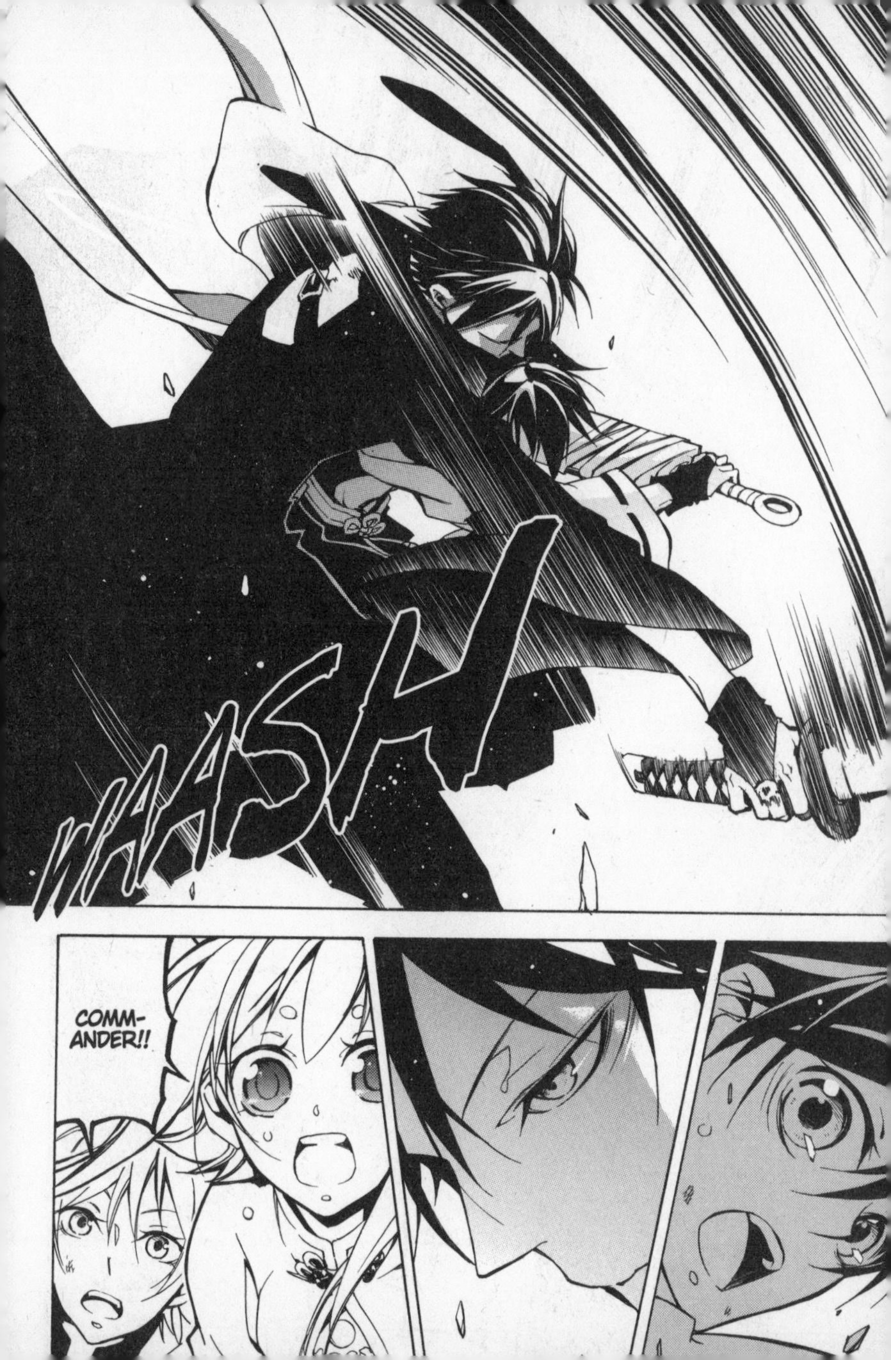
WAASH
COMM-
ANDER!!

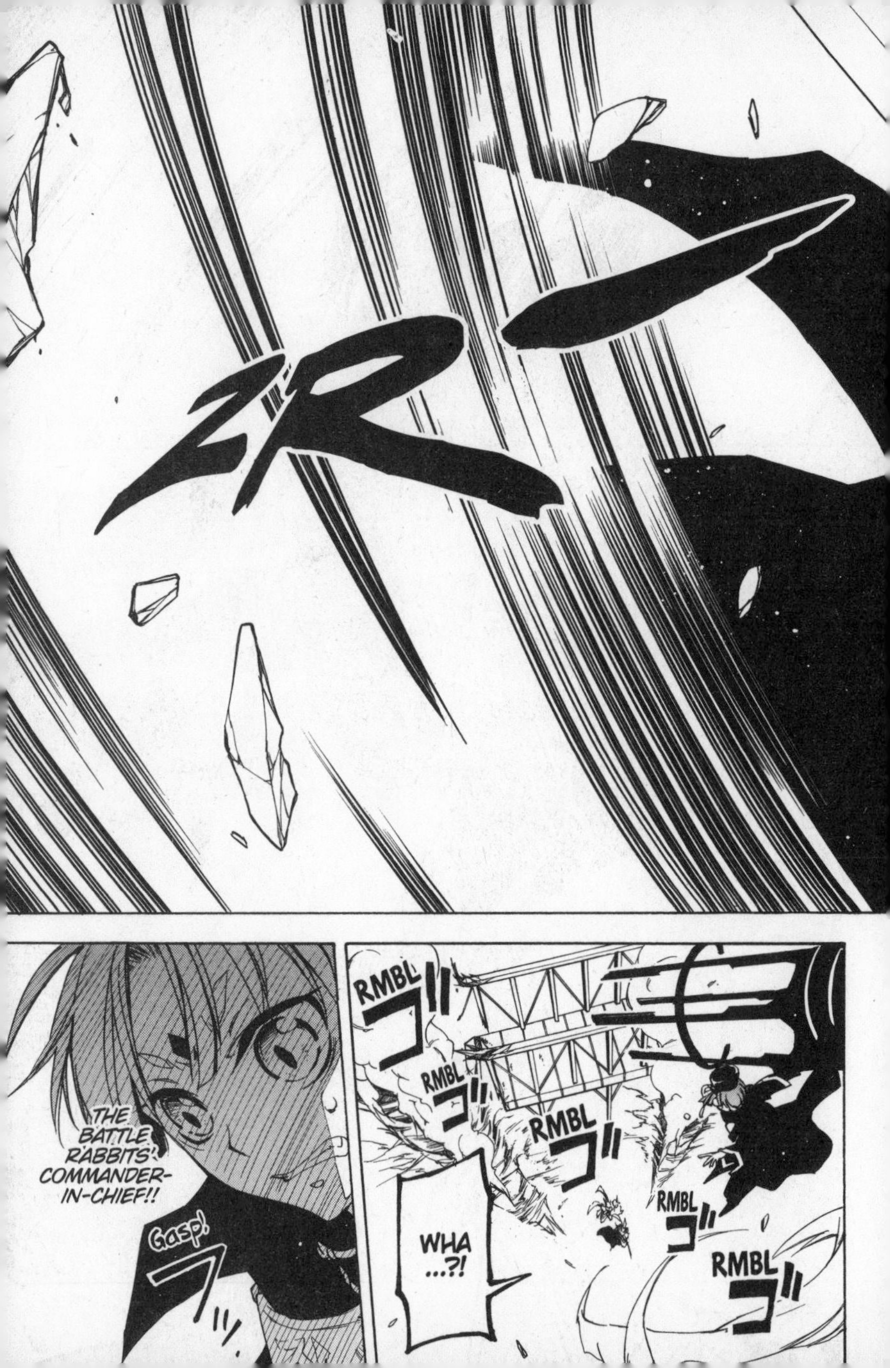
ZR
RMBL
RMBL
RMBL
RMBL
RMBL
WHA ...?!
THE BATTLE RABBITS' COMMANDER-IN-CHIEF!!
Gasp!

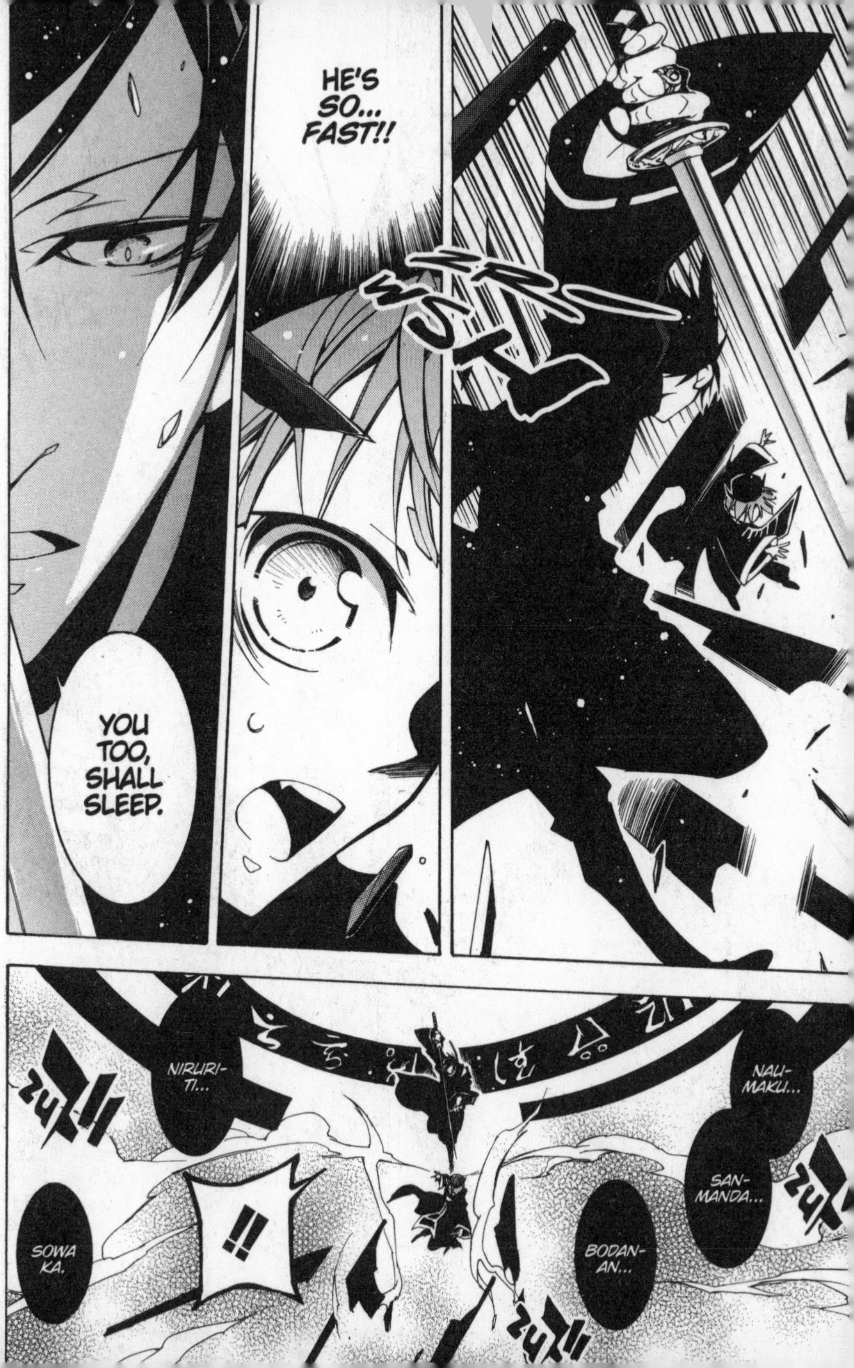
HE'S SO... FAST!!
YOU TOO, SHALL SLEEP.
NAU-MAKU...
SAN-MANDA...
BODAN-AN...
NIRURI-TI...
!!
SOWA KA.

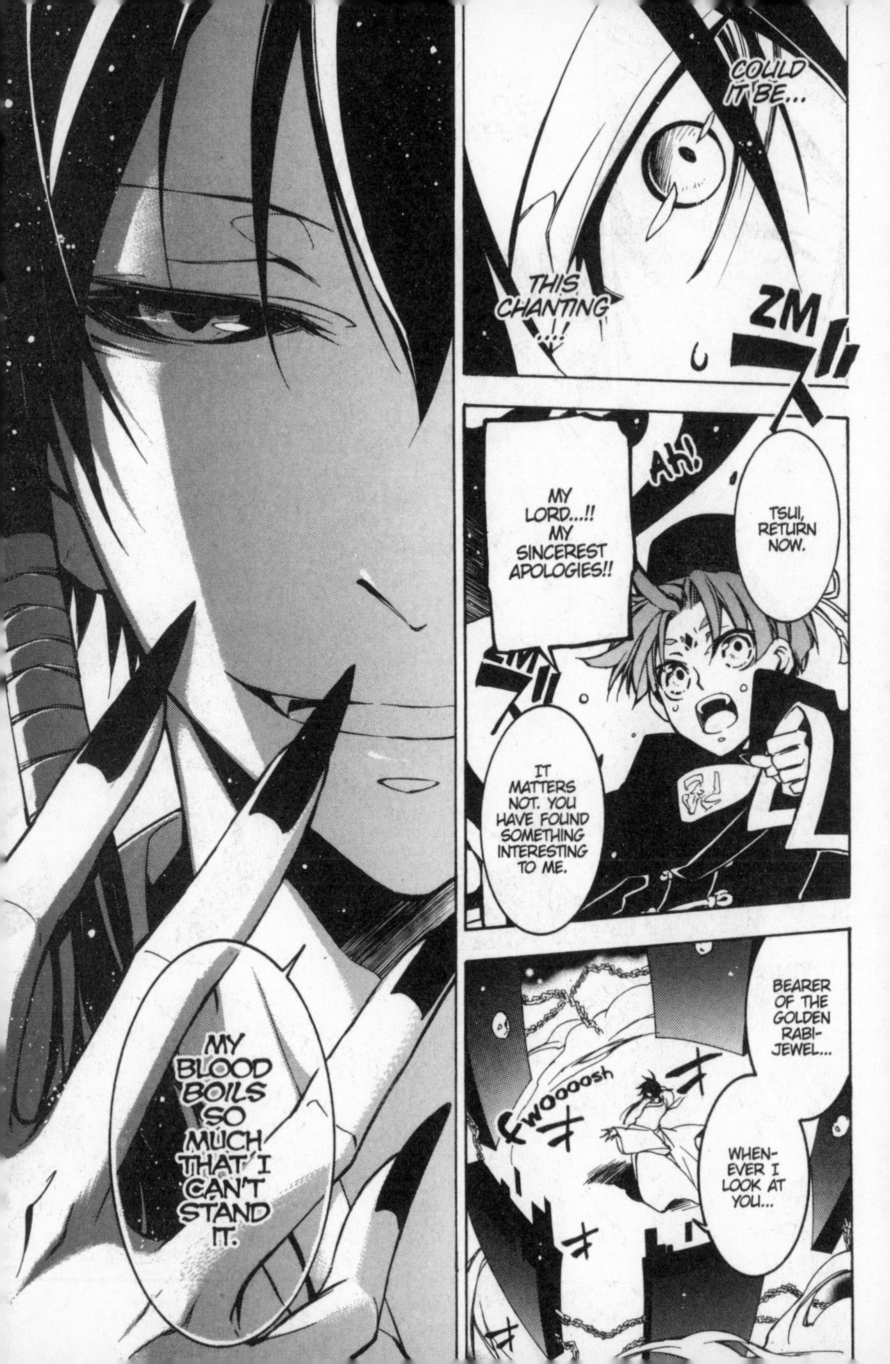
COULD IT BE...
THIS CHANTING...!!
ZM
TSUI, RETURN NOW.
Ah!
MY LORD...!! MY SINCEREST APOLOGIES!!
IT MATTERS NOT. YOU HAVE FOUND SOMETHING INTERESTING TO ME.
BEARER OF THE GOLDEN RABI-JEWEL...
FWOOOOSH
WHEN-EVER I LOOK AT YOU...
MY BLOOD BOILS SO MUCH THAT I CAN'T STAND IT.

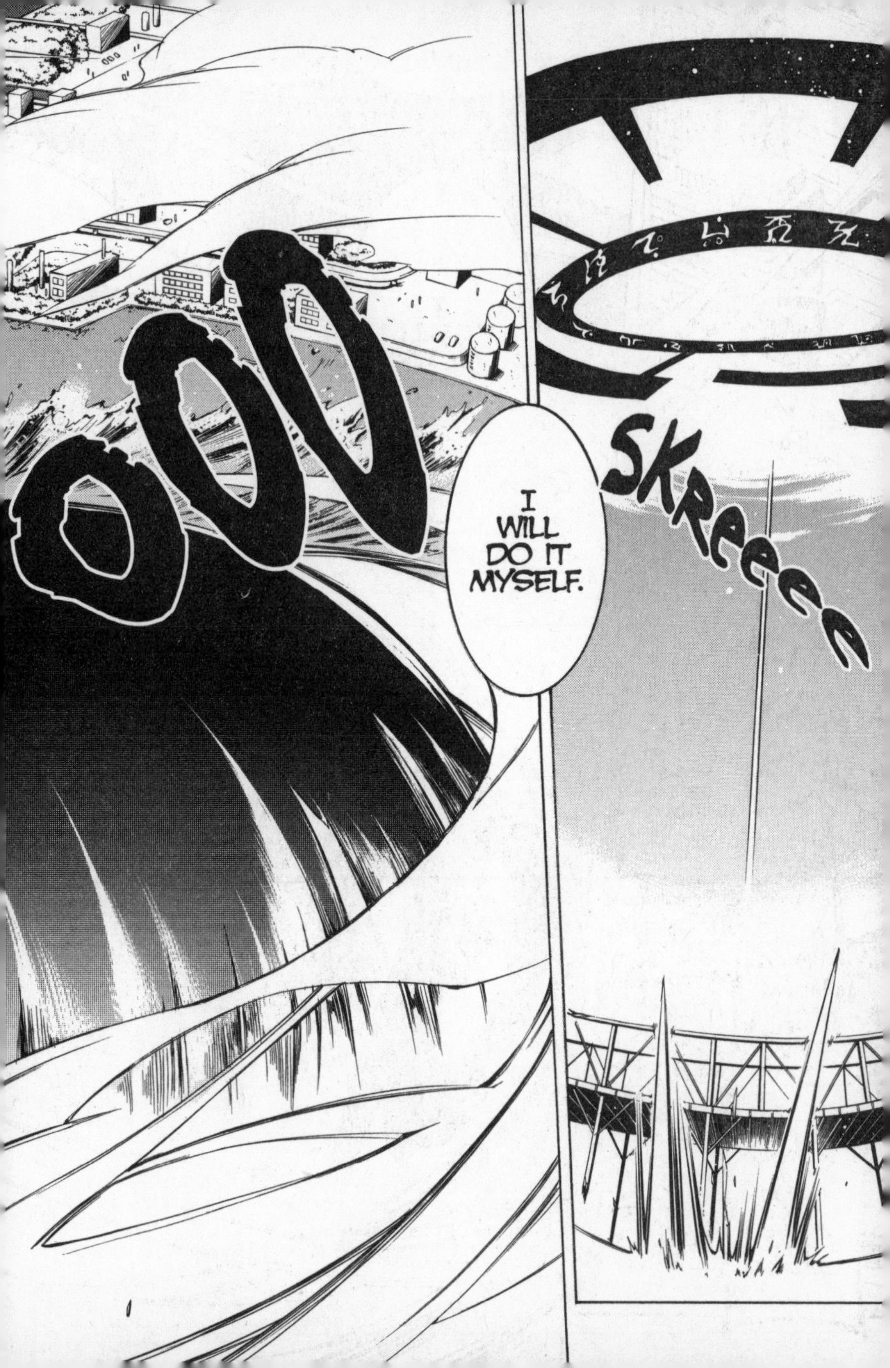
SKReeee
I WILL DO IT MYSELF.
DOO

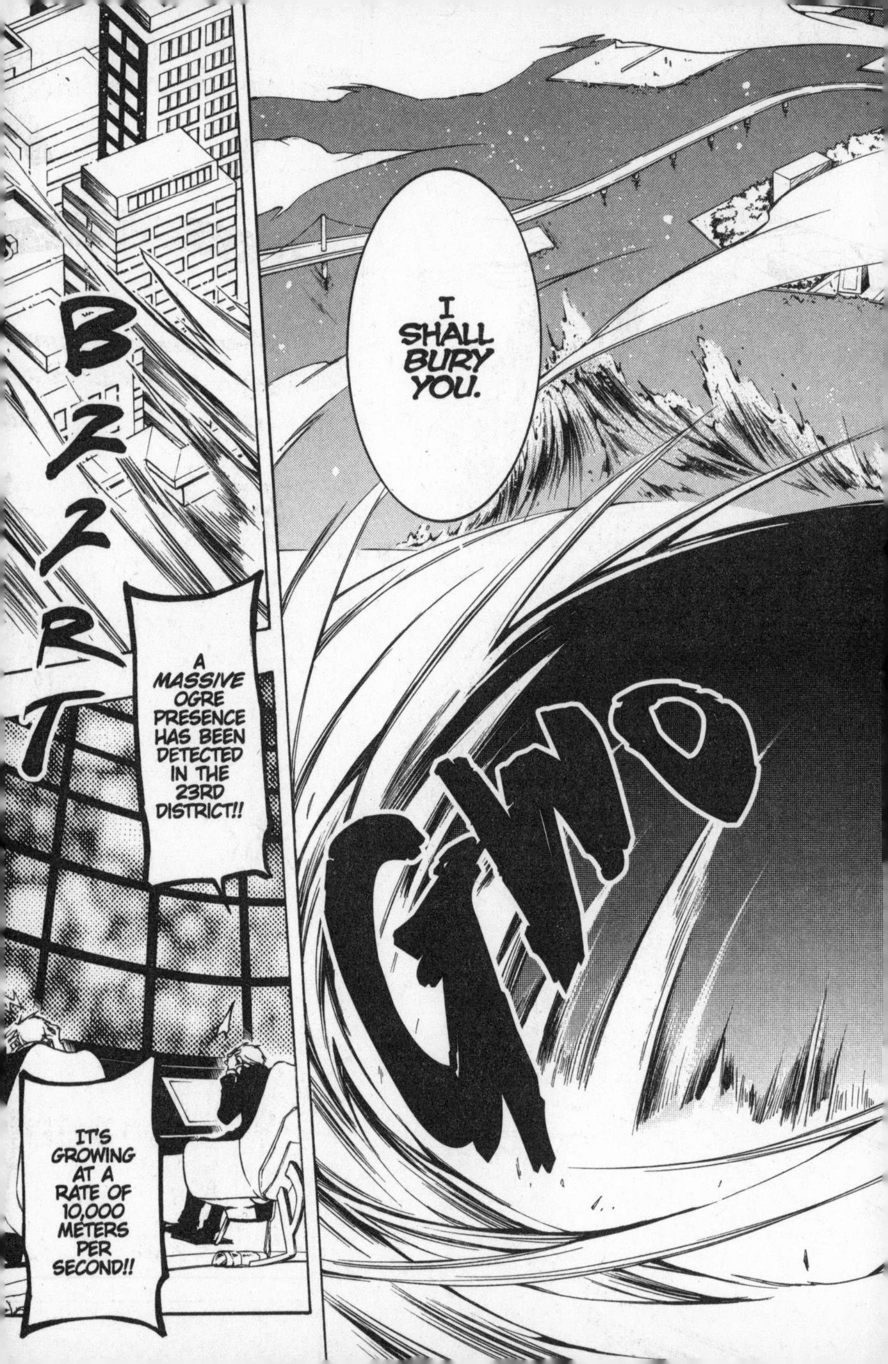
I SHALL BURY YOU.
GWO
BZZRT
A MASSIVE OGRE PRESENCE HAS BEEN DETECTED IN THE 23RD DISTRICT!!
IT'S GROWING AT A RATE OF 10,000 METERS PER SECOND!!

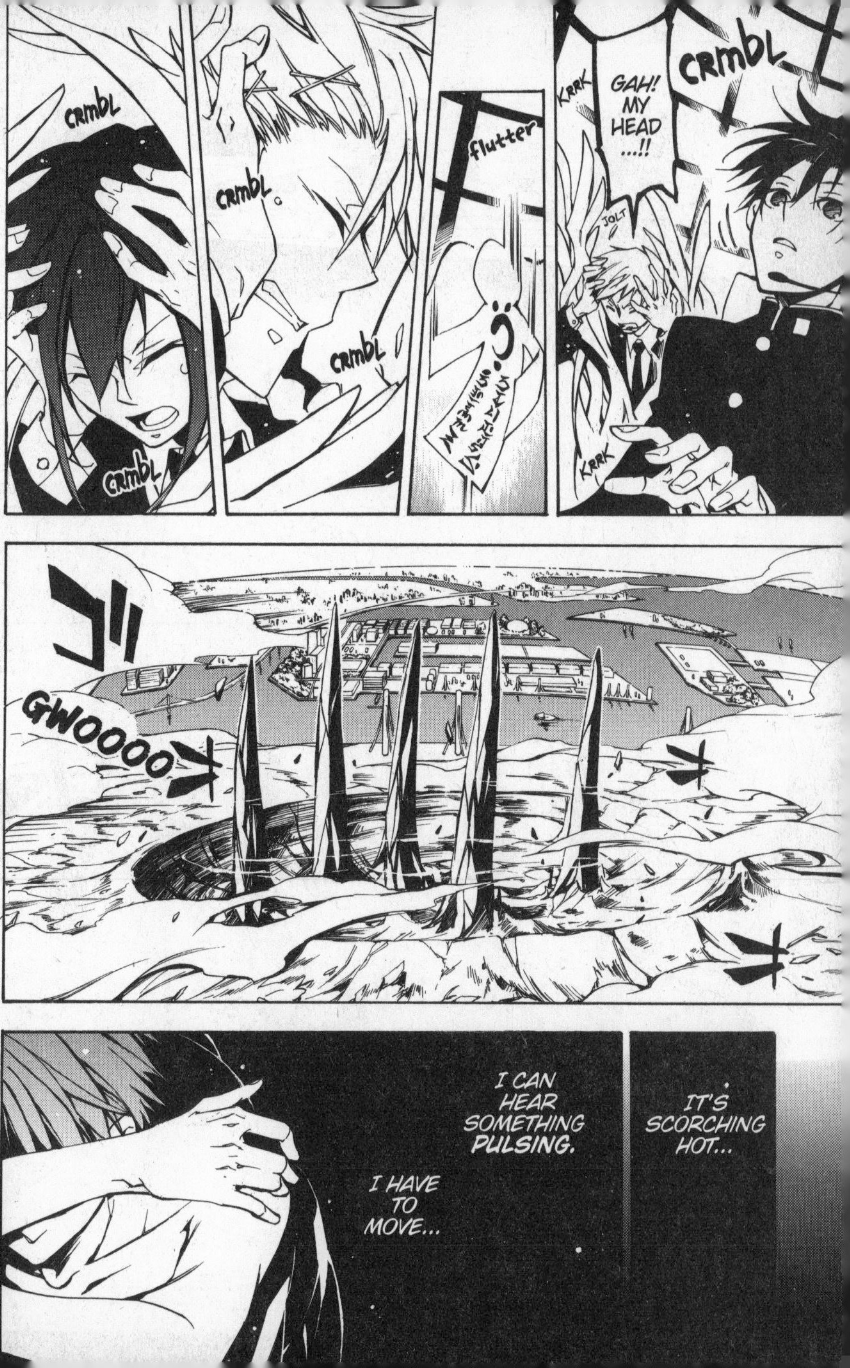
CRMBL
GAH! MY HEAD ...!!
KRRK
JOLT
KRRK
flutter
CRMBL
CRMBL
CRMBL
CRMBL
GWOOOO
IT'S SCORCHING HOT...
I CAN HEAR SOMETHING PULSING.
I HAVE TO MOVE...

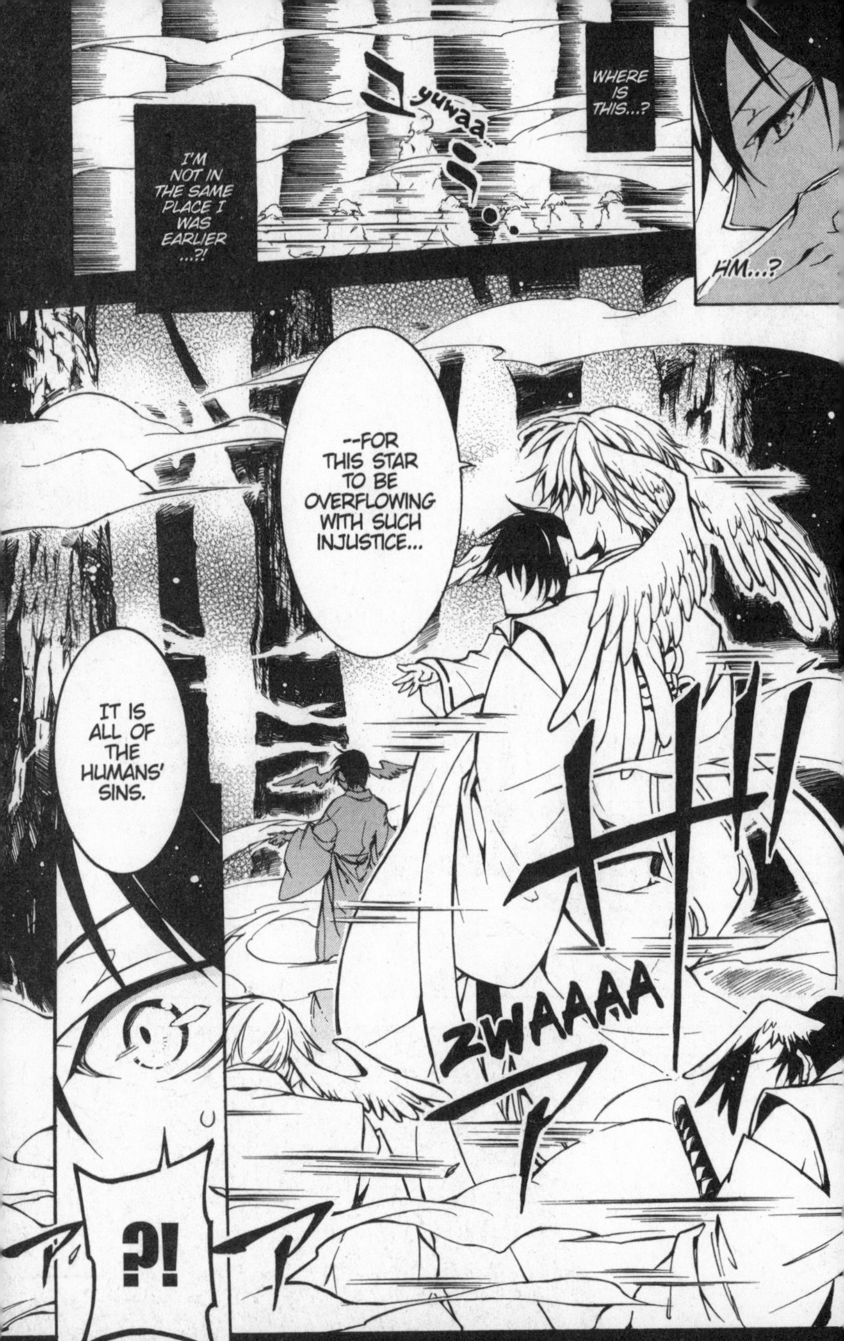
HM...?
WHERE IS THIS...?
yuwaa...
I'M NOT IN THE SAME PLACE I WAS EARLIER ...?!
--FOR THIS STAR TO BE OVERFLOWING WITH SUCH INJUSTICE...
IT IS ALL OF THE HUMANS' SINS.
ZWAAAA
?!

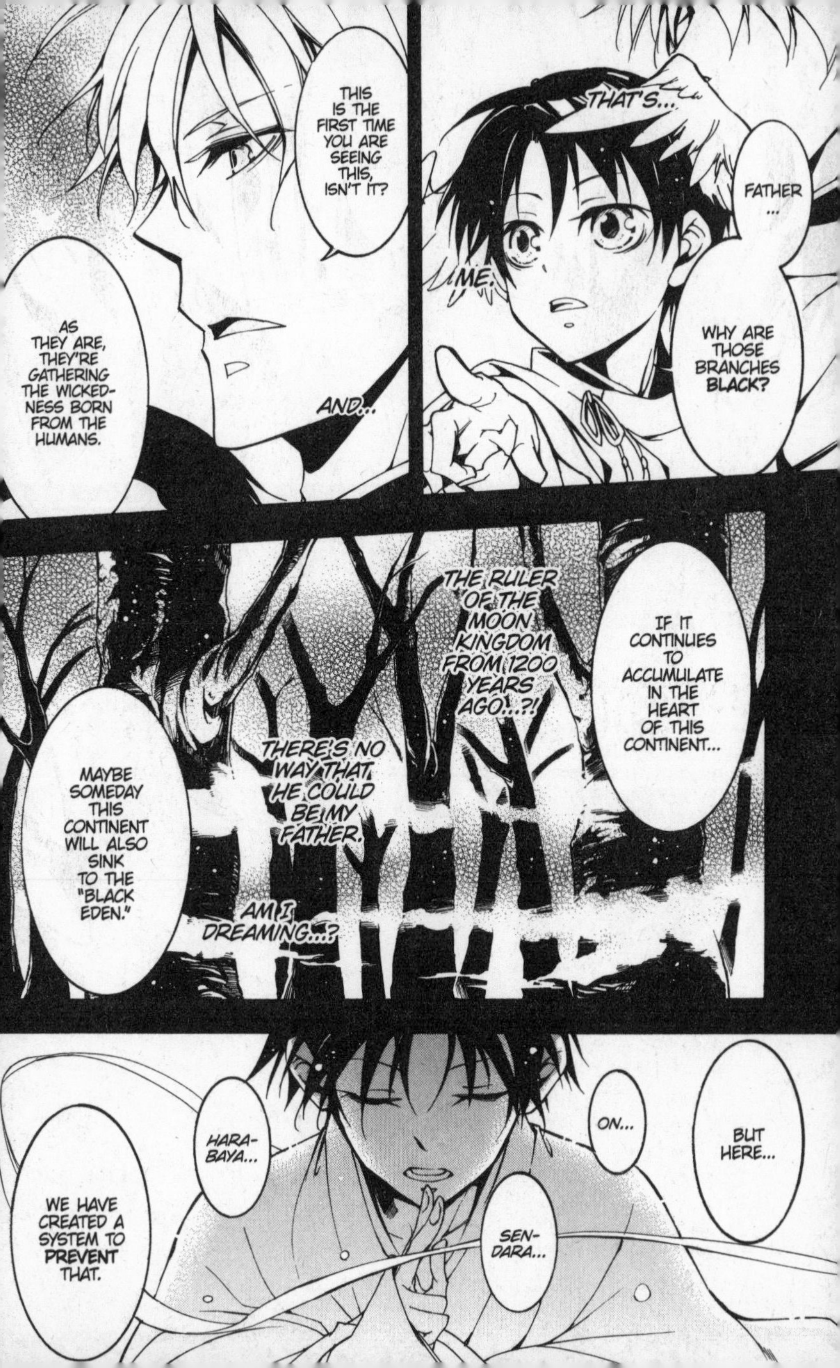
THAT'S...
FATHER...
ME.
WHY ARE THOSE BRANCHES BLACK?
THIS IS THE FIRST TIME YOU ARE SEEING THIS, ISN'T IT?
AND...
AS THEY ARE, THEY'RE GATHERING THE WICKED-NESS BORN FROM THE HUMANS.
IF IT CONTINUES TO ACCUMULATE IN THE HEART OF THIS CONTINENT...
THE RULER OF THE MOON KINGDOM FROM 1200 YEARS AGO...?!
THERE'S NO WAY THAT HE COULD BE MY FATHER.
AM I DREAMING...?
MAYBE SOMEDAY THIS CONTINENT WILL ALSO SINK TO THE "BLACK EDEN."
BUT HERE...
ON...
HARA-BAYA...
SEN-DARA...
WE HAVE CREATED A SYSTEM TO PREVENT THAT.

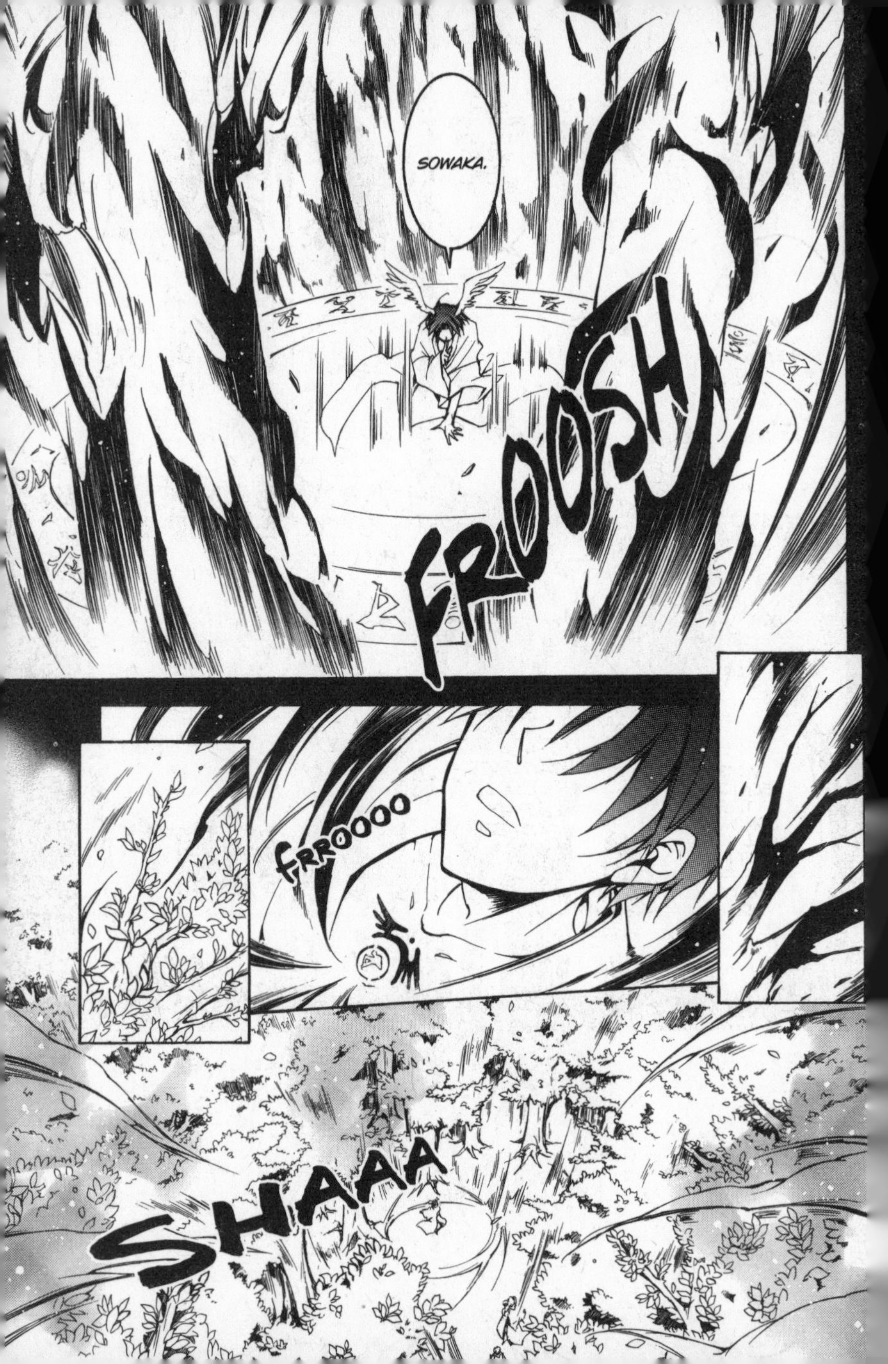
SOWAKA.
FROOSH
FRROOOO
SHAAA

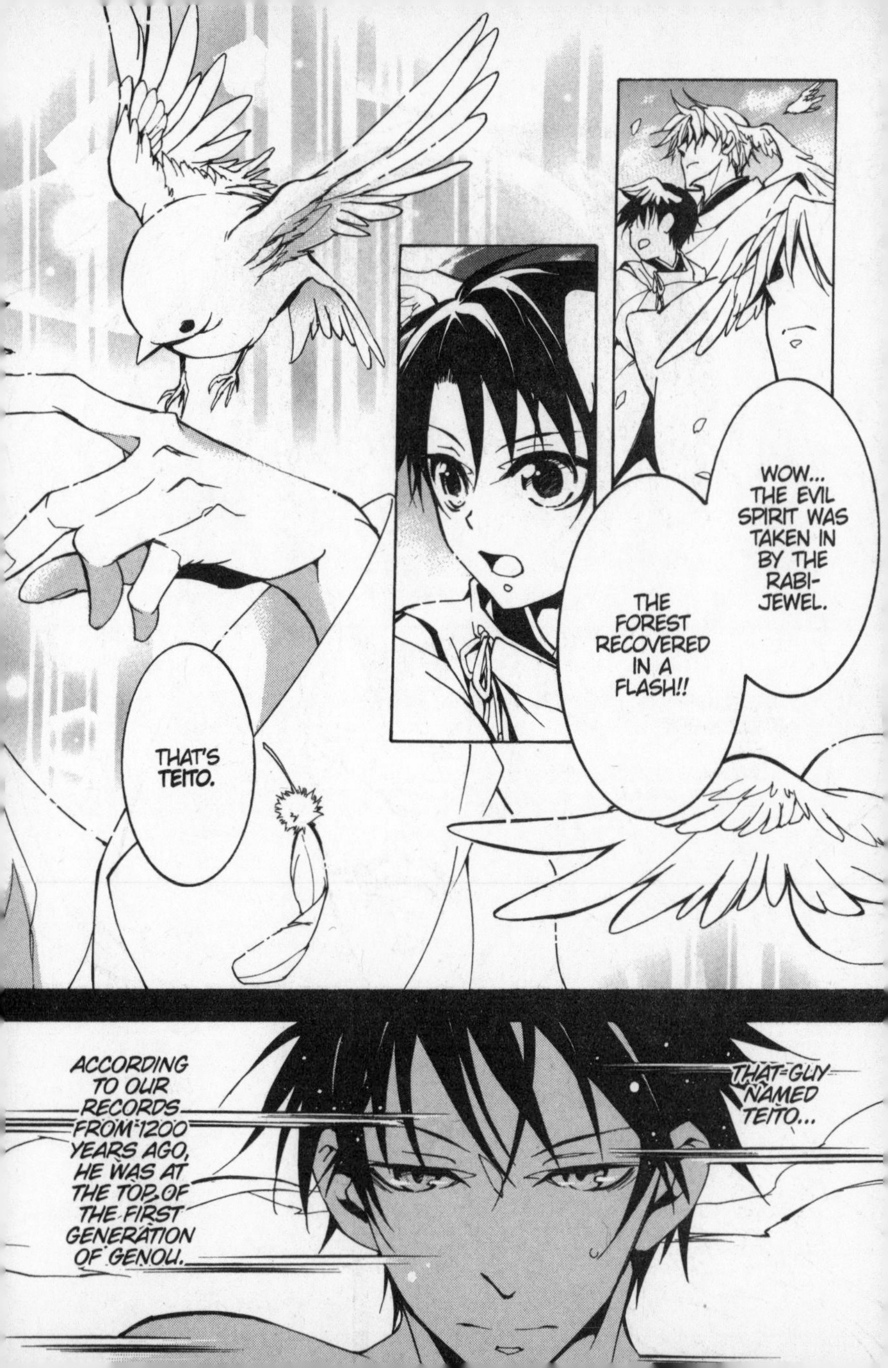
WOW... THE EVIL SPIRIT WAS TAKEN IN BY THE RABI-JEWEL.
THE FOREST RECOVERED IN A FLASH!!
THAT'S TEITO.
THAT GUY NAMED TEITO...
ACCORDING TO OUR RECORDS FROM 1200 YEARS AGO, HE WAS AT THE TOP OF THE FIRST GENERATION OF GENOU.

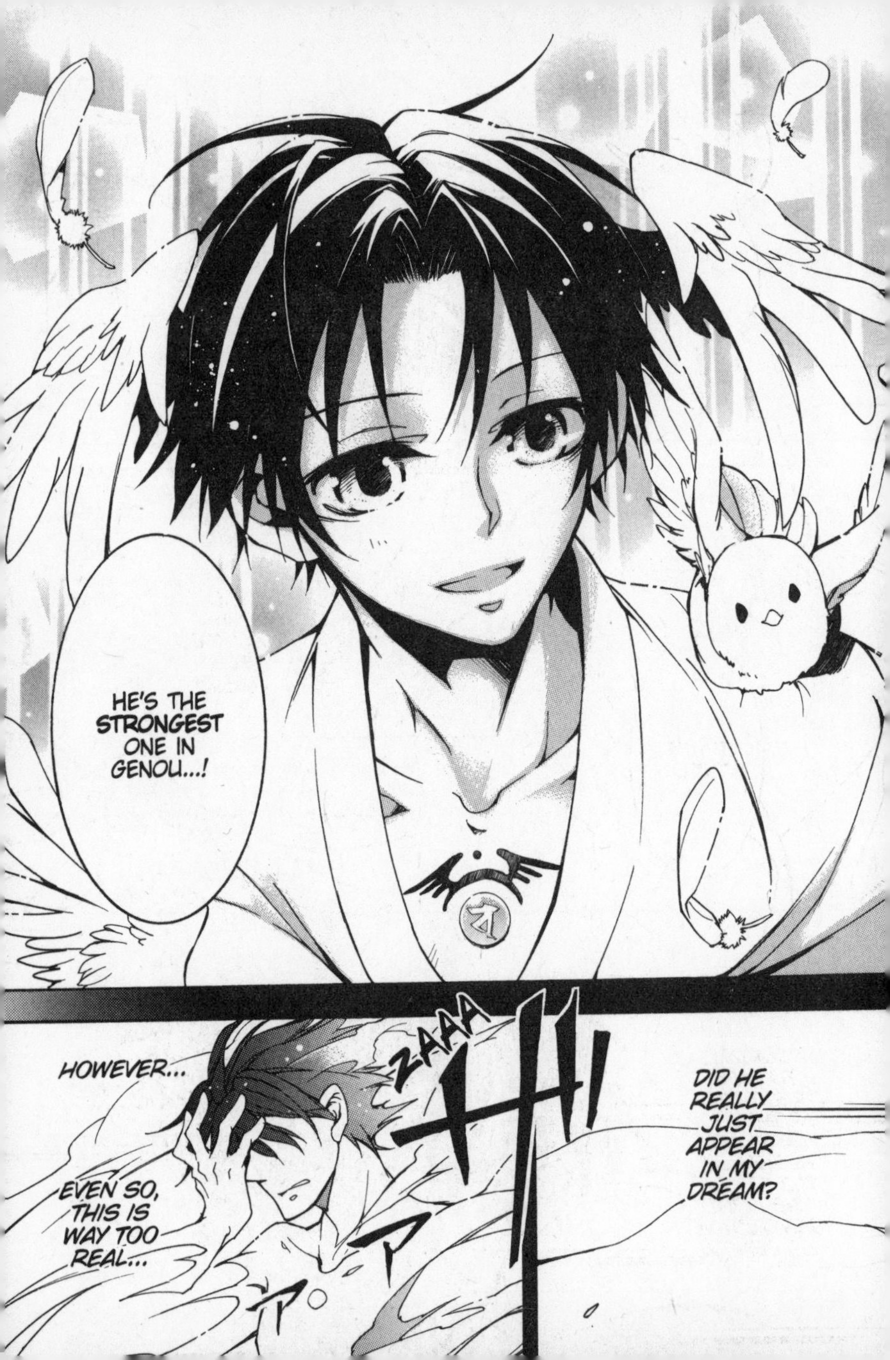
HE'S THE STRONGEST ONE IN GENOU...!
DID HE REALLY JUST APPEAR IN MY DREAM?
ZAAA
HOWEVER...
EVEN SO, THIS IS WAY TOO REAL...

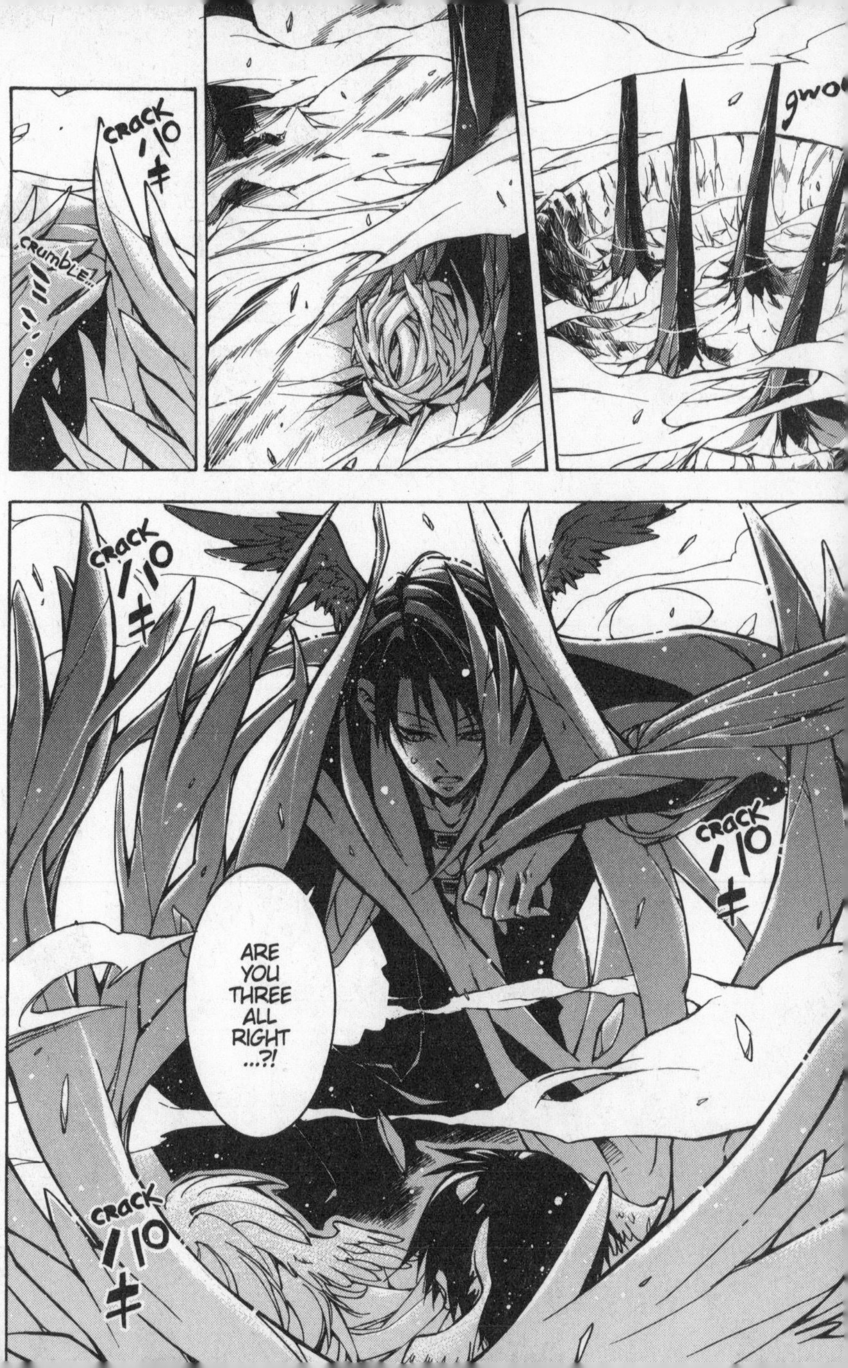
gwoo
CRACK
パキ
CRUMBLE...!!
CRACK
パキ
CRACK
パキ
ARE YOU THREE ALL RIGHT ...?!
CRACK
パキ

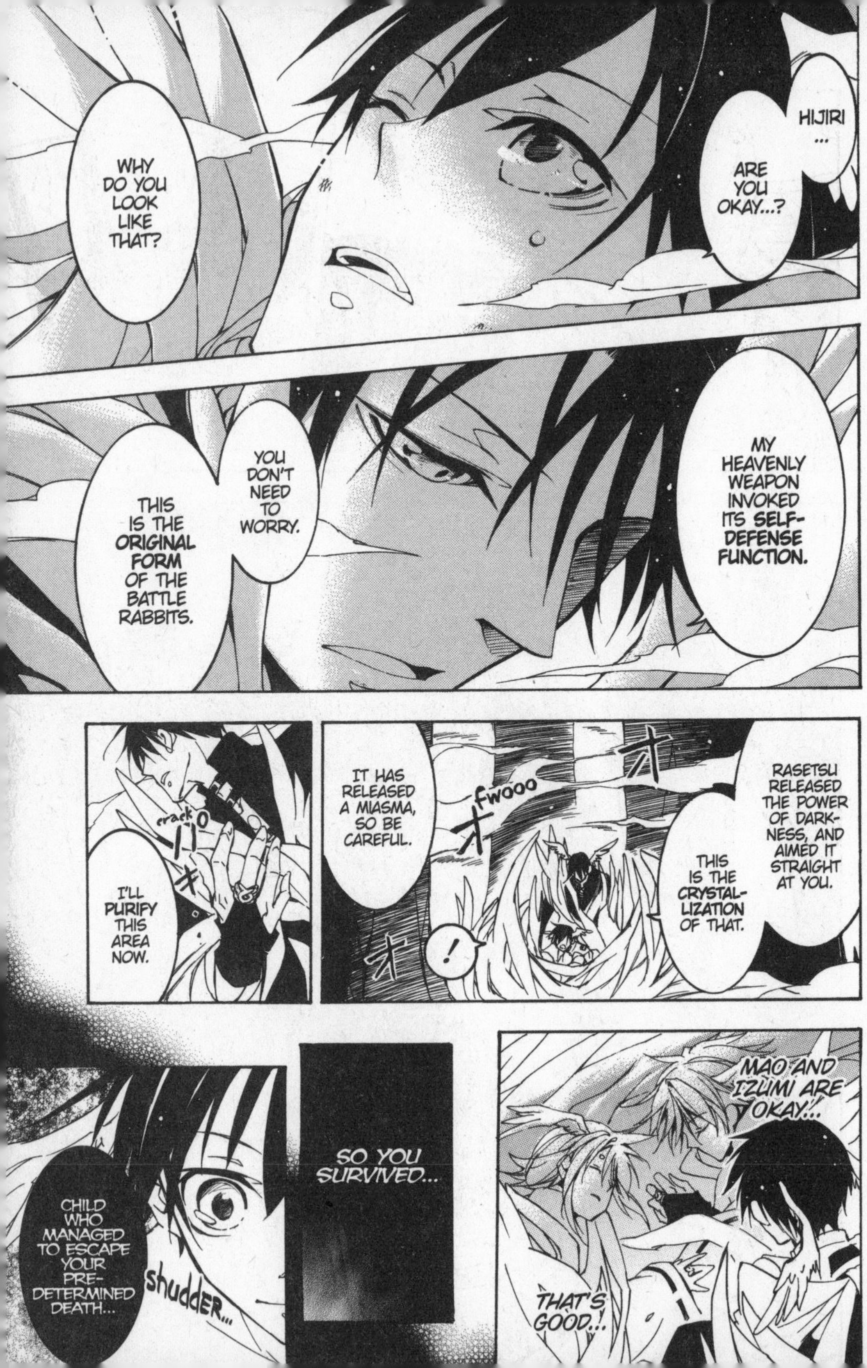
HIJIRI... ARE YOU OKAY...?
WHY DO YOU LOOK LIKE THAT?
MY HEAVENLY WEAPON INVOKED ITS SELF-DEFENSE FUNCTION.
YOU DON'T NEED TO WORRY.
THIS IS THE ORIGINAL FORM OF THE BATTLE RABBITS.
RASETSU RELEASED THE POWER OF DARKNESS, AND AIMED IT STRAIGHT AT YOU.
THIS IS THE CRYSTAL-LIZATION OF THAT.
fwooo
IT HAS RELEASED A MIASMA, SO BE CAREFUL.
!
crack
I'LL PURIFY THIS AREA NOW.
MAO AND IZUMI ARE OKAY...
THAT'S GOOD...!
SO YOU SURVIVED...
CHILD WHO MANAGED TO ESCAPE YOUR PRE-DETERMINED DEATH...
shudder...

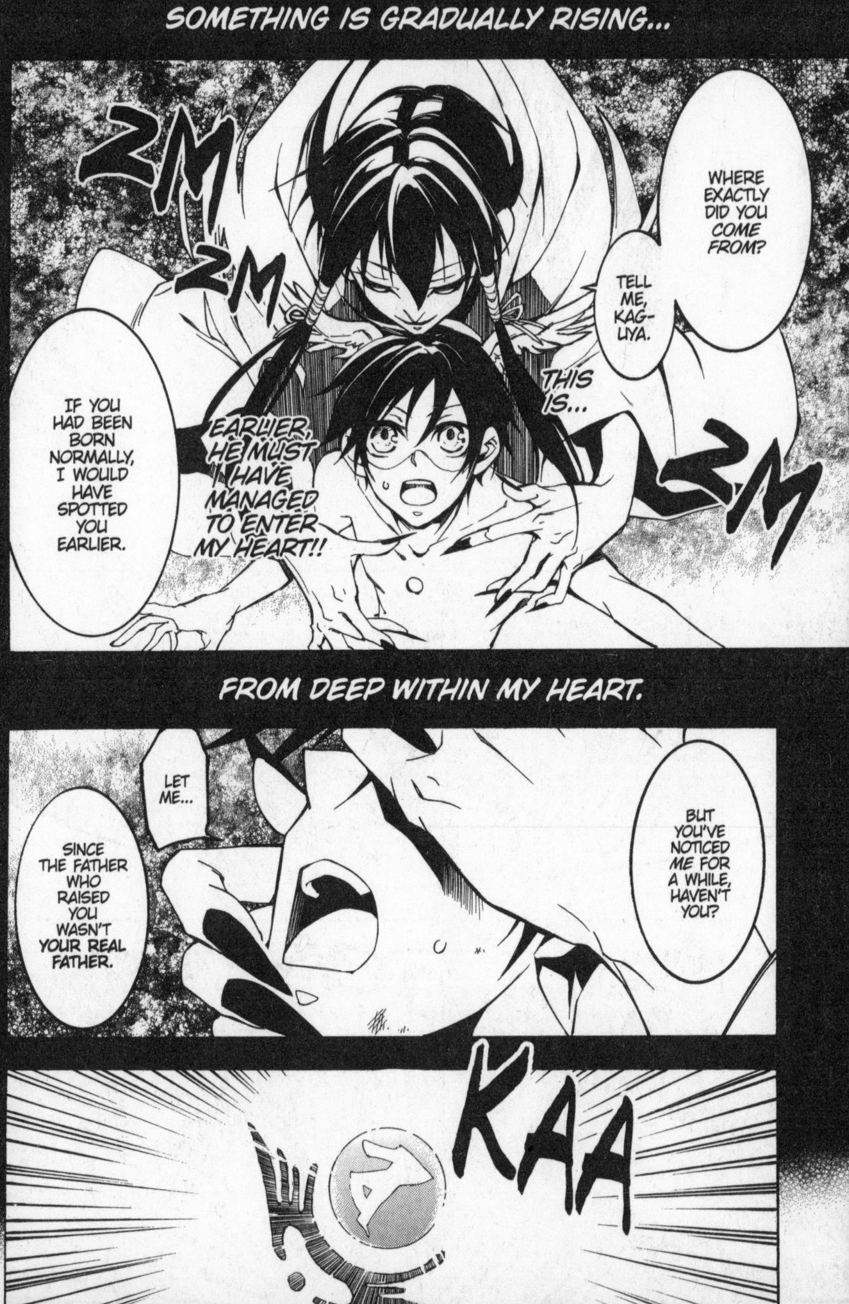
SOMETHING IS GRADUALLY RISING...
ZM
ZM
WHERE EXACTLY DID YOU COME FROM?
TELL ME, KAG-UYA.
ZM
THIS IS...
EARLIER, HE MUST HAVE MANAGED TO ENTER MY HEART!!
IF YOU HAD BEEN BORN NORMALLY, I WOULD HAVE SPOTTED YOU EARLIER.
FROM DEEP WITHIN MY HEART.
BUT YOU'VE NOTICED ME FOR A WHILE, HAVEN'T YOU?
LET ME...
SINCE THE FATHER WHO RAISED YOU WASN'T YOUR REAL FATHER.
KAA

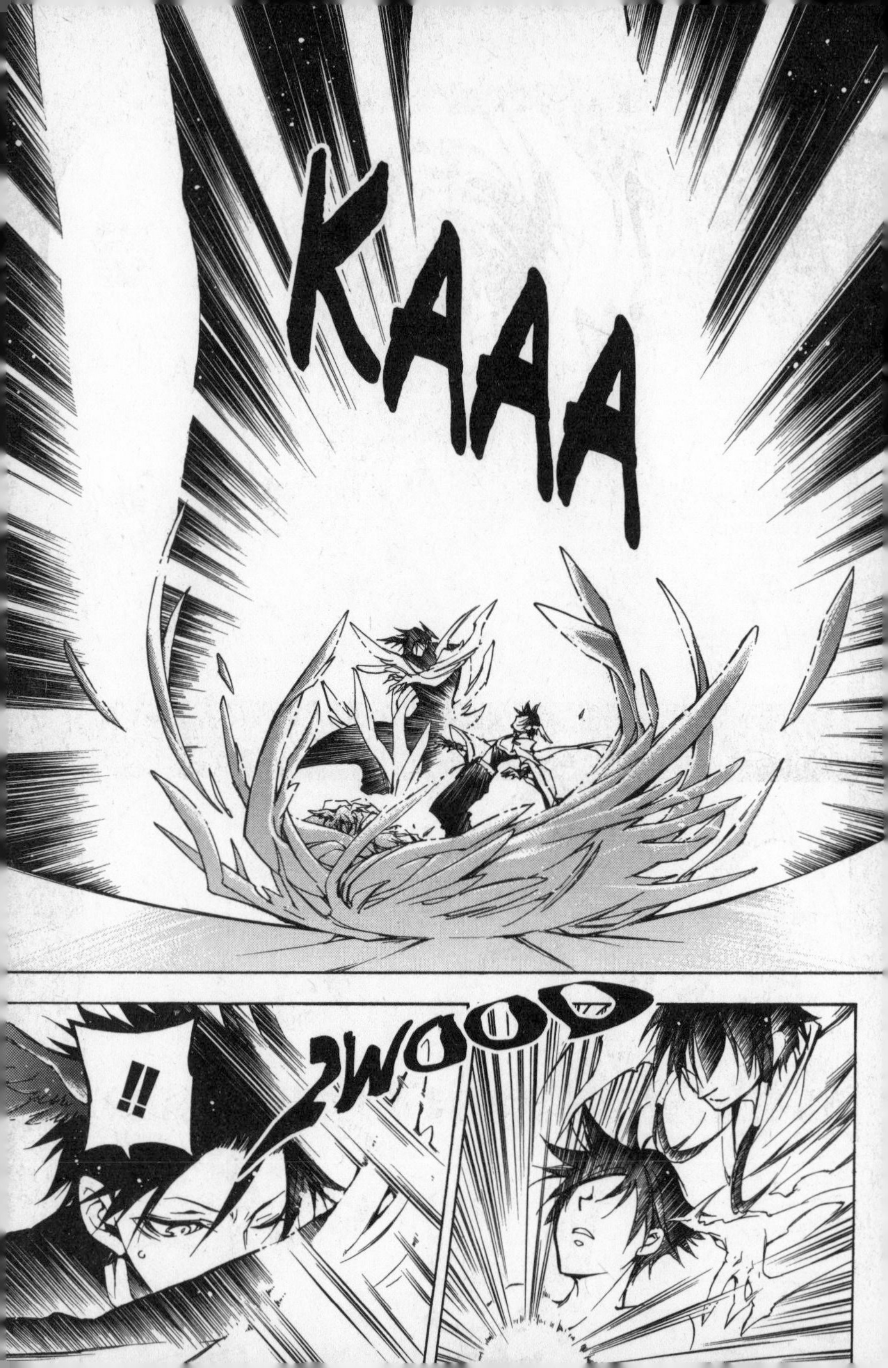
KAAA
!!
SWOOP

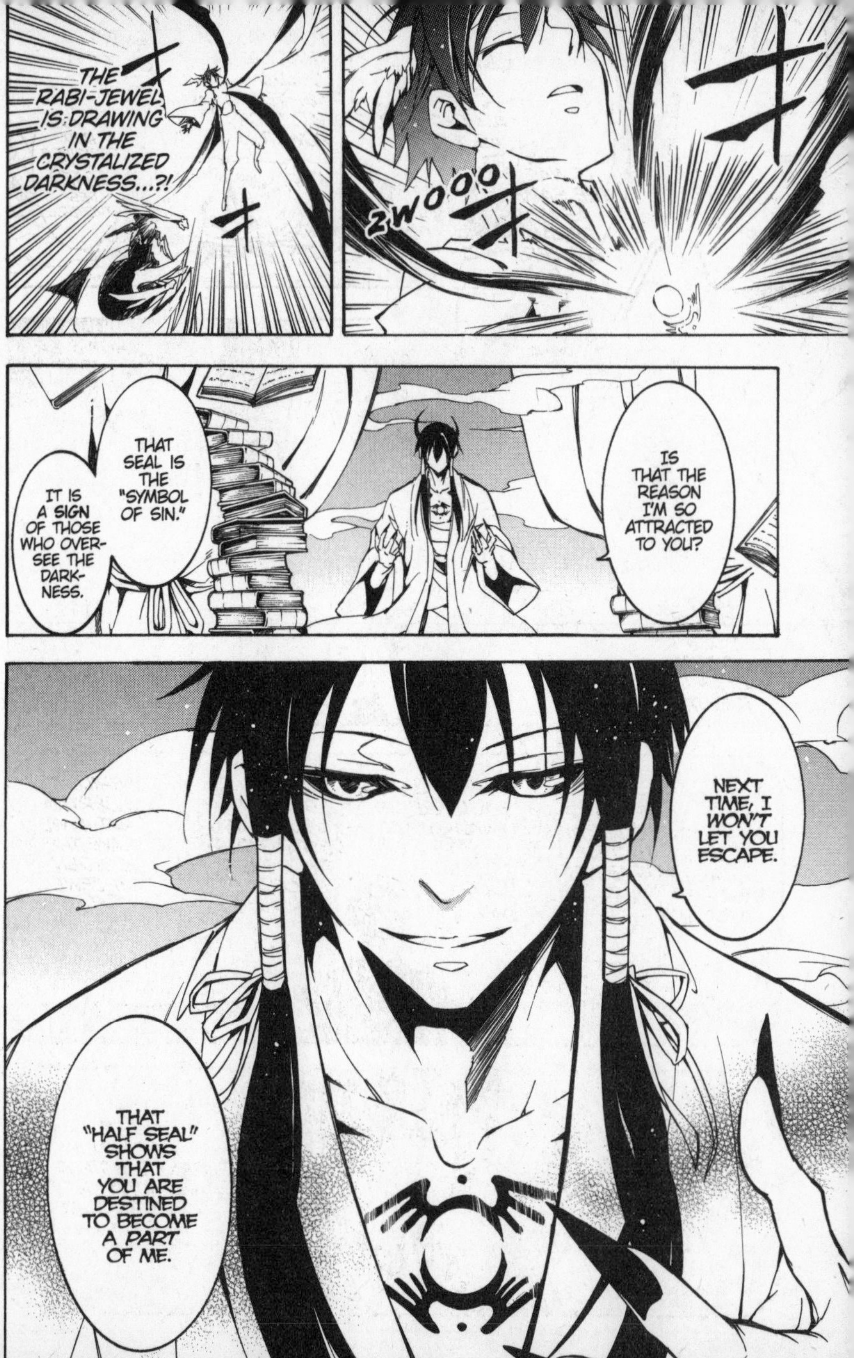
ZWOOO
THE RABI-JEWEL IS DRAWING IN THE CRYSTALIZED DARKNESS...?!
IS THAT THE REASON I'M SO ATTRACTED TO YOU?
THAT SEAL IS THE "SYMBOL OF SIN."
IT IS A SIGN OF THOSE WHO OVER-SEE THE DARK-NESS.
NEXT TIME, I *WON'T* LET YOU ESCAPE.
THAT "HALF SEAL" SHOWS THAT YOU ARE DESTINED TO BECOME A *PART* OF ME.

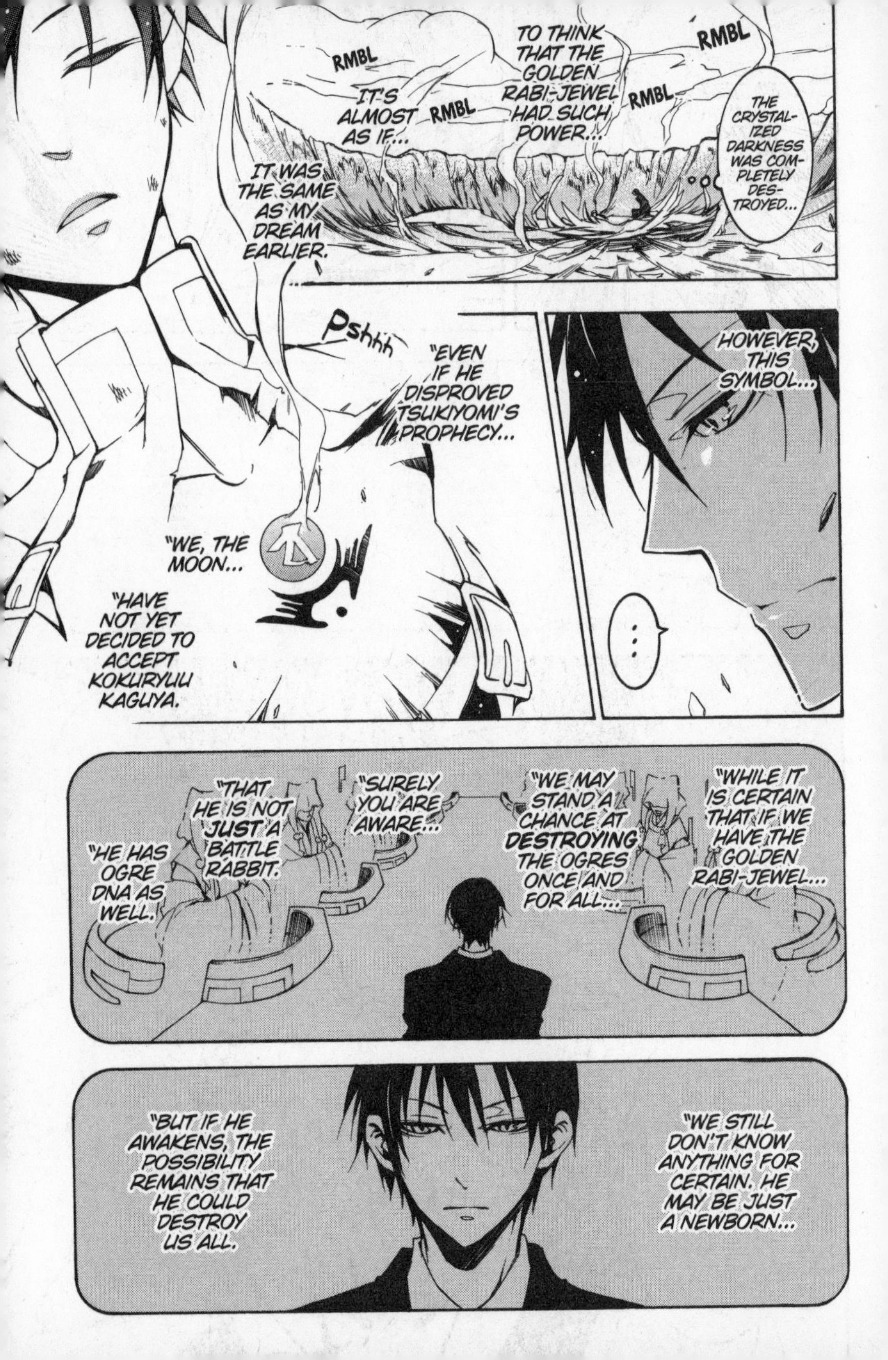
RMBL
THE CRYSTALIZED DARKNESS WAS COMPLETELY DESTROYED...
TO THINK THAT THE GOLDEN RABI-JEWEL HAD SUCH POWER...
RMBL
RMBL
IT'S ALMOST AS IF...
RMBL
IT WAS THE SAME AS MY DREAM EARLIER.
HOWEVER, THIS SYMBOL...
...
Pshhh
"EVEN IF HE DISPROVED TSUKIYOMI'S PROPHECY...
"WE, THE MOON...
"HAVE NOT YET DECIDED TO ACCEPT KOKURYUU KAGUYA.
"WHILE IT IS CERTAIN THAT IF WE HAVE THE GOLDEN RABI-JEWEL...
"WE MAY STAND A CHANCE AT DESTROYING THE OGRES ONCE AND FOR ALL...
"SURELY YOU ARE AWARE...
"THAT HE IS NOT JUST A BATTLE RABBIT.
"HE HAS OGRE DNA AS WELL.
"WE STILL DON'T KNOW ANYTHING FOR CERTAIN. HE MAY BE JUST A NEWBORN...
"BUT IF HE AWAKENS, THE POSSIBILITY REMAINS THAT HE COULD DESTROY US ALL.

"WE SHOULD KILL HIM NOW, WHILE WE STILL HAVE THE CHANCE."

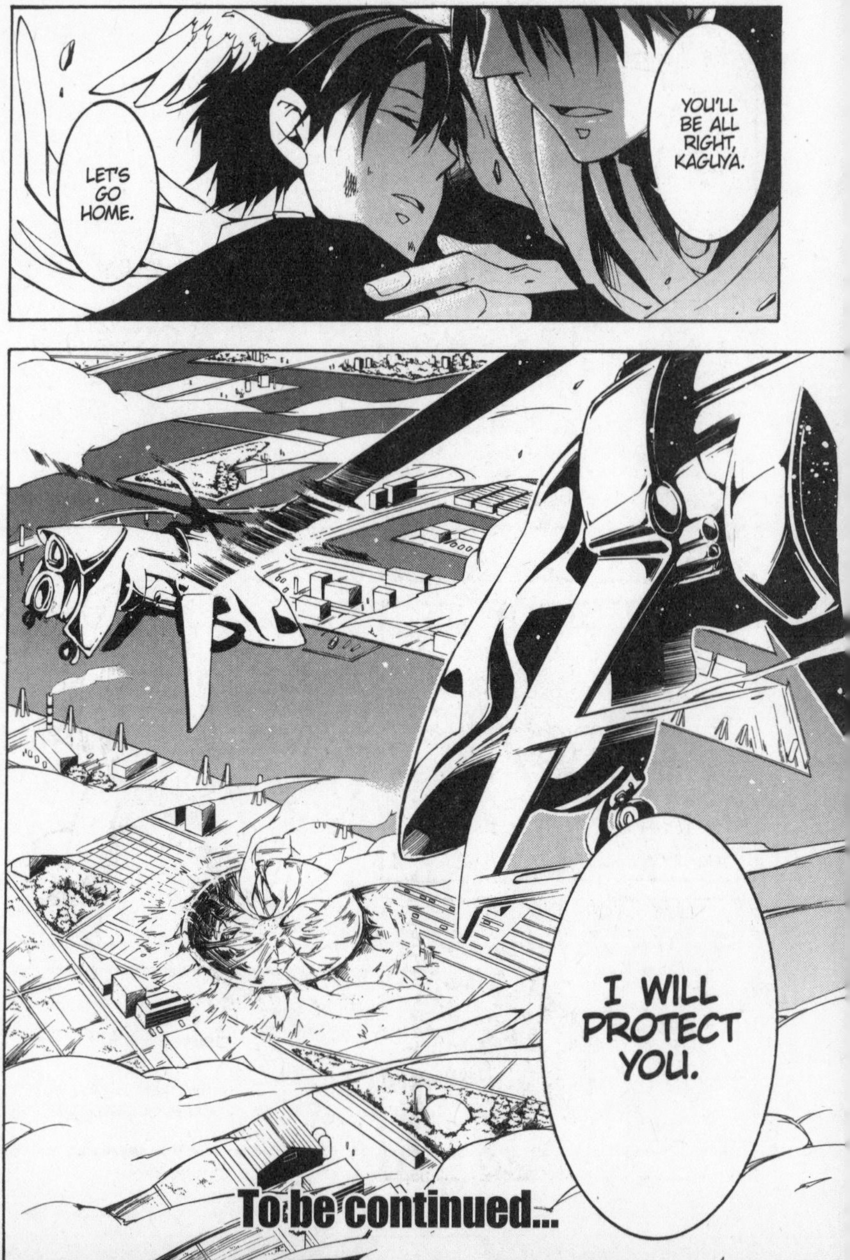
YOU'LL BE ALL RIGHT, KAGUYA.
LET'S GO HOME.
I WILL PROTECT YOU.
To be continued...

THE HEAVENLY WEAPON WAS INVOKED, AND NOW MAO'S EARS WON'T RETURN, *DESU.*

AND I CAN'T JUMP IN THE SKY, *DESU.*

Thank you very much for staying with us so far!

Ameichi ✿ Yuki Amemiya & Yukino Ichihara

Enjoying Shinigami Life

RELAX. I MAY BE THE GOD OF DEATH...
Waah!
BUT I PROVIDE PEACE OF MIND TO ALL WANDERING SOULS.
Waah!
Waah!
sob
RATTLE RATTLE
THUS...
I AM GIVING PEACE OF MIND TO THESE LOST CHILDREN WHO WANT THEIR MOTHER.
Mama!
Waah!
Waah!
HA HA HA... THERE YOU GO. I'LL BE YOUR MOMMY!
WAAAIIIIL
staaare
LAYING HIS OWN LIFE ON THE LINE... HE'S THE GOD OF DEATH ALL RIGHT, BUT HE'S SO FULL OF AFFECTION!!
SO YOU SEE, THAT'S WHY YOU CAN RELAX AND LEAVE YOUR SISTER ALONE WITH ME.
FWAP
...

SEVEN SEAS ENTERTAINMENT PRESENTS

BATTLE RABBITS

story and art by **AMEICHI**

VOLUME 3

TRANSLATION
Jill Morita

ADAPTATION
Janet Houck

LETTERING AND LAYOUT
Meaghan Tucker

LOGO DESIGN
Karis Page

COVER DESIGN
Nicky Lim

PROOFREADER
Danielle King

PRODUCTION MANAGER
Lissa Pattillo

EDITOR-IN-CHIEF
Adam Arnold

PUBLISHER
Jason DeAngelis

BATTLE RABBITS VOL. 3

First published in Japan in 2016 by ICHIJINSHA Inc., Tokyo.
English translation rights arranged with ICHIJINSHA Inc., Tokyo, Japan.

Seven Seas books may be purchased in bulk for promotional, educational, or business use. Please contact your local bookseller or the Macmillan Corporate and Premium Sales Department at 1-800-221-7945, extension 5442, or by e-mail at MacmillanSpecialMarkets@macmillan.com.

ISBN: 978-1-626923-81-2

Printed in Canada

First Printing: January 2017

10 9 8 7 6 5 4 3 2 1

FOLLOW US ONLINE: ***www.gomanga.com***

READING DIRECTIONS

This book reads from ***right to left***, Japanese style. If this is your first time reading manga, you start reading from the top right panel on each page and take it from there. If you get lost, just follow the numbered diagram here. It may seem backwards at first, but you'll ge

3
1
2
5
4
6
8
7
9

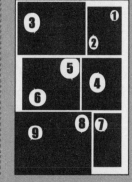